COMMUNISM AND NATIONALISM
IN THE MIDDLE EAST

Communism

and

Nationalism

in the

Middle East

---

by

WALTER Z. LAQUEUR

FREDERICK A. PRAEGER
NEW YORK

*Published in the United States of America in 1956
by Frederick A. Praeger, Inc.
Publishers, 150 East 52nd Street
New York 22, N.Y.*

All rights reserved

*Library of Congress Catalog Card Number: 55-11536
Printed in Great Britain*

Foreword

THE present study is the first in its field, and consequently entailed difficulties of a very special nature. The historical source material has never been systematically collected, and since much of it is made up of underground publications, certain bibliographical lacunæ have been unavoidable. In view of the fact that this attempt to trace the history of the extremist movements (and particularly of Communism) in the Middle East is the first to be undertaken, I cannot pretend to anything approaching completeness—a whole series of monographs would be needed for that purpose. I have felt that the almost certain unfamiliarity of the reader with the subject-matter obliged me first to make an historical survey of the movements dealt with before critically evaluating their past and present status. Persia has been left outside the compass of this survey, mainly because of the existence of several studies of Communism and the right-wing extremist movements in Persia—however fragmentary they may be—whereas there exists nothing of the kind for the other Middle Eastern countries. Some of the material in the chapters on Egypt and Israel has appeared previously (under the pen name M. Alexander) in *Commentary* (1952–53) and in the British monthly *Twentieth Century* (1953–54). Condensed versions of Chapters 19 and 20 appeared in *The Middle East Journal* (Winter, 1955), and *The World Today* (The Chatham House Review) (December, 1955) respectively.

I should like to express my thanks here to the many friends in various countries who have assisted me in procuring source material. Mr. N. Rogel has rendered invaluable help in checking and correcting the transliteration of names. I should like to record my obligation to Mr. G. L. Arnold and Mr. H. S. Deighton, who have read the manuscript and offered advice on a number of points.

Jerusalem and London WALTER Z. LAQUEUR
 July–December, 1955

v

Contents

CONTENTS

viii

CONTENTS

CONTENTS

x

PART ONE

A SURVEY
OF THE MIDDLE EAST
OF THE TWENTIETH
CENTURY

Chapter One

The Background of
the Crisis

I. SOME MISCONCEPTIONS IN TRADITIONAL
APPROACH

FOR almost two generations Western observers have been predicting imminent changes of decisive importance in the world of Islam. After World War I, when the "Mysterious East" and the "Soul of Asia" were rediscovered by the *terribles popularisateurs*, it was widely believed that a great revolution had started in the Middle East, the results of which would affect mankind everywhere. After World War II there was a fresh upsurge of interest in Middle Eastern affairs, reflected in a literature which, on the popular level, dealt with blood, oil, high explosives, strange lands, hate, and hope from Cairo to Ryadh and from Cairo to Damascus, and on a more sophisticated level commented on challenge and response, socio-cultural statics and dynamics.

Unfortunately, most of the observers of the first half of the twentieth century (with a few notable exceptions) have not excelled in political analysis and prediction. One reason was, perhaps, that the Orientalists cared little, if at all, for politics, while other observers laboured under various delusions and prejudices. A well-known British school had created the image of a noble Bedouin savage, which it was now seeking desperately all over the Middle East. For many years certain Zionist experts tended to deny (or at least to belittle) the existence of an Arab problem; the Turks were preoccupied with their own affairs, while the Arabs argued that if anything was indeed wrong with the Arab world, it was the fault of Western imperialism and Zionist aggression. In such a climate of opinion a realistic appraisal of the important political and social factors in the Middle East was a rare phenomenon.

Instead, various ideas and theories were voiced which may now seem

3

ludicrous but which were taken seriously at the time. On the eve of World War I, King Yahya of Yemen was the candidate of many Western observers for creating a great new Arab (or Moslem) empire. Ten years later, Ibn Sa'ūd was regarded as the up-and-coming man who would unite the Moslems from Cairo to Karachi. Still later, when the Arab League was founded, it was considered to be a new and potentially great power; after all these expectations failed, the "military socialism" in Egypt and Syria (up to early 1954) was declared to be not a mere *ultima ratio* but a socio-political movement of great significance and lasting importance.

It would appear that these observers were right in one assumption; namely that the Middle East is and has been in a state of ferment. But the hope that something significant and consolidated would somehow emerge, and not mere confusion and anarchy, has not as yet been realized. The situation in the Middle East has changed, and will continue to change. It is not static anywhere. But while events in Russia, in Eastern Asia, and in Eastern Europe have changed the course of human history, the Middle East has remained a vacuum between the big powers, the passive recipient, not the *subject*, of historical forces.

Historians of a later period may very well reach the conclusion that during the late 1940's and 1950's there was a conspiracy of silence regarding Communists and the religious and right-wing extremist movements in the Middle East.

A great deal had been written on Middle Eastern affairs, on politics and economics, on cultural and social affairs, on Islamic tradition and the Arab heritage, but hardly anything at all about the political movements which have emerged and which possess great and perhaps decisive importance. With apologetic and qualifying statements writers on Middle Eastern affairs introduced a few pages or lines in their books dealing with these issues. The real reasons for the lack of interest or actual ignorance in these fields have been simple. Journalists and diplomats are necessarily limited in non-democratic countries in their social intercourse; they are hardly likely to meet frequently with Communists or members of right-wing extremist movements, who, in their turn, see no cogent reason for establishing public relations bureaux in order to make their cause known to foreigners. Observers living outside the Middle East (and sometimes those within) have faced enormous difficulties when they tried to obtain illegal or semi-illegal extremist literature. It was natural to come to the conclusion that newspapers that were not sold at a news-stand or people who did not come to cocktail parties did not exist or, at least, were of no great importance, and that the strength and significance of Communism in the Middle East, like its right-wing counterparts, were highly exaggerated (if not altogether invented) by credulous people who had read too much cold-war literature.

4

2. THE "BULWARK OF ISLAM" THEORY

Up to very recently the "bulwark" theory has frequently bedevilled serious discussion of Communism in the Moslem world. Islam, it was stated, was altogether incompatible with atheist and materialist Communism, and since the vast majority of the inhabitants of Islamic countries were believing and practising Moslems, this movement stood no chance whatsoever of succeeding. Even today such ideas are occasionally voiced: Sayyid al Hāshimi, for example, in a recent article has described a public debate between a Moslem religious leader and a Communist in Pakistan. The Communist harangued the crowd, expounding the similarity between the essentially collectivist doctrine of Muhammad and present-day collectivism in practice. After the Communist's tirade, which appeared to swing popular sentiment in his favour, the Moslem Imām rose and asked to be furnished with answers to the following questions: "You say that Communism and Islam are the same in essence. Do you believe in God and the prophetic mission of Muhammad and the holiness of his book?" The embarassed reply was "No." "Do you believe that Marx, Lenin, and Stalin are as great as Muhammad or his four friends?" The reluctant answer was again "No." The third question was: "Do you believe that you may be wrong, that Muhammad may be right and may convert Communists and Christians to our way of thinking?" The answer this time, which came after a moment of obvious hesitation, was "Yes." Amid derision and open hostility the Communist and his comrades departed.[1] Such incidents, if true, must have become very infrequent; they may hold good for some parts of Pakistan, Yemen, and Sa'udia and the desert regions of Jordan, but the outcome of such a public discussion in Cairo or Beirut would probably be somewhat different—the emergence of strong Communist cells among the students of Al Azhar provides evidence to that effect. More and more outside observers have become convinced that Islam is no more (and probably is less) of a "bulwark" against Communism than Catholicism in France and Italy, and Confucianism in China or Buddhism in Indo-China. Some have reached the conclusion that the Communist groups in the Middle East consist in the main of "fellow-travellers" who hesitate to accept atheistic and materialistic Communist opposition to religion. But if they were compelled to make a choice between the present regime and Communism, they would probably opt for the latter.[2] Others have pointed to the affinity between Islam and Communism, both of which are all-embracing in their concepts, with, however, the important difference that the former is static and atomistic and cannot be incorporated any longer into people's daily lives. Hence the temptation for Moslem radicals to turn to another ideology justifying secular totalitarianism. They may view Stalinism, not as a materialistic system which rejects spiritual values

but as a monistic philosophy projecting spiritual values upon a materialist base.[3]

In fact, Communist leaders have pointed out ever since the period of
the Popular Front in the middle thirties that early Islam was indeed
Communistic (or at least democratic)—were not the Caliphs elected
by all the believers? And did not 'Omar ibn Khattab, for instance,
constantly ask the people for advice? Khālid Bakdāsh, the Syrian
Communist leader, wrote, " 'Omar ibn Khattab was a simple Bedouin,
and yet his opinion has remained important for all. How is it that workers,
peasants, and intellectuals in our days are not permitted to express
their opinions on their country, on affairs of the nation, and on the
government?"[4] Attempts to find Socialist or Communist parallels in
the Koran have been made by the left wing of the Moslem Brotherhood in Egypt and Syria. (Similar attempts were made in the European
labour movement in the nineteenth century when quotations from the
Old and New Testaments were used to establish revolutions as fore-
ordained, and the prophets were pictured as socialist revolutionaries.)
But the party propaganda based on religious references has been, on
the whole, of little consequence.

By now, the discussion about the affinity between Islam and Communism is no longer of vital interest. It was important so long as the
vast majority of the people believed in religion and Islam continued to
be the only active force in their daily lives. This, however, is no longer
true, for a considerable part of the intelligentsia in the Arab countries
and, to a growing degree, for the urban population in general. The whole
idea of the "Islamic bulwark" was based on the notion that the people
were, on the whole, ignorant of Communism and would remain so.
But ignorance has hardly ever contributed to the building of strong
bulwarks. It now seems clear that resistance to Communism can be
expected only in societies with a tradition of individual liberty.

If anything, the Arab countries are now more likely than most others
in the world to provide a favourable breeding-ground for Communism.
The problem of the affinity between Islam and Communism is, as we
said, of secondary importance at the present time. What is decisive is
that Islam has gradually ceased to be a serious competitor of Communism in the struggle for the soul of the present and potential *élites* in
the countries of the Middle East. This has something to do with the
fact that, although Western techniques are used in the East, the whole
development which preceded and produced them, including the
Renaissance, Protestantism, and the Enlightenment, are wholly lacking
in the history of the Islamic peoples. It was noted more than thirty years
ago by Zia Goekalp, the Turkish reformer and social thinker, that the
Islamic world was still in the Middle Ages; the self-critical spirit of the
Middle East has diminished since then, but the situation itself has not
changed fundamentally. Eighteenth-century Wahabism proved to be a

retrograde movement, while both Bahaism and the Ahmadiyya have affected only small numbers of people and have never been of great political significance. Professor E. A. Speiser has drawn attention to the inhibitive aspects of traditional Islam, which has affected the vitality of society as a whole.[5] The Waqf contributed to inequality in land tenure, education was restricted and reactionary, and social processes were stagnant. The international relations of these countries were hampered by their own numerous political and religious injunctions that were out of date by several centuries. Disestablishment (the separation between Church and State) would have been the obvious answer to stagnation; but then it should not be forgotten that Turkey (where Kemal Ataturk had carried out secular reforms) was heir to a more democratic tradition which predated Islam, that Islam was indigenous to the Arab world but an acquired, imported faith to the Turks. There have been attempts to infuse more liberal principles in Islam and to give it new vigour following a reform movement, but what has remained of Jamāl-ad-Dīn al Afghānī and Muhammad 'Abduh is mainly the stress on Pan-Islamism—not on reform. The failure of these attempts has been described by Orientalists from Goldziher to Gibb.

3. THE QUALITY OF NATIONALISM IN THE MIDDLE EAST

As late as 1906 Arminius Vambery wrote: "Religion absorbs the intellect of the Asiatic; it is stronger than his feeling for nationality, the latter is almost everywhere of second importance."[6] But by that time this observation was already not quite correct; Mustafa Kāmil's Nationalist Party was already in existence, and one of his fellow-countrymen calls him the first Egyptian thinker in whose works no trace of any culture other than the Western can be discerned. The "Young Arab" and "Young Turk" societies were intensely nationalist. And nationalism, needless to mention, was, in contrast to Islam, a European idea.

But in Europe nationalism had appeared until the close of the nineteenth century to be a liberal and democratic movement, "humanitarian in object and preaching." The doctrine of national self-determination had come out of the French Revolution—but it was certainly not the only aim of the French Revolution. The Middle East, however, received nationalism in isolation, without liberalism, democracy, and the humanitarian aims; and this has been the main reason why nationalism there, to this very day, has taken so much more frequently the form of chauvinism, of emotional aggression, and of opposition to everything foreign rather than that of genuine patriotism.

Some doubts have indeed been expressed by observers of the Middle Eastern scene whether these movements can be defined as national movements in the Western sense and whether the passion underlying them can be called "nationalism." The Western European and North American nation state is the result of historic development, and the outcome of conditions and ideas which did not exist in the East. It is based on democracy, not only in the central government but at every level down to small local units, and, of course, on individual liberty. All these prerequisites were absent in the Islamic East, and apart from Turkey, where development has been different, the transplantation of the Western idea of liberal nationalism has been a failure. The Arab nations are not "integrated nations," as Professor Kohn has pointed out, because they lack mobility of classes, because the country is divided into a minority of the rich growing richer and the mass of the poor growing poorer. And there are also the lack of a feeling of having a stake in the existence of the nation and the absence of readiness for creative action for the common good.[7] It is true that the attempt was made by Mustafa Kāmil and later by the Wafd, and again by General Naguīb, Colonel Nāsir, and the Cairo junta to overcome religious and ethnic divisions. Mustafa Kāmil preached the revolutionary doctrine that Moslems and Copts are one people united by patriotism. But soon after his death his own party was already mainly preoccupied in attacking Copts and Syrian Christians, and such relapses have recurred to this very day.

Western liberal nationalism never did have any deep roots in the Moslem countries, though a small upper class was fully Westernized, and the constitutions of some countries, such as Egypt, were modelled on the Western European pattern. But constitutions alone could not make democratic states, and parliamentary democracy was gradually discontinued or became a farce.

The nationalist inspiration that these countries received was thus mainly of the post- and anti-liberal era. This nationalism is distinguished by the over-estimation of one's own nation and the denigration of others, the lack of the spirit of self-criticism and responsibility, an ambivalent appraisal of the destiny of one's nation based on a feeling of inferiority, and a general tendency to attribute anything wrong with one's nation to the evil-doing of others, who should consequently be fought. The teachings of Fascism and National Socialism, as well as the Soviet theory of Russian superiority in all fields, have had more influence than the earlier liberal-democratic brand of nationalism. This does not mean that they were copied. The totalitarian movements, too, had grown in specific circumstances which were by no means identical with conditions prevailing in Egypt, Iraq, or the Levant states, nor could the qualitative differences between great- and small-power nationalism be disregarded. And a last reservation should be made: there were always, and there are now, to be found many sincere patriots in the Middle East who have regretted what they regard as retrogressive trends in the national movement of their country. But while modernism (the belief in a synthesis between Moslem tradition and Western culture) has prevailed in literature, this has not been the case in social life and in politics. There is a distinct trend which leads from the rationalism of Muhammad 'Abduh, who strongly influenced the founders of the Wafd, to Taha Husain (who reached the conclusion that Egypt was a Mediterranean and therefore a Western, not an Oriental, country), and to a social critic like Salama Mūsa. But these thinkers had been too much in advance of their time and people; their political advice was of no avail and probably could not be used. Western values meant little to the statesmen and politicians, who said (at the very best), as a young and promising Lebanese opposition leader did, that they wanted "to assimilate the best of all other great movements: Fascism, Communism, and Western Democracy."[8]

The new nationalism in the Middle East and most other Asian countries is quite different, then, both from the liberal democratic patriotic movements of the nineteenth century (a *nationalisme intégrale*, which found its classic ideological expression in the writings of the leaders of *Action Française*) and from totalitarian nationalism. It is probably nearest to what Hannah Arendt has called the "tribal nationalism of the 'pan' movements." Its leaders are mostly intellectuals, not members of the upper class who in some Middle Eastern countries more often than in Europe tend to be cosmopolitans.[9] They are authoritarian and anti-democratic—and here is an obvious similarity with the Communists, who also believe that the people are incapable of ruling themselves and that a small *élite*—namely, the intellectuals—must assume the task of ruling.

The new nationalism has found fewer friends outside Asia than the anti-colonial movement of a generation ago. Typical of this change are the pessimistic views of Professor Hans Kohn in 1952, who, a quarter of a century earlier, had been the historian of the national movement in the Middle East and welcomed the emergence of what then appeared to be progressive forces. But reviewing the course of events after almost three decades, he wrote:

"I regard nationalism, national self-determination, national sovereignty, a new nation state . . . as not a desirable good in itself. . . . There is no hope for Middle Eastern nationalism until the peoples learn that, if you wish to achieve a healthy nationalism, you must subordinate your personal strivings, your personal seekings, your class interests to what I call creative action for the common good. And there is little hope unless they learn to moderate their nationalism and to be ready for compromise solutions and accommodation, to outgrow their parochialism in an all-inclusive spirit of regional co-operation and beyond that in a larger community of nations."[10]

The inference is that the new nationalism is not an encouraging sign at all, and few people outside the Middle East will dispute this view.

Whether good or bad, this new nationalism is a fact—the most relevant political fact in the Middle East; it remains to be studied and understood. The most outstanding features of this new nationalism are, despite all apologetic explanations, chauvinism and xenophobia; the former, a "crowd phenomenon belonging to the sphere of collective behaviour where reflection is at a minimum and where the emotional processes are rampant" (Harold D. Lasswell), is certainly not something exclusively Middle Eastern. The fact that xenophobia appears now as anti-Westernism, not anti-Easternism, has of course to be explained by political and historical factors; viz. the circumstance that the West has been "in" for many years and the Soviet bloc has been "out," and for some years the Russians have taken great care to stress their passivity, and thus to make the Arabs forget both the geographic proximity of Russia and the fact that British imperialism has abandoned most of its positions in Asia.

It would not be difficult to find the roots and reasons for xenophobia in the history of Islam. But this would not explain, for instance, the different course taken by Turkey, another Islamic country. There is yet another factor which has profoundly influenced the national character of the Arab peoples—the impact of foreign rule, and later imperialism. No Arab country had been independent for many centuries; they have been ruled by the Turks and the Mamelukes and, during the most recent period, by the British and the French. H. A. R. Gibb has drawn attention to the psychological results of long centuries of misrule and oppression, supplemented by the tradition of quietism inculcated by the religious authorities and by an acquired habit of stoicism passing into fatalism. Eighteenth-century Arab chroniclers had reported time and again that mild, just, and peace-loving governors were not respected by the people:

"If the peasants were administered by a compassionate *multazim* (governor), they despised him and his agents, delayed payment of the taxes, called him by feminine names, and hoped for the ending of the *iltizām* (term of governorship) and the appointment of some tyrant without fear of God or mercy for them, so as to gain by that means their private ends by the alighting of his violence upon some of their number. . . .[11]

The passive attitude and fatalism, especially in the countryside, have been the source of much irritation to the intelligentsia. The same writers and speakers in Egypt, who publicly give excessive praise to the greatness of their people, will be usually the first to argue in private discussion (again exaggerating) that their people cannot be helped any more because the process of degeneration has proceeded too far and the people lack all initiative.[12]

But the urban masses have been aroused since World War I, and only they really matter for the time being in Middle Eastern politics. They have been taught that everything that is wrong in their country is the result of imperialist oppression and exploitation: economic and cultural backwardness, disease, illiteracy, low living standards, the absence of a highly developed industry, political instability, corruption, and so on. "Anti-imperialism" has become the great slogan; it is not, however, based on a belief in international solidarity; more often than not it covers up an *impérialisme manqué*: at the first opportunity the anti-imperialists display open imperialist tendencies.

We cannot pretend, within the bounds of this short survey, to reply to the question of whether imperialism has indeed been responsible for all or some of the evils mentioned and if so to what degree. It is largely a hypothetical problem because we do not know how this or that Asian country would have developed if it had been independent for the last one or two hundred years. (The little experience available does not provide conclusive results.) It would be difficult indeed to dispute the contention of all national movements that they want their *own* government—not *good* government. But the whole issue becomes complicated when practical and prosaic questions, such as those of economic development, are raised. England and France certainly did not occupy Asian countries for altruistic reasons, but we are here concerned with the objective results of their rule. Lord Cromer, who was surely the prototype of the imperialist at the end of the nineteenth century, can justly be accused of thwarting the development of a protected cotton industry in Egypt. But would the Egyptians have been able to build such an industry on their own? Would they have been at all able to extend cotton cultivation in the same degree as was done under British rule? A very big question-mark remains, to say the very least. But as things are now, the question of whether imperialism is indeed to be made responsible for all the evils and for the general backwardness has become largely academic. The whole matter has been transferred from the realm of facts to the sphere of political mythology. According to the myth created, imperialism had been guilty of every possible crime, and rational refutation of this has become irrelevant and, in any case, ineffectual. Occasionally one meets isolated intellectuals who take a different view, such as, for instance, Professor B. Himade of the American University, Beirut, who wrote in a recent Unesco study: "Xenophobia is declining and the Arab countries' economic under-development and political dependence is now recognized as due more to internal weakness than to foreign imperialism. There is a fuller appreciation of the modern conception of the State. . . ." We are concerned here, however, not with the opinions of a few political scientists but with the political beliefs of both the rulers and the vast majority of the politically conscious individuals, and, with regard to them, as events have shown during many years, such a conception (of internal weakness) is in utter contrast to their views and articles of faith. The source of the evil is the historical fact (for which nobody can be made responsible) that Asia has been trailing behind Europe by about three to four centuries, the period in which the modern world has come into being. G. F. Hudson has noted that the feeling of discrimination and humiliation which besets these people in view of their backwardness—the same people who once believed themselves to possess the highest culture—is in the last resort nothing but dissatisfaction with themselves. This feeling of inferiority is projected on to the West, and it continues to be active long after the real or alleged cause—imperialist rule—has ceased to exist. It becomes, to use a metaphor from another school of psychology, a conditioned reflex.[13]

Egypt has been independent for more than thirty years; Iraq for over twenty; Syria and Lebanon for the last ten years. The presence of British troops in the Suez Canal Zone and on certain airfields in Iraq was undoubtedly a source of anger and resentment for Egyptian and Iraqi patriots. But they had, on the whole, a free hand in the management of their countries' affairs, certainly during recent years. The citizens of Syria and Lebanon have had no points of discord whatsoever with Western imperialism since the end of World War II, apart perhaps from such minor issues as the management of the tramway system in Beirut. It would have been over-optimistic to expect that anti-imperialism would disappear with imperialism, but a lessening in its intensity was forecast by many observers. However, exactly the opposite happened; both the leaders and the led went on to attack imperialism and to charge it with the present dismal state of affairs, as if nothing had happened.[14]

Here we face another typical feature of this new nationalism: the preoccupation with national aspirations and foreign policy in general and, at the same time, the inability to sustain a constructive effort on the domestic scene. For a number of years now all the Arab governments have had the opportunity to instal progressive rule and to put an end to the "imperialist heritage" of corruption and mismanagement; but they have not succeeded, and not all have even tried. The well-intentioned government of General Naguïb which, when it came to power in July, 1952, stated that its main preoccupation would be to effect an internal clean-up, succeeded in persevering in this course for exactly eight weeks. This is perhaps the basic difference between Turkey and the Arab countries: once Kemal Ataturk had prevailed in his struggle against foreign intervention, he began to carry out his programme of internal reform, but did not engage in vainglorious dreams about the reconquest of the old European or Asiatic provinces of the Ottoman Empire. For him the primacy of domestic policy was self-evident; whereas the Arab rulers were unable or unwilling to follow this course.

The causes of this weakness, which makes the new nationalism mainly a destructive force, are manifold: one of the more important factors is undoubtedly the absence of the spirit of self-criticism and responsibility which has always been the indispensable corrective to nationalist excess. The admission of mistakes and faults has frequently been considered as something approaching treason, and those doing so were voices calling in the wilderness. One of the favourite pastimes of many politicians in recent years has been to put the blame for many of the evils in the Arab world on Zionism and Israel. To quote one example among many: the use of violence in the political life of the Arab countries and the many political assassinations have been explained on the ground of Jewish terrorism in Palestine.[15] Without trying to belittle the repercussions of the actions of the terrorist groups, a mere glance at the historical facts shows that this explanation cannot possibly hold. Beginning in 1910 with the murder of the Prime Minister, Butrus Ghāli, attempts have been made on the lives of many Egyptian statesmen; Iraqi and Syrian leaders such as Bakr Sidqi, Rustum Haidar, and Dr. Shahbandar were killed; and most of the political opponents of the Jerusalem Mufti in Palestine were assassinated before "Irgun" and the Stern gang had been founded. Too many of the anti-Western trends and other features of nationalism in the Arab and Islamic countries have been explained away in recent years by reference to Israel. Events in Persia in 1950, in Indonesia in 1953–54, and in other Islamic countries where Zionism and Israel was no political issue at all, have shown that the real reasons were far more complex.

4. THE ROLE OF THE STUDENTS

The great impact of student organizations on the national revolutionary movement in the Middle East (and in the East generally) have frequently baffled Western observers. American and British or French onlookers have found it difficult to understand that students could overthrow governments, or at least seriously endanger them, by mere demonstrations and strikes. Different outlets for surplus energy exist for college students in the United States,[16] and British students throwing their weight about have never been taken very seriously, certainly not by party politicians. French students have taken a more passionate interest in politics, but they, too, have been identified more with unpolitical clashes on the Boulevard Saint Michel and have not overthrown a government in living memory. German students played some role in their country's affairs after the Napoleonic wars and the days of the Burschenschaft, but this was more than a hundred years ago, and, even if the extremist movements found many supporters among the students in the Weimar Republic, students there never really influenced politics.

But the role of the student in the countries of the Middle East has been, and is, altogether different. It is certainly not unique; one tends to forget that in backward countries the intelligentsia is numerically small, and the weight of the students, frequently the only organized body considering the absence of political parties in the Western sense, is consequently great. On the other hand, the social position of the student in these countries is different, too. The rich can afford to send their children to universities abroad (from Jordan, for instance, to Beirut or Cairo, and from Egypt and Lebanon to Paris and London). But if they return after the completion of their studies, they find themselves again narrowly restricted both in their own careers and in their attempts to do something to overcome the backwardness of their country. Another consideration is, of course, that most, if not all, of the students lose in Europe the few religious convictions they may have had previously; they are now in a spiritual no-man's-land, lacking roots, and thus ready to adopt any *ersatz* religion that comes their way. Those who got their education at the universities at home are mostly from lower middle-class families and, sometimes, the sons and daughters of the poor. They live in extremely difficult conditions and frequently on the verge of starvation in order to complete their studies. At the same time, there is no certainty whatsoever that they will get employment thereafter; Egypt, for instance, used to have the highest academic unemployment figures in the world.[17] The students, not altogether wrongly, put the responsibility for this state of affairs not only and not mainly on the university authorities, but also on the regime as a whole, and they soon become its radical opponents. In the late 1930's semi-fascist movements had their heyday in the university, whereas recently the Moslem Brotherhood, since dissolved, and the Communists are the parties most influential there.

A similar situation existed in pre-revolutionary Russia and China. From the time of the big students' strike in 1899, which comprised all the institutions of higher learning throughout Russia, and which reached boiling-point when the Petersburg police dispersed student meetings with their *nagaikas* (whips), students have been in the forefront of the revolutionary movement. (Since the 1850's "student" had been in Russia, as in the Middle East today, a synonym for "revolutionary agent.") In China even the present-day Communist historians admit that the "anti-imperialist" struggle was headed, not by workers and peasants, but by the students, beginning with the famous "movement of May 4, 1919." Stalin is quoted to the effect that "nobody felt the imperialist yoke as acutely and felt consequently as deeply the necessity for the struggle against it as the youth in China." All but a very few of the leaders of the Communist party of the early period were students, and it is well known how important a role the students who were sent to Europe under the scheme of Chou En Lai played subsequently in the history of the Communist party. The suppression of academic freedom by the Chiang Kai-shek regime was instrumental in causing the bulk of the academic youth to join the Communist camp.

Another interesting parallel should be noted: the important, if unintentional, contribution of Western-sponsored schools and universities to the growth and promotion of nationalist and, later, Communist ideas. George Antonius begins his work on the *Arab Awakening* with the following words: "The story of the Arab national movement opens in Syria in 1847 with the foundation in Beirut of a modest literary society under American patronage . . . when five young men who had been educated at the Syrian Protestant College formed a secret society. . . ." And there can be no doubt at all that the college founded by the Lazarist brothers, the printing press installed earlier by the Jesuits, the Syrian Protestant College, and the Catholic schools in Syria and Beirut were the rallying-points of Arab nationalism.[18] Similarly, Western and missionary schools in China educated generations of nationalist leaders, and in our day it has been noted that the majority of the leaders of the Communist parties in Syria and Lebanon are graduates of the American University of Beirut.

The numerical strength of the student body in such cities as Cairo, Alexandria, Beirut, or Damascus should not be belittled; it is about 40,000 (with Al Azhar) in the two Egyptian cities, and about 6000 in the Lebanese and Syrian capitals. In political demonstrations and strikes the students are frequently joined by the pupils of the higher grades of the secondary schools. This was the case, for instance, during the demonstrations in Damascus under Shishakli in 1953–54; a British student who attended lectures at Cairo University (at that time Fuād I University) notes that many, perhaps most, of the student demonstrations reported in the Western press concerned not the university undergraduates, but the pupils of secondary schools.[19]

A Western educator in Egypt, quoting a colleague, gives the following account of the reasons for the frequent rioting and demonstrations:

"They strike . . . for all kinds of reasons—for a change of Cabinet, against a declaration by an Egyptian or foreign Minister, the high percentage of failures in public examinations, the low salary given by the state to graduates of an institution, to express their joy or disappointment on all kinds of occasions—in fact, for every reason under the sun. The student body turns into a proletarian dictatorship and the school or academic year actually shrinks to a matter of five months' work; at times even less."[20]

The political interest of the students is at constant high pitch, in stark contrast to the lack of interest in these things at the universities of the Western world. Back in the 1920's, Sa'ad Zaghlūl, the founder and first leader of the Wafd, had advised his aides to lean on the student:

"He is a power not to be overlooked." In the 1940's and early 1950's the danger of overlooking the student was not very great to be sure, and political leaders have tried to put a stop to these student practices by prohibiting political activities by students, by postponing the beginning of the academic year, or by closing the universities temporarily. Such an attempt was made, among others, by the military junta in Egypt. This, however, has aroused the ire of the students and their backers:

"The idea of a law to prevent students from occupying themselves with politics has caused concern among all free people. . . . This law would allow strangling the public opinion of the *élite*. The army knows perfectly well that the university students have paved the way and created the atmosphere for the deposition of the king. . . ."[21]

What is the relative strength of the various parties in the universities? In the American University of Beirut the Communists, together with their sympathizers, would appear to be strongest, and the extreme nationalists a close second. Partial elections, such as those at the faculty of law at Cairo University, have shown the Moslem Brotherhood and the "United Front" (a Wafdist-Communist front with the latter in the commanding position) to be of about equal strength.[22] There have been frequent clashes between the Moslem Brotherhood and supporters of the junta, whereas the Egyptian government crisis in February–March, 1954, was caused, as so many crises in the Middle East were before, by student demonstrations. The British observer quoted above relates that ". . . in their political ideas they are like students everywhere, vague and immature. A large proportion say that they are Communist, but very few of those know even the first thing about that creed. . . . Nevertheless the Communists seem to be an organized body among the students. . . . There is no doubt that many of the young men have identified Communism on the one hand with anti-Westernism: Russia is anti-West, they themselves are anti-West: Russia is Communist, so they too will be Communist. On the other hand, Communism has gathered in the bitter feeling against the great landlords of Egypt. Here some of the clearer sighted students see the drawbacks; but they accept them, nonetheless. 'We know,' they say, 'that to acquire economic freedom through Communism means sacrificing our political freedom; but it is we, the educated, who have political freedom to lose, and we are ready to lose it for the peasants' sake. . . .' It is very difficult to find out from the students what the policies of their various parties are. . . . The Moslem Brotherhood were particularly bad in that respect. They would not come down to brass tacks at all, but talked vaguely and without details of economic reform and a return to the principles of Islam. Only on the virtues of political assassination they were precise. . . ."[23]

As in the Russia of the 1840's and 1850's there has been a split into

"Westerners" and "Easterners." As far back as 1888 the French Consul-General in Beirut, Vicomte de Petiteville, wrote to the Minister of Foreign Affairs in Paris: "A revolution has begun here. The clergy is losing its influence more and more every day. It must be admitted that our colleges are to a certain extent the cause of this revolution. The young men who come out of them are not as docile under the episcopal crozier as their fathers were."[24] But the Westerners were Westerners only in one respect: that the Islam tradition was meaningless for them. Moslem youth wanted to be strong, to learn the technique of the West in order to beat the West. But the strength of the West was not an historical accident either, and if techniques could be copied, there were no short-cuts to building the social basis on which it had grown. However, Fascism, and later Communism, appeared to show that perhaps there were such short-cuts, after all. This admiration for material strength became one of the dominant features of student ideology (and of many intellectuals in general), and it has to be viewed in the perspective of Levantinism; Levantinism seen as a state of mind, a spiritual climate to be found in many countries outside the Levant. This explains, among other things, the switch-over in the allegiances of many students from vague pro-Axis sympathies to equally vague pro-Soviet sympathies. The last anti-Russian student demonstration took place in Cairo in 1942–43; since then only anti-Western demonstrations have been organized. The date does not lack significance.

Communism and extreme nationalism, frequently without a clear dividing line, are the two main forces among academic youth in the Arab countries.[25] Members of orthodox Moslem organizations and right-wing extremists collaborate closely with the Communists within the framework of various "fronts." The underlying reason for this state of affairs is the profound dissatisfaction with the existing regime, the belief in a patriotic duty to bring about a radical change. At the same time there is a feeling of impotence and lack of constructive and positive outlets. Whatever the outcome of this state of frustration (and there is admittedly more than one possibility), a democratic movement will hardly emerge. A radical change can be effected only by means of an authoritarian regime, a dictatorship. But the attitude of the students towards freedom (and here we have a general dilemma of the intelligentsia in the East) is highly ambivalent. They, too, suffer from a "fear of freedom," the democratic burden is too heavy for them.[26] But they are not prepared to stand (as the Turks did for many years) an authoritarian regime either, be it out of love for freedom or lack of national responsibility and discipline. They could not stand the corrupt parties of the parliamentary regime, but they do not like the "military socialism" of the subsequent period either. They would probably dislike Communism, too, because demonstrations would have to cease and the students would be asked to mind their own affairs. Two souls dwell in the student's breast, and the result has been, more often than not, anarchy—in a part of the world where anarchy will not be tolerated forever.

5. THE FAILURE OF PARLIAMENTARY DEMOCRACY

The fetishistic character (to paraphrase Marx) of nationalism in the Middle East and its mainly destructive features have expedited the growth of Communism. Elsewhere, as in Turkey, a strong national movement has created strong opposition to Communist designs of territorial aggrandizement and satellization. There are certain prerequisites for such a development: above all, the ability to make the state a going concern politically, socially, and economically—to provide a minimum of stability. In this task the ruling classes in the Arab countries have not yet succeeded. Parliamentary democracy has failed, but no stable regime has emerged to take its place.

Up to the 1930's the national movement in the East considered the parliamentary regime as both the "most efficacious means of self-expression and the most desirable political achievement they could offer their peoples."[27] There had been parliamentary governments in Egypt from the early 1920's, but the will of the parliamentary majority was counteracted from the very beginning by the throne and its appointed ministers—Ziwār, Muhammad Mahmūd, Sidqi, and others. The king remained the decisive factor in Egyptian politics up to the very day of his deposition in July, 1952. In Iraq there were no fewer than seven *coups d'état* in the course of five years (1936–41), and the army has been ready to intervene in politics at decisive moments ever since. In Syria there were the three consecutive *coups d'état* of Husni Za'īm, Sāmi Hinnāwi, and Shishakli, and if parliamentary government has not come to an end in the Lebanon, it is in all probability because the Lebanese army is not big enough to cope with the task. There has been a very large turnover in cabinets. In Iraq, for instance, there have been about fifty ministries during the last thirty years, or about one each eight months; and the situation in Egypt and Lebanon has not been very different.

The general reason for the discontent with parliamentary democracy in our time is well known and need not here be reiterated in detail: the growing complexity of state affairs, the absence of a collective popular will, conflicting interests which cannot be brought to a common denominator, the decline of the legislative and the reduced importance and influence of the executive power for the simple reason that state affairs have become more administrative and less legislative in character. In the Middle Eastern countries we find all this and a variety of additional factors detrimental to the functioning of democratic parliamentary government. Rondot names three essential obstacles: "Communal" or "denominational," "feudal," and "urban." "Denominational" in this context refers to the danger of an automatic transformation of denominational groups (in countries with religious and ethnic minorities) into parliamentary majority and minority factions. Such difficulties exist, it will be remembered, in Iraq and particularly in Lebanon. The "feudal obstacle" distorts the very principle of elections, because in most cases it is not a deputy who is elected but the chieftain who is acknowledged by the voter.

"Wherever tribal structures, still so frequent in the East, survived, the traditional chieftain was naturally elected to parliament. . . . But feudal influence extends even further. All the non-tribal settled populations of the plains, the entire rural population of the villages of the Fertile Crescent voted of necessity for the notables whose share-croppers and debtors they were and to whom they were bound in various ways."[28]

The urban obstacle, eventually, is the result of the preponderance of the towns over the countryside, though numerically the inhabitants of the former still are a small minority. But the big landlords reside in town and "because of the accelerated political development led by the middle class, and indeed confined to it alone, public affairs have become the portion, the sinecure, of a rather narrow *élite*."[29]

"This limited stratum is hardly ever recruited from the masses. It is extremely sensitive to the ardour and *élan* of the young semi-educated applicants for jobs, unemployed white collar men, students, and school youth, who are ever eager to swell the upper crust and are ever raising the stakes. It has also to reckon with the urban populace which, unlike the rural masses, is susceptible to violent reactions. Then there is the urban dignitary who will, when the occasion arises, mobilize the ruffians and reconstitute in his quarters with these 'abadayes' a kind of tribal nucleus which is devoted to him."[30]

A Lebanese observer gives the following description of the voting system in his country, which, it will be remembered, has the highest percentage of literacy among the Arab states:

"Certain powerful and influential individuals group themselves together and form what is called a 'list.' Your price for having your name on that list depends either on your financial ability (from 100,000–300,000 Lebanese pounds), or on how many votes you can buy from the district you are supposed to represent."[31]

The picture would not be complete without noting the damage done by the governments and the parliamentarians themselves. We refer to disregard of the constitution, to corruption, embezzlement, nepotism, falsification of election results, and so on. There have been popular movements, such as the Wafd in Egypt and, to a lesser degree, the National Bloc in Syria. But these popular movements, too, were corrupted in the course of time by what little power they got, and the leadership passed from the popular tribune (à la Mustafa Nahhās) into the hands of the rich boss-millionaire (such as the Sarāg ad-dīn brothers). These movements remained perhaps somewhat more popular than the rest, but faith both in them and in parliamentary democracy in general dwindled rapidly.

There is a great and growing literature on the failure in recent years of parliamentary government in the Arab countries, and we shall not dwell on these problems. What should be remembered is that parliamentary rule (or what went under that name) in England in the eighteenth century, and in many other countries, including Italy and Spain in the nineteenth, was not so very different from the state of affairs described above. Present-day Western democracy is, after all, a fairly recent achievement. But the important difference is, of course, that the ruling minority of a hundred or hundred and fifty years back, whatever its faults and drawbacks, was somehow able to cope with the (admittedly far less complicated) exigencies of government of the day. Ruling a country today with eighteenth-century methods has become an impossibility even in Jordan and Libya—even if only because of the provocative existence of more democratic or more efficient governments elsewhere.

6. "MILITARY SOCIALISM"

There has been no ideological revolt against parliamentary democracy in the Arab world. On the contrary, the dictators take great care to preserve, as far as possible, the cloak of parliamentary respectability, or, if this proves impossible, to promise the return of parliamentary institutions in the near future. While condemning the "tyranny of the parties," the politically conscious and active elements continue to regard the parliamentary regime as the only legitimate form of representative government.

But the feudal rulers have failed, and the popular movements headed mainly by the intelligentsia have not succeeded either. It is under these circumstances that the army has frequently taken over power as the last defence against complete anarchy; as the last institution which continues to function when the rest have broken down. Army rule has taken different forms in various countries: rule by a single dictator in Syria, and by committee in Egypt; but several observations as to the sociology and political intentions of the army movement can be made. These do not apply, however, to the commanders of the military forces in Jordan and Iraq, where the army command continues, for the time being, to support the king and the feudal forces.

The intervention of the army in the fight against the established social order is no specific Middle Eastern phenomenon; it happened earlier in South America (from Madero to Obregon and Péron) and on a wider scale. The Bakr Sidqi *coup* in Baghdad in 1936 brought to power the least reactionary regime Iraq ever had, and though Za'īm and Shishakli were certainly no revolutionaries, they were not particularly liked by the feudalists either. Under the Naguïb-Nāsir regime in Egypt, "feudal" became the worst invective, and the fat and boorish landowner became the favourite target of the cartoonists in the Egyptian press.

The officer group in the Arab armies does not, as a rule, consist mainly of the younger generation of the upper class; the social prestige and material benefits of the army are not attractive enough. Officers, including some in higher echelons, of lower middle-class origin are far more common than lower middle-class judges. The *élite* had not regarded the army as a suitable career for those willing to save the fatherland, in view of the record of army support for the powers-that-be and its collaboration with the mandatory power, such as France in Syria. But the situation gradually changed in the 1940's. Majīd Khaddūri has noted that not infrequently high-school teachers and lawyers, dissatisfied with their professions or believing that their ambitions could better be attained in the army, entered military schools and resumed their public careers in the military service.[32] This did not mean that selfless and disinterested patriotism was always (or usually) more important than personal ambition. Nor did it mean, on the other hand, that these officers had very clear social and political ideas. They were not socialists, though many of them used to call themselves so; not a few had vague and sometimes rather distinct pro-Fascist sympathies. This goes mainly for the Iraqi officers who had to leave army service in their own country after the suppression of the Rashīd 'Ali revolt in 1941 and joined other Arab armies. Such inclinations could be found among members of the Egyptian junta, too.[33]

Their political notions were almost invariably extremely vague. They usually thought that the country would have to be given more efficient government, that the army should be strengthened, and, in order to do so, certain social reforms would have to be carried out; such as the development of industry, agrarian reforms, etc. But they had no knowledge of the working of the modern state[34] (or politics in general), and tried their luck rather clumsily by trial-and-error, by adapting as far as possible army methods to civilian life (as by exploiting the army *mystique*). There were some undoubted achievements, from the deposition of King Farouk to the carrying out of limited agrarian reform, however fragmentary and amateurish; but the new regime raised far more hopes than it could possibly fulfil. The workers and peasants expected an immediate improvement in their situation, and the intelligentsia (and, above all, the students) had hoped for more than obligatory military training as a social panacea. Six weeks after he had taken power, Naguïb had to explain to "my children, the workers" that they

21

"should be not so naïve as to let themselves be exploited against their own best interests."[35] He admonished the peasants to continue paying rents, and said that "reform was not anarchy, and the sources of the general discontent would disappear with the reorganization which was prepared with the greatest rapidity." But the weeks and the months passed, and though new labour legislation was introduced which banned strikes, little if anything changed in the position of the workers and the urban middle class. The pashas had been overthrown and, in 1952, all parties called themselves "socialist," including the party of the big landowners, which protested against land reform. The official style of this period in speeches and newspaper articles was not dissimilar to the language of the French Revolution: patriotism, the appeal to be united and to fight against separatist trends, and brave phrases about social equality. But the new rulers were, if possible, more helpless in practical politics than the leaders of the old parties. They realized the necessity for mass support and both Naguīb-Nāsir and Shishakli established state parties called "Liberation Movements." The Egyptian movement came to number, after a few weeks, more than five million members, which means that it became, as far as registered members are concerned, the largest political party (outside America) in the free world. In fact these movements led a shadow existence; they existed on paper only and never became important political factors.

Following the rise to power of the military movements, there was an opportunity for the implementation of far-reaching reforms. Certainly no lack of good-will existed in Egypt, at least, but good-will alone was not enough. With the deposition of King Farouk and the dissolution of the old political parties, the military movement had spent most of its force; its domestic programme did not lead much farther. We do not even know for certain whether the members of the Cairo junta really intended to stay in power after overthrowing Farouk; it was the logic of events which compelled them to do so, in any case. In Syria military dictatorship was on a much more narrow, personal basis, and could therefore be more easily defeated.

Military leadership thus meant a step forward—but only one and no more. Having forced the old rulers to resign, the new government proved incapable of giving the country the lead which Kemal Ataturk had given Turkey in the early 1920's. The perpetuation of military rule in the absence of such a lead was tantamount to stagnation, to preoccupation with foreign policy. Absolute rule began to show its corrosive effect on the new rulers, and ever-recurring purges of the officer corps, including the original group of conspirators, caused a rift within the army. It is a process frequently described in the annals of history.

7. TURKEY AND ISRAEL, VARIANTS FROM THE MIDDLE EAST NORM

During the last generation Turkey has moved in a direction opposite to that taken by the Arab countries. This development was the result of the Kemalist reforms, the secularization of public and private life, the disestablishment of Islam, and consequently the "Westernization" of the country. The liquidation of theocracy was the prerequisite for all other reforms, and the enlightened dictatorship of Kemal Ataturk resulted, in our time, in a gradual passage to a democratic regime—an almost unique phenomenon.[36] How, then, has Turkey succeeded (where the Arab countries have failed) in modernizing its country, overcoming backwardness, and creating a strong feeling of patriotism free from xenophobia and Islamic superiority complexes? One of the reasons is the fact that, in contrast to the Arab peoples, the Turks were never oppressed and ruled by strangers, but had been masters in their own house; responsibility was not something new and frightening to them, and there existed a large urban middle class which could lead the nation as a whole. Even so, without belittling the very great importance of the Kemalist reforms, it has to be pointed out that the impetus of the original reform movement petered out in the late 1930's, and in the years thereafter the country did stagnate. Fresh vigour came only in 1946–50 with the "second revolution" when the country turned to the two-party system and, equally important, when the new industrial and agrarian revolution came into full swing and caused a very considerable economic expansion. The open Soviet threats and territorial demands (for a revision of the straits statute, for the *Anschluss* of Kars, Ardahan, and other regions) also had something to do with this. The simple geographical fact that Turkey borders on Russia (while no Arab country does), and that it feels, consequently, directly endangered, cannot in all fairness be disregarded when we compare Arab and Turkish attitudes. Economic expansion has its pitfalls, too, such as inflation, and its resulting social dangers, which need not be described here. Nor has the political influence of Moslem fanaticism been completely overcome even in the cities of Turkey. But the spirit of the nation, on the whole, has been one of optimism and confidence, reflecting political and economic progress, and very much at variance with the state of frustration and restlessness, the result of stagnation, in the Arab countries.

It is difficult to generalize about Israel because it is the country in the Middle East where matters are more in flux than anywhere else. It has often been called "completely Westernized," "a bastion of democracy and stability in that part of the world," but those who say so have in mind mostly the Jewish population of 1947–48, and tend to forget that the large immigration waves since then have brought into the country hundreds of thousands of Oriental Jews whose general educational level and feeling of civic responsibility is not considerably higher than that of the average citizen in the neighbouring countries. Israel thus appears half-Westernized and half-backward, and though in such a society the more forward elements are almost certain to prevail, the process will take many years. But there have been other factors, too, conducive to a crisis—apart from the economic dependence of the country on outside factors and a frequently narrow communalism which tends to disregard altogether the existence of an Arab problem and the importance of relations with the Arabs. Zionism itself, the movement which brought about the rebirth of a Jewish state, underwent a profound crisis when immigration nearly ceased in 1952. Zionism had brought the Israelis up to that point, but it did not automatically provide an answer to many questions which were now asked. What was to be the tie between the members of the new nation which comprises so many greatly differing individuals and groups? It could not be religion, and was the common experience in Israel—the necessity to withstand strong outside pressure—alone sufficient to provide a permanent basis? Could the state survive without, in the long run, finding its place in a community of Middle Eastern nations? But how could it be integrated in a world which was itself in a state of dissolution; how could it adapt itself to the spiritual values of the Moslem Brotherhood, or to the intelligentsia in the Arab countries, who were vacillating between Communism and extremist nationalism? These and other questions produced a spiritual tension, quite apart from the day-to-day political crises, and there were no ready-made answers available; the years after 1952 were a period of anticlimax to the great wave of enthusiasm of 1947–49. Cultural provincialism and the almost exclusive preoccupation with Israeli domestic and foreign politics (conditioned, we must add in all fairness, by the intensity of the struggle for physical survival) made greater issues, including the West–East conflict, appear all too frequently in an exclusively Israeli perspective—all depending upon the single criterion of whether it was good or bad for the Jews (to put it somewhat crudely). This moral and political parochialism in due course contributed to the growth of neutralism in certain quarters.

8. THE ECONOMIC SETTING

The economic status of the Middle East has been more fully investigated than most other aspects of the affairs of this region, and we shall note only the most important trends that are relevant in this context. The outstanding characteristics of the economies of the Arab countries (and Persia) are, according to a U.N. research unit[37]: a rapidly growing population, which in some countries is pressing heavily on the means of subsistence; a low hygienic and educational level, which manifests itself in the form of high mortality, widespread disease, and low literacy rates; a paucity of known mineral resources with the important exception of oil; a marked concentration on agriculture, in which the greater part of the population is engaged and which provides the bulk of the national income; a marked shortage of capital and consequent dependence on foreign sources for investment; and a lack of technological advancement, which, coupled with natural and social causes, leads to low productivity. These characteristics result in low national output, the economic and social consequences of which are aggravated by the unequal distribution of wealth and income. The predominance of the rural population in all Middle Eastern countries except Israel (only 20-25 per cent. living in towns) does not, however, mean large agricultural crops. The small amount of capital investment, as well as the use of antiquated methods of work, coupled with unfavourable natural conditions, result almost everywhere in the region in low agricultural yields. Average production figures of the major crops show a considerable increase during the last fifteen years in such food crops as rice, sugar, and potatoes; of the staple foods, wheat, also increased by 10 per cent. But the total population increase during the same period was 20-25 per cent., which means that agricultural production has grown less rapidly, and the gap between it and the natural growth of population has become even wider than before World War II. One of the main hindrances in the way of agricultural development (and certainly the one with the gravest social and political implications[38]) is the prevalent system of land tenure, especially in such countries as Iraq and Egypt, where most of the land belongs to a few hundred rich landowners. The other two main obstacles are insufficient water supply and irrigation works, development of which on a large scale has frequently been prevented by political squabbles; on a lower level, a lack of initiative for reform and improvement has been felt. Only in Turkey and Israel has modern machinery been used extensively; modern fertilizers are not in common use either, in the Middle East, except for Israel. Light consumers' goods account for the bulk of industrial production in Turkey, Israel, and Egypt, the three most industrialized countries of the Middle East. But even in Turkey only 15-18 per cent. of the national income is contributed by industry, and in Egypt less than 15 per cent. Many industries have remained close to the handicraft stage, and have continued to use obsolete methods. The traditional crafts still account for a sizeable part of the total output; they completely dominate certain fields, such as rug-making, and play an important part in pottery-making, etc. In certain industries a partial adaption of the craft to modern conditions has taken place through use of power-driven machinery to supplement hand work. In consequence, industry in the Middle East presents a wide variety of methods ranging from archaic crafts to the use of modern equipment. But with a few exceptions, even the modern enterprises are not capitalized to an extent in any way comparable with similar industries in Western countries and with the Middle Eastern oil industry. (It should be noted that mining, in general, has expanded more rapidly than manufacturing.) But oil operations have had only a limited effect on the general economic situation. They have stimulated certain activities and retarded others, and have frequently caused inflation. Up to very recently the profits of oil operations have exclusively benefited the ruling family in Sau'dia and a very small section of the population in Iraq; and there has been no over-all economic plan or development scheme for the rational use of the proceeds from these dwindling natural assets.

At the present time the Middle East, one of the poorest and most backward regions of the world, possesses natural resources of great importance, such as the unused land and water reserves of the region which, in bygone days, were cultivated and provided food for a much larger population than now. The Director-General of the F.A.O. stated in 1948 that "owing to the unique natural resources of this region . . . increased production of food to relieve the world shortage can take place more quickly in this region than in any other." But the vicious circle of a lack of investment keeping output down, and low output failing to provide the necessary surplus for investment, has prevented economic development in agriculture as well as in industry, and in several countries (including Egypt) the standard of living actually declined over the last thirty to forty years.

"Low national incomes, unequally distributed among the population, result in a restricted volume of savings, imperfectly channelled by under-developed money markets and financial institutions and in a scarcity of long-term and medium-term credit, with its consequent shortage of investment. The gap created by the inadequacy of domestic savings has been filled only to a limited extent by foreign capital, which by its very nature can supplement, but not substitute for, local capital, while the contribution to the economy of the region of royalties paid by oil companies and of sterling balances has also been limited. The scarcity of investment funds is reflected in all branches of the economy: in the inadequate transport system, which in many countries retards production; in the primitive methods often used in agriculture; and in the low capitalization and productivity of industry. . . . The poverty of Middle Eastern countries limits the scope of government action by restricting the size of budgets. Moreover, the fiscal systems in general are not progressive. The bulk of the revenue is derived from taxes on consumption."[39]

We find an economic setting, in other words, similar in most respects to the under-developed countries of Southern and South-Eastern Asia, with aggravating circumstances, such as great and growing differences between rich and poor, generating social unrest and political instability, and the weakness or absence of a non-Communist reform movement willing and able to work for social and economic change. It is the ideal breeding-ground for Communism, which promises swift progress by doing away with many of the obstacles which now seem unsurmountable. The intelligentsia is attracted by the bold perspective of overcoming backwardness by the application of radical measures, and the peasants and workers are told that they have nothing to lose but their chains.

PART TWO

EGYPT

Chapter Two

Nationalism and Communism
in Egypt 1919-39

I. ATTEMPTS TO FORM A COMMUNIST PARTY

THREE men met in Alexandria late in 1920 and founded what was later to become the Communist Party of Egypt. The three were Joseph Rosenthal, a jeweller who would soon be expelled for "right-wing deviationism"; Husni al 'Arābi, who became the party delegate to the Comintern and whom we later locate in Nazi Germany teaching Arabic; and Antūn Marūn, a lawyer and the first secretary-general of the party, who was to die in an Egyptian prison in 1924.

The three men founded a party, but they did not bring about a revolution. They soon disappeared from the Egyptian political scene. The party itself went into a state of hibernation for many years. Even its present existence is wrapped in dense, almost impenetrable, clouds of mystery.

A British Communist leader said in 1952 that there exists in Egypt a Communist movement with a long tradition of struggle, but that the various groups which make up the movement have been unable to establish a united party because "of the many difficulties created by the police."[1] The history of Communism in Egypt is therefore that of a movement rather than a party, and the movement consists of many factions, some of which have had a total membership of *one*. Communism as an overt political activity became illegal in 1924-25, and ceased to exist despite several attempts to revive it shortly afterwards. It became a political factor of some importance only after World War II.

The story is long, complicated, and occasionally tedious, even if we concentrate on the main trends and refrain from tracing the fortunes of the smaller groups with their endless splits, mergers, and bitter polemics.

Communism appeared on the Egyptian scene in the early twenties, at a time of national revolt and considerable social ferment. In order to understand it properly, we have first to cast a backward glance at the origins of the national movement in Egypt. This takes us back to the eighties of the last century.

The Ahmad 'Arabi *coup* of 1882 was the first outward sign of this national movement. It was preceded by the activities of various Masonic lodges and of a "National Party" sponsored by army officers of fellah stock.[2] The 1882 movement was a short-lived one, though it was the first to awaken political interest in wide circles. It came to an abrupt end with the military defeat and the arrest of its leaders. In the 1890's a new National Party came into being upon the initiative of Mustafa Kāmil; in contrast to the former organization, this was not a semi-secret society, but one that considered its main task to be political propaganda for constitutional reforms among the intelligentsia. However, the events of 1905–8 in Russia, Turkey, Persia, and elsewhere, which had given a strong impetus to the demand for a constitution, faded into the past, and after 1908, the year Mustafa Kāmil died, the movement faded out, although the party continued to exist, and Egyptian students and a few political leaders in Europe continued their anti-British propaganda, voicing the demand for independence in two national congresses in Geneva and Brussels.

2. THE WAFD

An historian of political parties in Egypt has noted that while the national movement in Egypt during 'Arabi's days was essentially religious and emotional, the movement initiated by Mustafa Kāmil (though in certain respects a revival of the former) appealed to the mind and was led by the small Europeanized middle class. "The dream of a reformed Islam gave place to a well-organized demand for political freedom and self-government. This was not merely a change from Islamic agitation to political xenophobia, but to party organization and propaganda in the European manner, with the political elements dominant."[3] Only after the end of World War I, with the emergence of the Wafd, did the national movement begin to influence and organize the masses. The war had contributed not a little to the general ferment. The constitution, promised on the eve of the war, had been indefinitely postponed, and when it was eventually published in 1918 it provoked a storm of protest because it was so far from what the Egyptians had anticipated. The promise of national self-determination, which had been the avowed aim of the Allies in the war, had given rise to great expectations which were soon disappointed; Britain appeared to be in no mood to abolish the protectorate. When the British High Commissioner refused to permit a delegation (Wafd), headed by Sa'ad Zaghlūl, to proceed to Britain to voice its demands, a wave of protest spread through the country. The leaders of the new movement were arrested in March, 1919, and deported. This was followed by mass strikes and demonstrations, led by the students. Egyptian women participated for the first time. After a few days the general strike spread to the countryside, and Cairo, where some people had already been killed and wounded in clashes with the army, was practically cut off from the rest of the country. In a number of smaller cities, such as Al Minya and Zifta, independent local "republics" were proclaimed. After the arrest of the leaders during the following month, the passive resistance and boycott campaign continued, and under its pressure a "collaborationist" ministry had to resign.

The Wafdist movement had no immediate success, and a renewed strike wave in December, 1921, resulted in the British "Declaration of Independence" of 1922. This was rejected by the Wafd as not going far enough towards meeting its basic demands: viz. that the complete independence of the Nile Valley be recognized, that the British troops be evacuated, and that the new constitution be worked out by representatives of the Egyptian nation, and not by foreigners. The Wafd was realistic enough, however, to accept the 1922 Declaration as an initial compromise solution. In the autumn of 1923 parliamentary elections took place. The Wafd received a large majority. Its leader, Zaghlūl, formed the first government under the new constitution early in 1924.

3. THE GROWTH OF THE SOCIALIST-COMMUNIST PARTY

The first revolutionary socialist cells in Egypt came into being as early as 1918 in the major cities, such as Alexandria, Cairo, and Port Said.[4] A Socialist Party was founded two years later, in 1920, by the Alexandria jeweller Joseph Rosenthal. Initially, this party had no clearly defined aims, nor had it decided which of the international socialist bodies it would join. The majority favoured a *rapprochement* with the Comintern, and the party delegated one of its members to the third Congress of the Communist International (without, however, being a member of that organization). In 1922 it was recognized as a member party of the Comintern, accepted the "21 conditions," and changed its name to "Communist Party of Egypt." Rosenthal, who belonged at that time to the minority opposing the merger, was expelled from the party.[5]

The sources do not agree on the numerical strength of the Socialist-Communist Party. According to one contemporary source it had 1500 members in 1921 and 1000 after the split in 1924.[6] Others mention that the party had 650 members in 1923 (among them 80 per cent. Egyptians and the rest foreigners), and reached 2000 in 1924.[7] According to independent reports received by the author from early members of the Socialist-Communist Party in Egypt, these figures are exaggerated. The party never had more than a few hundred members—and this at a time when membership was based neither on the paying of membership dues nor on absolute ideological identification, but rather on a vague declaration of sympathy and occasional participation in party activities. Of the total party membership, 80–90 per cent. were foreigners, not Egyptians; only during World War II did the Communist groups gradually become Egyptianized. The party even had some difficulty in finding a suitable native candidate as a delegate to the Comintern. Husni al 'Arābi, who went to Moscow, was far from being an ideal choice. He left both the Communist Party and the Soviet Union in the late 1920's, and became an Arabic language teacher in Germany.

In December, 1921, before joining the Comintern, the party had published its political credo[8]; it is an appeal directed to the "manual and non-manual workers of the world," and the "brutal aggression by which British militarist and colonial officials have replied to the sacred demands of Egypt" is sharply denounced. "The Socialist party of Egypt will place itself in the vanguard of the national movement," it is stated, and "the Egyptian intellectual proletariat will cease all collaboration with the oppressors." "The Socialist ideal, which is the expression of the rebirth of the peoples of the world, has appeared in Egyptian political life. Let the intellectuals go to the peasants to create a united political and economic front which is to act at the same time as a counterbalance to the influence of the *bourgeoisie*."

The Socialist-Communist Party programme did not diverge greatly from the national aspirations formulated by the Wafd, apart from the proposed alliance between the intellectual proletariat and the fellaheen, which was impractical for many years in Egypt (though not in other Asiatic and African countries), and the general attitude of suspicion towards the middle class, which was the mainstay of the Wafd. After the party had joined the Comintern, it worked out a political platform which was published in mimeographed tracts in French and Arabic, and later it issued the party paper, *Al Khisāb*. This programme provided for labour legislation, a working day of eight hours, factory inspection, the freedom to found trade unions, equal wages for European and Egyptian workers and employees, recognition of shop stewards, and the establishment of producers' and consumers' co-operatives. There were hardly any differences between it and the Wafd in its foreign political programme: it demanded union with the Sudan, the nationalization of the Suez Canal (the Wafd at that time would have been content with mere neutralization), the repudiation of all state debts, and the abolition of all extraterritorial rights, by which foreigners had many special privileges in the country. More interesting and more specific

34

was the programme on agricultural affairs, though there is some reason to doubt whether these details were based on a real study of the situation of the fellah. The widespread practice of renting land for half of the crop was to be abolished. All the debts of peasants with less than 30 feddan of land should be revoked, all the fellaheen who had less than 10 feddan should not pay taxes at all. The programme also provided for the distribution of the big latifundia; the maximum amount of land to be owned by an individual was fixed at 100 feddan (as compared with 200 under the 1952–53 agrarian reform). There was not a single manual worker among the early members of the Socialist-Communist Party, and the group saw its most vital task as reaching the Egyptian worker by the organization of trade unions. This task was not easy, because few party members spoke and wrote Arabic, and fewer still knew how to approach the Egyptian worker, who was generally a fellah on seasonal work in the city. The Communist movement in Egypt never was (nor is it now at the time of writing) a working-class movement, but it has always tried to win a mass basis among the industrial workers (the effort of the 1920's was even greater than the one made later, although less successful). This mainly took the form of founding trade unions in which individual Communists held the key positions, or of attempts to take over existing trade unions.

Workers' organizations had been in existence in Egypt for many years before the emergence of a Communist movement (apart, of course, from the medieval workers' guilds, some of which continued to exist, but would hardly qualify as trade unions in this context). There had been widespread strikes in Cairo in 1899, demonstrations in front of government buildings, and clashes with the police, and, on the whole, the public supported the workers.[9] In the latter year the tobacco workers' union was founded, and in 1908 there were big strikes in which the tobacco workers were joined by the tramway employees. In 1909 'Omar Bey *Lutfi* founded the "Manual Workers Union" on behalf of Mustafa Kāmil's Nationalist Party, and two years later it contained eleven unions.

Immediately after World War I a new strike wave, the biggest up to that date, shook the country. Factory workers, tram drivers, and even waiters and lamplighters (whose organization was soon to become one of the Communist strongholds) went out on strike. The reasons were not hard to find. The war had brought prosperity to the feudal landowners and to some of the factory owners, but inflation had hit the workers and lower middle class hard and a twelve-hour working day had become quite general. Between 1918 and 1921 many new trade unions were founded in Cairo, Alexandria, Port Said, and other cities, and according to official statistics there were 38 such associations in Cairo in 1922, 33 in Alexandria, and 18 in the Canal zone. Some of them had only a few dozen members, and most lasted only for a few weeks or months, but the relevant fact is that the general trend was towards the organization of workers, however primitive and limited in scope the organization might be.

The strike movement and the demonstrations were followed with misgivings by the government of the day, and a first warning had been given to the trade unions in January, 1921. But the Socialists-Communists went ahead in their efforts to organize the workers (as did the other parties and the independent unions). They were instrumental *inter alia* in organizing the lamplighter strike in Alexandria, and the members of the executive committee of the party were arrested in March, 1922, after demonstrations in the two big cities.[10] They were scheduled to appear before a military court, but were released when martial law was abolished several weeks later.

The Communists were certainly not alone in this field. There existed trade unions which were sponsored by the Nationalists and by the Wafd politicians, and which appeared as independent unions; as well as a few sponsored by Socialists such as Maḥmūd Sāgib and Sabri. In a trade-union congress scheduled for October, 1925, 668 delegates were to represent more than one hundred trade unions comprising 70,000 members.[11] But the congress never took place, although by that time non-Communists had already taken over the leadership.[12] The right to strike had already been limited by the government in 1923, when the workers in public utilities were forbidden to stop work. Some members of the Communist Party central committee were arrested by the police in 1923, and further members were arrested after the general strike of February–March, 1924. This strike provoked violent clashes when workers in Alexandria seized a factory and held it for three days. But the Wafdist government under Saʿad Zaghlūl, which had just come to power, did not hesitate to act, and on July 1, 1924, the principal leaders of the Communist Party were brought to trial. Their trial dragged on for many weeks, and was eventually held behind closed doors because of the risk of "endangering public security."[13] The sentences given to the Communist leaders were comparatively mild, but Antūn Marūn, the leader of the Communist trade unions and the first secretary-general of the party, and an Alexandria lawyer, died in prison.

The main office of the Communist Party was closed by the police, but the party had not yet been declared illegal and it still pursued its activities. By the end of 1924 a new central committee was established which replaced the leaders in prison. At the same time both a legal newspaper (*Al Khisāb*) and an illegal one were published for the first time in Arabic. But on June 5, 1925, the Aḥmad Ziwār government, appointed by the British and the Palace and replacing the democratically elected Wafd cabinet, had the whole Communist leadership and almost all the militants arrested. Among them were Jaboux, who had edited *Al Khisāb*, and Charlotte Rosenthal.[14] The party became illegal, and, in fact, ceased to exist.[15] Among the Communist front organizations which had even earlier ceased to exist was the Egyptian branch of the "Red Help" (M.O.P.R.) in Alexandria, which had collected £1000 (Egyptian) for the victims of starvation in Russia.[16]

4. OBSTACLES TO THE GROWTH OF EGYPTIAN COMMUNISM

The reasons for the failure of Communism in Egypt in the 1920's are obvious. The party had not succeeded in gaining a foothold among the native population and had found its adherents almost exclusively among the minorities: Greeks, Jews, Armenians, etc. Its programme had no relation at all to Egyptian social realities. It did not yet understand the two basic rules for success: First, that the intelligentsia was the main reservoir for enlisting support for the party—instead of regarding the working class as the *mass basis* of the party, they were busy trying to find manual workers for the leadership. Second, instead of laying the main stress on the struggle for national liberation, they concentrated almost exclusively on the class struggle. It was only in the late 1940's that the Communists in Egypt began to adapt themselves to these two basic tenets. This adaptation did not derive from preconceived ideological notions, nor was it even openly admitted. They were simply learning from experience, which in present Communist strategy overrides all other considerations, whatever lip service may be paid to doctrine.

There were certainly enormous difficulties to be overcome. Let us consider for a moment the conditions facing the Egyptian Communists. The living standards of the Egyptian workers and peasants are among the lowest in the world. According to an I.L.O. mission which visited Egypt in the early 1930's, the average daily pay of a skilled worker was 50–80 cents, the pay of an unskilled worker 20–30 cents. The average income of the fellah was said to be 5–6 cents for a working day of twelve hours. Wages have gone up since then, but the cost-of-living index has risen even faster. Illiteracy is general, and an estimated 20–25 per cent. of the city workers are women and children. Housing conditions are appalling. The workers live in filthy hovels; overcrowding in the Cairo and Alexandria slums is fantastic. A writer in the chief Egyptian business periodical, commenting on this dismal state of affairs, reaches the conclusion that "however much one may blame the imperialist power for omissions and commissions, one cannot help the thought that its acceptance by the propertied classes testifies to the depth of moral degradation to which they have sunk."[17]

The state of health of the population is even worse than in China and India: trachoma, bilharzia, and other tropical diseases are endemic. Tuberculosis is widespread, and there are almost yearly outbreaks of epidemic diseases which have not appeared for generations in most other parts of the world. The Egyptian army regards only four of every hundred recruits as capable of being enrolled without medical treatment, and the great majority are rejected for military service altogether. Attempts have been made in recent years to improve the standard of living of the worker, but it will remain low so long as there is such a degree of agricultural over-population in the country.

A diseased, illiterate working class, vegetating below the bare subsistence level, will not, as a rule, produce a fighting and class-conscious organization. It may take part in sudden outbreaks, but it will be unable to sustain a long-term effort. Politically it will tend to gravitate to ideas even more primitive and emotionally attractive than those propagated by the Communists; the Moslem Brotherhood stood a better chance, on the whole, so long as it persisted in social-demagogic slogans. The possibility of propagandist work in the village is restricted. In fact, no Egyptian party has ever succeeded in gaining a real foothold in the villages. The situation of the fellah is even worse, in most respects, than that of the urban worker. Eighty per cent. of all Egyptian farmers own no land. Of those who have land, more than 80 per cent. have less than 2 acres, which is considered the absolute subsistence minimum. Attempts to carry out agrarian reform have been made in recent years, but equally important is the burning question of irrigation. And the problem of agricultural over-population can be solved only by reclamation of part of the desert—a gigantic task which, if ever tackled seriously, will take a long time to show results. The Egyptian village is politically indifferent. The rule of the feudal landowner is still absolute, and the system of control prohibiting political agitation is foolproof in most villages.[18] The village teacher, who makes up the revolutionary element *par excellence* elsewhere in the world, is more often than not a member of the Moslem Brotherhood and not a radical socialist. There has occasionally been agrarian unrest, but this was restricted to a few regions of Upper Egypt and did not last long. Some pre-conditions for a revolutionary agrarian movement on the Chinese model do exist, although it is unlikely that such a movement would be country-wide, except in the wake of a foreign or a civil war or the permanent crippling of the central government.

Another difficult problem, which for many years has caused considerable heart-searching among Egyptian Communists, is the attitude to be adopted towards the national movement. In the beginning the party supported the Wafd, without however contemplating closer alliance—or without any hope of being accepted by the Wafd even as a junior partner in such an alliance. In 1925 Stalin gave what became for many years the classical description of the "immediate tasks" of the revolutionary movement in dependent countries: "In such countries as Egypt or China, where the national *bourgeoisie* is already split into a revolutionary party and a compromising party, but where the compromising section of the *bourgeoisie* cannot yet become *welded* with imperialism, the Communists can no longer make it their aim to form a united front against imperialism. In such countries the Communists must pass from the policy of a united national front to the policy of a revolutionary bloc of the workers and petty *bourgeoisie*. In such countries this bloc may assume the form of a single party of workers and peasants like the Kuomintang, on condition, however, that this peculiar kind of party shall actually represent a bloc of two forces—the Communist Party and the party of the revolutionary petty *bourgeoisie*. The task of this bloc is to expose the temporizing spirit and inconsistency of the national *bourgeoisie* and to wage a determined struggle against imperialism."[19]

These views gradually underwent considerable modification, mainly in view of the sad experience of the Comintern in China in 1927.

5. THE 1930–40 DECADE

After 1928 the Communist movement in Egypt was to be guided by the resolutions of the Sixth Congress of the Comintern (1928). The Egyptian Communist Party, it was stated on that occasion, will be able to play an important role in the national struggle, but only if it bases itself on the organized proletariat. "The organization of trade unions among Egyptian workers, the strengthening of the class struggle, and leadership in the class struggle are, consequently, the first and most important task of the Communist Party. The greatest danger to the trade-union movement in Egypt at the present time lies in the *bourgeois* nationalists getting control of the workers' trade unions. Without a decisive struggle against their influence, a genuine class organization of the workers is impossible. One of the essential defects of the Egyptian Communists in the past has been that they have worked exclusively among the urban workers. A correct setting out of the agrarian question, the gradual drawing into the revolutionary struggle of the masses, constitutes one of the most important tasks of the party. Special attention needs to be devoted to the building up of the party itself, which is still very weak."[20]

In the early 1930's criticism became even stronger, and it was stated that "the national reformist movement in the dependent and colonial countries was the main brake of the revolution—just as the Second International in the imperialist countries"; and the Egyptian Wafd was named specifically among those "traitorous pseudo-nationalist movements."[21] The main assignment of the Communists was to undermine the mass influence of these movements by uncovering their "betrayal."

It is not difficult to divine what the Egyptian Communists thought when these instructions reached them. They had a few dozen adherents in Cairo and Alexandria, almost exclusively foreigners, and the "national movement" did not greatly care whether the Communists decided to join them in the national struggle or to combat them. The party had been on the decline since 1925.

The Comintern executive decided, in the middle 1920's, to send a number of emissaries to Egypt in an attempt to revive the leaderless and practically extinct Communist Party. In 1925 a Russo-Turkish trade company was established in Cairo, which was headed by an American citizen, Ignaz Semenyuk. In 1927 a further trade agency, which called itself "Textilimport," was founded in Alexandria by Alexei Vasiliev and Hugo Rudolf, a German Communist. Semenyuk's attempts to re-establish an Egyptian Communist Party came to an end in 1928, and the above-mentioned heads of "Textilimport" were requested to leave the country in 1929, though the agency under different management continued to exist up to 1932.[22] In 1934 a Syrian Communist, Mahmūd Wahīb Malik, was sent to Egypt in the hope that he would succeed better than his European predecessors, but his activities resulted in the arrest of almost all the forty militants who then made up the party's cadre.

The Comintern emissaries published fairly optimistic reports about the situation. "There were mass strikes, armed workers had built barricades, and only after three days did the police and the army succeed in reoccupying the Boulak Quarter of Cairo."[23] The masses, generally speaking, were looking for a revolutionary solution, and the Wafdists knew about their state of mind; but "the danger of a revolution, the fear of the fellaheen and the workers holds them back."[24]

In the meantime new attempts had been made to resurrect the trade-union movement. Big strikes had taken place in 1926-27, but the attempt to convene a new trade-union conference in the autumn of 1927 was thwarted by the government. In 1928 the political parties, including the Wafd, and later the "Liberal Constitutionalists" and Prince 'Abbās Halīm, a royal prince, became interested in working-class support and founded trade unions of their own. A new trade-union congress, which benefited from a liberal spell between two semi-dictatorships in December, 1930, purported to represent fifty-five unions. But the government of Sidqi Pasha brought new restrictions and the eventual cessation of these activities the following spring. The trade-union leaders succeeded, nevertheless, in contacting both the International Labour Office and the Second International, and both those institutions sent delegations to Egypt; their conclusions did not, however, bring any change in the lot of the Egyptian worker, nor of the workers' organizations.

There were widespread strikes, demonstrations, and clashes with the police (resulting in dead and wounded) in June, 1934, and new life at the same time was given to the trade-union movement as a result of the competition between the Wafd and Prince 'Abbās Halīm. The following five years were not very eventful from the point of view of labour relations.

Eventually, Parliament could no longer ignore the demands for better working conditions, and during the second half of 1939 new and more progressive labour legislation was adopted by the Chamber, only to be rejected by the Senate. The "Fellah Party" meanwhile launched a political campaign, culminating in a hunger strike which attracted wide attention. Inside the Wafd, too, the left wing was on the upswing. It claimed that if the Wafd prevailed, workers would not be persecuted any more and would get a fair deal.[25]

Small Communist groups continued to be active in Cairo and Alexandria, but there was no contact between them and the Comintern, and the members of these groups did not like everything they read in the Moscow publications. They took exception particularly to the Moscow trials, and sometimes voiced, in their leaflets and periodicals, highly unorthodox views betraying a "Trotskyite deviation." Such a group, founded in 1938, was headed by George Hunain and Anwar Kāmil,[26] who published a periodical *At-Tatawwur* (Evolution), only to be suppressed by the authorities after less than a year.

In July, 1940, strikes were banned by order of the government and trade-union activities came to an end for the duration of the war. But the extreme wing of the nationalists continued its propaganda against any Egyptian involvement in the war, and the Communists, though few in number and limited in their influence, were among them. The Wafd, on the other hand, had come to consider post-1935 Italian Fascism as a greater danger to Egyptian independence than British control. After the signing of the Soviet-German agreement in August, 1939, the Egyptian Communists demanded absolute neutrality and denounced British aggression; their stand was identical with the attitude of the government of the day, which refused to declare war against Italy despite the Italian invasion after July, 1940.[27] At this juncture the early history of Communism in Egypt ends; the new groups which came into existence in the later years of the war are a new beginning, unconnected with whatever party activities took place in the country prior to 1940.

Chapter Three

Factional Disputes, 1941-55

I. THE "MARXIST STUDY CIRCLES"

IN the winter of 1941-42, "Marxist study circles" were founded in
Alexandria and Cairo and subsequently became the nucleus of a
new Communist movement in Egypt. Their history from their
foundation up to the present time is enormously complicated. More than
twenty different groups, frequently changing their names and the names
of their publications, have taken part in the competition to become the
only true Egyptian Communist Party. Only the development of the
major factions can be traced in the following account.

Out of the Marxist study circles two political groups emerged in
1942: M.E.L.N.,[1] headed by Henry Curiel, the owner of a Cairo book-
shop; and Iskra,[2] led by Hillel Schwarz—together their membership
numbered no more than thirty. Differences of opinion between the two
factions centred mainly on the practical problem of a Communist
movement in Egypt—should it try to become a mass movement or
should it rather try in its initial stage to educate cadres? Should it attempt to get as many native Egyptians into the ranks of the movement,
though this would necessarily involve lowering the level of political
maturity? Real interest in Marxism, real "class consciousness," was,
after all, much more prevalent among the foreigners resident in Egypt.
Disputes on these issues continued for many years. M.E.L.N. saw the
party cell as a fighting unit (*cellule unite de lutte*), while Iskra put the
stress on preparing cadres and preferred a *cellule unite d'études*. M.E.L.N.
stood for "Egyptianization" and "proletarization" of the party, while
Iskra maintained that under present conditions most cadres would have
to belong to the "intelligentsia," and frequently to the national minorities, and no artificial attempt should be made to attract to the movement
elements which would lessen the Communist character of the party. In
September, 1943, a further split occurred when a number of M.E.L.N.

42

members seceded and founded an organization of their own, Taḥrīr ash-Sh'ab (People's Liberation), which was, in theory at least, to emphasize even more the necessity of Egyptianizing the party.

2. THE INFLUENCE OF SOVIET MILITARY SUCCESSES

Between 1943 and 1945 several other Communist groups came into being in a general atmosphere of pro-Sovietism which had received its main impetus from the Soviet military victories. (Diplomatic relations had been established between Egypt and the Soviet Union in 1943.) Among these factions *At-Talīa* (The Vanguard) should be mentioned in the first place. This was a group of Wafdist students and intellectuals, mainly concentrated in Alexandria, who came to be swept more and more into the Soviet orbit; this flirtation was to continue and grow in intensity subsequently. Other groups included the Marxist League, Citadelle, and Al Fagr al Gadīd (The New Dawn), which published for some time (1945–46) a widely read Communist weekly of the same name. It would lead us too far afield to analyse in detail the programmes of the smaller groups, none of which numbered more than thirty to forty members. The New Dawn charged the M.E.L.N. with deviating from Marxist-Leninist orthodoxy because it put too much faith on classes other than the proletariat. In one of its publications it accused the M.E.L.N., more specifically, of expecting revolutionary action from the lower middle class, and of working for a popular front while neglecting to build strong party cadres. However, despite these internal struggles and the lack of efficient leadership, M.E.L.N. (and to a lesser degree the other Communist factions) continued to grow because the general political climate of anti-Fascism was extremely favourable, and dis-satisfaction with the government was widespread among the intelli-gentsia. By the end of the war the number of active Communists was 1000, perhaps slightly higher, and it continued to rise. On the trade-union delegation which represented Egypt at the W.F.T.U. Congress in Paris in 1945, two out of four members belonged to M.E.L.N., while in the National Committee of Workers and Students founded shortly there-after, all of the Communist factions were represented. When this organization (in which the Moslem Brotherhood and the Wafd had originally taken part as well) broke down, a new front (the Egyptian Students' Association) was founded, in which the M.E.L.N. took the leading part. M.E.L.N. also headed several big strikes, including the Shubra al Khaima textile workers' strike (in May, 1947), the largest of all, while the other groups, notably Iskra and The New Dawn, ap-parently kept aloof and were subsequently charged with lack of assist-ance by the M.E.L.N.

3. THE FORMATION OF COMMUNIST FACTIONS

In July, 1946, the Isma'īl Sidqi government clamped down on Communism in Egypt. But the arrests affected mainly the smaller groups and the pro-Communist Wafdists, while M.E.L.N. and Iskra did not greatly suffer from the measures adopted. If the arrests had any effect at all, it was to cause a *rapprochement* between the main factions in Egyptian Communism. In the winter of 1946–47 talks took place between the leaders of both groups, and after lengthy debates they decided to merge in May, 1947; the new movement became known under the name of "M.D.L.N." (*Mouvement Démocratique de Libération Nationale*; "D.M.N.L." in English; "HADITU" in Arabic). This new union lasted for about one year, until July, 1948. Several months previously the "People's Liberation" and Citadelle had ceased to exist; some of their members had joined the M.E.L.N., others went to Iskra. Only Talī'a remained outside, though the Iskra leaders had tried very hard to win them over.

When the two main factions in Egyptian Communism merged, Iskra reported 900 members and M.E.L.N. 500; both estimates were somewhat exaggerated, especially the figure given by Iskra. But M.E.L.N. statistics were also open to grave doubts. According to their statement, 250 of their members (50 per cent.) were workers, 90 "youth," 80 students, 25 per cent. soldiers or army officers, 25 pupils of Al Azhar, the Moslem Seminary—no intellectuals and no non-Egyptians were reported by them.[3] After the merger had taken place, the majority of Talī'a joined the new group, while the small groups which had remained outside, including the Marxist League[4] and The New Dawn, united in an opposition bloc, denouncing M.D.L.N. as "Fascist, imperialist, and Zionist," with the latter replying in kind. But the honeymoon lasted only four months. Already in September, 1947, the old quarrels were renewed, and there were frequent changes in the ten-man party executive (five from each faction). The old M.E.L.N. faction insisted on the popular (national) "Front" tactics, while Iskra maintained that it had been right all along in its belief that more cadres should be trained first of all, and this should be the main assignment of the new party. There were new factions, too. Sulaimān demanded that Hillel Schwarz and Henry Curiel should be expelled from the leadership in order to give the party a more "Egyptian character" (and presumably in order to give Sulaimān more influence).[5] There were differences of opinion, too, on the Palestine question. The M.E.L.N. faction approved of the Soviet stand in favour of partition; while the head of Iskra founded, in the winter of 1947–48, the Jewish League against Zionism, which, however, found little response and was dissolved after a few weeks of existence.

In November, 1947, the party executive decided to establish a new central committee in which the M.E.L.N. was to get nine seats out of fifteen, Iskra five, and Tali'a one. This increase in the influence of their old rivals was resented by Iskra, who agreed, however, that an effort should be made to stamp out factionalism. At the same time they insisted on the need for greater party democracy within the movement and criticized the "terroristic methods of the new Central Committee." But Iskra proved incapable of rallying a united front against M.E.L.N., and it split into no fewer than three different subfactions.[6] Iskra, which had been even more non-Egyptian than M.E.L.N., now demanded that the leadership of the party should be Egyptianized (in order to oust Henry Curiel), and it declared in its publications that, owing to its preoccupation with front organizations, the M.D.L.N. had, in fact, become a front, rather than a Communist, party. M.E.L.N. countered by pointing to the necessity both of creating a party according to the example given by Lenin and Stalin and of collaborating with other "mass organizations."

Both these arid discussions and the stringent measures taken by the police in the spring of 1948 weakened the M.D.L.N. In April it was decided to convene a party congress to reach a decision about the future of the party. But Iskra demanded that sympathizers, too, should be permitted to take part in the congress,[7] while M.E.L.N. was opposed to the suggestion. When Egypt decided to enter the Palestinian war in May, 1948, these discussions came to a sudden end. One hundred Communists were arrested immediately after the declaration of martial law on May 15. In July, 1948, the remnants of the party executive again convened and demanded that the principle of "democratic centralism" should be adhered to strictly by all party members; in other words, the instructions of the executive (with a M.D.L.N. majority) should be accepted without question.

Both 'Ādil's group and the other Iskra subfactions continued to resist and called for the convocation of the congress, which under conditions of martial law was, of course, impossible. At the same session 'Ādil's friends established themselves as a new party, "M.D.L.N.—(O.R.)."[8] Other militants proclaimed the foundation of a second group, Nahu al hizb ash-shuyu'ī al misri, or the N.H.S.M. (*Vers un Parti Communist Egyptien*).

All these decisions were, however, of little if any importance, for martial law continued to be in force in Egypt from May, 1948, until February, 1950, and during that period there was little overt Communist activity in the country. The number of those incarcerated in the concentration camps of Huckstep and Abukir reached 3000, but only a minority of these were party members. The number of the Moslem Brotherhood, Jews, and even Wafdists was larger. M.D.L.N. lost contact with its branches outside Cairo and Alexandria, and although a few issues of illegal magazines were printed and distributed[9] they neither reached wide circles nor had any appreciable influence. The whole party organization had been dislocated, but in a long-range view, the new allies and friends won in the concentration camps were more important for the future development of the group than its temporary eclipse. Many Wafdists, members of the Moslem Brotherhood, and non-party people there met Communists in the flesh for the first time, and the very fact of their arrest on a charge of Communist or other subversive activities was bound to make Communists or at least sympathizers out of people who had been very far from the movement when they first entered Huckstep or Abukir. It is there that the foundation was laid for the "National Front" of 1951-52, through which the Communists achieved their greatest successes in the history of their movement.

Most Communists were released from the concentration camps by the end of 1949 or early 1950, and the M.D.L.N. renewed its activities at once in Cairo and Alexandria. The attitude of the authorities (the Wafd at that time) was not consistent. The party was outlawed but "Front" organizations, as a rule, were tolerated. These included the "Peace Movement" in 1950-51 and the "National Front" in 1951-52. Actual Communist activities, however, were not allowed, and arrests took place frequently. Among those arrested late in 1949 were Dr. Sharīf Hatāta and Kāmil 'Abdul Halīm, both leading members of the M.D.L.N.[10] In the summer of 1950 Henry Curiel, Hillel Schwarz, and others were re-arrested, and the following summer the printing press of the movement was seized; Henry Curiel was deported to Italy in August, 1950.

The troubled years of 1951-52, the nationalist agitation aided and abetted by the government, and the impotence of the Wafdist leadership created ideal conditions for the growth of Communism; M.D.L.N., which had numbered not more than 100-200 members when martial law was abolished in February, 1950, had 2000-3000 followers by the end of 1952, and the other Communist groups grew correspondingly. M.D.L.N. had regained its influence in leading trade unions; it claimed to have established branches or at least "contacts" in villages (thirty in 1951, a hundred in 1952). It had founded "Democratic Councils" in the Egyptian army and air force, and it had greatly strengthened its hold on the students' organizations.

As a result of the arrests and deportations, a number of M.D.L.N. found themselves outside Egypt, and several M.D.L.N. branches were founded in Europe. One in London attempted, without much success, to convince the British Communists that M.D.L.N. should be recognized at last as the official Communist Party in Egypt. At first the British Communists tended to accept this claim,[11] but later, after it appeared that much of the information supplied by the M.D.L.N. had been false, wiser counsels prevailed. In any case it was not for the

British Communists to decide. The M.D.L.N. branch in France engaged both in trade and in the publication of a news-sheet, and there were other branches in Italy and Austria. What should be noted in particular is that although many of the non-Egyptian old-timers were compelled to become inactive after 1950 or to leave the country altogether, the M.D.L.N. had found enough native cadres to ensure continuity in its activities. Among those who took over from the old leadership was Sā'ad Kamil, a lawyer (and a nephew of Fathi Ridwān), who became the leading force in the "Peace Movement," and Sa'īd Sulaimān Rifā'i, a mechanic, who became the secretary of M.D.L.N.[12] The development of the smaller groups between 1950 and 1952 was less clear. Al Fagr al Gadīd (The New Dawn) continued to exist; Iskra had been dissolved after two of its leading members, in prison, announced their adhesion to M.D.L.N. Other Iskra members continued to be active in the Communist Party of Egypt (C.P.E.) or Towards a Communist Party Egypt (N.H.S.M., the initials in Arabic). Early in 1952 negotiations for a possible merger between this group and the M.D.L.N. took place, but were, however, unsuccessful. Other small groups which published occasional leaflets or showed other signs of activity during the same time included Red Star, Popular Democracy and the Nucleus of Egyptian Communist Party (Nawat al Hizb, etc.). There was also at least one Communist opposition group among the trade unionists headed by Yusūf Mudrik, who had led the delegation to the W.F.T.U. Congress in Paris in 1945. Most of these organizations—very few of which lasted for more than a few months—opposed the M.D.L.N. "fronts" and its "Fascist allies," and *Popular Revolt*, a bulletin published by Al Fagr al Gadīd (which had absorbed parts of Tahrīr ash-Sha'ab) openly attacked the Communist Peace Movement sponsored by M.D.L.N.[13]

4. THE JUNTA OF JULY, 1952

This fantastically complicated situation appeared to become more simple when General Naguīb came to power in July, 1952; only the M.D.L.N. and the Egyptian Communist Party (under its different names) continued to exist. But after a very short time new groups came into being, both legal and illegal; and to make confusion worse confounded for the outside observer and the historian there were splits within the M.D.L.N.

The *coup d'état* of July, 1952, and the deposition of Farouk in July, 1952, were reported by the M.D.L.N. to the other Communist Parties in the world as an action engineered by its representatives in the army. The organ of the British Communist Party was indeed taken in by these reports and wrote: "The Free Officers Committee, it is claimed, represents an almost equal combination of M.D.L.N., Moslem

Brotherhood and Independents. . . . M.D.L.N. appears to have considerable influence in the armed forces."[14] In Egypt the M.D.L.N. wholeheartedly supported the *coup* and distributed leaflets, both on the day of the *coup* and during the week thereafter, expressing complete and unreserved support. It claimed that it had known all along about the preparations for the *coup*, that two of the members of the junta (Yūsnf Sādiq and Khālid Muhi ad-Dīn) were party members and that others were sympathizers. Subsequent events have shown that M.D.L.N. may have had (and may continue to have) sympathizers among the fringe of the junta, but it most probably had only one in its inner circle (Yūsuf Sādiq). Another friend was Captain Mustafa Kamāl Sidqi, a former commander of King Farouk's bodyguard,[15] an adventurer rather than a convinced Communist, and one who had dallied with the M.D.L.N. as he had with the "Free Officers" and other organizations.

During the first months after the *coup* all but fourteen political prisoners were released, and the parties obtained almost unrestricted freedom of action. Two legitimate groups, in competition with each other, were established by the Communists, although both had the unofficial backing of M.D.L.N. The National Liberation faction (At-Tahrīr al Watani) was headed by the "Red Pasha," Kāmil al Bindari, former Egyptian ambassador to Moscow and leading "fellow-traveller" in the country, and one of the richest landowners in Egypt. He was joined by Yūsuf Hilmi, Ibrahīm Hilmi, as well as Sa'ad Kāmil, all leading members of M.D.L.N. In their published programme they demanded the revision of the constitution by Parliament; nationalization of all monopolist companies, including the Suez Canal Company; distribution to the poor peasants of all the land not cultivated at the present time; defence of local industry and Egyptian capital; the right of workers to organize; the granting of political rights to women, etc.[16] The government refused, however, to recognize this group. It may be of some interest to note that the leaders of the group combined support for the new military regime with defence of the Wafd, which was just then under attack from many quarters.[17] Kāmil al Bindari was perhaps repaying an old political debt.

The other "legal" Communist party was Fathi ar-Rāmla's Democratic Party, which also tried in vain to obtain official recognition, but which was permitted to publish a magazine *Al Mu'ārada* (Opposition). Fathi ar-Rāmla, who had been a member of the Wafd in the early 1940's, first became known as a popularizer of Socialist and Communist literature in 1943-44. In his magazine he argued that the junta was not willing to carry the revolution to its end; many of the enemies of democracy in Egypt had not yet been arrested, Point Four and other agreements with America had not been denounced, the reactionary laws (to combat Communism) had not been revoked. Ar-Ramla also came out in his magazine in favour of peace with Israel, because it "would be stupid to open a second front in our fight against Imperialism."[18]

Whereas M.D.L.N. enjoyed a large degree of freedom during 1952, all the other Communist groups, which had opposed the military junta from the outset, were less well treated. Ibrahīm 'Arafa and some other leaders of the P.C.E. (Communist Party of Egypt) were arrested in September, 1952, and the activities of this faction were paralysed for several months.

But relations between Naguīb and the M.D.L.N. in their turn rapidly deteriorated in the autumn of 1952. There was the Kafar ad-Dawar incident, in which police clashed with strikers following a big demonstration provoked by opposition elements.[19] The Naguīb government wanted to put domestic reform first, while the Communists demanded that the "national struggle" should be given priority. M.D.L.N. opposed both the purge of the administrative bureaucracy, which was carried out by the new regime, and the willingness to reach a compromise with Britain on the future of Suez. It attacked agrarian reform and reclamation as mere eye-wash—though there is some reason to believe that it was afraid of these schemes, trying to copy Lenin who had at one time, in very different conditions, pointed to the danger of Stolypin's reforms. The M.D.L.N. representatives abroad were given new and quite different instructions, a situation which must have caused considerable embarrassment. Only as recently as August, Naguīb had been hailed as a friend and ally—now they had regretfully to inform the Communists abroad that he was, after all, an imperialist agent who had aligned himself with the West.[20] When Naguīb faced growing opposition from the political parties, he again reinstated political control, and by January, 1953, all the semi-legal Communist groups and their organs (*Al Malāyīn, Al Mu'ārada, Al Kātib*, etc.), were again banned. One hundred members of the M.D.L.N. and the other factions were arrested at the same time; they retaliated by declaring open war on the regime in their leaflets and stressed the necessity "to uncover his real class face and to tear off his national and democratic disguise." The M.D.L.N. leaflets protested against the arrest of "progressive free officers," among them Yūsuf Sādiq, who had been, according to them, one of their representatives in the junta. The "Peace Movement," on the other hand, was hardly affected by this deterioration in relations. A big delegation was permitted to proceed to the Vienna Congress and the Communists were allowed to establish new peace councils in the factories and the universities. It appears likely that the Naguīb government, in order not to offend Russia, did not interfere with these activities; the junta wanted to maintain good relations with the East in order to have greater bargaining power in its relations with the West.

During 1953 M.D.L.N. reached working agreements with both the Wafdist leadership and, in particular, with the Moslem Brotherhood; agreement for co-ordination in the common struggle against the military regime was also reached. Pro-Soviet Wafdist groups, who had co-operated with the Communists in 1944-45 (*At-Talīa al Wafdīyya*, the Wafdist Vanguard), again established themselves as a political group with Al Gabha al Dimukratīyya al Muttahida (United Democratic Front) under Abu Bakr Saif an-Nāsir and Ibrahīm al Bikār.[21] Another organization partly overlapping with U.D.F. was the National Democratic Front (N.D.F.), also consisting of Communists, Wafdists, and "Independents." In their literature they called for the overthrow of the military regime and the intensification of the struggle against "Western imperialism," as well as for general support for the declared aims of Soviet foreign policy.

5. THE ATTACK ON COMMUNISM

M.D.L.N. again split in July, 1953, for reasons incomprehensible to an outside observer (but probably largely personal reasons), and a faction calling itself "The Revolutionary Trend in the M.D.L.N." emerged. In August, 1953, a wave of arrests of Communist leaders started, which lasted for one year, affecting in December, 1953, both the M.D.L.N. and two sections of the Egyptian Communist Party (Nahu and Nawah) and, eventually, in the spring and summer of 1954, the U.D.F. and the N.D.F. This followed Communist-inspired demonstrations in February, 1954 (at the time of the Naguīb-Nāsir crisis), and in July and August against the Suez agreement. The regime of Colonel 'Abdul Nāsir took even more stringent measures against the Communists than had General Naguīb, and in a series of trials in the autumn of 1954 many Communist leaders and militants were given long prison sentences.[22] Information which came to light about the relations of the Communist movement with the Iron Curtain countries and with certain diplomatic circles in Cairo have strengthened the government's hand in dealing with Communist penetration and have sharpened its sense of danger, according to *The Times* correspondent in Cairo.[23] "Pseudo-Communist cells were formed by the security services wherever the Communists were suspected of operating; infiltration of real Communist cells by government agents followed," according to the same source. But "Communist leaflets continue to circulate, Communist doctrines are popular in university circles, and the organization, with some 7000 members, seems to remain in being."

6. COMMUNISM EGYPTIANIZED

This statement defined fairly accurately the state of affairs at the end of 1954. The Communist movement continued to be split, despite new attempts to unify it in 1954 and the establishment of a "co-ordination committee," but it has, nevertheless, made considerable headway since 1950. Government repression seriously impeded its work, but the working alliance with the Wafd and the Moslem Brotherhood made it possible to reach wide circles and to win new friends and sympathizers. In free elections the Communists would not stand a chance of competing with the big political groups, but in conditions of underground work neither the Wafd nor the Ikhwān are a match for the Communists, who are better organized. They are probably by now the most strongly organized political group in the universities, and they have regained some of their prestige in the trade unions. The movement has not quite been "proletarized," but it has certainly become Egyptianized. There are Jewish and Greek and Armenian cells, but they are by now only a fraction of the Communist movement, and the leadership is exclusively Egyptian: Sulaimān Rifā'i and Khalīl Turk, Muhammad 'Ali 'Amr and Hasan 'Abdur-Rahmān, Mubārak 'Abdul Fādil, and Muhammad Tāhīr al Badri.[24] The Egyptian authorities have not substantially changed their attitude towards Communism at home as the result of the *rapprochement* with the Soviet Union in 1955. Whether the members of the junta will be able to go on indefinitely to praise the Communist Party of the Soviet Union while denouncing the Communist movement in Egypt is a different question. The Egyptian Communists, on the other hand, have dropped their attacks against the foreign policy of the government. Their criticism of the junta's domestic policy has been considerably softened, though not discontinued altogether. In October, 1955, Gamal Abdul Nāsir ceased to be the "slave of Dulles," and the junta, "essentially Fascist" up to that date, became now essentially Democratic-Progressive. (February, 1956.)

The weakness of Communism in Egypt is the fact that most of its new adherents are "fellow-travellers" rather than convinced party members. From the Communist point of view, the acceptance of vague pro-Soviet slogans does not provide a safe and lasting basis; it only creates possibilities.

Chapter Four

Egyptian Communism in Action – a Résumé

1. THE TRADE UNIONS

THE attempts of M.D.L.N. and the other Communist groups to gain a decisive hold on the Egyptian labour movement go back to 1944. In December of that year the "Congress of Workers' Unions" was founded by Communist initiative. This was a federation of several trade unions that came into being on an *ad hoc* basis following the announcement that a World Federation of Trade Unions (W.F.T.U.) would be founded in Paris early in 1945. The Congress was intended to be recognized in Paris as the representative of all, or at least of most, Egyptian workers. It represented, according to its own statement, 103 unions with 80,000 members, and it chose Muhammad al Mudrik as its representative. The figure was vastly exaggerated, and Mudrik was certainly not recognized as the representative of all Egyptian workers, not even within the Communist camp. Another Communist delegation to the W.F.T.U. Congress was to be headed by David Fuād Nahoum, Muhammad 'Abdul Halīm, and Murād al Kaliubi (the latter two did not actually attend), and there were several independent representatives.[1] At the time of the Paris Conference agreement was reached among the Egyptian representatives, but it did not last, and after the delegation's return to Egypt there was founded the Workers' Committee for National Liberation, which was affiliated to the M.D.L.N. Its programme, as announced in Paris, was a working week of forty hours, one paid rest-day each week, social insurance, and work to be provided for those who had been employed by the British army during the war (300,000 workers!). The other demands, points 5 to 10 of the programme, were political: evacuation of the Nile Valley by the "imperialistic troops," opposition to the "Fascist Zionist movement," a fight against Fascism and reaction everywhere in the world, etc.[2] Several leaders of this group were arrested in January, 1946; though subsequently acquitted, they were re-arrested in the course of the arrests of Communist militants and sympathizers in July, 1946. However, the internal splits were more damaging than government persecutions. Apart from the fact that many unions, and among them the strongest (such as the tramway workers), remained under the leadership of non-Communists, the various Communist factions continued to quarrel among themselves. The attempt to call a general strike on June 25, 1946, was an unmitigated failure. This came as a sequel to many small-scale strikes, mainly in the Shubra al Khaima area (a concentration of textile factories), where hardly a week passed during the winter of 1945–46 without a walk-out. Many of these strikes were political, and the workers ceased to support the leaders of the Congress after realizing that Congress activities were not helping to promote their own demands. In September, 1947, there was another big strike in the Mahalla al Kubra section of Cairo (also mainly textile workers), in which four workers were killed and forty wounded in clashes between the police and the workers, who staged a sit-down strike. After the Mahalla al Kubra violence there was a lull of almost four years in the activities of the Communist trade unions. The condition of the workers in the post-war years undoubtedly offered fertile ground for Communist propaganda. But the Communists—even if we may disregard for a moment their own internal divisions—were far more interested in fomenting general unrest, for reasons not quite obvious to most workers, and thus weakened their position in the trade unions. A new upsurge in their activities came only with the abolition of martial law in 1950 and the general reorganization of Communist groups. The strike movement became more intense in 1950, and in the same year another "Preparatory Committee" was founded by the Communists to bring about the establishment of a new federation of Egyptian workers. According to Communist sources, this Committee was said to represent 104 unions and 65,000 workers—a more modest figure than the one given in 1945.[3] This initiative, too, was not crowned with success, and at least three groups of Communist-dominated, and several independent unions, continued to exist.[4] Most resented by the Communists was a "yellow transport workers' union headed by the British agent Zain ad-Dīn," as one of their leaflets stated.[5] The Communist factions had individual workers among their leading members, and some, such as Anwar Makkār, Muhammad Shata, and Muhammad 'Ali 'Amr (all three belonging to M.D.L.N.), were active trade unionists who had great personal influence among the workers. But M.D.L.N. was much more interested in strengthening its various "national fronts" in 1951–52 than in extending its strongholds in the trade unions. This, moreover, would have created serious political difficulties; it would have caused a deterioration in the relations with the Wafd, and would have "split the united anti-imperialist front." As a result, the Communists failed to exploit all the possibilities open to them in the trade-union field in 1951–52.

When General Naguīb came to power his regime was enthusiastically greeted by both the "Confederation of Trade Unions" (the former Congress) and the "Union of Egyptian Trade Unions."[6] Both upheld the stand of the junta on the Kafar ad-Dawar incidents, strongly denouncing the *agents provocateurs* who had staged the demonstrations. Several weeks later, when the M.D.L.N. decided to come out against the new regime, it appeared that it had lost much of its influence in the trade-union movement and had to start over again almost from scratch.

During the first months of the new military regime a number of labour laws had been promulgated, such as the conciliation and arbitration laws, and the trade-union law, which, while encouraging the formation of unions, made government control obligatory. (By the end of 1953 the number of trade unions was reported to have exceeded 900!) At the same time most of the Communist militants in the unions —apart from those who had come to support Naguīb and Colonel 'Abdul Nāsir—were expelled from key positions.

Gamāl 'Abdul Nāsir, in particular, realized the political importance of the workers, and placed his aides in strategically important positions in the unions. Following demonstrations by these unions, the tug-of-war in the junta was decided in his favour in February, 1954. An appraisal of the social character of the military regime in Egypt is outside the scope of this study; though Gamāl 'Abdul Nāsir has learned much from Péron, he is not as obviously wooing the *descamisados* as Péron did. But from the point of view of the workers, military rule was preferable to the old regime—not only of King Farouk but also of the Wafd, neither of which had done anything for the worker. It was for this reason that the Communist-Wafdist alliance in 1953–54 attracted little sympathy among the workers, and labour remained the weakest spot in Communist activities.

2. STUDENTS

University students and the pupils of the upper forms of the secondary schools have played, together with the army, the most important role in recent Egyptian history. The background of the student movement and its support for extremist parties in the Middle East has been given in Chapter One, but additional details relevant to the situation in Egypt will have to be provided.

The various Communist factions contained a high percentage of students, and there were separate Communist students' sections. In

February, 1946, the National Committee of Workers and Students was founded in Cairo, and it headed the big demonstrations which took place during that month in several Egyptian cities. Following an unsatisfactory exchange (from the Egyptian point of view) of notes between London and Cairo on the future of the country, the student leaders called a demonstration for February 9, in which they demanded full independence and the evacuation of British troops. The demonstrators clashed with the police on 'Abbās Bridge, and there were several dead and wounded. The students' tempers were running high; the following day an executive of 115 members was elected from the various Cairo schools and universities (in the presence of their teachers), in order to continue the struggle. Contact was established with the workers of Shubra al Khaima, who had been on strike, and a National Committee was established. Among its members were representatives of the Communist factions, the left wing of the Wafd, and the Moslem Brotherhood, who left the Committee, however, after a few days. A girl student, Surāya Adham, and a worker, Husain Qāsim, were elected secretaries of the Committee. The Committee called for a general strike on February 21, and said in its manifesto that on this day "the Egyptian people will show Britain and the world that it is ready for a fight which will not end until it achieves its independence."[7] There were large-scale demonstrations in Cairo, Alexandria, and elsewhere, and dozens of casualties occurred, but the storm blew over as suddenly as it had started. The Committee ceased to exist after a few weeks. The reason given for this by a Communist writer, viz. that the failure of the Committee to establish contacts with the peasants was the cause of the breakdown, is unconvincing.[8] The Communist cells in the universities continued to exist, and were strengthened by the influx of new members following the decision of the Wafdist "Vanguard" group to secede from the Wafd. The usual Communist activities in the high schools and universities continued, and there were small-scale strikes, demonstrations, meetings, publications of nationalist slogans, etc.

But all in all, Communist influence was at a low ebb among the students during 1948–50; only with the coming to power of the Wafdist government were new attempts made to found a Democratic Union of Students as well as a Congress of Patriotic Students, and similar front organizations. The Students' Congress published a "National Charter"[9] in which it asked, among other things, for "the recruitment of the people in an armed struggle," as well as "opposition to any regional bloc" and "to fight side by side with all the people of the world for peace, for the decisions of the Warsaw Congress and those of the Committee of the 'Partisans of Peace' in Egypt and Sudan."

The heyday of student demonstrations came in 1951 and in the first half of 1952. The following short list of "student activities" in the course of a mere three weeks in October, 1951, comes from a Communist source, and has to be taken with the usual grain of salt. But it, nevertheless, conveys a typical picture.

October 6, 1951.—Beginning of the school year in Egypt.

October 9, 1951.—General strike in all Egyptian schools and universities to protest against the unequal treaties with Great Britain. Tens of thousands of students demonstrated in the streets all over the country against imperialism and the "Middle East Command." Port Said students organized a demonstration in front of the British warships anchored in the harbour.

October 10, 1951.—Sudanese students organized mass demonstrations against British occupation. In Cairo, secondary-school students marched to Fuād University, where they decided unanimously and with great enthusiasm to give their entire support to national demands. In the evening students marched in the streets with torches, demanding an energetic struggle against imperialism. Students were on strike in the whole country.

October 11, 1951.—Ten thousand students from Cairo and surrounding districts held a public assembly in Ibrahīm Pasha Square in the centre of Cairo. They decided to boycott the products of the imperialist states . . . to set up battalions for the defence of national sovereignty.

October 16, 1951.—Students in Isma'ilia resisted aggressive action of the occupation troops . . . schools are closed down in the whole Suez Canal area.

October 17, 1951.—Three pupils were killed by the occupation troops: Ramadān Hasan, 12 years old; Farūq 'Abdul Hamīd, 11 years old; Nabīl Mansūr Fidda, 11 years old.

October 18, 1951.—Alexandrian students, gathered in a general assembly, asked the government to decide on general mobilization and to create people's battalions.

October 19, 1951.—Representatives of the students, participating in a meeting in Alexandria, decided to organize the people's fight against imperialism.

October 21, 1951.—In Tanta, secondary-school pupils drove British inspectors from their schools. In Cairo, thousands of students in Fuād University mingled with delegates of the workers. Amid great enthusiasm, the creation of a National Committee of Workers and Students is announced. The following resolutions are unanimously passed: . . . pact of friendship and non-aggression with the Soviet Union, wholehearted support for the world Peace Council. . . .

October 22, 1951.—The professors of Farūq University in Alexandria decided to participate actively in the national struggle and protested against imperialist actions. At Ibrahīm University in Assiout students held a general assembly and demanded the creation of people's battalions.

October 24, 1951.—Several thousand students in Omdurman (Sudan) demonstrated under the slogan, "Long live the revolution against imperialism." Gordon College in Khartoum was closed down following a general strike of the students.

October 26, 1951.—All professors of Fuād University decided to take an active part in the national fight.

October 28, 1951.—In Shindi, Port Sudan, Omdurman, and elsewhere in the Sudan, there were great popular demonstrations against imperialism. . . . Secondary schools were stormed by British troops, students and professors were arrested. . . .

October 29, 1951.—General strike of Omdurman students to protest. . . .

October 30, 1951.—Students of Hantoub secondary school in Wādi Madani went on strike. . . . Students occupied their school and refused to leave it.[10]

Elsewhere we have dealt with the historical and social causes of the prominent part of students in the Communist-front movements. It has also been pointed out that many, probably most, of the demonstrations were launched by secondary-school pupils (the 13–18-year-olds) rather than university students! But it may be misleading to give students a central place in Communist activities. Students were, and are likely to remain, a revolutionary element in the Arab countries. They will always be against the party or group in power. They were, and are, ready to engage in short bouts of hectic activity, but not in a sustained effort. They readily accept, moreover, the popular-front slogans (national liberation, etc.), but are far less willing to submit to strict party discipline. So long as the Communists were moving with the general trend of public opinion, the students could be relied upon, but once the Communists clashed with other political forces inside the country, student support could not be depended on.

Nevertheless, student demonstrations, organized by the Communists and their front organizations (in collaboration with the Wafd and the Moslem Brotherhood), remained one of the main sources of concern for the military junta in 1952–55. The beginning of the scholastic year was frequently postponed when the government wanted to make important decisions and did not want to run the risk of student demonstrations.

3. "PARTISANS OF PEACE"

The Partisans of Peace were less active in Egypt than in most other Arab countries. This was only natural in view of the fact that after 1949 the Communists put "armed resistance to imperialism" far above peaceful coexistence propaganda. Altogether, 12,000 signatures for the Stockholm appeal were collected in Egypt in 1950, and about 100,000 for the other appeals in 1951. Among the bigwigs of the movement in Egypt were the "Red Pasha," Kāmil Bindari, formerly Egyptian ambassador to Moscow, Mrs. Siza Nabrāwi, deputy president of the Egyptian feminist association (the "Daughters of the Nile"), Hafni Mahmūd Pasha of the Liberal party (a former minister of trade), some parliamentary deputies belonging to the left-wing Wafd, such as Ibrahīm Tala'at, the late 'Azīz Fahmi, Dr. Hanīf ash-Sharīf, Dr. Muhammad Mandūr, and others, as well as political leaders of the semi-Fascist right, such as Ahmad Husain and Fathi Ridwān. The latter participated in some of the peace congresses in Europe, notably the Vienna Congress.[11] The Partisans of Peace also published a periodical, *Al Kātib*, which claimed a circulation of 22,000 and which 'Ali Māhir prohibited in February, 1952. The fact that the party lacked prominent, and above all reliable, "fellow-travellers" and personalities willing to act as a front for the Communist movement, caused M.D.L.N. to make one of its leading members, Sa'ad Kāmil, a poet, head of the peace movement. The general secretary of the peace partisans was Yūsuf Hilmi, a Communist lawyer, who had originally belonged to the pro-Fascist wing of the Nationalist Party.

4. COMMUNIST RELATIONS WITH OTHER PARTIES

Relations between the Communists and other political parties in Egypt have not undergone basic changes during the last five years. Most interesting is their relationship with the nationalist and Moslem extremist groups. Until 1949 both Ahmad Husain's party and the Moslem Brotherhood were bitterly denounced and attacked as Fascist groups. "Fascists are Fascists wherever they are," the editor of the M.D.L.N. journal wrote in January, 1948. "Their supreme aim is to break the unity of the struggle for freedom. The Moslem Brotherhood is one of the Fascist groups in Egypt. . . ."[12] Ahmad Husain was attacked in even more violent terms, and occasionally called a "British agent" as well.[13] After the abolition of martial law early in 1950, the "National Front" came into being and the M.D.L.N. began a period of close collaboration with both Ahmad Husain's followers and the Moslem Brotherhood. The other Communist groups were not ready to co-operate with the right-wing extremist groups, and this opposition was one of the main stumbling-blocks in the way of unity in the Egyptian Communist movement.

It is difficult to say whether the decision to modify its attitude towards the "Fascists" was taken by the M.D.L.N. upon instructions from abroad, or whether this new approach was home-grown. It may be assumed that members of the main group of Egyptian Communists realized on their own that the establishment of a broad "anti-imperialist front" was the order of the day, and that all other considerations should be subordinated to that necessity. In order to justify this policy an ideological explanation was found which was so revealing that it must be given here in full:

"After 1950 Ahmad Husain's party becomes a Socialist party. The wing of the 'National Party' headed by Fathi Ridwān and *Nur ad-Dīn* Taraf becomes a champion of neutralism fighting against an alliance between Egypt and the Western World, demanding a non-aggression pact with the Soviet Union. On the domestic scene a progressive wing of the Moslem Brotherhood openly affirms the necessity of collaborating with the Communists against imperialism. It is impossible to talk about real Fascism in colonial countries, though para-fascist organizations may exist, and this happened in Egypt too. But the concrete conditions in which these para-fascist movements came into being do not exist any more. At that time, twenty years ago, a national democratic trend did not yet exist in the national movement. Now it is all different: These (para-fascist) organizations have been transformed as a result of their own experience and the growing prestige of the international democratic (Communist) anti-imperialist movement."[14]

If it had been "scientifically" proven that Fascist parties could no more exist in the colonial and dependent countries, large potentialities were of course open to M.D.L.N., and the party was not slow to exploit them. It should be noted that collaboration with the Moslem Brotherhood continued until the abolition of the latter, and the Communists backed the anti-reform wing of Hasan al Hudaibi against the rival pro-reform faction of Sālih Ashmāwi for the simple reason that Hudaibi opposed the Cairo junta, while his opponents were willing to co-operate with the "Free Officers." Communist collaboration with the nationalist extremists went through a crisis after the "Black Saturday" of January, 1952, and also after both leaders of the "neutralist" Nationalist wing decided to join the army government, which appeared to them, after all, more congenial. But on the whole this co-operation has continued.

Relations between the Communists and the Wafd have always been excellent, so long as the Wafd was out of power. Under Naguīb and Gamāl 'Abdul Nāsir, too, the Communists always appeared as defenders of the Wafd, the "political party of the national *bourgeoisie*, the greatest obstacle to the consolidation of the military regime," as they said in their literature. For the working class, it was stated, the alliance with the Wafd was "absolutely indispensable" for the creation of a broad anti-imperialist front—without which there could be no hope of victory over the dictatorship. This alliance with the Wafd was a clever move tactically, but it was a difficult policy to defend in public. The Wafd demonstrated quite clearly, when it was in power in 1950–52, that it was no more than a shadow of the great party of Zaghlūl (and of a younger and better Mustafa Nahhās). It was inefficient and corrupt, and it maintained a mere façade of parliamentary democracy. It was the best guarantee (apart from King Farouk, who had been removed from the scene) that no political and social reforms would ever be undertaken, that the country would stagnate, that the Wafd leaders would grow richer, and the Communists more powerful. It was, in short, an ideal solution for all concerned, but a majority of the population did not apparently share the Communists' predilection for the Wafd, and this alliance proved far less effective than the Communists had hoped. Whatever the drawbacks of the military rulers, they were at least not corrupt, and it was difficult to convince the Egyptians that it was their patriotic duty to restore to power an inefficient and rotten party.

Relations between the Communists and the government of Naguïb and Gamāl 'Abdul Nāsir have been surveyed elsewhere in this book. After a brief flirtation in July to October, 1952, M.D.L.N. turned against the junta, and became one of its most bitter enemies and the chief force in the various opposition fronts organized in 1953–54 against the government. The leaders of the junta became "Naguïb-Hankey," "Gamāl 'Abd–Dulles," and "Salāh–McCarthy" in the Communist literature.[15]

5. THE PROGRAMME OF THE M.D.L.N.

The programme of the M.D.L.N., adopted in 1950 or 1951, reflects to a large degree political conditions prevailing in Egypt at that time. The political changes which have taken place since July, 1952, have necessitated a complete reorientation, so that the programme is now partially out of date; Egyptian Communists no longer regard the right-wing Wafd, the other parties, and the Palace as "the bloc of treason, the enemy of the people."

"The M.D.L.N.," it says, "is the fighting organization of the working class. It defends the interests of all the classes and all the patriotic groups of the nation. The M.D.L.N. takes as its guide in its struggle the theory of Marx–Lenin–Stalin, and has as its aim the establishment of socialism and, later, Communism in Egypt."[16]

Part one of the programme is headed: "For complete independence, for a people's democracy." It says that ". . . all imperialist armed forces have to be expelled, all the chief monopolies nationalized. The free national capitalism of medium and small enterprises has to be protected in order to gain the support of these strata for the popular struggle against imperialism. They will be placed, however, under the control of the people in order to give the workers the necessary guarantees, especially decent wages, and in order to assure reasonable profits for the medium and small national enterprises."

The confiscation of the great rural properties is demanded, as well as the abolition of all feudal privileges. "The property of medium and rich peasants should be protected." The other demands are conventional: free education and medical services, social security systems, etc. In order to carry out this programme it is considered necessary to form an Egyptian Communist Party which is to have "the same qualities, the same nature, and the same aims as the movement" (the M.D.L.N.). At the same time a popular front should be established, an alliance between the workers, peasants, the lower and medium middle class, and the democratic intellectuals. This popular front should be directed by the working class, and it should engage in an armed popular fight as the only political means of achieving the people's aspirations. A democratic government should subsequently be established, including the classes and strata united in the popular front, under the leadership of the working class. "This will be the dictatorship of the people against imperialism, its allies, and lackeys. This government will give the people full democratic liberties. . . ." Other paragraphs deal with co-operation with the Arab countries, the common struggle of the Sudanese people, and "adhesion to the democratic camp headed by the Soviet Union." The second part of the programme deals with the immediate aims of the party, and it says, among other things, that Egypt should refuse any suggestion that the Security Council deal with its conflicts with the British. (This was written before the all-conflicts-can-be-peacefully-solved era, inaugurated in Moscow after Stalin's death.) As for the Palestine question, the programme demands the establishment of an independent and democratic Arab state in Palestine and, generally speaking, the implementation of the U.N. decisions on Palestine of November, 1947.

The M.D.L.N. also stands for the "integral application of democratic liberties and their extension." Among other things, it demands the separation of state and religion, abolition of all the laws restricting civil liberties, release of all political prisoners, and the abolition of the political police. The rest of the programme deals with various economic and social problems, which are of little interest because they are identical with the standard programme adopted throughout the non-Communist world by Communist Parties in 1950–52.

6. THE FUTURE

The future of Egyptian Communism is a matter which cannot be dealt with in isolation. At the time of writing, the Communist movement in Egypt continues to be split, and it will probably remain so for some time to come. The M.D.L.N. is the strongest faction, but it has not yet been given official recognition by the Cominform authorities. This internal split has weakened Communism in Egypt, but it has not prevented its growth. From a few dozen members of Marxist study circles in 1942 it has grown to an estimated 7000 in thirteen years. It has attained key positions in the political life of the country—such as in the students' organizations—and to a lesser degree in the trade unions. It has established "popular" and "national" fronts, together with the Wafd and the Moslem Brotherhood, and through these instruments has organized and led mass demonstrations. To a limited extent, M.D.L.N. and other Communist sections now have working-class cadres among their members. But their main support still comes from the intelligentsia and, above all, the student organizations. The popular-front tactics have in certain situations proved very effective from the party point of view; this is at the same time one of the sources of weakness of Egyptian Communism. It succeeded in infusing some, and occasionally many, of its slogans into the United Front, but it has not been able to *lead* these fronts most of the time; the moment it had to follow (for one reason or another) a line of policy which was out of step with the general trend, it found itself isolated or left in the lurch by yesterday's allies.

Any relapse into parliamentary democracy in Egypt would be, under present conditions (and in the foreseeable future as well), only of short duration. What Communism has to fear most at present is an Egyptian version of Kemalism. Such a regime could put an end to the conditions in which Communism prospers. It is therefore on the willingness and the ability of the Cairo government to carry out domestic reforms that the future of the Egyptian Communists depends. Kemalism would probably mean that Communism in Egypt would be doomed to impotence, just as it is in Turkey. Any other policy will ultimately lead towards an increase in Communist power in Egypt and a repetition of the ominous events of 1951–52 on a more dangerous scale. The preoccupation of Egyptian "Military Socialism" with foreign affairs, and the evolution since 1952 of the regime in general, recall Italy in the nineteen-twenties and thirties rather than Turkey during the same period.

Chapter Five

The Sudan

I. THE SUDAN COMMUNIST PARTY (THE S.M.N.L.)

THE Sudan Communist Party, the S.M.N.L.[1] is an offshoot of the Communist movement in Egypt. The first Communist cells were established among Sudanese students in Cairo in 1944; later they became a section of the M.D.L.N. Their organ (*Umdurmān*) belonged to the M.D.L.N.; close contact has been maintained between the two groups to this day.

Sudan is a predominantly agrarian country, and the number of industrial workers is negligible; of its eight to nine million inhabitants only 1–2 per cent. are believed to be literate. Nevertheless, in spite of the lack of both a numerous working class and a developed native intelligentsia, Communism has made much progress in the Sudan during the last ten years, and would probably have been even more successful if the leaders of the movement in Khartoum had been allowed a modicum of independence in their policy. The absence of permanent splits makes the history of Communism in the Sudan easier to follow than in Egypt, and this has probably been the main reason for its spectacular progress.

The Sudanese students who were the core of the S.M.N.L. in Cairo numbered about twenty-five to thirty. But their periodical soon attracted attention[2] among the thousands of Sudanese students in the Egyptian capital. There were not many newspapers and magazines which dealt exclusively with Sudanese affairs. *Umdurmān*, moreover, was not suspect of "Egyptian Imperialism" among them. It stood for the common struggle of the Egyptian and Sudanese peoples, and proposed granting the Sudanese the right of self-determination rather than a merger under the Egyptian crown—the latter solution being the one proposed by all other Egyptian parties, the pro-Sudanese feelings of which were not believed to be altogether altruistic by many Sudanese.

The exaggerated stress given to "Egyptian rights in the Sudan" had, in fact, provoked a negative reaction in Khartoum, where this kind of propaganda encouraged separatist trends.[3] *Umdurmān* wrote: "Those who call for unity (without self-determination) in Egypt are not less dangerous than the separatists in the Sudan."[4]

2. EGYPTIAN COMMUNISTS AND THE SUDAN

In the Sudan, 1946 was the year in which a first "national front" was organized, one in which Communists played a prominent, though not a decisive, part. There had been a small national movement in the Sudan since the early 1920's (the "White Flag"), which received fresh impetus in 1936 when the Alumni Association of Gordon College (Khartoum) was founded; it later changed its name to the "General Congress of University Graduates." There was a student strike in March, 1946, and a Sudanese delegation was sent later in that year to Cairo. The United Nations started to deal with the Sudanese issue in August, 1947, in response to Egyptian demands. This debate had no tangible results, however, and the constitutional reforms decided upon by the British government in 1948 were boycotted by most political parties in the country.

During this period (1947-48, when the Communist movement in Egypt was united) there were serious differences of opinion in the M.D.L.N. as to the policy to be pursued in the Sudan. Finally a resolution sponsored by Henry Curiel was adopted, which said that Egypt should hold a protectorate over the Sudan under U.N. control until the Sudanese should be ready to exert their right of self-determination. In its political programme after the split of 1950-51, the M.D.L.N. preferred not to take a clear stand, and merely stressed that "we should support the struggle of the Sudanese people against British imperialism, etc., and co-ordinate the fight of the workers, peasants, students, and all [sic] the political organizations in the two countries."

Co-operation between the two groups continued, however, and became even closer after the abolition of martial law in Egypt in January, 1950. Sudanese party members were added to the central committee of M.D.L.N., and Sudanese cadres were sent for training to Egypt.[5]

3. THE PARTY LINE

The mainstay of Communist influence in the Sudan, outside the intelligentsia, is the Railway Workers' Union, which has more than 20,000 members. It headed a series of strikes in 1946, one of which lasted for thirty-three days. In March, 1949, a Sudanese Workers' Federation of Trade Unions was founded under the ægis of S.M.N.L., which, according to Communist sources, included sixty-two unions, comprising 180,000 workers. (It is noteworthy that the total number of workers in the Sudan is less than 100,000.) These activities were followed by the proclamation of a general strike in 1950, which, however, did not come off in the end. But it brought Sudanese workers new labour legislation, including the right of free association and the right to strike, and greatly strengthened the prestige of the Federation, which was also behind the police and student strike of 1950. Communist activities among the peasants were restricted to the Moslem areas, such as Gazīra province, where the party helped organize a strike movement against high taxes in the winter of 1951–52. S.M.N.L. also organized the first congress of a peasant union at Atbara in August, 1952, in an attempt to form units on the Chinese and Indian (Kisan Sabha) pattern. The Sudanese Communists admit, in fact, that "we have learnt from the glorious Chinese Communist Party a lesson which is confirmed by experience in our country."[6]

There were new large-scale labour conflicts in 1952. In January there was a three-day general strike to reinforce the railway workers' demand for a 75 per cent. increase in pay. In April, 1952, the president of the Federation, Muhammad as-Sayyid Salām, and its first secretary, Sa'īd Fādil, were arrested and brought to trial after refusing to sign a pledge of good behaviour. This again provoked a general strike, and more arrests and a trial against seventeen trade-union leaders in May, 1952. This time the two Federation heads agreed to sign the pledge and were released.[7]

Propaganda of the Partisans of Peace was comparatively weak in the Sudan. Even Communist sources reported only 10,000 signatures collected for the Stockholm appeal and 25,000 for the Berlin appeal. The National Peace Council, founded in 1950, was later banned by the authorities.

In 1952 the main interest shifted to the international scene. After lengthy negotiations between Britain and Egypt (where General Naguīb had come to power), agreement on the future of the Sudan was reached in February, 1953. This pact provided for elections in 1956 in which the citizens of the country would be able to decide for themselves about the future of their country. The first elections (which were not, however, decisive) brought victory to the pro-Egyptian groups; but it would be precipitate to consider the trend of public opinion in 1953 to be a reliable barometer of future events.

The party line on relations with Egypt did not reveal much political acumen. In 1951 the S.M.N.L. had participated, together with a number of non-Communist groups, in the United Front for Sudanese Liberation. Rejecting the draft constitution for Sudan (which followed the Anglo-Egyptian agreement of 1952), the Communists argued that it would retard the "political freedom" they were campaigning for. Naguīb was described by the Communists as the liaison man who was assisting further penetration of U.S. imperialism in the Sudan. But had not the Sudanese Communists given their approval to General Naguīb and his policy as late as November? But the party had been mistaken, they said; it had not understood the real character of the new Egyptian rulers, who were "running dogs of American imperialism."[8]

But the Cairo government succeeded in enlisting Sudanese public opinion in support of the agreement. The United Front for Sudanese Liberation (U.F.S.L.) broke up, and the Communists, insisting on opposition to the Anglo-Egyptian agreement, were isolated. The Federation of Workers in their annual convention in January, 1953, again called all parties to unite in the U.F.S.L. and to resist "all imperialist schemes and intrigues." Instead of helping the Communists, this only provoked serious discontent within the ranks of the Federation. For some time it appeared that the Communists in key positions would be ousted and replaced by non-Communist trade unionists. The Communists realized in time, however, that they had over-played their hand and decided to go slow on their stand towards the Cairo agreement rather than lose their positions. The loss of Communist influence at that period was reflected by the results of the elections to the Khartoum University College; this had been a Communist bulwark for some years, but now the Communists failed to get even one out of the ten seats. (The Moslem Brotherhood received nine seats.)

During the second half of 1952 a dissident faction broke away from the S.M.N.L. and established itself as the "Sudanese Democratic Organization." It opposed the dependence of the party on instructions from abroad, and, more particularly, the negative attitude towards the Cairo agreement which had, in its opinion, needlessly antagonized all other groups. But the new faction did not become a serious rival to the S.M.N.L., and in the summer of 1953 a further split occurred in the minority faction when several of its members who sympathized with the National Unity Party (formerly Ashigga) were expelled.

When the Communists realized that their attempt to attack the Cairo-Sudanese independence pact had misfired, they established a new "progressive" front organization, which took part in the elections with a national and social programme in which everything was promised to everybody. Muhammad as-Sayyid Salām, the president of the Communist "Federation," declared that the trade unions were not political organizations, and that their members were free to vote as they pleased. He advised them, however, to vote for such candidates as would favour national self-determination and their social interests, and who would oppose the "new laws restricting freedom, and, above all, the law directed against subversive doctrines."[9]

The Communists (appearing as "Anti-Imperialist Front") were not successful in the 1953 elections,[10] and throughout that year there were further attempts to restrict Communist influence within the S.I.U.F.

Efforts to stage new political general strikes in July and August were bitterly fought by an independent group, the Socialist Labour Party, which emphasized in its propaganda that Sudanese interests should be put above the tactical exigencies of the international Communist movement.

It would be wrong, however, to regard the temporary setback suffered by the Communists in 1952–53 as decisive. The S.M.N.L. prevailed in the struggle against its competitors within the trade unions as a result of its superior cohesion and organization, its ties with the Cominform, its training of cadres abroad, etc. Its isolation in 1952–53 was overcome by a better adaptation to the new situation created after the introduction of self-government. In its "immediate programme," published in the spring of 1954, the S.M.N.L. called for the immediate withdrawal of British troops, the amendment of the constitution, and an "anti-imperialist government to carry out liberation and social reform." The issue of self-determination was neatly circumvented by stating that "we stand for united action with the Egyptian people," which, of course, left the question of co-operation with the Egyptian *government* quite open. S.M.N.L. renewed its overtures to Al Azhari's National Unionists, and a national manifesto for the preservation and development of the constitution, initiated by the S.T.U.F., was supported by the National Unionists.[11]

4. RENEWED EFFORTS

More important, however, than these political manœuvres were the great efforts made by the Communists to strengthen their position among the intelligentsia and the peasants, and to regain their hold on the workers' organizations; opposition had appeared even in the railwaymen's union, which was the traditional stronghold of the S.M.N.L. These efforts were aided by the dissension of the non-Communist parties, which culminated in the March 1 riots in 1954, when the followers of Al Mahdi (many of them tribesmen) demonstrated against the new government on the occasion of the convocation of the Sudanese Parliament.

Communist activities among the intelligentsia and the youth (which have been specially marked in the last two years) follow the usual lines: "Front" organizations are established for fellow-travellers—such as the National Committee for the Defence of Democratic Rights, Women's Progress Society, or the Sudan Students' Congress. Communist influence is predominant in the Khartoum and Omdurman teachers' associations, and the students' organizations in Kosti, Port Sudan, Omdurman, and Khartoum. Youth festivals are arranged and efforts are made to send big delegations to the meetings of the international front organizations. The only interesting feature in the propaganda of the S.M.N.L. and its satellites is perhaps the distinct pro-Islamic and anti-Christian bias in the party press, which complains that "there is no freedom of conscience in the Sudan." "Though the majority of people in the north are Moslems, only Christian missionaries are allowed to proceed to the south and to preach there."

Propaganda among the peasants is an important part of Communist activities. The Sudan is the only Middle Eastern country where Communists have succeeded in "organizing" peasants on the Chinese-Indian pattern.[12] Out of many local peasant unions a few central peasant unions have been formed: the Nuba Mountain cotton growers (with 20,000 members, according to Communist reports), the Gash peasant union, the Northern Province peasant union, and the Gazīra union (the Gazīra region being the richest agricultural region of the country). The demands of the Communist-dominated unions are, to quote the Ten Point Demands, as follows:

1. *Land.*—The preservation of peasant ownership so that lands do not fall into the hands of big landowners, merchants, and the Sudan government, through (*a*) resisting confiscation of the land of indebted peasants; and (*b*) the improvement of agricultural production through co-operation, good farming methods, easy irrigation, etc.
2. *Contracts.*—Cancellation of unfavourable contracts between peasants and private water-pump owners; and between the peasants and the government, promoting the interests of the peasants.
3. *Taxes.*—Opposition to new taxes and all rises in taxation; reductions of old taxes, such as water taxes, land taxes, fruit-tree taxes, palm-date taxes, cattle taxes.
4. *Improvement of Production.*—Through introduction of fertilizers and the adoption of modern methods in their use; mechanization of agriculture as far as possible; scientific seed selection, etc.
5. *Crop Marketing.*—Supervision of the sale of crops inside and outside the Sudan, the protection of peasants against money-lenders, and the removal of bans on certain agricultural products. [The remaining demands deal with transport (improvement of transport to the cities), housing, the establishment of social clubs, prevention of floods, education, and "removal of government suppression of the peasants," i.e. a weaker central government.]

The demands of the Northern District union do not differ in substance from the demands of the rest. It is of some interest to note that Gazīra is the most developed agricultural region of Sudan (and perhaps of the whole Nile Valley); it was nationalized in 1950 and its 26,000 peasants are not allowed to cultivate more than about thirty acres each—there are no big feudal landowners among them. This regulation was introduced in order to prevent the emergence of an agricultural proletariat on one hand and the growth of big latifundia on the other. What should be noted, therefore, is that the peasants of Al Gazīra are far better off materially than those in the rest of the country, and that their strikes and protest demonstrations are directed against the government rather than against any exploiting class. The Communists are appearing here as the spokesmen of *sredniaks* (middling peasants) and even kulaks, but it is, of course, completely irrelevant to mention that these peasants would lose their land in a popular democracy (which is the official programme of the S.M.N.L. since the spring of 1954). This the peasants cannot possibly know. At the present time the peasants regard the Communists as the main champions of their cause. The latter are ready to exploit any source of conflict in a non-Communist regime, and the peasant movement serves them as a powerful political weapon.

S.M.N.L. has made some inroads into the Sudanese defence forces, the country's small army. There has been no party progress worth mentioning in the south, though attempts in that region have been made. The Communists oppose the separatist trends of the south, and try to explain to the southern tribes that they need not be afraid of domination by the north.

The further growth of Communism in the Sudan depends mainly on the ability of the new government in Khartoum to cope with its tasks, and the ability of the non-Communist parties to establish mass organizations and not to let their differences of opinion paralyse the development of the country as a whole. Basically the economic situation and the social structure of the Sudan are far sounder than those of Egypt. But, as a result of clever leadership, hard work, devotion, a knowledge of the basic principles of political organization, and a strong will to power, the 1500 Sudanese Communists have succeeded in infiltrating into many key positions. The other Sudanese parties have been deficient in most of these qualities.

PART THREE

ISRAEL

Chapter Six

The Rise of Communism in Palestine

I. PALESTINE IN 1919

IN Israel, Communist ideology collided head-on with a powerful rival force, which was, in the final event, to determine the future. This rival force was Zionism, of course, and it was Zionism which brought the third and subsequent waves of Jewish settlers to Palestine from Eastern Europe after World War I; the very small number of Communists who appeared among them were in a paradoxical or even quixotic position from the very beginning. Zionism had a strong nationalist strain, and also had its own "heretical" brand of socialism, its own prophets, and its own sense of Messianic mission. The small, struggling Jewish community of post-war Palestine could have little patience with a political movement which denied its very right to exist, banned Hebrew in its "second fatherland," exiled Russian Zionists to Siberia, and in the 1920's and 1930's made common cause with Arab rioters and terrorists. By identifying themselves with forces which the Jewish community felt to be a threat to its elementary security, the Communists found themselves utterly isolated and ostracized, a fact which became evident even to them, in spite of all their dialectical double-talk and their acrobatic dance on the party line.

It is not easy to trace the history of a movement the origins of which are shrouded in obscurity, and which, torn by incessant internal strife, tended to break up periodically into splinter groups; a number of times the movement even ceased to exist but was always revived. With patience, however, we shall be able to find our way through the labyrinth, and shall come to discern the patterns, policies, and metamorphoses of the Communist Party.

Communism in Palestine goes back to 1919. The first world war had

73

ended the previous year; in Russia, Hungary, and Bavaria Communist governments had been set up, and the revolutionary movement seemed to be spreading like wildfire through Eastern and Central Europe. The Communist leaders were absolutely convinced that victory was in their grasp and that the final convulsive struggle was only a few months off, perhaps even a matter of weeks. They were almost exclusively absorbed in the European scene, so that the famous Baku Conference of 1920 (which appealed to the peoples of the Orient) remained a mere colourful episode not to be followed up at the time.

The revolutionary upheaval had its repercussions in distant, diminutive Palestine, which was then in the process of becoming a British Mandate as a result of the Turkish defeat, the Balfour Declaration, and the occupation of the country by General Allenby's army. The Jewish population of Palestine numbered less than 80,000 and was not organized; the workers' parties had only a few hundred members, and their activities, like those of all other parties and public institutions, had practically ceased as a result of wartime dislocations. There were no trade unions worth mentioning, and when the General Federation of Jewish Labour (the Histadrut) was founded in Haifa in 1920, a mere 4500 persons was all the Federation could muster under a somewhat high-sounding name. The very establishment of the General Federation had been rendered possible only by the "third immigration wave" from Eastern Europe, which brought about 30,000 new-comers to Palestine. A detailed survey of the motivating causes of this and subsequent immigration waves would be outside the scope of this study; it would involve the history of Zionism and the Jewish question in general between the two world wars. It was probably a result of the general ferment in Eastern Europe, which seethed with revolution, counter-revolution, and civil war, and had witnessed the emergence of new states, most of which were strongly nationalistic. The young Jews who decided to come to Palestine to build a Jewish homeland were, nevertheless, a small minority; the mass of East European Jews was not interested, whereas Jewish Communists considered Zionism a reactionary movement which aimed at cutting off the Jewish worker from the general struggle for national and social liberation, in which he should participate side by side with his Russian, Polish, or Hungarian brethren. The Communist leaders—and many others as well—saw Zionism as a mad delusion and they believed that the fears, doubts, and apprehensions of the Zionists as to the future of Eastern and Central European Jewry unfounded if not downright "propaganda." Why should young Jews migrate to a little country far away from the centres of political activity and revolutionary struggle just to strengthen the hold of British imperialism "objectively"? This argument seemed very convincing. There were many Socialists among the new-comers of 1919–20, but—apart from several semi-official emissaries of the Comintern—very few Communists. Some of the *halutzim* (pioneers) became Communists during the first years of their stay in the new country—there was no lack of good reasons for heartbreak and disappointment—but most of these soon left the country.

There was an extraordinary lack of continuity in the Palestine Communist Party during its first twenty years of existence, and thus Jewish Communists in Palestine differed in one important aspect from Communists everywhere else in the world. A British, German, or American citizen by becoming a Communist revolted against the existing social order, but he did not for a moment consider leaving his country in protest. Yet this was just what happened in Palestine. Once the Palestinian Communist had realized that Zionism was a reactionary, utopian movement, what earthly reason was there for him to stay any longer in the country? He had come there, he realized, as a misguided idealist, but as the Jewish national home was not going to be built (nor should be built either, he thought), there was no longer any reason for him to regard it as his country. The very motives which brought him to join the Palestine Communist Party made him, as a rule, leave the country again. The party became a transit camp, and this rapid turnover, besides complicating the historian's task, was a source of grave concern to the party chiefs, who saw their organization seriously weakened. But anti-Zionism did not have merely organizational consequences; it also had unique political results, about which more will have to be said presently.

2. THE M.O.P.S. (SOCIALIST WORKERS' PARTY)

The small groups which had split away from the Jewish Labour parties in Palestine and Eastern Europe (*Poale Zion*, Workers of Zion) established themselves as a political organization at a conference on the Jewish New Year in September, 1920. This party did not yet reject Zionism altogether, but favoured, to quote its leaders, "proletarian Zionism." This, however, could be achieved only within the general framework of the social revolution, which was the only guarantee for the realization of the progressive kernel to be found in Zionism.[1] They opposed the "constructivism" of other Socialist Zionist groups and, to quote a later Communist account, "they dreamed that the mighty Red Army would cross the Caucasus and the Taurus and bring them a Soviet Palestine."[2] Gradually they came to reject the idea of *binyan ha'aretz* (the upbuilding of the country), the one slogan which united all other Zionist groups. Nevertheless, they took part in the foundation of the General Federation of Jewish Labour and obtained seven out of eighty-seven seats in the first election in December, 1920—a percentage larger than any they gained thereafter. It was typical of their confusion that they attributed paramount importance to the language dispute (Yiddish *versus* Hebrew). Nor did they propose to join the Third International at once, as they undoubtedly should have done; their hesitations were probably motivated by the wish to attract members from wider circles which might have been antagonized by a too close attachment to the Comintern.

The M.O.P.S. (*Mifleget Poalim Sozialistim*, Socialist Workers' Party) was active for less than one year. Its existence came to an abrupt end as a result of the May Day riots of 1921, when a separate Communist demonstration in Jaffa provoked a clash with the General Trade Union demonstration, and in the ensuing confusion Arabs attacked the Jewish quarters of Jaffa. The M.O.P.S. was charged with responsibility for this attack (among the many Jews killed was the important Hebrew novelist and critic, J. H. Brenner); most of its leaders were arrested and deported by the British Mandatory authorities. A Communist source admits that there was much heart-searching in the party following the events of May Day; they wondered if it had really been worth while organizing the demonstration. But no, concludes the Communist chronicler, even if it had meant that the party would be destroyed, abandoning the demonstration would have been tantamount to an opportunist deviation.

Among those deported were all the main leaders of M.O.P.S.—Khalidi, Wolf Averbach (Abu Sian), Gershon Dau (Avigdor), and the main ideologist and most capable of all, Yitzchak Meirson. They all went to the Soviet Union. Khalidi disappeared, and Averbach, after a spectacular Comintern career, was shot during the great purge. Dua worked in the Middle East and Polish departments of the Comintern, and died in Poland after World War II. Meirson was imprisoned for many years in Siberia, and after his release, old and broken, he applied for a visa at the Israeli legation in Moscow in 1952.[3]

At about the time that the M.O.P.S. ceased to exist, another group made a fresh attempt to establish a Palestine Communist Party. But this time the initiators did not begin by trying to build a separate party. They concentrated their efforts within a left-wing Zionist party, the *Poale Zion* (Workers of Zion), "both to gain a legal front and to disrupt the party from within," to quote again an official Communist source.[4] Only after they had gained some strength did they decide to build their own illegal Communist Party. But the new illegal party was beset with internal dissension from the very beginning. If *Poale Zion* debated whether they should join the Third International or not, the Communists quarrelled among themselves as to whether they should collaborate with the "proletarian Zionists" (on the tacit assumption that these would gradually get over their harmful illusion), or whether such collaboration should be opposed altogether. The leadership of the Communist Party, the so-called "Menachem-Elisha" group, belonged to the "appeasers" and were supported by the majority. At the fourth party conference in September, 1922, the extremist minority split away and established itself as a rival Communist Party, the K.P.P., their main political slogan being: "Leave the Zionistic hell!" The majority at the conference had approximately 300 members and sympathizers, the minority, the K.P.P., about 150, and they fought each other ferociously during this ten-month split, which was healed only at the time of the fifth party conference in 1923.[5] Both groups established semi-legal "fronts," a "Workers' Fraction" and a "Proletarian Fraction," but as a result of the internal struggle their attraction for outsiders was strictly limited. In 1923 the majority accepted most of the tenets of the minority and the latter rejoined the party. "It is the main task of the Party," it was now stated, "to fight against Zionism in all its forms, to expose the bankrupt Zionist bluff." The struggle against Zionism was to be waged not only in Palestine but also in Europe, and Jewish youth was to be warned not to emigrate. The struggle against "proletarian Zionism" was especially urgent and was to be intensified.

The progress made in Palestine by a party which had hitherto disassociated itself rather hesitantly from Zionism, and which now began to fight it openly, was duly noticed in Moscow, where K.P.P. was officially recognized as a member of the Comintern in February, 1924. But the newly established unity did not last long, and early in 1924 we again find the party in a state of disintegration—the old minority complained about discrimination (they had been given only three out of eight seats in the Politburo), and there was, moreover, to make things worse, a split *within* the old party majority. The "Menachem-Elisha" leadership was accused of defeatism and inactivity (the party membership was by now only a third of what it had been two years previously) and, what was worse, of "liquidatory intentions." They had suggested launching a Communist "educational organization" to replace the Bolshevik-type party—thus anticipating Earl Browder by twenty years, and with similar results.

At the fifth party conference in July, 1924, the old leadership was deposed and new activist forces (the so-called "Emek-Nachum-Litvak" group) took over. "Out of the Jewish Ghetto!" was the commandment of the hour, they said, repeating what Karl Radek had told them a few weeks before.[6] *The success of the party depended on its becoming an Araq mass party*; "Arabization" became the slogan for the first time, and was to remain so for many years to come.

But this was easier said than done. The party had burned its bridges leading to the Jewish camp, and was consequently ousted (in April, 1924) from the Histadrut (the General Federation of Jewish Labour), which stressed that the "Fraction" (the Communist front organization —the Communist Party not appearing as such) was removed, not for its political views but for its subversive activities: demonstrations against the Histadrut, assaults on local workers' councils, and virulent attacks in the Palestinian and European Communist press upon the "yellow Fascist" Jewish workers' organization. The Communist Party attempted to regain admission to the Histadrut in 1926, when the Comintern tried its hand at an unsuccessful popular front experiment (the so-called "Anglo-Russian Committee"), but this honeymoon was short-lived, and the Communists in Palestine had to drop the unity campaign even before it had reached the general public.

The Afula Case of November, 1924, did more than anything else to isolate and ostracize the Communists in the Jewish community of Palestine. The Jewish National Fund had purchased part of the Valley of Jezreel, and the Zionist settlers proceeded to colonize the area. Several dozen Bedouin and fellaheen attacked the settlers, there was a clash, and the police had to intervene by force; there were several casualties. The Communist Party and not the Arabs was generally held responsible for the bloodshed, because it had called on the Arabs to fight the Jews on the very eve of their settlement, which was to "colonize the country on the ruins of the fellaheen village." The Zionist contention was that the Communists aimed at inciting hatred between Jews and Arabs, and wished to foment civil war by their direct appeal to Arab nationalism. The Jews were especially embittered, since Arab peasants were not displaced as a result of Jewish colonization in a majority of cases; Afula, for example, was considered an uninhabitable swamp till the Jews came there. It is possible that the Zionist exaggerated the importance and the effect of Communist propaganda, but there can be no doubt that they correctly appraised their intentions, for the Communists claimed that the Arabs were the rightful owners of the country, that the Jews were imperialist (later, "Fascist") invaders, and that the fight against them was part of the general anti-imperialist struggle in the colonies. The Afula pattern returned frequently during the late 1920's and 1930's.[7]

The year of the fourth immigration wave, 1925, produced a boom in Palestine which, however, proved to be a mixed blessing for the country in the long run; 36,000 new-comers arrived in the single year of 1925, but in contrast to the 1919–20 immigration wave, there were few *halutzim* (pioneers) among them, and the lower middle-class elements predominated. This sudden influx did not strengthen Palestine's economy so much as one might have expected, and real-estate speculation in the cities produced artificial prosperity; after a few months there was a crash, resulting in widespread unemployment. The difficult economic situation caused a sudden drop in immigration, and in 1927 more Jews left the country than came in. Only in 1929 did Palestine overcome the effects of the 1925 "boom." The Palestine Communist Party, which was the only openly and actively anti-Zionist party, profited considerably from the disillusion and disappointment which pervaded part of the population after the 1926 crisis. But the party could not depend for lasting support on people who had come to Palestine expecting a good and easy life, and who now preferred to return to the fleshpots of Europe rather than engage in a dangerous underground struggle. It was comparatively easy to go to the *Assefat Hanivharim* (the prototype of the Israeli parliament) with the slogan: "The illusions of Jewish autonomy and self-government in Palestine have been buried; no serious and honest man can believe in them any more."[8] The party could win more than a thousand votes on that platform—but it could gain no lasting benefit by basing itself on a wave of resentment, on frustrated hopes, individual disillusionment, or various other purely negative motives.

It was at that period that Communist propaganda began to concentrate its attacks on the "illusory character" of the Zionist movement: Zionism was not only incapable of contributing to the solution of the Jewish question, it even endangered the lives of the 130,000 Jews in Palestine. Why should it call East European Jews to leave their homes, where they were perfectly safe, and participate in the fraudulent Zionist experiment? The Communists had a scientific ideology, and could therefore correctly appraise the world situation in general and the position of the Jewish people in particular; the Zionists were at best mere utopians, engaged in an adventure which was doomed from the outset.[9]

We have already mentioned the urgent call for "Arabization." The party leaders continued to pay lip-service to this most important of all Moscow's instructions. But, in fact, the party remained exclusively Jewish up to the late 1920's, and the Communists had great difficulty in finding, not only Arab candidates for party membership but even sympathizers and potential allies. The Communist Party called on its members to support the extreme wing of the Arab national movement in elections (such as the Jerusalem municipal elections in 1924) and in its demonstrations, but the latter, mainly the group of Mūsa Qāsim and Haj Amīn al Husaini (the ex-Mufti of Jerusalem) did not reciprocate at that period, and Communist-Arab Nationalist collaboration was a somewhat one-sided affair. There were differences of opinion within the Communist leadership as to how far to go in support of the Husainis, and these differences caused a split in the party on the eve of the "Seventh Arab Conference" in Jerusalem in June, 1928. A minority group calling itself the "Jewish Workers' Council" addressed the conference in an open letter, stating that "the homeland of a Jew is wherever he happens to be born, while Palestine belongs to the Arabs. . . . It is our sacred duty to fight side by side with the Arabs and arouse the people of the world against the Zionist danger."[10] The Communist Party majority censured the view taken by the minority that all Jews in Palestine were connected with Zionism and should be considered therefore as beyond salvation. Their address to the Arab National Congress, while emphatically denouncing Zionism, Jewish immigration, and Jewish settlement, was somewhat more moderate, and the Comintern decided in favour of the stand taken by the majority; the minority were expelled from the party.[11] But less than a year later Moscow had second thoughts on the whole issue, and then it appeared that the stand of the majority had been tantamount to a "dangerous pro-Zionist deviation" and that the minority had, after all, been basically right.

The first and only major success of the Communists in Palestine in the 1920's was the splitting of the *G'dud Avodah* (Workers' Battalion). This group of several hundred pioneers filled an important role in the history of the collective settlements in Palestine. The Battalion was founded in 1920, and was made up of a group of newly arrived *halutzim* (pioneers) who were building a road near Tiberias; other groups joined the Battalion at a later date until, in the middle 1920's, some of these collectives became agricultural settlements. All the members of the Battalion were Socialists—many were radical Socialists. But they were Zionists too, otherwise they would hardly have come to the country. Their Zionism was put to a very hard test, since the economic position of the collectives in 1926 was extremely shaky, there was widespread unemployment, and occasionally the after-effects of that terrible time can be observed in many middle-aged patients in Israeli clinics and hospitals today—the results of semi-starvation. And, on the other hand, there were the speculators in the cities who had won easy profits in real-estate deals and building contracts—what did the pioneers have in common with these, whom they regarded as purely parasitic elements?

Thus there was much dissatisfaction in the Battalion and the Communists found a fertile field of action. "Your constructivist socialism is bankrupt," they wrote. "Its *raison d'être* was to pave the way for the capitalist infiltration. But now you are not needed any more, and therefore your whole movement and its nationalist-romantic ideology are doomed."[12] Communists infiltrated the Battalion and paralysed its activities; the Zionist elements therefore resolved to force a decision. In the decisive vote of December, 1926, the Zionists had a majority of some thirty, and the Battalion split. Those who remained founded agricultural settlements like Tel Yosef, which have become the main pillars of the *Kibbutz* movement in Israel. The main group of the Communist opposition, which was headed by M. Elkind, departed for the Soviet Union and were given a "much bigger and better farm, 'Via Nova,' near Eupatoria in the Crimea. . . . We are very happy here and have received every possible help from the Soviet government. At last we are no longer subject to the terrible pressure of British Imperialism and Zionism."[13]

The Elkind group was not the only one to leave Palestine. When the

Soviet government decided in 1925 to promote Jewish agricultural settlement, the Communists in Palestine made considerable efforts to recruit candidates there through a special agency, Agro, which appeared as a non-political institution. Leaflets published by Agro were, however, fairly suggestive: "We are leaving Palestine because Zionism cannot solve the Jewish question, because the whole Zionist camp, up to the very left, is one black reactionary force. Under the cover of Zionist and socialist ideals, the Jewish worker is turned into a Czarist Cossack, a weapon against the toiling masses."[14] Those who left for Biro Bidjan did not want to be accessories to such a crime, but hoped, as they said, to build a Jewish state with the help of 160 million Russians in the Far East. No more than forty or fifty families migrated from Israel to Biro Bidjan, and organized emigration ceased altogether in 1933.

The aforementioned Afula clash was no isolated incident; clashes between Jewish settlers and Arab Bedouin at Wadi Hawarit (midway between Haifa and Tel-Aviv) began in 1928 and continued sporadically for several years, and there were similar incidents elsewhere. The Communist Party attempted with varying success to give additional impetus to the Arab demonstrations and attacks as a "link in the chain of peasant uprisings against imperialist colonization in all colonial countries." Their argument ran as follows: We Communists are not against Jewish colonization—we are in favour of agricultural settlement in Russia. In Palestine, however, it is our task to organize the amorphous mass of fellaheen and to give direction to their struggle. The agrarian movement should become a great revolutionary force.[15] But did this not mean calling upon Arabs to kill Jews and fomenting racial hatred in general? "No," they replied. "Only degenerates and impostors can argue that way."[16] Actually the problem was a complicated one, and the party leadership solved it by saying one thing in their Hebrew and Yiddish leaflets, and something else again in their Arab publications, assuming that only a very few people would get hold of and understand all its literature. The newspapers and leaflets scheduled for Jewish consumption stressed, as a rule, the necessity for Jewish-Arab solidarity, while the Arab periodicals called on every patriotic Arab to go out and fight to save his home and country against the invaders.

Such tactics did not make the Communists very popular among the Jewish workers and settlers, but with their remarkable tenacity and typical stubbornness they did not give up the attempt to win new adherents among the Jews, although the "objective situation," they admitted, was not very favourable. But the propaganda aimed at the Jews soon brought them up against another most intricate problem: the "Conquest of Labour" drive, which was sponsored by the General Federation of Jewish Labour (Histadrut). Most of the Jewish owners of orange groves in Palestine employed seasonal Arab workers from southern Syria and Jordan, while the Jewish labour movement vehemently opposed this practice, and voiced both nationalist and social-ist arguments against it. First of all, they argued, we are against cheap, unorganized labour always and everywhere; the owners of the orange groves should not be allowed to get away with it, especially as their workers are not local inhabitants but "Houranis" from abroad. And then, of course, there was the Zionist motive—Jews should be employed by the grove owners in order to increase the absorptive capacity of the country. The Communist Party at once took issue with the "Conquest of Labour" slogan, and defended the Arab seasonal workers against the Jewish attempts to oust them. This attitude was perfectly logical, if one accepted their basic assumption that Zionism was a reactionary move-ment which should be combated at all costs; but it placed them in a most ludicrous position. Their allies in the fight against the Jewish trade union became, on the one hand, the Jewish capitalists (who pre-ferred, of course, using "cheap labour"), and, on the other hand, the unorganized "yellow" seasonal workers.[17]

Apart from such demonstrations against the "persecution of Arab labourers," the activity of the party was restricted to the traditional demonstration on May Day and on November 7 in the cities. The first party delegation went for a visit to Russia in 1927, and in the subsequent years the first group of students left for a prolonged course in the Comintern academy. But in spite of its anti-Zionist enthusiasm, the party had not yet succeeded in attracting Arabs, and a few years later this period was characterized (somewhat ungraciously) by Nadir, the representative of the Syrian party in Moscow, in the following way: "Anti-revolutionary Zionist elements dominated not only the Palestine Communist Party, but had even infiltrated the leadership of the Syrian and Egyptian parties and retarded the development of these parties."[18]

3. THE 1929 RIOTS

The 1929 riots, which started in Jerusalem and spread throughout the country, were a milestone in the history of Mandatory Palestine, and at the same time a turning-point in the development of the Pales-tine Communist Party.

Early in 1929 the Central Committee of the party convened to dis-cuss the resolutions of the Sixth Congress of the Comintern and to apply them to local conditions. This Congress, it will be remembered, adopted very sharp resolutions against the traitorous *bourgeois* parties in the East (such as the Kuomintang in China), which had betrayed the Communists, who had themselves worked so hard to establish an anti-imperialist alliance with these parties. The "new course" in the Middle East meant, therefore, that Nahhās Pasha in Egypt, Hāshim al Attāsi in Syria, and Jamāl Husaini in Palestine, all of them imitators of Chiang Kai-shek, who had passed to the reformist camp, could not be trusted because they had already given up the struggle, afraid as they were of a general agrarian and proletarian revolt.[19] In view of this "betrayal" there was little sense in voicing general nationalist slogans, and the main stress from now on should be on class differentiation and class struggle. This meant, in fact, that the previous demand for a democratic parliament in Palestine should be replaced by the revolutionary slogan: "For the establishment of a workers' and peasants' government."[20]

As it appeared later, the "new course" was only a short intermezzo and the "big revolt" of August, 1929, put a sudden end to that policy. During several years Communist leaders had talked and written much about the impending revolt and its revolutionary and progressive character. But they had not taken into account the possibility that the "big revolt" might not be directed against the "imperialist power" but only against the Jews, and that it would not differentiate at all between Zionists and Jews. On the contrary, they had published a number of articles during 1928–29 warning against the "British intrigues" to stir up trouble between Jews and Arabs and to propagate "fratricide."[21] One week before the first clashes occurred in Jerusalem, the party published a leaflet in which it called on the "toiling masses, Arabs and Jews alike, to combat racial hatred and incitement and all attempts to unleash a civil war."[22] How could they possibly foresee that only a few months later their stand would be branded as utterly wrong and muddle-headed, and that the correct tactics would have been not to combat the revolt but to head it?

The riots broke out in Jerusalem in mid-August, 1929, and were directed exclusively against Jews (in contrast to the 1936–39 events). There were 133 Jewish dead and about 300 wounded—most of them not in the Zionist settlements but in such cities as Hebron and Safed, which had centuries-old Jewish communities, orthodox communities which had no sympathy whatever for secular Zionist colonization. Everything happened contrary to expectations—and the text-book saws about colonial uprisings were absolutely useless. How did the Palestine Communists react?

Their first reaction was one of utter confusion. Not that anyone expected them to do anything spectacular; after all, the party was small and illegal, and contact between the Central Committee and the few Arab comrades was cut as the result of the state of war. But should they not at least have taken a correct ideological attitude? It would seem that technical difficulties prevented the publication of the party organs during the critical months of August–November, 1929. During the first four weeks of the riots the party continued to hold to the old "pacifist" line. It took part in defence of the Jewish quarters of the cities and even held the government responsible for the pogroms. It noted approvingly the fact that the politically conscious Arabs in the cities did not take part in the pogroms.[23] It may be interesting to note here that the reaction of the European Communist press was not unanimous either. In some cases a favourable view was taken (especially *Inprecorr*, the central Comintern publication), and the German *Rote Fahne*, which even said *expressis verbis* that the anti-Jewish concomitant of the revolt was a natural development which should not be regretted.[24] But a Profintern spokesman, Smolenski, pointed out in September, 1929, that the "objective revolutionary sometimes uses reactionary means not unlike the Narodniki," which in his opinion was something to cause concern, though eventually the movement would reach a "higher stage" and things would somehow be straightened out.[25]

The party was able to begin reorganizing its ranks only at the end of September, when there was a lull in the fighting. Meanwhile, new instructions had been received from Moscow and the plenum which was now convened had to accept a policy diametrically opposed to the old line. A purge was decided upon, and every party member had to re-register and to reply to a questionnaire which included such questions as: "Do you accept the view that the August uprising was the result of the radicalization of the Arab masses?" The Comintern executive had sharply criticized the Palestine party line: "It is not enough to be a Communist ideologically—the main task is the day-to-day work of winning the confidence of the local, viz. Arab, proletariat. The main weakness of the Palestine party is its failure to become an Arab mass party."[26] Which meant that notwithstanding the appeals and warnings since 1924, little or nothing had been done towards Arabization.

Reorientation began with the September plenum and, if larger groups (including the majority in such key branches as Haifa) refused to go along, and even if the party leadership passed into entirely different hands, it did not greatly matter to the Comintern, because the main task was now to make the party an Arab group rather than an "immigrants' section." First of all, the revolt had to be reassessed: "In a country like Palestine a revolutionary movement without pogroms is impossible."[27] This, in a nutshell, was the new line. Could a real revolutionist argue that such a movement should be disapproved of and discouraged merely because there was a danger of pogroms? Of course not. If the Arab proletariat had not been so weak, pogroms would not have occurred at all. And how did the Mufti succeed in dominating the revolutionary movement? Well, this was the responsibility of the social-fascists of the Jewish Federation of Labour (Histadrut).[28] The Zionist ideology was the real culprit, but the Arab revolt, the pogroms, and the national struggle in general had given Zionism a death blow from which, in all probability, it would never recover. The main assignment for the Communist Party was to encourage the Arab revolt, to broaden it, and to lead it. But the Communist leaders had switched too late to these new tactics. By the time they decided to lead the national revolt it was all over, and nothing remained for them to do but sing its praises in retrospect and to publish leaflets every year on the anniversary of the Jerusalem uprising (up to the time of the new riots of 1936)—leaflets in which the Arabs were called upon to rise again against their Zionist and British oppressors.

The December, 1929, plenum decided to oust the opposition which refused to adopt the Arab line. From the point of view of the internal struggle going on in Moscow at about the same time, the Palestine opposition came to be called "rightist" and "Bukharinist," although there was, in fact, very little in common between Bukharin, who had probably never heard about the intricacies of the Palestinian revolutionary movement, and the majority in the Haifa branch of the party. The resolutions adopted by the plenum were extremely optimistic: "The revolt was victorious, it was not suppressed. We are on the eve of bigger uprisings," and so on.[29] These assumptions were not borne out by subsequent events. The main error of the party, and especially of its leadership, was said to be its loss of contact with the masses, and its failure to get hold of the main positions of command in the revolutionary movement. "The party had been lost in a morass of opportunism and vague anti-imperialist slogans. The party had forgotten that the fellaheen and Bedouin waited for leadership and wanted to be shown what to do with their knives and revolvers."[30]

Such Bolshevik self-criticism was a prerequisite for taking over the national revolutionary movement, and the idle talk about "pogroms" had to cease immediately. But it all came too late. The revolt was over, and all the party could do was to prepare itself for another great revolutionary wave and to make a point of being prepared the next time. It was, as was said before, a turning-point in the history of the party. Most of the Jewish rank-and-file members left and new statutes were adopted, according to which the majority of the Central Committee had to be made up of Arabs. As for the Jewish members of the party, it was stated that those who should prove themselves sincere and reliable would also be permitted to remain in future.[31] This rider, however, was hardly necessary, because the Communist Party had, in fact, become a part of the most extreme wing of the Arab nationalist movement. It had been anti-Zionist before, but there was, of course, a great difference between political anti-Zionism (which was shared by other Jewish groups such as the ultra-orthodox *Agudat Israel*) and the call to destroy Jewish settlements in Palestine by acts of violence. Previously, the Jewish parties had more or less ignored the Communists, but now these had become a dangerous enemy, actively inciting pogroms. The party was deliberately antagonizing the Jews, but this had most probably been taken into account by the Comintern—was it not infinitely more important that the Palestine party should strike root and thrive among the Arabs, who made up the vast majority of the population?

Chapter Seven

Arabization

I. COMMUNISM AND ZIONISM

THE 1930's were the era of the struggle against "social fascism," i.e. against the Socialist Parties in Palestine. Soon after the new Communist line had been introduced the party leadership had to face a "liquidatory trend" among the rank and file. "Well," they said, "the Jewish worker is hopeless. Either he is a Zionist or he leaves the country. We cannot possibly hope to convince him."[1] But the party executive did not accept this view. "True enough," it stated, "Zionism is national madness. But we have never made a real all-out effort to explain the situation to the Jewish worker. Surely he'll support us once the Zionist delusions have been destroyed."[2]

But the new slogans were hardly apt to make the Jewish worker more sympathetic. "It is the task of the Jewish trade unions to make the worker a fascist"[3]; or "The collective settlements [*kibbutzim*] were socialist utopias at first—now they have gradually become fascist bases."[4] "But the day is near when the Arab peasant will rise again and no imperialist force, no Jewish fascist cohorts, will be able to prevent this explosion."[5] Such propaganda could not hope to gain many supporters among the Jews, and there were, moreover, several finer ideological questions which caused considerable embarrassment to the party. Everywhere in the world, their critics said, "You put the main emphasis on the urban proletariat, and there is only one country in which you make an exception and attribute to the peasants a more 'progressive' role than you do to the proletariat—because the proletariat is Jewish." But the party was in no mood for such scholastic discussions.

The centre of gravity had definitely shifted from Jews to Arabs—to the Arab factories in Haifa, the railway workshops, the clubs of the Arab youth groups, and the nationalist parties. But the number of Arab cadres was small, and in order to strengthen them, more than thirty Arabs were sent for extended courses to the Soviet Union between 1929 and 1935; the first group went even before the 1929 riots broke out, the second and largest, in 1931, and some of its members returned only in 1934.[6]

In Jerusalem the party extended its activities to the neighbouring villages; leaflets were distributed on market days. One of the demands constantly reiterated in this party propaganda was for the release of the prisoners who had been arrested during or after the 1929 riots. The party attempted in every way possible to overcome the distrust of the Arab nationalists and to "refute the calumny" that the party was pre-dominantly Jewish. "No," shouted the secretary, "not a single worker will believe any more what the Effendi tell him—that we are a Zionist party!"

The Yiddish party monthly, *Forward*, ceased to appear in 1931, but an Arab monthly by the same name (*'Ala'l Amām*) continued to be published. The disappearance of the Yiddish monthly may have re-sulted from various causes. The number of Jewish supporters and party members, and consequently the local financial resources, had dwindled. It should be recalled, moreover, that though the party opposed the use of Hebrew in principle, it was gradually compelled to use it for the simple reason that the majority of those addressed failed by now to understand Yiddish. And the new but legal and unofficial party organ *Ha'or* (The Light), published first in December, 1930, was already in Hebrew.[7] In the winter of 1930 several of the new party leaders (Sidqi Najāti among them) were arrested by the police, and the party, while protesting against the arrest, proudly pointed to the fact that "Arabiza-tion" was now a fact, and that the Arab public had been shown that the party was no longer Jewish.[8] However, in the absence of the few Arab cadres that the party had been able to gain, there was, as could only be expected, a new relapse into "Jewish nationalism," and this rightist deviation made a new intervention of the Comintern executive neces-sary. "All those who wish to delay the process of Arabization have to be removed from the party," it was again said.[9] And the new leadership, to remove all doubts, was for the first time not *elected* but *appointed*. Nevertheless, the years 1931–34 did not bring the party spectacular successes among the Arabs, and it was only with the return of "Mūsa" from the Soviet Union and his appointment as secretary-general in 1934 that party affairs became somewhat more stable.

The few Arab workers in the cities were simply not interested in Communist ideology, and the fellaheen preferred the religious brand of anti-Zionism as served up to them by the ex-Mufti. Among the intelligentsia Soviet Russia became interesting and fashionable only after the battle of Stalingrad. The party did not have great hopes for success among the Jews, and the December, 1930, elections (to the

Assefat Hanivharim, the prototype of the Israeli parliament), showed that the party had lost about half of its adherents compared to 1925—and many more, taking into account that the population of the country had grown considerably since then. One of the reasons for the drop was the vacillation of a weak leadership, which declared at one stage of the election campaign that it would boycott the elections and later changed its mind. Another, probably more important, reason, was the fact that the Communist Party was attacked by all other Jewish parties as a group of "pogromists," an accusation which seemed to be borne out by appeals to the Arabs issued by the party at that time "to march on Tel-Aviv" and to use force if arguments did not convince "misguided and incited Jewish workers."[10] These Communist leaflets had little effect, but their intention was indeed unmistakable and the reaction of the Jewish parties all too natural. The Histadrut (General Federation of Jewish Labour), for instance, came to be called by the Communist Party "the Nazi Histadrut" as a matter of routine.

Another source of their weakness was their stand on the issue which was to become the crucial one in subsequent years—the problem of immigration. There had been only a few immigrants in 1930, but the rise of Nazism in Germany caused the figure to rise steadily and the Communists were the first to sound the tocsin against "the danger of the renewal of Zionist invasion."[11] They still regarded the whole idea as utopian; and a speech by a member of the Jewish Agency Executive at that time, Dr. D. Eder, in which he declared that one day a million Jews would live in Palestine, was in their eyes "mere idle talk."[12] In their Arabic leaflets the party called upon the national movement to arise and fight against the renewal of Zionist effort, and warned it against hoping that the government would intervene and stop immigration. The ex-Mufti's attitude was far too moderate for them. He as well as the other national leaders would act only if they felt considerable pressure from below.[13] And they, the Communists, were to exert that pressure by using the nationalist clubs, by openly attacking the national leaders for trying to restrain the masses rather than calling upon them to demonstrate on November 2 (the anniversary of the Balfour Declaration), and also upon various other occasions. The radicalism of the youth, it was said, would bear no fruit except in the struggle against "the traitors who called themselves national leaders." And even more outspoken was an appeal on the occasion of the third anniversary of the 1929 riots: "The agreement between the gang of robbers calling themselves national leaders and the imperialist government and aggressive Zionism is a solid one. . . . But just on this very day after the execution of three of the rebels, we should demand more than ever the release of the prisoners of the riots and the continuation of the struggle."[14] These slogans were undoubtedly popular among some sections of the Arab population, although it is more difficult to understand what benefit the party thought it would derive from the publication of such a leaflet in Hebrew and Yiddish, too. Perhaps it was intended only to demonstrate that the party had nothing more to hide, in contrast to its position in the 1920's, when different, and frequently conflicting, lines of policy had been advocated in each of the languages used for party propaganda.

It was about this time that the slogan calling for an Arab federation was first used by the party; this, however, was not to be identical with an "imperialist federation." The party also showed considerable interest in the Muslim conference in Jerusalem in 1931; when an Egyptian delegate to the conference was deported from Palestine for particularly violent anti-Jewish and anti-British declarations the party was among the first to lodge a protest.[15] The Egyptian delegate, incidentally, was 'Abdur-Rahmān 'Azzām, the future secretary-general of the Arab League.

2. THE YEAR 1933

The disorders of 1933 were in most respects entirely different from both the 1929 riots which preceded them and the 1936 revolt which followed. They lasted only several days, nor did they spread throughout the country, and most of the clashes that occurred were between the demonstrators and the British police. The immediate reason for the disorders was the protest strike which had been proclaimed by the Arab Higher Committee for October 13 against Jewish immigration. There were demonstrations in the cities, government buildings were attacked, and in the ensuing clashes 27 people were killed and 250 wounded. Some of the Arab leaders (notably Jamāl Husaini and 'Awni 'Abdul Hādi) were arrested, but they claimed that they had not participated in the demonstrations. The government promised to reduce the semi-annual immigration quota for Jewish workers from 20,000 to 5600; after a few days, tension decreased and the riots were over.[16]

According to the line taken by the Communist Party in its publications, the 1933 revolt was a natural and desperate reaction of the exploited masses against their Zionist oppressors who wished to drive them from their land. Only strong and sudden pressure from below had compelled the hesitant Arab leadership to act. This opinion was not, however, shared by other observers. Harold Beeley (who can hardly be accused of lack of sympathy for the Arab National Movement in Palestine and elsewhere), writes[17] that the striking contrast between the respective fortunes and prospects of the Arab peasantry in the hill country and in the plains (which latter had been the main theatre of Jewish agricultural colonization) was another proof that Jewish immigration cannot have been the cause of the distress of the Arab peasantry in the hill country. Their distress was, on the contrary, mitigated and relieved by the general prosperity, both private and public, which Jewish immigration had brought in its train. But a deliberate effort had been made to spotlight the plight of this "obscure local community of fellaheen" before the Arab world at large, and thus to turn it to political account in order to attract and concentrate massive Arab opposition to Zionist aims. Nor did Mr. Beeley agree with the assertion that the riots were spontaneous. "The date originally fixed for the demonstration was the twentieth of October, but it was said that this was afterwards altered to the twenty-seventh because of the Jaffa lawn tennis tournament. A starving peasant does not postpone his outbreak for a week in order to make sure of getting in a tennis party."[18] There can be no doubt about the resentment felt by the Arab leadership in regard to Jewish immigration, and these feelings were shared by part of the Arab urban population. But there was no "class angle" whatsoever in the 1933 disorders, the fellaheen did not participate (as some of them had done in 1929), and economic exploitation was neither a principal nor a secondary motive.

One of the more interesting features of the 1933 disorders was the close collaboration achieved at the time between the Communists and the newly founded Istiqlāl (Independence) Party, and more particularly with its left wing. This party's leaders were mainly intellectuals from the cities, who were more radical than the Arab Higher Committee; they put rather less stress on Islamic tradition, and had vaguely liberal sympathies. The left wing of the party was headed by Hamdi Husaini from Gaza, who had visited Russia in the early 1930's.[19] The slogan invented by the Communist Party with regard to Istiqlāl was "March separately; strike together." It is interesting to note in passing that in 1933, while the party called for an "armed uprising," in its official publication it expressed, on the other hand (in a communication directed to its leading members), the fear that the revolt could come too early and therefore would be easily suppressed.[20]

The party press descriptions of the clashes in the cities hugged the political line: "Ten thousand Arabs, mainly workers, peasants, and Bedouins, artisans, and intellectuals participated in the demonstrations, which were headed by revolutionary elements, such as the leaders of the left wing of the Istiqlāl."[21] And the Communist papers were bitter about the "falsifications" of the Zionist newspaper *Davar*, according to which the demonstrations had been headed by the members of the Arab Higher Committee, and especially the religious aides of the Mufti, such as Shaikh Muzāfir. What was even worse was that the Mandatory government appeared to share this view, and that it did not arrest the revolutionary leaders of Istiqlāl but rather Jamāl Husaini, Ya'qūb Ghusain, Shaikh Muzāfir, and the other national leaders.

The party publications attacked the Jewish parties sharply for not having supported the "national revolt" and its leaders' demands for the cessation of Jewish immigration—mainly from Germany, where Hitler had come to power. Most "impertinent" of all were, as usual, the Jewish workers' parties, which demanded that more Jews should be allowed to immigrate from Germany at the very time of the disorders. "Even the white reaction in Shanghai did not reveal so much cruelty when the Chinese were killed. . . . But history never forgets, and you should not complain and ask that others feel sorry for you when you are brought to account."[22] The line of intimidation became more and more frequent and intense. "The Jewish masses do not yet realize what a terrible fate is in store for them in Palestine."[23]

The Communist Party had not taken any prominent part in the 1933 disorders. Some of the Arab party members had been arrested, together with many other demonstrators, while some Jewish militants had tried to gain admission to the ranks of the Arab national movement, but had failed to do so. The Communist Party press sponsored an appeal to collect money for the relatives of the victims of the clashes, and demanded the release of all those arrested. On the whole, the 1933 disorders were far less important, seen in the wider context of party history, than the 1929 riots. They did not cause important changes in either the party line or the constitution of the party leadership and the cadres. They are chiefly significant, perhaps, as a prelude to the events of 1936–38.

3. THE PALESTINE COMMUNIST PARTY *versus* THE REST

When we survey the relations between the Palestine Communist Party and the other Jewish parties during the 1930's, and analyse their attitudes towards immigration, which is the *central issue*, we receive the impression that the right-wing and centre parties were virtually ignored by Communist propaganda, which aimed its guns only at the left-wing Zionist groups. This trend, which holds true for most of the history of the party in Palestine, can easily be explained. The Histadrut (General Federation of Jewish Labour) and Mapai (the Palestine Workers' Party, headed by Ben Gurion, Ben Zvi, Sharett, and the since deceased Haim Arlozoroff and B. Katzenelson), were together the strongest single political factor in the country (Mapai was and still is the majority and controlling party in the Histadrut). They led the great majority of the workers, but their leaders (substantially the same individuals) were at the same time national figures; their "Zionist radicalism" was certainly not less fervent, and was frequently even more so than that of members of other parties. Their "reformism" alone would not have sufficed to explain the violent Communist attacks against them; their cardinal sin in Communist eyes was undoubtedly their strong nationalism. This applies, in even a greater degree, to the Marxist-Zionist parties to the left of Mapai, such as *Poale Zion* (Workers of Zion) and *Hashomer Hatzair* [the Young Guard, later Mapam (United Workers' Party)]. Though opposed to the leadership of the Jewish community and to Histadrut, these groups became the the Communists' worst enemies during the late 1930's. The dividing line did not run according to the Comintern pattern at all; it ran between those who regarded Zionism as the national liberation movement of the Jewish people, and those who denied the existence of a Jewish people altogether and considered Zionism a reactionary movement and a servant of British imperialism.

In most other countries there was a definite change in the attitude of the Communist Parties towards the Social Democrats when the former changed over from the slogan of "Social Fascism" to the Popular Front line after the Seventh Congress of the Comintern. There was no such change in Palestine. "The Jewish worker in Palestine does not belong to the type of worker who mistakenly believes in Social Democracy," it was said[24]; "chauvinism blinds the Zionist worker, and the darkest national instincts have made him believe in miracles. He really thinks that this country will be able to absorb tens of thousands of Jews each year during the next fifteen to twenty years. He believes in the absorption of millions and the establishment of a Jewish state. The Jewish worker errs far more seriously than the Social Democratic worker in Europe." The nationalism of the Jewish worker happened to be at that time a particular source of irritation in Communist eyes—nationalism had not yet been rediscovered in the Soviet Union. There was nothing more ludicrous than the primitive belief in a national movement; moreover, "mankind has already passed its stage of development within national frameworks."[25] And hence the recurring polemics against the Zionist leaders who called upon East European Jewry to come to Palestine. "Why are the millions of Polish Jews doomed—as maintained by the editor of *Hapoel Hatzair* [The Young Worker, the mouthpiece of Mapai]. Do Polish Jews really have no chance whatsoever of finding work in agriculture and industry? Will the reactionary rulers always continue to be in power?"[26] Obviously not. And therefore the attempt to ask those Jews to leave their countries was most reprehensible. "You Zionists do not believe in the future of East European Jewry and its peaceful development; you always tell them that the Poles will devour them."[27]

The only two groups which the Communists did not fight were the non-Zionist, orthodox, Agudat Israel (with whom there was little contact), and the Zionist "minimalists" of the Brith Shalom (Peace Covenant; later the League for Arab-Jewish Rapprochement) headed by Dr. J. Magnes and M. Kalvariski. Party members infiltrated the Brith Shalom, though it must be added at once that its politics were never influenced by the Communist Party. The Communist Party praised the Brith Shalom because it was the only group which had "realized that one cannot revolt against historical truth."[28] They were the only ones who understood how serious and how critical the position of 160,000

Jews could be among the Arabs of Palestine. In 1939, however, with the beginning of World War II, Brith Shalom favoured a united Arab-Jewish defence of Palestine against Nazism and Fascism, and this change of position became the object of heavy Communist attacks. As the Communists saw it, the commandment of the hour was not the defence of Palestine, but rather a common struggle *against* the call to defend the country.[29]

Anti-war propaganda took on considerable importance. As early as 1932 there were leaflets against the "establishment of an Anglo-French base in Palestine for the war against the Soviet Union."[30] In the following year this line reached its first peak of intensity. "During the one year of 1933, 50,000 new soldiers of the Zionist-Imperialist-Fascist army have entered Palestine."[31] Every new immigrant was a potential soldier for the invasion of the Soviet Union (which the Western democracies would launch, according to Communist predictions), each railway line, road, and new harbour was tantamount to the establishment of a new military base. And thus additional arguments were provided for the opposition to Jewish immigration and to the building up of the country in general.

With the Nazi rise to power in Germany immigration nevertheless began to increase, and this became a matter of much concern to the party. Its attitude was one of absolute opposition, and the line remained consistent to the very end. At the very beginning, during the first weeks after January 30, 1933, there was no official party declaration on that issue. All over the world emergency committees were set up to save German Jews, and there may have been doubts among the party leadership as to whether this would be the proper moment for such a public statement. But these initial hesitations were soon overcome and already in June, 1933, the first new appeal against immigration was published. "The Zionists wish to exploit the murder of Haim Arlozoroff (one of the most gifted and important Zionist leaders) to get 10,000 immigration certificates in order to bring in Zionist-Fascist soldiers for the war against the Arab national movement and the Soviet Union."[32] And at the same time further arguments were provided. "The whole Zionist movement is fascist." Party propaganda did not fail to draw the attention of the British authorities to the cunning devices used by the Zionists to bring in more Jews from Germany than were permitted. "The 13,000 certificates granted mean that 26,000 new immigrants have to be expected because every *halutz* (pioneer) will contract a fictitious marriage with a girl immigrant."[33] Party propaganda did not fail to point out the "remarkable similarity" between Nazism and Zionism ("Only two parties exist today in Germany—the Nazi Party and the Zionists"[34]) and, as evidence, it referred to the fact that the Zionist newspaper published in Germany did not attack the Nazi regime in its columns.[35] It drew attention to the fact that Zionism exploited the persecution of Jews in Germany (only the day before, Zionism had been charged with painting too grim a picture of the future of European Jewry!). But were only Jews persecuted in Germany? What about the millions of workers, Catholics, etc., who were persecuted, too—all of them could not emigrate, so why should the Jews leave? Was it not utterly irresponsible to propose that Jews should leave Germany and come to Palestine at a time when a decrease in the price of the citrus crop could cause a serious economic crisis?[36] But irresponsible Zionists were, of course, not to be moved by such inhibitions and scruples. Another argument was mentioned in German-language leaflets distributed among new immigrants from Germany in Haifa harbour in 1936, urging them to return at once. "There are enough unemployed in this country!" Our slogan should be, "An end to immigration and Zionism in general!"

Intimidation of the new immigrants was the most recurrent theme in party propaganda. "What are the results of immigration? Blood and fire, destruction and hell!" This was the main argument against immigration after the 1936 riots broke out. And the obvious conclusion was: Ask your leaders to stop immigration![37] But at the same time immigration was severely restricted, anyway, by the Mandatory government, and the situation of Central European Jewry deteriorated rapidly. In 1937–38 some of the cadres had their first doubts with regard to the party line. But this minority position was not reflected in official party publications until much later. After the Nazi occupation of Austria and parts of Czechoslovakia in 1938, the party organ *Kol Ha'am* (People's Voice) admitted that the situation of Central European Jewry was really becoming serious. But the transfer of 100,000 Jews from the *Reich* to Palestine would not help at all. "What should become of the remaining 700,000, and what of the Czechs and the Catholics and Protestants who are persecuted too?"[38] The conclusion was that the "demand for 100,000 immigration certificates was a crime, one of the holy lies of the nationalist reactionary leadership." The propaganda against immigration did not come to an end when World War II broke out. "More than half of the Jews in this country have no future whatsoever. They have been led out of Europe and brought here by the Zionists under false pretences."[39] At the same time Communist propaganda was concentrated against "B" Immigration (illegal immigration), which had considerably increased following the sharp reduction in the official immigration quota. In an article, already mentioned, which was fairly typical of the line taken as late as May, 1941, it was stated that "during 1939–40, Europe, and particularly the Balkan countries, had been flooded with Zionist emissaries who created an atmosphere of emigration approaching panic."[40] The disillusionment of many began even on the ship—"If we had only decided to return at that time!"[41] But they continued their trip and came to Palestine, and did not have enough to

94

eat now. It is interesting to note that the Communist line, which changed in every other respect after Hitler's invasion of Russia in June, 1941, remained as it was in one field: the stand on immigration was not affected, only the argumentation changed. Hitherto immigration had been wrong because it strengthened the war effort of the Western imperialists. From then on immigration had to be opposed because it was "detrimental to the Allied war effort."[42] "Those who drowned," one leaflet said of the passengers of a vessel from South-eastern Europe, which was torpedoed by a German U-boat, "were the victims of the Gestapo and the Zionist *conquistadores*, the mass murderers and robbers who 'save' them by packing them into floating coffins."[43]

It is impossible to deny that the stand of the Palestine Communists on immigration was consistent to the end—the end of European Jewry. It must be presumed that they thought during the first years after the rise of Nazism (1933–36) that their scientific analysis was correct and the utopian Zionist line was all wrong. By 1938, and certainly after 1941, even the more obstinate among them must have realized that their prognosis with regard to European Jewry had been utterly mistaken. But they were loath to admit it.

4. THE 1936–39 REVOLT

The nature and the extent of the 1936–39 revolt were different from previous disorders and riots in Palestine. They soon affected the whole country, and made necessary the concentration of large military forces in order to combat them. For almost three years a minor war raged up and down the country; it petered out early in 1939, but came to an end only with the outbreak of World War II. The events of those years have been given various explanations and most contain some truth. Opposition to Jewish immigration and settlement, for example, had undoubtedly reached a new high among the Arabs. On the other hand, parallel developments on the international scene cannot be ignored. The British position in the Mediterranean was weakened, the Italians and Germans propagandized and planned conquests, and there were also contacts between the Berlin–Rome axis and Palestine Arab leaders, such as the ex-Mufti, Haj Amīn al Husaini.

There have been many descriptions of the 1936–39 rebellion and its origin by both Zionists and Arab nationalists. The following conclusions were reached by an outside observer several years later:

"The Arabs had no love for the Jews or for the British, and were quite prepared to support the rebellion and enjoy whatever benefits the rebellion might bring them, provided that the rebellion and their support of it was not likely to cause them much trouble, expense, or inconvenience. A certain number of them gave it their active support from the first, either because it appealed to their patriotic instincts, or because it provided them with a source of income, satisfied their love of adventure, or their religious fanaticism. Later, many of them supported the rebellion because it became advantageous from the point of view of business, social popularity, or even of personal safety to do so. In the early days of the rebellion—that is to say, during the general strike—it may be said that although there was not a great deal of active enthusiasm for it, there was at least very little feeling against it. A large part of the Arab population would have been glad to see things return to normal at the end of the strike, but that feeling was not sufficiently strong, nor sufficiently organized, to constitute anything in the nature of opposition to the rebellion. The active rebels were in a minority from the beginning, but like many resolute minorities they succeeded in establishing complete ascendancy over a majority that was uneducated, unorganized and irresolute.

"The villagers felt far less strongly than the townsmen about the point ostensibly at issue. For instance, land sales. The grievance that the Jews were continually pushing the Arabs off the land, which was the most publicized and the most sympathetically received of all the Arab grievances, was far more bitterly felt by the townspeople, who had no direct interest in the question, than by the villagers, who were the people who were supposed to be suffering. This fact cannot be reasonably attributed to the altruism of the townsmen. Such spontaneous animosity as the villagers felt against the Jews was more due to religious fanaticism and general xenophobia than any sense of economic grievance. In fact, in normal times relations between Arab villagers and the Jewish settlers, who were alleged to be squeezing them out of existence, were reasonably good. . . .

"Thus the rebellion was not a national movement in the sense that it commanded the active support of the majority of the Arabs in Palestine. But the rebellion would not have been possible without the existence of a strong national movement under cover of which it was able to develop. It developed in the same way as fascist movements in various European countries have developed, under the cover of nationalist or patriotic revivals. These movements are cheered and helped in their early stages by more or less disinterested patriots who think that the country is 'going to the dogs,' and by less disinterested magnates who think they can make use of these movements for their own purposes. Then these patriots and magnates wake up and find that they have helped a dangerous gang of hooligans into power, and that, instead of being able to use them, they are used by them. So it was with the rebellion." [John Marlowe, *Rebellion in Palestine* (London, 1946), pp. 229 *et seq.*]

The Palestine Communist Party had announced as early as November that a new revolt was brewing; it called upon the Jewish masses to support the Arab revolutionary movement and denounced the "Zionist Fascists and chauvinists for waging war on the Arab people and killing fellaheen."[44] At the same time the party demanded in its propaganda that the Hagana, the Jewish defence organization, should be outlawed and disbanded. On the eve of the riots representatives of the party met the Jerusalem Mufti in order to hammer out a working agreement. This had been preceded by discussions in the party executive which had resulted in a decision that "the Arab Communists should actively participate in destroying Zionism and imperialism, while the Jewish members should do their share by weakening the *Yishuv* [Jewish community] from within." As a result of the agreement between the party leadership and the Arab chiefs, two Communists were attached to the general staff which was planning and co-ordinating the revolt. One of them, Nimr 'Uda, became one of the "Intelligence" chiefs of the Arab military units, since he had useful contacts with Jews via the party. The second Communist representative, Fuād Nāsir, became deputy to the commander ('Abdul Qādir Husaini) of the gangs in the Hebron-Jerusalem region.[45]

In the first party appeals published in Hebrew a fortnight after the riots broke out, the party fully supported the demands of the Arabs, which included abolition of the Balfour Declaration, cessation of Jewish immigration, the establishment of a popular democratic state council, etc. At the same time, the Jews were urged to "Join the Arab liberation movement"; though it was not explained how this was to be done, which made the appeal somewhat impractical, since the Arab units made a point of shooting Jews at sight and asking questions afterwards.[46] The tenor of party propaganda was aimed at arousing panic and despair—the Jews were lost, and there was no future for them in Palestine. At the same time there was an attempt to show that it was the Zionist leaders who were really responsible for the Jewish bloodshed, and the Mandatory government was attacked for having announced a new immigration quota of 4500 despite the outbreak of the revolt.[47] "We are against the bloody adventure of a Jewish state."[48]

But one should not attribute exaggerated importance to party propaganda in 1936–37. The party again suffered from internal dissension up to and including the very leadership. At the Seventh Congress of the Comintern, one representative, Tajar, said that it was "our task to show the Jewish workers that their national and class interests are connected with the victory of the Arab liberation movement," while another spokesman expressed quite a different line of thought—"The Jewish minority in Palestine is a colonizing minority by its very nature."[49] In 1934 a "Trotskyite group" had been expelled from the party; early in 1936 the "Volodya group" was ousted; and when the riots started and the Jewish party members were asked to take part in terrorist acts sponsored by the party and directed against Jewish workers' organizations in Haifa and Tel-Aviv, all but a small group preferred to leave or to become inactive.[50] Among the acts carried out by order of the party were attempts to blow up the workers' club in Haifa, and several cases of bomb-throwing in Tel-Aviv—which, it should be added at once, were carried out in a very amateurish way and caused little damage with no casualties. Once again there were stormy debates among party members, and when the editor of the American Communist newspaper *Morgenfreiheit*, Meleh Epstein, came to visit Palestine at that time he told the party leaders[51] that such incidents would create an extremely bad impression abroad if they became known. At a later date, events in 1936 were characterized in the following manner in a memorandum of the "Jewish Section" sent to the Comintern:

"The party executive established the thesis of two fighting camps, the one Arab and progressive, the other Zionist and imperialist. The Jewish party members were asked to aid the progressive camp in the same way as the Arabs, by fighting. While the Arabs began to engage in partisan warfare, the Jews were to throw bombs in the Jewish quarters—bombs which were not meant to kill people but to increase the general panic. What were the results of this mistaken policy among the Jews? The party was completely isolated and openly hated. The Jews held the party responsible for the bombs used in the workers' clubs, and thus a dangerous weapon was given Zionism for the struggle against us."[52]

But the rival faction did not share this opinion, and in their view the reasons for the failure of the revolt—and the failure of party policy—were quite different: "The lack of leadership in the Arab National Movement, the egotism and opportunism of the leaders, . . . the decentralization of the guerrilla command which allowed hooligans to enter the ranks of the partisans, and last but not least, the weakness, especially the numerical weakness, of the Communist Party."[53] The party leadership of 1936–37 thought that there was no room for any "popular front" initiative in Palestine, and instead they published leaflets about the "destruction of the Zionist settlements and the acts of sabotage and partisan attacks by which the Arab Liberation Movement would put an end to the continuation of Zionist colonization."[54]

There was a lull in the riots when the Arab general strike came to an end in October (and when the citrus season started). The Communists were not happy about the decision of the Arab leadership to discontinue the revolt, even temporarily, and they wrote in their Arabic leaflets about the "shameful betrayal" and asked the masses to continue the struggle regardless of what their leaders decided.[55]

The riots did not cease altogether, but there were no major attacks between October, 1936, and August, 1937, when the situation again deteriorated. This time the revolt affected most parts of the country and the Mandatory government decided to outlaw the Arab Higher Executive. The Jerusalem Mufti escaped to the Lebanon, but big guerrilla units were organized in the north of Palestine. Only in October, 1938, did the Mandatory government turn over the task of restoring order to the army and then, in the course of a few months, the revolt was suppressed. In the meantime, however, terror was rampant, in the Arab camp itself (it is believed that more Arabs were killed as a result of internecine family and political feuds than perished in the fights against the Jews and the British army), and among the Jews the more extreme elements of the Irgun Zvai Leumi (I.Z.L.) inaugurated their policy of retaliation in the summer of 1938.

The state of the party in mid-summer, 1937, was one of almost complete disintegration. Of the Arab militants, who had never been very numerous, some had been killed or wounded in the fighting, others (including the military leaders Fuād Nāsir and Nimr 'Uda) had been arrested. Among the Jews whole party branches (including the largest one in Tel-Aviv) had been dissolved for insubordination, and the members, insofar as they did not leave the party altogether, were sent to Spain. The party press continued to denounce the "mad, chauvinist, militarist incitement of Zionists" (i.e., their opposition to the Arab attacks), and, although it dissociated itself for the first time from "individual terror" which "causes the Liberation movement much damage,"[56] it was at that time that support for the Arab leadership, mainly the Jerusalem Mufti, reached the stage of full identification. This became obvious after the Bludan (Syria) Conference in the summer of 1937, when the party backed up the declarations of the Arab representatives and their proposals for a solution of the Palestine question. The party had protested previously against the deportation of the Mufti from Palestine,[57] and the Jewish leaders were now accused of not accepting the "very reasonable proposals of Haj Amīn al Husaini."[58] At a later date, in September, 1938, the party organ published the appeal of one of the major gang leaders, 'Abdul Rāziq.[59]

By that time contact between the executive and the party cadres had virtually come to a standstill. The party executive continued to publish occasional leaflets while the exclusively Jewish branches, such as that in Jerusalem, published propaganda material of their own which was not at all identical with the extreme pro-Arab line of the party executive. By 1937 it had become fairly obvious that Haj Amīn al Husaini and the other leaders of the revolt received substantial support, in both money and arms, from Rome and Berlin. But it was only in May, 1939, when the revolt was practically over, that the party executive first began to change its policy, realizing that it had collaborated in fact with Fascist and Nazi satellites. But the only such admission is contained in a "Letter to the Party Cadre" of November, 1939.[60]

"The Arab nationalist leaders wanted to continue the riots of 1937 because they erroneously thought the international situation favourable. The revolt spread but the party did not take part, because the masses were weak and unorganized and we were afraid of Fascist infiltration. But it was the mistake of the party not to explain its opposition to the renewal of the riots. When the revolt spread we, nevertheless, decided to participate after some hesitation. We decided in favour of participation because of the mass character of the revolt, and also in order to combat Fascist influences."

But this explanation, which, incidentally, confines itself only to a tactical level and never gets down to fundamentals, does not mention what the "Jewish Section" said very clearly, "that the Arab Communist militants joined the nationalists and later refused to carry out any instructions from the party executive."[61]

The party suffered a severe setback among the Jews as a result of the 1936–39 riots, and it ceased to exist among the Arabs. It had to begin from scratch in order to gain the influence it did win among the Arabs in later years. The leaders and militants of the time of the riots make up only a handful of the members of the present Communist Party. Contact with the Comintern had ceased in 1937, mainly, it would seem, as a result of the purge in Russia, and there was no supreme authority to give direction and material assistance. In 1939 there existed a party executive without followers, and there were several Communist factions refusing to take orders from the executive—but no Communist Party.

Ever since the riots had begun in 1936, the British government had tried to remedy the situation by political proposals of various kinds. The Peel Commission, which came to Palestine late in 1936, proposed the partition of the country. This suggestion was rejected, however, by both the Arab leadership and the majority of the Zionists. A second inquiry commission, which came to Palestine in April, 1938, was also opposed by the Arab Higher Committee and the Zionist parties, who considered it even less favourable than the Peel project. The British government then shelved these plans and published in May, 1939, a "White Paper" which envisaged the establishment of an independent Palestinian State within ten years, the immigration of 75,000 Jews during the first five years (and the total cessation of immigration thereafter), and the prohibition of further purchase of land by Jews in most parts of the country. The "White Paper" was violently opposed by the Jews, while most Arab groups, though not approving it in so many words, considered it an important achievement gained in their struggle. In fact, the "White Paper" was intended to create a more favourable sentiment among the Arabs in view of the danger of war, the assumption being that the good-will of the Arabs in a state of emergency would be far more important than that of the Jews, who would have to support the British anyway.

The Communist Party was against partition because it did provide, though on a very small scale, for the establishment of a Jewish state.[62] The first issue of the new party periodical, *Kol Ha'am* (People's Voice), depicted an (Arab) fist crushing the miniature Jewish state.[63] It supported the stand of the Arab leaders against partition and coined the slogan: "The Arabs want peace, the Jews do not want peace"[64]; and this at a time when the revolt was renewed on an even larger scale. At the same time it was pointed out that the fight against partition was "part of the wider struggle throughout the world against Fascism."[65] This statement, too, was not recalled with much relish by the party leadership in later years. On the other hand, there were some differences of opinion regarding the "White Paper." The party executive gave it a favourable reception without reservation. "The party viewed it as an achievement of the Arab liberation movement and as a first step towards full liberation of the country."[66] And it complained about the line taken by the "Jewish Section," which, it said, was apt to create the impression that it opposed the "White Paper," and furthermore insisted that arguments identical with those of the British imperialists should not be used, so that the party should not be totally isolated among the Jews, and needlessly at that. The party executive said that this whole mistaken attitude was based on the assumption that a popular front with the Jewish left-wing parties was possible and desirable.

A critical survey of the publications of the "Jewish Section" tends to show, however, that the charges of the party executive were greatly exaggerated. The "Jewish Section" stated (in a leaflet issued several days after the publication of the "White Paper") that what "we need now is a return to normalcy; we oppose all the Revisionist and semi-Revisionist slogans of a constructive revolt."[67] This attitude had the unexpected consequence of making the Communists the only party in Palestine which was in almost full agreement with government policy— for the first time in its history. The Jews were strongly opposed to the "White Paper," the Arabs were more or less satisfied but did not show it openly; thus the Communists were the only ones who approved and justified government policy. Indeed, the only two complaints they made were that the "White Paper" had been issued by the Chamberlain government and that it did not go far enough on some points. In their criticism of the law which restricted Jewish land purchases (a law engendered by the "White Paper" policy), the Communists wrote that in spite of all protests the law still left room "for the continued colonization of the country."[68] In the restricted area which had been left open for land sale to Jews, the "Zionists would still be able to purchase 700,000 dunams" (70,000 hectares). And the party demanded that the authorities put an end to this remaining opportunity for the expropriation of the Arab fellaheen. This line did not change during the war years, and the party occasionally criticized the Mandatory authorities for compromising with Jewish demands on minor points of interpretation of the "White Paper" (mainly concerning immigration).

The expulsion and disappearance of successive generations of party leaders and militants in the 1920's has already been described. The situation in the 1930's was no different. Yizhak Barzilai, Litvinski ("Emek"), Ze'ev Birman, Hofshi, Bahiri, and many others left Palestine or were deported. Some were killed in Spain, many more were shot during the purges in Russia. To the best of our knowledge, not one of these is still alive; the Palestine Communists do not now have a single member in their midst who has belonged to the party from the very beginning—or even from the early years. There have been so many abrupt interruptions in the history of the party that it has achieved the peculiar position of being one of the very few Communist Parties in the world which has carefully refrained from writing its own history (not even publishing articles on the subject). It does not celebrate anniversaries, and even abstains from quoting the party press of bygone years. Though one of the oldest parties in Palestine, it is, or at least wishes to appear as, a party without a past.[69]

A few words on the "Communist type" of the 1920's and 1930's may be called for here. He was very different from the opportunist type of later years, who merely wishes to float on what he believes to be the crest of the wave of the future. The early Communist was a revolutionary and an idealist who could expect little more than prison and deportation, or at the very least to be treated as an outcast and pariah. His ideas did not lack a certain consistency; he was fighting for a higher aim than mere Jewish nationalism. The world revolution took precedence over all national movements, and certainly over the Zionist movement, which was a late-comer among the national movements, and affected one of the smaller peoples. He was called a traitor by his enemies among the Jews—but he was certainly not a traitor in his own eyes, since one cannot betray what one does not believe in. The Palestine Communist was absolutely convinced of the justice of his service as a soldier in the cause of world revolution; the era of nationalism was over; only the Zionists, whose political ideas were utopian and unscientific, refused to realize it. Though the more educated and sophisticated youth rejected Communism, many young Jews, once they were out of the Polish ghettoes, found in Communism a veritable spiritual revelation, an incomparably nobler idea than ossified Jewish orthodox tradition could offer them, and actually the only other *Weltanschauung* (apart from Zionism) they could possibly know. Democracy for them was some remote abstract idea—where could they have seen it in practice? They knew little about economics, philosophy, or psychology, and next to nothing about history, apart from what Marxism had taught them; Marxism alone appeared to show the way out of the stifling narrowness of the lower middle-class conditions and atmosphere in the villages and small towns of Poland and Rumania—some of which had indeed been transplanted to Palestine. The life of a Jewish Communist in the 1920's and 1930's was not an enviable one, convinced as he may have been of final victory. There may have been a few adventurers among them, but certainly no opportunists, attracted by external considerations and personal ambition. However warped and perverse its way of thinking and its unrelenting opposition to the interests of its own people may have been, the Palestine Communist Party of the 1920's was undoubtedly a revolutionary party—the "revolution from above" had not yet been invented.

Chapter Eight

During World War II
and After

I. COMMUNIST FORECASTS

THE German-Soviet pact of August, 1939, was the supreme test for all Communist Parties, and the Palestinian party certainly proved its loyalty, though its position was undoubtedly the most untenable of all. A French or British or American Communist could argue, wrong-headedly but with some semblance of veracity in the eyes of those who had been taught to think dialectically, that this was just another imperialist war, and that it was wrong to support one imperialist power against another, just as it had been wrong to back the Entente against the Kaiser. The Jewish Communists, however, had realized by now that at least one small (but for them, decisive) difference existed between the two "imperialist camps"—one of which, whatever its crimes of commission or omission, was not out to destroy all Jews. Nevertheless, they hesitated no longer than did the other Communist Parties outside Russia in informing their own rank and file and the world at large that Hitler was now the ally of the Socialist fatherland, while the enemy to be fought was the one at home, viz. England and the imperialist West. The party had very much shrunken after the 1936–39 riots; there were rather fewer than 300 Jewish members and hardly more than a handful of Arabs left. But these were the hard core, the cadres, and they did not flinch.[1] They stood the test honourably, at least from the Comintern point of view. On August 1, 1939 (their annual anti-war day), the party executive had published one of its traditional appeals—"International Fascism wants to occupy the Middle East and Palestine. But all patriots will defend their homeland. There is no room for neutralism today—neutralism means assistance given to the Fascists."[2] The international scene of the following four weeks has been frequently described, and need not be gone into here in detail. The news of the Moscow pact came as a deep shock to the Palestinian party. Its first reaction was to support the war against Hitler (the exact parallel of Harry Pollitt's "errors" in Britain or Terracini's position in the Italian party—for parallels in France the reader is referred to Rossi's standard work).[3] The party executive wrote that "the agreement has completely isolated the Hitlerite gangs"[4] and the "Jewish Section" even approved of the enlistment campaign launched by the Jewish Agency. In September the old "anti-Fascist" line was continued; when the Soviets entered eastern Poland, the "Jewish Section" described the occupation as "a knife-stab into the face of the Hitlerite bandits."[5] But meanwhile some things had been said in Moscow about the friendship of the two peoples being sealed in blood, and Mr. Molotov himself had declared that the ideology of Hitlerism could be accepted or rejected, but should not be fought with arms. The party executive was the first to rally from the shock; as it could not very well admit that the party line had somersaulted, it now held that Hitler had changed his character. "The Hitler against whom Chamberlain is now fighting is no more the same Hitler who intended to fight the Soviet Union. He has ceased to be Chamberlain's and Daladier's gendarme and has to do what Moscow tells him."[6]

Several weeks later, when the first Palestinian Jewish soldiers were sent to the Maginot Line in British units, the party executive, in a special appeal, went even further and said that they were sent to fight not Hitler but the Soviet Union on behalf of international finance. At the same time party cadres were told orally by the executive that Hitler had to be regarded as an ally and friend of the Soviet Union, though this could perhaps not be so clearly explained in the party propaganda.[7] It was on this point that the "Jewish Section" (whose pro-enlistment leaflet had been subject to sharp criticism as a nationalist deviation), refused to go along with the party executive. They believed that both sides in the world dispute were equally evil and at fault, but did not share the opinion of the executive according to which Hitler was a lesser evil than the British and French governments. But both sections agreed that the main slogan would have to be in future, "Down with the war," and that the fight against mobilization would have to be the rallying-point of their activities. While the British were falling back on Dunkirk, the Haganah (the Jewish underground) became the main target of Communist attacks, since it had offered the imperialists "Jewish soldiers as cannon fodder."[8] This, they said, was clearly tantamount to suicide. The only realistic policy was the one proposed by the Communists—to declare Palestine an open country, thus safeguarding the lives and property of its inhabitants.[9] At the time of the Battle of Britain, when British defeat appeared imminent, the campaign against the defence of Palestine was stepped up. "Imperialist mobilization has failed despite all the efforts made by the Zionist criminals." The party press of 1940 is full of news from various places in Palestine about organized and spontaneous resistance to army recruitment and similar defeatist propaganda. The words "Hitler" and "Fascism" had temporarily been struck out of the dictionary.

Once again the Jews of Palestine were a source of desperation to the party—they were dead but did not know it. The Arabs had revealed a much more progressive attitude. "The Arab peoples have understood clearly the character of this imperialist war, and they have realized that their task is to fight against this war and those responsible for it."[10] The Arab countries had refused to break off relations with Nazi Germany and were highly commended for this stand. Only the Zionists were all-out for a war against Germany. But there was still hope that the Jewish worker would not blindly follow the criminal call to fight the Nazis. "They understand very well that this is not their war and, together with the Arab masses, they will fight Britain and its Zionist agents."[11] All this was in direct consequence of the directive ("active opposition to enlistment") which had been issued in January, 1940, and of which the "Maginot Line Leaflet" was the first example.[12]

Communist propaganda opposing the war against Hitler is of little interest politically, because it did not affect the course of events to any appreciable extent. And yet, for the understanding of the character of the party, no period in its history is more revealing, because the line taken was so patently absurd. It is obviously not difficult to "gain friends and influence people" on the basis of popular-front slogans which everybody can readily accept. The real test comes when the cadres have to appear with a political line they do not understand themselves, which is based solely on the belief that "the party can never be wrong." A leaflet of July, 1940 (literally recalling W. Liebknecht's appeals against the 1870–71 war), was typical of many of those published by the various party branches. "Do not give imperialism a single soldier, a single farthing. The Communist party declares at this critical moment that a Jewish army under the command of the traitorous Zionist gangs and British imperialism is sharply inimical to the vital interests of the Jewish masses in this country....Fight the warmongers! Demonstrate your opposition to the war effort in all its forms!"

The ideological justification was given elsewhere the same month— "Goebbels and Mosley say that this is a Jewish war. But the Jewish masses know that this is not true, they never wanted a war. The Jews do not want war because they are always its first victims. It is a crime to argue that this war is our war! Where can they [the Jews] escape if the war should reach this country?" The defeatist propaganda of the party press centred around the following points: (a) Nobody wants to join the army. (b) Conditions in the army camps are intolerable. (c) Soldiers are beaten in the camps by their officers, and everybody wants to run away. (d) The families of the soldiers do not receive support. The following quotation from a "letter from an army camp" by a "newly enlisted private," published in the party organ, indicates the general tone: "Frequently I think we have to fight against our officers and not for them. What difference is there between them and the Fascists?"

Another favourite subject of the party press was the struggle against the Haganah (the Jewish underground para-military organization), which made at that time great efforts to strengthen Jewish military resistance in preparation for a possible Nazi invasion, and continued at the same time to organize "illegal immigration" to save Jews from destruction in Nazi-occupied Europe. *Kol Ha'am* violently attacked this transfer of thousands of Jews by an organization of "pirates and smugglers" robbing and exploiting their poor victims instead of leaving them in peace in Europe.[13] It is highly unlikely that the writers of these articles and leaflets did not know by that time that this was the "peace" of concentration camps and cemeteries.[14]

Early in 1941 the threat to Palestine became more acute as a result of the offensive of the Axis troops in North Africa, the infiltration of Axis agents into Syria, and somewhat later the Rashīd 'Ali *putsch* in Iraq. The party executive considered itself obliged to intensify the struggle against the war effort, and sharply attacked the slogan coined at that time by M. Sharett of the Jewish Agency about "fighting with our backs to the wall."[15] Only once did the party appear to have had certain doubts about its own line. At the time of the pro-Nazi Rashīd 'Ali revolt in Iraq it published leaflets in Arabic and Hebrew calling on both Britain and Germany not to intervene in Iraq.[16] Mentioning Germany in this context was no doubt an important innovation, as was the fact that Rashīd 'Ali was called an "Axis agent."[17] But the Rashīd 'Ali revolt was no turning-point in the attitude of the party. A few days later it realized that its appraisal of the situation had been all wrong. The Soviet Union was the first to recognize the Rashīd 'Ali regime, and the Palestinian party was again compelled to retreat.

In May and June, 1941, tension came to a head. Allied units entered Syria in order to forestall a *coup* by Vichy and German forces. The party reacted as usual. "All these actions are a criminal extension of war-sabotage."[18] Allied soldiers throughout the Middle East were asked in a special leaflet in English to demand that they be returned home from overseas. The Palestinian masses were at the same time admonished that they would not be saved from the horrors of the war by the British or German armies.[19]

Nor should "counter-revolutionary slogans be given any credence, such as the one that the Soviet Union would shortly enter the war because the war was approaching its frontier." "Mr. Churchill would naturally like such a development," it was added.[20] The Communists' confusion increased each week, but they saw no sound reason for changing their line. "We oppose the slogan of defending the homeland," they reiterated. "Workers come to ask us what to do, they want concrete advice. We tell them, 'Well, it is true that the German and Italian armies are at the gate. . . . But it is also true that Churchill's armies are in this country. And our first task is to fight the enemy within."[21] The party set up in place of the slogan "defence of the homeland," its own catchword, "peace and bread," and criticizes sharply the continued efforts to enlist the youth of the country and the exertion of pressure to that end.

Several days later, the German army invaded the Soviet Union.

2. THE PARTY IN 1941

The Palestine Communists had been cut off from the Comintern since 1937. One of the results of the state of isolation was the existence of various splinter groups rather than one united party. Another consequence was the lack of orientation, which emerged most clearly during the weeks and months after June 22, 1941. Both main groups, the Executive and the "Jewish Section," continued to oppose the very idea of a common "anti-Fascist front" and a war effort in Palestine. The Executive, in its first leaflet after the Nazi invasion, stated that the Zionist-Imperialist mobilization campaign should be opposed, the workers should strike at their places of work, in order to demonstrate their solidarity with the Soviet Union.[22] The "Jewish Section," equally intransigent, wrote in its organ that the "attack had been the result of an agreement between Fascism and Western democracy, and enlistment in Churchill's army is therefore tantamount to support given to the enemies of the Soviet Union."[23] The official line during the four months after June 22 was that the old attitude of opposition to the "imperialist war" should be continued in the colonial countries. As late as August, Kol Ha'am declared that "although the Palestinian workers were ready to give their lives for the Soviet Union . . . nothing has changed their attitude towards enlistment in the army."[24] Only in October, 1941, did the party announce that a united front "from Tobruk to Leningrad"[25] had been created; now the order of the day was to join the British army, the "comrade in arms" of "the heroic Red Army." At a still later period, the party admitted having been mistaken in having correctly appraised the new situation created after the Nazi attacks only at this late date. Most of the party leaders had been arrested by the police in the late spring of 1941, among them the party secretary "Mūsa," his Jewish deputy, S. Mikunis, as well as S. Sabri and others. They were to be brought to trial on several charges concerning their fight against the anti-Nazi war effort, but meanwhile the international political situation changed as the result of the Nazi attack on Russia, and they were released. The secretary of the Tel-Aviv branch, S. Mironianski, died while under arrest, and the Communist Party accused the police of having killed him.[26]

The party line after autumn, 1941, underwent considerable metamorphoses. Both main groups decided for the duration to play down the demands for Jewish national independence and in their propaganda material there appeared new slogans about a "Greater Syria." The attacks against Zionism were also toned down for some time (although not in the material distributed to the cadres). Up to June, 1941, Zionism had been attacked as the ally of British imperialism. Between July and September, 1941, Zionism was denounced as the "agency of Fascism in Palestine." Between the autumn of 1941 and the summer of 1942 a close season was declared on Zionism, but thereafter Mūsa again returned to the old anti-Jewish line, which in 1943 caused another split in the party. The struggle against Zionism now took on mainly the form of attacks on the forces which "sabotaged" the war effort. "Zionism has remained an adventure of British imperialism, but the Jewish *bourgeoisie* is worse than the American and British middle class."[27] The Jews, and especially Jewish youth, were accused of not displaying the necessary enthusiasm for the fight against Hitler, compared, for instance, with General Mikhailovitch's partisans in Yugoslavia. The continuation of Jewish immigration from Europe was one of the forms of Zionist sabotage, and the Communists in the Jewish units of the British army were instructed to inform their officers about all the "extracurricular" activities of the Zionist soldiers, and to protest against the nationalist atmosphere created there in general.[28] Generally speaking, the party opposed the establishment of Jewish units from Palestine as "narrow provincialism," and advised its members, wherever possible, to join other units (Czech, etc.). As for saving Jews from Nazi-occupied Europe, especially from the Balkan countries, nothing could be done (nor should be done) before the Red Army's liberation of East European Jewry. At that time there was much sympathy for the Red Army and the Soviet Union in general in Palestine, and the two Communist groups were instrumental (among others) in creating the "V" (for Victory) League, which was to promote friendly relations between the two countries.

3 · THE LEAGUE FOR NATIONAL LIBERATION

The 1943 split, about which more will be said presently, put an end to the existence of the "territorial" (i.e. mixed Arab and Jewish) Communist Party in Palestine; only in 1948, after the state of Israel had come into being, were Jewish and Arab Communists reunited. The education of indigenous Arab cadres had been considered the main assignment of the Communist Party in Palestine from the very beginning. The first leaflets in Arabic were published as early as 1921, and in the late 1920's the Haifa branch issued a magazine of its own: *Al*

Munbih (Tocsin).[29] Soon thereafter the regular party monthly, *'Ala'l Amām* (Forward), began to be published and at the same time the first Arab Communist (Khalīl Shanīr) was sent to the Moscow Comintern School.[30] By 1934 the party politburo had an Arab majority. We have dealt elsewhere with the part the Arab Communists played in the 1936–39 revolt.

The immediate reason for the party split in 1943 was certainly not of momentous importance. Mūsa and other Arab party leaders denounced a strike [which had been declared early in May of that year by the Histadrut (General Federation of Jewish Labour)] in the army camps as "contrary to the war effort"; while the Jewish members of the party executive, drawing attention to the fact that Mūsa had not hesitated to support such strikes when Arab workers were concerned, refused to go along with the stand taken by the party general secretary. Feeling had been running high for some time, and Mūsa decided to expel the Jews from the party leadership, while the latter published leaflets in which it was announced that Mūsa and his friends had been expelled.[31] The split was precipitated by the publication of an appeal by one of Mūsa's lieutenants, Emil Habībi,[32] in which the Jewish Communists were accused of a nationalist deviation. "The truth is that the Palestine Communist Party is a national Arab party, though it contains individual Jews, who accept its national programme."[33] It was also stated on the same occasion that the party (that is, Mūsa) welcomed the dissolution of the Comintern, since this made it possible for the first time for the party to approach "national elements" that had previously hesitated to join the party. This was more than the Jewish Communists could stomach, and they decided to make a clean sweep. The "cancer of Mūsa'ism" (as it now came to be called in the letters to the cadres) was to be cut out. If Mūsa had thought that he would benefit from the dissolution of the Comintern, and the *rapprochement* with nationalist forces, he was greatly mistaken. There was an increase in Arab Communist activities after 1944, but it mainly affected the young intellectuals in Haifa, Jaffa, and Jerusalem; and Mūsa, a leader without education and no pretensions to culture, was obviously not the man to head these activities. The leadership passed into the hands of others like Emil Tūma and Emil Habībi (later joined by Fuād Nāsir), who founded the League for National Liberation in 1943–44. The League (Usbat at Tahrīr al Watani) had grown out of a number of intellectual circles which existed throughout the country.[34] It saw its main tasks as working for the war effort, and demanding a "new deal" in the political organization and representation of Palestinian Arabs. It also played a certain part in organizing the Arab Workers' Congress.

Their opposition to the old Arab leadership, of which only the *dei minorum gentium* had remained (the Mufti, Jamāl Husaini, and other leaders of the first rank being out of the country), reflected a conflict of generations even more than of ideas. The League fought for the democratization of Arab leadership, but its own policy did not differ radically from that of the Arab Higher Committee after the latter was reorganized in 1945. While the Mufti was prepared to admit to his independent Arab state only those Jews who had been in Palestine prior to 1918, the League was ready to admit all Jews then living in the country. After the Bludan Conference of the Arab rulers there were further differences of opinion between the League and the Arab leadership. The League proposed that the Palestine problem should be dealt with by the United Nations, while the Arab rulers opposed this idea. The League was expelled from the Arab Higher Committee, but it kept in close contact with the Mufti and Jamāl Husaini, and its representatives frequently visited the "National Leaders"[35] in Cairo and Beirut. When the Mufti escaped from Paris, where he had been held because of war-crime charges, the League weekly wrote: "The Arab people, which has remained faithful to its leaders, celebrates this holiday throughout the country."[36] When the Mufti demanded that the League should not appear before U.N.S.C.O.P. (the U.N. inquiry commission in 1947) and give evidence, it complied with his wish, though it had previously declared its willingness to appear.

After the Gromyko declaration in May, 1947 (which recognized—for the first time—Jewish rights in Palestine and the Jews' right to immigration), the position of the League became extremely difficult. On the one hand they declared in their publications that they supported all the steps taken by the Arab leadership to "liberate Palestine and preserve its unity,"[37] which by that time meant the preparation of an armed revolt and perhaps even war; their delegation, which came to meet the Mufti a few weeks before the outbreak of the riots, stressed its loyalty emphatically. But in the meantime two groups had formed within the League: one, headed by Fuād Nāsir and Emil Habībi (the extreme nationalists of former years), now defended the Soviet position, while the second group, led by Emil Tūma and Mūsa Dajāni, opposed partition.

When fighting broke out late in November, 1947, both groups acted according to their previous stand. Emil Tūma joined the Haifa National Committee which organized the anti-Jewish struggle, and later escaped to Lebanon. (He returned to Israel in the winter of 1948–49.) Other League leaders, such as Fuād Nāsir, continued to be active in the parts of Palestine occupied by the Arab armies. Many of them were arrested by the Egyptian authorities and sent to Abu Ageila concentration camp in the Sinai desert, from which they were released only after the offensive of the Israeli army in the winter of 1948–49. It is they, in collaboration with a group of militants from Haifa who returned meanwhile from the Lebanon (including Emil Habībi, Tawfīq Tūbi, and others), who rebuilt the Arab Communist Party in Israel. Even previously, in August, 1948, there had been tentative talks between the head of the Jewish Communists (now assuming the role of senior partner) and the remaining Arab militants, with a view to restoring party unity. These talks were successfully concluded in the autumn of 1948.

It is not difficult to find, in retrospect, the source of Arab Communist successes between 1943–48, which were far in excess of the achievements of their Jewish comrades. (Nor did matters change much after 1948.) The Arab Communists appeared as a nationalist party among the Arabs, part of the main stream of the national movement, and not in opposition to the national aspirations of their people, as did the Jewish Communists. They were the only real Arab party in the modern sense, the others being mere pressure groups of the leading families. All the other groups were conservative, at a time when hardly anything worth-while remained to be preserved, except the privileges of the Husainis, Nashashībis, and Dajānis. Among the Jews there were other political parties, left-wing, right-wing, and centre, and the national institutions were democratically elected. The League, on the other hand, with its vaguely "social" and democratic programme, was the only force among the Palestinian Arabs to voice even these modest demands. Therefore it is not surprising that a majority of those among the younger generation of Arab intellectuals who were politically conscious should have come to regard the League as the most progressive and democratic group of all.

For more detailed consideration of the splits in the Communist Party, the reader is referred to Appendix II.

4. AFTER WORLD WAR II

When the war ended in 1945 the Communists had tried for some time, and not without success, to become a "respectable party" like all the others in Palestine. Their new leaders were indeed quite different from the wild revolutionaries of the 1920's. New bureaucratic types had replaced the professional revolutionaries, the chief figures being Meir Vilner and Ester Vilenska among the Jews, and Emil Tūma, Tawfiq Tūbi, and Emil Habībi among the Arabs. The Jewish party was not Zionist and did not fight for a Jewish state—nor did a number of other groups and political parties. It was in favour of close collaboration with the Soviet Union and the "world of Socialism"—so was practically everybody else in 1945, apart from a few "incorrigible warmongers." Its Socialist programme was certainly no more radical than that of the Zionist left-wing parties. Since it exploited the Soviet Union's soaring prestige, the influence of the party was considerably strengthened. The party remained non-Zionist, but its former militant anti-Zionism had vanished. From time to time it had to express its opinion on national questions, but it took care to do so in a sufficiently vague and ambiguous way so as to be prepared for all eventualities. It demanded, for instance, that the country should be "democratized" and the British Mandate abolished, but it did not state exactly how this was to be brought about. The "Fascist terror" of the I.Z.L. and the Stern Gang were strongly condemned. As for the future of the Jewish community, well, "the establishment of a democratic and independent republic would guarantee full rights to a Jewish minority."[38] Meanwhile it was the task of the party cadres to explain to the masses the anti-Jewish and anti-popular nature of the adventurist plans of the Zionist leaders for a Jewish state.[39] This was in 1944. Two years later the party line was again somewhat modified; now it was argued that "the state which is to be established will not be exclusively Arab or Jewish, but an independent, democratic Arab-Jewish state."[40] The Jewish party suggested an arrangement according to which one-third of the key positions in a Palestinian popular democracy should go to the Jews and two-thirds to the Arabs, but the League refused to accept this proposal in spite of the fact that it had received the backing of British Communist leaders. The change in the party stand came only as a result of the completely unexpected Gromyko speech at the U.N. Special General Assembly on Palestine in the summer of 1947, when the Soviet representative declared that a bi-national state would indeed be preferable, but if this was impossible, then the establishment of two separate states would be the best solution. This, of course, came as a terrible shock to the Jewish Communists, for whom the very idea of a Jewish state had been anathema for more than twenty-five years, and it was catastrophic from the point of view of the Arab Communists. The first reaction of the Jewish Communists was to argue that Gromyko had been misunderstood or wilfully misinterpreted. But after a few weeks of party executive sessions the line was adjusted. It had been realized, meanwhile, by the party leaders that the shock they had received would, in the long run, be a salutary one. The anti-state record of the party would gradually be forgotten, and, on the other hand, much more favourable working conditions for the party would exist in future. Nevertheless, it was decided to favour the bi-national solution, and as late as October 13, 1947, the party organ sharply attacked the United States for its support of the "adventurist" partition project.[41] But, as it happened, the Soviet delegate in the U.N. (Zarapkin) came out on that very evening in favour of partition, too, and the party had to adjust its line once again. The first reaction was as usual, that Zarapkin had been misunderstood and that he regarded partition only as a temporary solution, not desirable in itself[42]; on second thoughts (after more party executive sessions), the party came to swallow this pill, too. Now, its programme on the national question was for the first time almost identical with that of the Zionist movement. The party called its militants and members to take part in the defensive war of 1948–49; it approved the occupation of the Negev, and complained only about the Prime Minister having given orders to discontinue the offensive in the direction of Suez (when Britain intervened in January, 1949). But the patriotic honeymoon did not last very long. It came to an abrupt end following the Jerusalem interlude, which, though in itself not of very great importance, reminded the citizens of Israel that the Communists were not, after all, a party like all others. On September 17, 1949, the party executive had published an appeal to the people and the government "to include Jerusalem immediately in the state of Israel because American imperialist intrigues wish to internationalize the city. In order to thwart this intrigue [to separate Jerusalem from the state] a counter-offensive should be launched immediately."[43] Following this appeal, mass demonstrations and meetings were organized, but the whole project was brought to a sudden end when the Soviet delegate in the U.N. declared that he, too, like the Americans and the Catholic powers, was in favour of internationalization. The Israeli Communist Party (M.A.K.I. as from October, 1948) had to switch its stand and explain its "opportunist errors" committed only a few weeks before. "We have mistakenly tried to find a solution to one part of the Palestine question, and forgot that this would be in contradiction to the supreme interest of the anti-imperialist struggle."[44] Party propaganda was now to stress the vital necessity of internationalizing Jerusalem, articles were written, meetings arranged, and the new drive was in full swing, when the Soviet representative in the U.N. declared (in late spring, 1950) that his government had reconsidered its stand on Jerusalem and did not now think that internationalization was practicable. Once again the Communists had to adjust the party line, but this time there were no lengthy explanations.

In spite of these somersaults, which, from the point of view of the party leadership, were not amusing at all, and despite the gradual deterioration of Israeli-Soviet relations (following the stepping-up of the "anti-cosmopolitan" campaign), the party received, in 1951, 25,000 votes and five seats in the Knesset (about 4 per cent. of the total) in comparison to 15,000 votes and four seats in the first Knesset elections in January, 1949. This apparent paradox can, nevertheless, be explained with comparative ease. Several hundred thousand new immigrants came to Palestine in 1949–51, and of those not a few had been Communists or sympathizers in their countries of origin. Iraqi and Bulgarian sections came into being in Jaffa, Ramla, and the other concentrations of new immigrants. These immigrants (and they were in 1951 already a majority of the inhabitants of the country) were not very much interested in the past record of the Communist Party; they cared much more for such immediate issues as housing, food, and working conditions.[45] Inevitably, a certain percentage of the new-comers were disappointed with what they found (just as in 1925 and 1936–37), and their grievances were exploited by MAKI (the present party name, formed from the initial letters of its full name).

There were two other objective reasons which made Israel, in the years after 1949, fertile ground for Communism despite what was going on in the Soviet world. First, the increase of Communist influence among the Arabs must be mentioned. At the time of the 1949 elections, Communists polled 50 per cent. in Nazareth, and, generally speaking, half of the votes of the Communist party came from Arab-populated areas.[46] Apart from the general reasons which made it comparatively easy for the Communist parties to gain followers in the Arab world, there were several motives specific to Israeli Arabs. In 1948–49 the Arab Communists (who were then believed to belong to a non-hostile or at least democratic party) were given key positions by the Israeli authorities in the Arab-populated areas (e.g. as heads of labour exchanges). At a later time, when the line of the party had become openly anti-Israeli, it was still the only anti-Zionist group permitted to exist, and thus succeeded in uniting all discontented elements on the basis of a national Arab, anti-Jewish platform. The existence of a single Arab nationalist party would have put an end to this Communist monopoly, but among the mistakes of Israeli Arab policy was that of giving the Communists a long start and preventing the organization of effective competition.

MAKI had also made considerable inroads into MAPAM (the Socialist Workers' Party), which was much larger than the Communist Party and which, for a number of years, had been steadily moving towards Stalinism. It appeared in 1952 that the Communists stood a fair chance of taking over the party, or at least a majority of it, but then, as frequently before, unforeseen events on the international scene intervened. Dr. Moshe Sneh[47] and several other prominent MAPAM leaders (such as Y. Riftin) had reached the conclusion that there was no hope that Moscow would ever accept the MAPAM brand of Communism (i.e. that Russia was right everywhere in the world but in Israel), and that the time had come to throw Zionism overboard. Their influence in the party had steadily grown, and, in fact, they dominated the party by having a majority in the larger of the two factions of which MAPAM then consisted. But in November, 1952, news about the Prague trial and the undisguised anti-Jewish drive was more than MAPAM could stomach, especially in view of the fact that one of its own leaders, M. Oren,[48] was included in the "amalgam" produced by the prosecutor as an Anglo-American spy and subsequently given a lengthy prison sentence. Several weeks later came news of the arrest of the group of Moscow physicians, most of whom were Jews, and Dr. Sneh and his group were put on the spot. The non-Stalinist faction demanded that the party should openly dissociate itself from the anti-Semitic line, while Sneh countered with a demand for complete identification with

Prague and Moscow. This, of course, was the worst possible moment to do so, and when Dr. Sneh was expelled from MAPAM in January, 1953, he carried with him only a small minority (a few hundred), who later established the Left Socialist Party, a small splinter group, identical in everything but name with the Communists. MAKI decided, however, that the Sneh group should not join the Communists, but continue to exist as a separate group with an eye to its attracting members and thus helping to bring about the disintegration of MAPAM. However, although the international situation was considerably eased after Stalin's death and the rabid anti-Semitic propaganda was discontinued, the Sneh split had caused so much bad blood and mutual recrimination that he had, in fact, become the least likely candidate for attracting MAPAM to the Communist camp. Eventually, the Sneh faction came to join MAKI (in November, 1954).

MAKI, on the other hand, passed the tribulations of 1952–53 unscathed, on the whole. The party had justified both the Prague trial and the Moscow accusations, and though it lost most of its periphery during these difficult months, there were no substantial defections among the cadres. Of the "fellow-travellers" many returned to the party after Stalin's death, being convinced that the "unfortunate episode" was now over.

MAKI, on the whole, is an ordinary Communist Party like many another, but it is far more difficult to find a parallel for MAPAM (the United Workers' Party). It could be likened to Nenni's Socialists in Italy, but this would be somewhat misleading, because Nenni has no Zionist issue to face, nor are there *kibbutzim* (collective agricultural settlements) in Italy, and MAPAM is predominantly a *kibbutz* party. Up to World War II, MAPAM, or rather Hashomer Hatzair (The Young Guard), its main component,[49] was a Marxist radical left-wing party, in sharp opposition to the Comintern on the Zionist issue and critical of the Moscow trials, the pact with Hitler, and the Finnish war. It had established contacts with the Independent Labour Party in Britain, with left Socialists in France and elsewhere, but not with the Comintern. Since then, however, a radical change affecting most of its leaders has taken place, due to a multiplicity of factors that are hard to define in relation to each other. The importance of the Soviet Union's change to a favourable attitude towards the Jews in Palestine in 1947–48 should not be minimized, though it was largely cancelled by such subsequent events as the Slanski trial and the "anti-cosmopolitan" trend in general. A search for the sources of this development would probably lead us back to the 1920's, when the present-day leaders of MAPAM were students in Poland and Rumania, and adopted Marx, Engels, and Lenin as their highest authorities in philosophy, politics, and history. Non-Marxist or more recent Western thought has hardly ever reached them, and few have had the time, the quiet, and the inner impulse to sit down and re-examine their basic assumptions and attitudes. For them the Soviet Union has not basically changed since the middle 1920's, and the Russian Revolution, as far as they are concerned, is still in its early romantic and heroic period, engaged in the building of a new society, proclaiming internationalism, equality, and cultural freedom to the world.

Clinging to Leninism, they concluded after World War II that their anti-Stalinism had been a symptom of their infantile form of leftism. What counted for them now—after the impact of Fascism, followed by the Russian victory—was that the means of production in Russia and the "People's Democracies" had been socialized; as Marxists they felt that this was the decisive criterion. Besides, the Soviet Union owed its high prestige not only, and perhaps not chiefly, to its ideas, but to Russia's military victories and to the successes of Communism since the war. MAPAM would like no longer to struggle for lofty but abstract ideals in the wilderness, slandered and attacked all the while by the Communists as traitors to the cause. It would prefer to be a small spoke in a big and powerful wheel. It is an opportunism which does not aim at immediate political or material advantage; though the anti-Israeli stand taken by Moscow in 1955-6 has badly shaken them, they continue to believe that the Soviet Union is real (in the Hegelian sense, i.e. a powerful political force), and that it will become even more real in the future.

MAPAM continues, however, to collaborate with the Zionist parties, and it joined the government coalition after the July, 1955, elections. A severance of relations with the Zionist movement would hurt the material interests of the *kibbutzim*, which are now the main source of strength for the party. In the ideological sphere the party stands for the territorial concentration of the Jewish people, and criticizes the "cosmopolitan attitude" of MAKI, which opposes Zionism and denies the existence of a Jewish people. MAPAM has argued for many years now that it, and not MAKI, should be regarded as the Communist Party of Israel, but the relevant authorities have apparently not been impressed by these arguments.

Generally speaking, it can be said that MAPAM appeals to the more literate sections of the population in Israel, while MAKI caters for less-sophisticated Marxist tastes. MAKI has no intellectual "fellow-travellers," while MAPAM, through various front organizations, notably the Centre for Progressive Culture, the Workers' Library (one of the largest publishing houses), and its daily newspaper *Al Hamishmar*, and several literary periodicals, reaches a comparatively large section of the intelligentsia, especially of the younger generation. MAPAM support among urban workers has decreased as a result of the many splits which beset the party in 1952–54, and is not much larger now than that of the Communists. The party is extremely weak among the Arab population of Israel, despite its many efforts to gain an Arab following, but about half of the members of the agricultural collective settlements (*kibbutzim*) belong to it.

MAKI has about 4000–5000 members at the time of writing, among them at least 2700 Jews and 1300 Arabs. There are no exact figures about the social composition of the party, but several facts have emerged in recent years. One is that the party is relatively stronger among Arabs than among Jews; the other, that it has more members among new immigrants than among that part of the population which was born in Israel or had come to Israel prior to World War II. The third fact is that there are comparatively few workers among the members and that the lower middle-class element prevails.[50]

The Central Council of the party numbers fifteen, eleven Jews and four Arabs, a proportion which is maintained in all the leading organs of the party. A secretariat of five, headed by Shmuel Mikunis, is responsible for the management of day-to-day affairs, and there are sub-committees for trade unions and army work, for women and youth, and for various other activities. The party publishes a daily newspaper in Hebrew (*Kol Ha'am*), the circulation of which is about equal to the number of Jewish party members, and an Arab weekly, *Al Ittihād*, as well as a theoretical magazine, *Baderekh* (On the Way). The Hebrew daily is, political considerations apart, on a low level, and cannot hope to compete with the rest of the Hebrew press; it has to rely on the enthusiasm of its readers rather than on any intrinsic interest. The influence of *Al Ittihād* is much larger and its cultural level higher. *Baderekh*, the theoretical organ, is issued by very cautious editors; most of the contributions consist of translations. There was a change for the better in 1954. The party maintains a large number of front organizations, some of them more or less openly Communist, others outwardly bona-fide organizations to which non-Communists belong, persons who do not recognize, or do not want to recognize, or do not mind the Communist background. To the openly Communist organizations belong the Democratic Women's Organization, the Association for the Promotion of Trade (with the U.S.S.R.), the Committee for the Defence of Children, etc. To the second group belong the League for the Defence of the Arab Minority, the League for the Defence of Human Rights, and such *ad hoc* and rather specialized affairs as the Committee for the Return of the Histadrut to the W.F.T.U. and the Committee for the Defence of the Interests of the Shoemakers. Considerable efforts have also been made to establish a progressive Rabbi's organization, without much success until now.

Apart from the fronts which have been exclusively sponsored by MAKI, there are front organizations common to MAKI and MAPAM, which, however, in a majority of cases have caused much friction. These include the friendship leagues with the Soviet Union, Rumania,

Poland, Czechoslovakia, Hungary, and Bulgaria. Most of them have broken up, and each party has established friendship leagues of its own. The only front which has not been affected by the disputes since 1950 is the Israeli "peace movement." But even there a crisis was reported in the winter of 1955 on the background of Soviet Middle Eastern policy.

5. CONCLUSION

The Israeli Communist Party has been moderately successful in recent years in certain respects. MAKI has become an important party among the Arabs of Israel. On the other hand, it has remained relatively uninfluential and unpopular among the Jews; it has not been able to live down its past, though it has gained in experience and learned from its past tactical mistakes. Such neutralist and even pro-Soviet sentiment that exists has found expression in various front organizations, but there has been little readiness to support the party the moment it has appeared with some slogan more outspoken than the struggle for peace in its most general form. The experience of several years shows that such fronts may have contributed towards the spread of a neutralist climate, but the party as such has not greatly benefited from it

PART FOUR

JORDAN

Chapter Nine

Feudalism and Communism

I. THE EMIRATE OF TRANSJORDAN

FOR many years Jordan had been thought to be a quiet country. Here at least, it was believed, there was stability and effective government in that Middle Eastern maelstrom of *coups d'état*, student demonstrations, and confusion worse confounded. Jordan, most outside observers assumed, was the country least affected by Western influence (excepting, perhaps, the nomads of the Arab peninsula), interest in politics was low, left-wing and reformist trends practically unknown. Here at least horsemanship and chivalry and piety and the other traditional Arab virtues were the criteria by which a man was judged; new-fangled ideas could not possibly make much headway under such conditions. Some closer observers of the Jordan scene, including the British Major-General John B. Glubb, late commander of the British-financed Arab Legion (hardly to be charged with ill-will towards Jordan), did indeed take issue with this superficial view and had drawn attention to quite different and more sinister developments which had taken place in recent years. But their voices went unheard, and the events of October, 1954 (and even more, the events of December, 1955—March, 1956), came as a shock to most Western statesmen. There had been a major revolt in that quiet country, headed by Communists and their allies. It spread throughout the country, was suppressed by the army with considerable difficulty and resulted in many casualties. All of a sudden it had become clear how precarious the position of the government was; that many sections of the population, including the most vocal and influential ones, had been estranged; and that new forces had emerged which were willing and able to head this opposition movement. Among these opposition forces the Communists and their "fellow-travellers" from the National Front took a leading part in many places.

123

How had the Jordanian party succeeded in the course of a very few years in attaining such a position of strength?

The Emirate of Transjordan came into being in 1921. Emir 'Abdullah was made a king in 1946, and his country, after the merger with parts of Palestine, became the "Hashemite Kingdom of the Jordan." Transjordan proper was one of the smallest and economically least-developed countries of the Middle East. The number of persons employed in industry did not exceed a few hundred. The regime was authoritarian up to King 'Abdullah's murder in 1951; in contrast to Iraq and Egypt, most of the land in this predominantly agricultural country was not concentrated in the hands of a few dozen owners. The merger of Transjordan, which had a population of about 450,000, with Arab Palestine (700,000–800,000 inhabitants, about half of them refugees) created countless problems. The country had been given a constitution in 1947, but the rights of members of parliament were fairly restricted and there could be no doubt about the fact that effective rule had remained in the hands of King 'Abdullah. His son, Prince Talāl, and Talāl's son, Husain, took a more liberal line, but real power remained in the hands of a comparatively small group of officials in Amman, and in those of the Arab Legion command. Obstinate parliaments have been dissolved, and political parties critical of the regime have been banned. Palestinian Arabs have, as a rule, been given only half the seats in parliament and the cabinet, despite their numerical superiority. They complain bitterly about discrimination against them in many walks of life by the Jordan officials who continued to hold most key positions in government, army, and police. The Cisjordan Arabs have, as a rule, a broader non-religious education and are incomparably more critical of the tradition preserved and taken for granted on the other side of the river. This pertains not only to religion but to their attitude to life in general; whereas Jordanians, except for a small minority, are Arabs of the nineteenth century—i.e. religious and strictly adhering to the code of honour of bygone days—they are probably closest to the romantic image of the T. E. Lawrence–Freya Stark school. The Cisjordanian urban Arab belongs to the twentieth century; he is strongly nationalist, but is frequently no longer a pious Moslem.

2. THE LEAGUE FOR NATIONAL LIBERATION

The story of the Jordanian opposition begins with Dr. Subhi Abu Ghanima, a member of the Istiqlāl party in Palestine (which was courted at that time by the Communists), who founded in Amman in the early 1930's *Ittihādu'l 'Ummāl al Urduniyyīn* (Union of Jordan Workers). This union, which existed for several months, had fewer than

2000 members, and was the first, and for several years to come, the last of its kind. A new attempt to revive trade unionism and workers' organization in general, was made by Qāsim Milhim in 1936, but he and some of his pro-Communist friends were refused entrance permits by the Amman government. They continued to be active, however, from Syria, where Dr. Ghanima had found refuge, and there were reports about sporadic arrests of members of the Jordan Arab party (sponsored by him) and the Free Jordan Youth, another opposition group. The Communist press in the neighbouring countries published occasional leaflets in 1945–46 which were issued by groups with various fancy names but were of obviously Communist inspiration, such as, for instance, the appeal of the Conscious Young Transjordanians on the occasion of the Anglo-Jordan Treaty in March, 1946—"We would not have been silent . . . were it not for the cruel conditions and the military courts. Freedom of speech, of press, of assembly, all these are absent in our country. Four governments exist in our country—the rule of imperialism, of the king, of the government, and of the ruling class." The appeal goes on to demand the abolition of the Anglo-Jordanian Treaty and the instituting of free elections for a parliament.[1] These demands were certainly not very extreme and revolutionary, but the powers that were in Amman steadfastly refused to carry out any changes in the political regime, and the Communist newspapers abroad, on the other hand, were among the only ones to serve as a platform for the dissatisfied elements in Jordan. But up to the merger in 1949 the number of active opponents of the regime was very small and the number of Communists among them even smaller. From the Communist point of view, Jordan was simply too small and unimportant; the peasants did not revolt, industrial workers were few and far between, and there was no intelligentsia willing to spearhead the movement. The British, moreover, though in effective control, were not much in evidence, and there was less xenophobia and anti-Westernism than in most other Middle Eastern countries.

The change came with the merger, when several leading Palestine Arab Communists were delegated to work in Jordan; they were headed by Fuād Nāsir and Rushdi Shahīn.[2] Many outside observers had expected that since favourable conditions had been created for the growth of party influence in the refugee camps, its activities would now be concentrated in the camps—just as the Greek Communist party developed in the late 1920's mainly in the refugee camps of the repatriates from Turkey. "The most threatening hotbed of Communism [in the Middle East] is found among the Palestine refugees who were torn away from their houses and lands," writes Najla 'Izz-ad-Dīn in her book[3]; this opinion, typical of the prevailing ignorance of the character and methods of Communism in the Middle East, was shared by the majority of experts, both Arab and Western.

In fact, the exact opposite happened. Nāsir, Shahīn, and the others had learned well the lessons of the Palestine League for National Liberation; viz. that organizing the masses was something to be done through special channels such as trade unions, but that the first and most important task was to find and educate reliable cadres. And the cadres would be found, according to past experience, mainly among the intelligentsia. Teachers, physicians, and lawyers were approached and cells were established in the upper forms of secondary schools, and these became the backbone of the party. As in all the other Middle Eastern countries, the main stress was not on a revolutionary mass struggle; the approach was entirely different. In party propaganda the feudal regime was attacked and democratic reforms were demanded. Why was power in the hands of a few feudals in Amman and not in the hands of those who by education and calling were predestined to lead the people? (If the Communists appealed to *class* interests at all, it was the class interest of the intelligentsia and not of the proletariat!) In foreign policy the country's dependence on Britain was denounced and the dissolution of the Arab Legion, the pillar of "feudal rule," was demanded. But the main appeal was based on the realization of the necessity (shared by all) for developing the country as rapidly as possible, to industrialize it. And what more shining example could possibly be found than that of the Soviet Union? What could the West offer apart from phrases about the desirability of democratic values and the wickedness of totalitarian regimes? But what did this mean in practice to a country which had never known democracy and whose main problem was to overcome the national backwardness?

The central organ of the League for National Liberation (as it continued to be called), *Al Muqāwama ash Sha'biyya* (People's Revolt), was first published in the summer of 1949, and one of its first tasks was apparently to clarify the position of the party in Jordan and Israeli affairs. In one respect the attitude of the League has not been changed; like the Israeli and all other Middle Eastern Communist Parties, it regards the U.N. decision of November 29, 1947 (i.e. the establishment of both a Jewish and an independent Arab state in Palestine), as the basis of its programme. But the vacillations in Soviet policy (for which the Palestine issue was, after all, a rather unimportant one) occasionally caused the League serious difficulties. At one time, in 1949, the Soviet Union supported the internationalization of Jerusalem according to the original U.N. decision. Accordingly, the League published articles demonstrating that "the U.N. resolution for the internationalization of Jerusalem was a victory of our cause."[4] A few weeks later the Soviet Union announced that it had reconsidered its stand and reached the conclusion that internationalization was now impractical; then the League had to explain that the U.N. decision on Jerusalem had, after all, not been a victory but a defeat for the cause. The party press sharply and consistently attacked Zionism, but it usually did not display a very friendly attitude to the Mufti either. The main attacks were directed against the "Anglo-Hashemite rulers."

The year 1949 was devoted to preparing cadres, mainly in the old strongholds of the League under the British Mandate—the Old City of Jerusalem, Bethlehem, and Nablus, where members of the leading families, such as the Bandaks in Bethlehem and the Tukkāns in Nablus, supported them. They tried to infiltrate the Arab Palestine Workers' Association in Jerusalem,[5] but without much success; the number of adherents was small and Communist infiltration therefore all too obvious, and when the Association was dissolved by order of the government the Communists did not make a serious effort to re-establish it on an illegal basis. It is interesting to note that though Communist activity was restricted in 1949, one of the few people to note its potential wide appeal was Major-General Glubb.[6]

Early in 1950 the party leaders believed themselves strong enough to appear in public and to try to reach a wider circle with their propaganda. When the National Guard was established at that time (i.e. home guards in the border region), the League opened a propaganda campaign against it, and also launched protest demonstrations against the Western proposals for a Middle Eastern command. But the main event of 1950, so far as the League was concerned, was the election of April 11, 1950.

The party, which had been weakened just then by a number of arrests,[7] called upon the population of Palestine to boycott the election. "The people remain indifferent to the electoral comedy of King 'Abdullah. The vast majority boycott the elections because they oppose the annexation of their country by the British colony called 'Transjordan.' The appeal for the boycott launched by the 'League' has been given wide attention. . . . Palestine Arabs fight for the independent Arab state as provided in the U.N. decision of November, 1947."[8] Whether the Communist boycott slogan was effective is a debatable issue; the followers of the Mufti and other groups had issued similar instructions. But this propaganda, as well as the Nablus incidents on the eve of the elections, served at least to put the Communists on the political map. In a Communist-inspired meeting in Nablus, anti-Jordan speeches had been made, and it had ended with a demonstration in front of the local District Commissioner's building, which was dispersed by Arab Legion forces. About thirty people were arrested and marched off on foot to a concentration camp. One of those arrested, a member of the Sa'īd Qilāni family, died on the way from exhaustion. This incident caused much resentment, and the Communists gained much sympathy in the country.[9] It was exploited by party propaganda in denouncing the "'Abdullah–Ben Gurion–Bevin plot against the establishment of an independent Arab state."[10] When the then Jordan

Prime Minister, Sa'īd al Mufti, brought the draft bill of an anti-Communist law to the Jordan parliament, he had considerable difficulty in overcoming the opposition of several deputies from Cisjordan. Notwithstanding sporadic arrests,[11] the party continued its activities, especially in the Palestinian cities where the population was not over-friendly towards the Jordanian police officers, and hardly ever collaborated with state officials in revealing the whereabouts of leading Communists. The League collected 4000 signatures for the Stockholm "peace" appeal in the winter of 1950–51, and more in 1951; it organized minor demonstrations against UNRWA (the U.N. relief association aiding the refugees) and, for the first time, a May Day demonstration (1951) both in the Palestinian cities and in Amman.

3. THE GROWTH OF COMMUNISM AFTER 1950

New elections were held in Jordan after the murder of King 'Abdullah in August, 1951. Only three months before, leaflets issued by the League had announced that the Communists would again boycott the "pseudo-elections,"[12] but a few weeks later the Central Committee announced, referring to many quotations from Lenin and Stalin, that the previous course had been mistaken and correct tactics now required it to take part in the elections. There appear to have been differences of opinion on that issue among the party leaders, and the decision was made after referring the whole issue to the Cominform authorities. The party appeared in the election campaign on a popular-front platform, with the usual "democratic" progressive and "anti-imperialist" demands which practically everybody could accept. The main difficulty was therefore to point out the differences between the "Popular Bloc" (this was to be the name of the party in the elections) and other parties which appeared with similar names and programmes, particularly the left-of-centre Ba'ath (Renaissance) Party, which, consisting mainly of Jerusalem and Ramalla intellectuals, had been for some time both ally and competitor of the League. The League charged the Ba'ath with lack of consistency (some of its members had agreed to be ministers in the Amman government), and relations between the two parties deteriorated. The performance of the League in the elections was not bad, though probably below the expectations of the party leaders. The two candidates in Nablus, Rushdi Shahīn and Dr. 'Abdul Majīd Abu Hajla, polled more than 5000 votes each, or about 25 per cent. of the total in that area. (It should be added, however, that each elector could give his vote to several candidates at the same time.) The party candidate in Amman, Mahmūd Mutlaq, received more than 2000 votes out of a total of 14,000 in the capital.[13]

The party platform for the elections was not without interest. The struggle for peace and the fight against "all intrigues to involve our country in a war" was given first place, with the demand for the abolition of the Jordan-British treaty a close second. Next followed a demand for freedom of speech, demonstrations, and strikes; and proposals for the legalizing of political parties and trade unions. The Palestine problem was to be solved according to the November, 1947, U.N. resolution, and the United Nations' Observers were to be removed from the country. Government lands and the property of the feudalists should be distributed among the fellaheen. Existing industries should be given protection and new ones established to provide work for the unemployed. The level of teaching in the schools should be raised, and education should be provided free of charge.

This programme was of particular interest because two months earlier (in June, 1951) the League of National Liberation had published a first platform for the elections, which was now superseded and watered down by the popular-front demands. The original platform had been far more radical, as it had counterposed American imperialism and the Soviet Union (the "bulwark of freedom") and had urged a republican regime. Women were to be given freedom in all fields and "released from the chains of reaction," there should be a "struggle for restoring a democratic peace with Israel." Education should be freed of its present radical-nationalist-imperialist taint. All factories owned by foreign imperialists must be nationalized, a popular army must be established, and the Bedouins settled on arable land.

At about the same time the League had decided to discontinue its policy of boycotting the Jordan parliament, the executive was convened (in June, 1951) and decided to change the name of the League to "Jordan Communist Party."[14] This, of course, was not a mere change of name, it signified also a change in tactics. The party had put up with the fact that an "independent Arab state" in Palestine was not to emerge in the foreseeable future, and it adjusted itself to realities; from now on and until further notice Jordan as a whole was to be its field of activity. At the same time a purge of "Titoist" elements as well as of "Government spies," who had allegedly infiltrated the party, was to be carried out. The party was by now standing on its own feet. If in 1949–50 it had yet needed the advice and material help of the comrades in Israel, Syria, and Lebanon, it had by now both the cadres (700 party members by the end of 1951) and a fairly wide fringe of "fellow-travellers" and supporters willing to give both their names and their money to help the party. The manner in which the 1951 "peace campaign" was carried out testified to the ability of the Jordan Communists to attract public figures who were not at all suspect of Communist inclinations. Four thousand signatures had been collected during the winter of 1950–51 and about 15,000 more during 1951. The "peace movement" published a stencilled bulletin on behalf of the Partisans of Peace, and later (in November,

1951) a printed bi-weekly, *Al Fajr al jadīd* (The New Dawn).[15] Among the public figures who signed and expressed support were four members of parliament; the former senator, Sulaiman Haj Farūki; the former minister, Sulaimān an-Nabūlsi; members of the municipal councils of Jerusalem, Hebron, Bethlehem, and Jericho; the writer Kāmil Nāsir (from Bi'r az-Zait); 'Abdullah Bandak of Bethlehem[16]; and the heads of the workers' organizations in Jerusalem, Nablus, and Ramalla, such as Mahmud Hammād and 'Abdur-Rahīm Irshid.

A temporary executive of twenty-four members was established, and among them, for the first time in Jordan politics, were four women. The "peace movement" came to serve as the semi-legal framework of the party for its sympathizers (not unlike the League for National Liberation, which had been a looser organization than a Communist party), since it was open to all who were interested. The "peace movement" came in fact to deal in its propaganda with many problems which had no direct bearing on world peace, and it carefully refrained from commenting on the one concrete war-and-peace issue in Jordan—namely, peace with Israel. Some of the "peace movement" leaders were arrested in March, 1952, among them Hasan an-Nabūlsi, the editor of the organ of the group. Most of them, however, were released after several months and represented their group in various international meetings of the world peace movement, as, for example, Dr. Ya'qūb Zayā Dīn (a physician at the Augusta Victoria Hospital in Jerusalem), who took part at the Vienna Congress of the Peoples in 1952, and was elected a member of the executive of that organization. He was arrested soon after his return; as were Musallim Bassīsu (owner of the pro-Communist weekly *Al Hawādith*), Dr. Nabīh Nashidāt, Mahmūd Mutlaq, and Fā'iz ar-Rusān, after their return from the Bucharest Conference of the "peace movement."[17] In the meantime the activities of the party had been temporarily interrupted as a result of the arrest of Fuād Nāsir, the secretary-general, together with several other leading party workers,[18] by Jordan police in Amman at the printing press of the party.

Once identified, Fuād Nāsir did not deny any of the charges against him, and attempted by sharp attacks against the political regime in Jordan to turn the court into a propaganda show trial. However, this attempt was cut short by the decision to hold the sessions behind closed doors. Fuād Nāsir was given a ten-year sentence, the other defendants received six years each. It was stated in the verdict that the behaviour of the accused in court had been considered an "aggravating factor."[19] But by this time the party apparatus was working very well, and the shock of the arrest of some of the leaders was overcome after a short period. It was perhaps a fitting comment on the efficient work done by Fuād Nāsir that on the very day the verdict against him was announced (two months after his arrest), the Jordan police revealed that Communist cells in the Amman high schools (including the girls' college!) had been uncovered.[20]

The years 1952 and 1953 showed a further growth of the party, mainly among the intelligentsia, but serious attempts were now made to reach the masses as well. According to figures from Communist sources which cannot be verified, 20,000 leaflets were printed and distributed on the eve of May Day, 1953, and 30,000 on the occasion of the visit of John Foster Dulles to Old Jerusalem.[21] Dr. Zayā Dīn was released from prison following a decision of the Jordan High Court, and, following much pressure in parliament and the press, a number of other Communist internees in the concentration camps were released, too. Police attempts to combat Communism were, on the whole, inefficient. Party militants were arrested and released at frequent intervals, but the sympathy gained by these arrests was worth more than the damage done to the party. The practice of government policy was indeed one of adopting laws against Communism which did not prevent its spread at all, such as the law to combat Communism, adopted in December, 1953,[22] according to which every member of a Communist organization would be arrested for an indefinite period, and those contributing money or distributing literature would be given prison sentences ranging from one to three years.[23]

Ironically enough, Communist influence in Jordan never made so much progress as it did in the months immediately following the adoption of the law. New Communist legal magazines appeared (such as *Al Jabha, Ar-Ra'i*), and the first successful attempt to establish a popular front (Al Jabha) was made. Before dealing with this new Communist venture, some further remarks about the reasons for the Communist success seem to be called for.

Communist reports about bloody repression and persecutions under King 'Abdullah had, of course, been greatly exaggerated. His was, for a feudal regime, a benevolent and paternal rule. His successors gradually introduced liberal reforms. But the intelligentsia, and especially the younger generation, continued to believe that nothing was really changing in Jordan, that foreigners continued to be the masters of their country (while their fellow-Moslems had ousted the strangers from Egypt, Persia, and other places), and that the ruling classes at home were not prepared to share power with the people (or rather with the intelligentsia, who appeared on behalf of the people). Under these circumstances, and in view of the absence of strong liberal and reform groups on the one hand and the impossibility of preserving the old order on the other, the Communists could indeed appear as the party of a general popular revolution and national liberation. They were, moreover, the only outspokenly republican party, and this at a time when the more developed Arab countries had opted for republican regimes. The discrimination against the leading Palestine Arab families, which brought many of their members into the camp of the popular front, has already been mentioned.[24] In addition, it should not be forgotten that the education given to the younger generation (which was supposed to make them faithful subjects of his Hashemite Majesty, if not really active citizens) was hopelessly irrelevant to the real issues which occupied them. Islam had ceased to be a living spiritual force as far as they were concerned, nor could they possibly think in terms of exclusive Jordanian nationalism. A void was thus created which would be filled by the most plausible creed and the one most easy to understand and to practise.

Al Jabha al Wataniyya, the Communist-led national front, first appeared in the open in the spring of 1954. Among the sponsor members were three members of the Jordan parliament, several well-known physicians and lawyers, and even a feudal landowner and the Jordan equivalent of Robin Hood, Fakhri Marraka, a highwayman from the Hebron region who had cherished anti-imperialist pretensions ever since he participated in the 1936–39 riots. (A full list of the sponsor members was published in *Al Jihād*, May 23, 1954.) But the Jordan authorities refused to recognize the new party or to grant it a permit, arguing that it had not pointed out in its platform that it wanted to achieve its aims by legal and peaceful means. Al Jabha published no fewer than four weeklies, which were widely acclaimed; they were closed by the Jordan authorities in May and June, 1954.

Jordan government restrictions prevented the Communists from openly contesting the elections of October, 1954, although several members of the Communist-sponsored national front (Jabha) appeared as candidates. One of them, 'Abdul Qādir Sālih, a member of a well-known Nablus family, was elected in his home town.[25] Another, Rashād Maswada, was returned for his native Hebron. Those who failed to be elected, such as Qadri Tukkān and Dr. 'Abdul Majīd Abu Hajla (who got 8000 votes), had missed election very narrowly; the successful candidates had polled 9000 votes. The restrictions affected the left-wing and liberal elements hardly less than the Communists (most of their magazines had been banned two months before the elections), and they induced the Ba'ath to make common cause with the Communists in the struggle against the government. Several candidates declared on election day that they would withdraw since a free election campaign had been impossible. This declaration was the signal for demonstrations in Amman by students (soon to be joined by others), who actually took over the centre of the city for several hours; they burned the U.S. Information Centre. The army had to intervene, and in the clashes that followed more than twelve people were reported killed and many dozens were wounded. Martial law was at once imposed, but the riots spread to Irbid, as-Salt, Nablus, Ramalla, and other towns of the kingdom. In these disorders, the most serious since the Hashemite Kingdom came into being, the Communists took a leading part. But they would not have succeeded in enlisting thousands of demonstrators if a short-sighted and reactionary government policy had not brought about, almost intentionally, the co-operation between Communist and non-Communist opposition groups.

This was the beginning of far greater trouble for the Jordan government, which has (like the Iraqi government) succeeded in a few years in antagonizing the whole intelligentsia. Numerically, to be sure, the intelligentsia is still weak; there are even fewer workers in Amman than in Baghdad, and the response of Palestine refugees has been below party expectations. King Husain, moreover, has the Arab Legion to suppress disorders. But if the present process of ferment goes on and broadens and develops, one may well doubt whether the Arab Legion will remain an instrument readily available for each such occasion. It is believed that the Jordan Communists have intensified their efforts to establish their cells in the army and to gain the support of non-commissioned officers and subalterns, inciting them against the British commanders of the Legion. The riots of December, 1955, and January, 1956, which eventually caused General Glubb's dismissal in March, 1956, tend to show that this tension has reached a fairly advanced stage. The Jordan Communists are now among the leaders of the Jordan opposition which has overthrown one Jordan government and dictated its policy to another. (March, 1956.)

There has been less greedy exploitation in Jordan than in the other Hashemite kingdom, that of Iraq, and less abject poverty. Despite the prevalence of absentee landlordism, the government has been less corrupt and more efficient and paternal, though still reactionary. But it has been lagging by about thirty years behind the political and social development of the country, and these have been thirty fairly eventful years in the history of Jordan. In 1921 Amman was a small village of 2000; today it has more than 160,000 inhabitants. But the means of governing the country are still in line with the exigencies of 1921—not with those of 1956.

PART FIVE

SYRIA
and
LEBANON

Chapter Ten

Syria under the French Mandate

I. GENERAL BACKGROUND

THE Communist Party of Syria and Lebanon is the strongest and best organized of all the Communist Parties in the Middle East. Though not the oldest, it has functioned for many years now as a sort of foster-parent to the other parties in the Arab world. It is the only party of which it can be said that its leading cadres have neither vanished nor been purged in the course of its existence. Most of the present-day leaders were already prominent as militant Communists fifteen or even twenty years ago—in contrast to the situation elsewhere in the Middle East, where a rapid top-level turnover is the rule.

The Communists in the Levant have had particular advantages and drawbacks. They have been hampered by the fact that in Lebanon no single party can hope to encompass all the heterogeneous and mutually antagonistic social forces in the country, as well as by the fact that in Syria there is not the enormous contrast between feudal luxury and splendour and the most abject poverty that can be found, for example, in Iraq. On the other hand, a tradition of permanent misrule, an inefficient and unstable administration, the almost complete frustration of the intelligentsia, the inability of the middle class to produce leaders and leadership, and the weakness of the other political parties (except for minor reformist groups)—all these have created a fertile field for intensive Communist cultivation, ideal conditions under which the Communists have gained spectacular successes in the past, with even greater promise for the future.

For many centuries Syria and Lebanon, the countries of the Levant, have been in closer contact with the West than any other part of the East. It is the most Westernized of Oriental countries, but also the one most beset by the general malaise of Arabic society: Levantinism. The

Levant is a region of the spirit no less than a region of the globe, says one contemporary historian of Syria[1]—"it is the spirit of a man who has been brought up simultaneously on the edges of more than one civilization and who in consequence is at home in none." But the Levant was also the place where the initiative for the Arab revival appeared first. The ties with the West have been manifold, as the geographical situation of the country on one of the world's most ancient trade routes, the emigration to the West (there are sizeable Syrian and Lebanese communities in North and South America), the existence of a strong Christian Arab element in Lebanon, and Western missionary activities and Western schools and universities have all contributed to this situation. Most of the leaders of the first groups of the Arab nationalist movement in Beirut and Damascus were alumni of these Western educational institutions; Lebanese and Syrian intellectuals, in their turn, have considerably influenced the intellectual life of other Arab countries, such as Palestine and Egypt, where for many years most of the press was in Lebanese hands.

2. THE FRENCH MANDATE

With the defeat of Turkey in World War I, it was decided by the Peace Conference (following previous secret agreements) that the system of Mandates of the League of Nations should be applied to Syria and Lebanon. The American King-Crane Commission recommended that Iraq and Syria should be treated as a unit and ruled by a constitutional monarch, but the Conference of San Remo gave the Mandate for Syria and Lebanon to France. Meanwhile, Syrian representatives had offered the country's throne to the Emir Faisal—to the extreme displeasure of the French. The French brought military forces to the country and sent an ultimatum to Faisal, who was compelled to leave Syria in the same year (1920).

The French Mandate was of the "A" class, according to which self-government was to be given gradually to the countries concerned. But constitutional progress was slow (in Syria even more than in Lebanon), and the French policy of strengthening the existing ethnic and religious subdivisions added fuel to the nationalist fires which had been burning from the very inception of Mandatory rule. The French did not succeed in winning the support of any important political group in Syria, and even in half-Christian Lebanon, which was much closer to France in many ways, the majority of the population was antagonized by Mandatory rule. One of the main charges against the Mandatory power was that of French corruption and maladministration. When, however, the historian considers the Syrian and Lebanese record since 1945, he will have to take such allegations with some reservation. The complaint about the lack of self-government is probably to the point, as is the general desire to get rid of the foreign protectors. A wave of unrest originating in Damascus and the Jebel Druze swept the whole country in 1925, and soon turned into a full-scale revolt threatening French rule throughout the Levant. The revolt was suppressed by the end of 1926, but the Mandatory authorities had been forced into realizing the need for making concessions; consequently a constitution came into force in Lebanon in 1926. In Syria the first elections for a constituent assembly were held in April, 1928, and they resulted in the victory of the "National Bloc" (the nationalists), who stood for complete independence. Since the French High Commissioner could not reach an agreement with the Nationalists, he dissolved the assembly in 1930 and promulgated a constitution on his own initiative. Elections in 1932 produced a majority of moderates, but a nationalist cabinet was, nevertheless, constituted, which tried, without success, to conclude a treaty with France on the pattern of the Anglo-Iraqi Treaty of 1930. After the nationalists' failure, the moderates returned to power, but their draft proposal for a treaty did not fare any better, and in November, 1934, the Chamber was dissolved and the country returned again to rule by presidential decree, and so it remained till the advent of the Popular-Front government to power in France, when a new chapter was opened in the relations between France and the countries of the Levant.

There were no political parties in Syria prior to 1920, only small secret societies. After the breakdown of Turkish rule, the pro-Faisal elements united under the ægis of Istiqlāl, the Independence Party. During the 1920's the leaders of the national movement were active mainly outside of Syria. The "Syrian-Palestine Committee" was founded in Geneva in August, 1921, and its chief political demands were full independence for Syria and Lebanon, as well as for Palestine, and the evacuation of French and British troops. Within Syria the first mass party was founded by Dr. Shahbandar in 1924; he was backed at that time by Fā'iz al Khūri, Lutfi al Haffār, and other influential politicians. This group (the People's Party) was active in the 1925 revolt, but the participation of the Druze in the anti-French campaign was at least as important, if not more so, and there was no direct connection between Druze anti-French resentment and the struggle of the Syrian national movement. The National Bloc (Al Kutla al Wataniyya) was founded in 1928, and it became subsequently (during the late 1930's and the 1940's) the chief factor in Syrian political life. It was the mainstay of the national movement and included many of the old Istiqlāl supporters as well as followers of Dr. Shahbandar (though not he, himself) and representatives of the leading families of Damascus, Aleppo, Homs, and the other cities.

In Lebanon the two main camps were the Unionist Party (headed by Emil Edé) and the Constitutionalists (led by Bishāra al Khūri). The political difference between them was not very great, but the former tended to be less anti-French and saw their chief aim as Lebanese rather than Syrian independence, because they feared Syrian and Moslem domination. During the early 1930's more political parties came into being, some of them on semi-fascist patterns, among which were the Syrian National Party (led by Antūn Sa'ada) or the "Nationalist Action Party," a group consisting mainly of Syrian intellectuals, as well as the various para-military youth organizations and the Phalange in Lebanon.

About 60 per cent. of the inhabitants of Syria are Sunni Moslems; the 'Alāwi, Druze, Greek Orthodox, and Armenian minorities, though occasionally of some importance during elections, have not, on the whole, constituted serious political problems in recent Syrian history. The situation in Lebanon is entirely different. There, about 50 per cent. are Christians, subdivided into Maronites (the largest single community), Greek Orthodox, Greek Catholics, and Armenian Orthodox, to name only the more important sects. (The balance has been temporarily upset by the influx of Moslem refugees from Palestine, who are not, however, recognized as Lebanese citizens.) Lebanese Moslems are subdivided into Sunni (more than 20 per cent. of the total), Shī'i (about 16 per cent.), Druze, and others. The clan spirit is of paramount importance in Lebanon. Most members of a community regard themselves first and foremost as Maronites, Shī'ites, etc., and only secondarily as Lebanese. This sectarianism has been strongly criticized, and is indeed the main stumbling-block to political and social reform; but up to now political division has remained in accordance with communal lines. The President of the Republic has to be a (Maronite) Christian, the Prime Minister a (Sunni) Moslem, and so on; elections and political organization down to the lower echelons are set up according to religious and ethnic groups and lists.

Two-thirds of the inhabitants of the Levant states are employed in agriculture, the percentage being somewhat higher in Syria than in Lebanon. Syria is self-supporting in most foodstuffs; Lebanon is not, and tries to readjust an adverse trade balance by commerce, tourism, and the influx of currency from Lebanese living abroad or returning to their homeland. The polarization of land tenure is far less glaring in the Levant than in such countries as Iraq or Egypt, but in certain regions of Syria and Lebanon feudal landowners still wield decisive economic and political influence.

Industry developed rapidly during World War II, but output decreased in most fields thereafter. In addition to light consumers' goods, such as sugar, paper, and textiles, cement is produced in both countries and, following the laying of pipelines, oil-refining has reached sizeable proportions in Tripoli and other Mediterranean terminals of Iraqi and Saudi-Arabian pipelines.

3. THE RISE AND THE SUPPRESSION OF THE COMMUNIST PARTY

The Communist Party of Syria and Lebanon was founded in 1930.[2] But there had been several attempts in the early 1920's to establish a Communist Party following the return of a delegation of Arab Communists who had studied methods of agitation and propaganda in Moscow, as well as Marxism-Leninism generally.[3] These attempts were abortive and reached only small circles; some of the emissaries did not even remain in the party. In Lebanon the Communists appeared for the first time on the political scene (though not as yet in their own name) in 1924–25, and again, after an interval, during the 1929 elections, when they demanded that the workers should not give their votes to "capitalist and pro-imperialist parties," but ask for the establishment of their own working-class lists.[4] At the same time there was some Communist activity in the trade unions, which sufficed to irritate the government into suppressing it in the spring of 1931. At about the same time a first attempt to publish a legal semi-Communist periodical (*Sawt al 'Amal*, Workers' Voice) had been made, but after two months the authorities intervened and banned this publication.[5]

After the failure of this attempt, the party proceeded to publish an illegal organ *Al Fagr al Ahmar ad-Dāmi* (The Red Dawn), which appeared for several months during the winter of 1930–31. But then the police discovered the printing shop (in a garage), and the editor, Artin Maduyan, who was also the first party secretary of that period, was arrested.[6] There was also a party organ in Armenian at that time, as the vast majority of the early party members were Armenians. The Syrian and Lebanese press, which was staunchly anti-Communist at that time, demanded the intervention of the authorities, and there were even suggestions that all Communist Armenians be deported to Soviet Armenia. But Communist activities were then confined almost exclusively to the organization of demonstrations on May Day and on November 7. On November 7, 1931, there was a demonstration in Beirut (200 participants), according to contemporary sources,[7] though in Damascus the party failed to enlist enough supporters for a demonstration, and distributed leaflets instead. In 1932 the Communists fomented several strikes, such as the railway strike in August and the strike of the oil-refinery workers in Tripoli.[8] The demonstration on the anniversary of the Russian Revolution was celebrated, this time by a fair-sized turnout, which was noted, in contrast to former years, by all local papers.[9] In 1933–34 the leadership of the party was taken over by a number of Syrian and Lebanese Arabs, among them Khālid Bakdāsh, Mustafa al 'Arīs, Fuād Qazān, and Nikola Shāwi.[10] Most of them had been in the Soviet Union during the Seventh Congress of the Comintern, or even before, and underwent several months' training in Russia. But the new local leadership could do very little until the adoption of the new Popular-Front line put an end to the anti-religious propaganda and the exclusively "proletarian" orientation. The years 1934 and 1935 were, therefore, lean years from the point of view of the party, although a certain amount of activity did continue in the few existing Beirut trade unions, and the printers' strike in the Lebanese capital in 1934 was Communist led. In 1935 a new party organ was published illegally, though it had to be discontinued following a police search. Only in 1937 did *Sawt ash Sha'ab* (People's Voice) become a legal journal.

In the same period, party activities extended to the Arab elements in northern cities, such as Aleppo and Homs, where formerly it had been confined to the local Armenian inhabitants. But at the same time there was much friction between the Armenian and the Arab sections, and the Communist attitude to the national movement caused several splits in 1933–34 which weakened the party considerably. Those who demanded closer collaboration with the Arab national movement were ousted as deviators from the party line.

The first big change in the fortunes of the party (whose membership had not previously exceeded 100–200) came in 1936. The French authorities, who saw the emergence of a Communist Party as a matter to be dealt with by the Sûreté Générale rather than as a political and social problem, reported (retrospectively) about the events of 1936:

"In the course of this year the party intensified its activities and changed its methods of work. It is not content any more with putting up illegal posters on the walls, but wants to recruit new members, exploiting the economic crisis. The party organizes new trade unions, and it has had a part in a number of strikes declared after the devaluation of the franc, with the intention of getting higher wages and shorter working hours. . . . In the speeches in the party cells the leaders have approved the French-Syrian Treaty and opposed the French-Lebanese Treaty. The party has declared itself in favour of Syrian unity. Some of its chiefs are now on good terms with the members of the government in Damascus and hope for their party to be recognized officially in Syria."[11]

It was at this juncture that the Popular-Front coalition came into power in Paris. The initiative for the "treaties" of 1936 had already come from the new French government. The treaties provided for the gradual abolition of the Mandate and the grant of independence, self-governing institutions, and eventually admission to the League of Nations. The Maronites in the Lebanon and some other Christian elements demanded a similar alliance, which, however, offended the Syrian nationalists and the Moslem communities in the Lebanon, who stood for Syrian unity (i.e. annexation of Lebanon). The political negotiations lasted for more than two years, and ended with French rejection of the treaties. Meanwhile the attitude of the Syrian nationalists also had stiffened as a result of the separation (and eventual annexation by the Turks) of the Sandjak of Alexandretta and because of the problem of the Jazīra, the north-eastern province of Syria, which was to be given special status. The Communists saw imperialist intrigues and a continuation of the traditional policy of divide and conquer in the French-Lebanese Treaty, and although favouring the Franco-Syrian Treaty, they opposed the secession of the Sandjak and expressed grave concern over the future of the Jazīra.[12]

The party had now become semi-legal. A propaganda campaing in which Khālid Bakdāsh's pamphlets served as the basis of discussion penetrated wider circles.[13] All the outspoken revolutionary demands had been dropped. "Our party has adopted a national policy and the principal demand has become national liberation," the party executive stated retrospectively; the Syrian party had already become more independent of the Comintern after the Seventh World Congress, and there was no contact with the Comintern executive committee after 1938.[14] "People's libraries" were founded throughout the country, and in 1935 the first of many "front organizations" was established in protest against the Italian invasion of Abyssinia. It was headed by Antūn Thābit, who became in later years the main party specialist in organizing "fellow-travelling" groups and in leading them.

The main foes of the Communists were the Maronite Christian groups in the Lebanon, notably the Phalange (the most radical exponents of Lebanese nationalism), and Antūn Sa'ada's Syrian National Party, a pro-fascist movement. The Maronite press complained that the authorities were giving the Communists a free hand in the very heart of Beirut on May Day, and demanded police intervention. But by that time the Communists had become a legal party, and if *Sawt ash-Sha'ab* (now appearing freely) was suppressed in October, 1937, it was permitted to reappear a few days afterwards. The party took part in the Lebanese elections of October, 1937, without, however, gaining spectacular successes. Farjalla al Hilu, Nikola Shāwi, and Fuād Qazān, who appeared as straight Communist candidates, were not elected; neither were several crypto-Communists, who appeared as candidates of the Democratic Party and various other fronts.[15] Nor did the attempt to establish an alliance with non-Communist Armenian parties have much success. In its relations with this minority the party leadership tried acts of political tight-rope walking which frequently boomeranged. Some of the central figures in the party executive were still Armenians (such as Natsir), but elsewhere, including strongly Armenian Aleppo, the Armenian members had been ousted from the local party leadership to make place for Moslem Communists. Such manœuvres had made a bad impression on the Armenian community and hardly contributed to the success of election alliances. On the other hand, the leaders of the National Bloc, the strongest group to have emerged in the Syrian national camp, did not reject Communist overtures; nor did they oppose the opening of party headquarters in Damascus, but they were not ready to deal with the Communist leaders as equals.

In November, 1937, Khālid Bakdāsh went to France, heading an official Syrian Communist delegation,[16] and in May, 1938, a return visit was paid by two French Communist deputies, Virgile Barel and Jacques Gresa.[17] Between these two visits there occurred the pre-war spate of Communist successes in the Levant, to be equalled only after 1943. The French Communist deputies came, "not to interfere" in Levant politics but merely "to study the situation," to quote their declarations. They spoke at large mass meetings in Damascus, together with such Communist leaders as Bakdāsh and Rafīq Rida, but they also went out of their way to see nationalist leaders. They visited the tomb of Ibrāhīm Hananu, the hero of the Syrian national movement, and paid their respects to Sultan al Atrash, the Druze leader. But time was fast running out. In France the Popular Front came to an inglorious end, and the changes in France were soon reflected in the reversion of the Syrian and Lebanese Communists to their former extremist opposition to the local French authorities. It was also mirrored in a message sent by the Communists to the National Bloc in July, 1938, in which the government was at last criticized for not restricting the "privileges of the feudal landowners"—"Our national rebirth will be brought about only by the people." This deterioration in the relations of the two led to a new, and this time extended, ban on *Sawt ash-Sha'ab*, and in September, 1939, four weeks after the outbreak of the war, it resulted in the suppression of the party.

4. FIELDS OF COMMUNIST ACTIVITY

The main fields of Communist activity during the two years preceding World War II were the trade unions and the "front" organizations. The beginnings of modern trade unionism in the Levant go back to 1914, when the Beirut printers established their first organization, which, however, ceased to exist during World War I.[18] It was reorganized in 1922, and it established a labour exchange and published an internal news-sheet. Other professional associations founded in the 1920's included the truck drivers' union (which, however, included employers as well as employees)[19] and the union of the workers in the Damascus power-plant. But these and similar attempts in Tripoli, Aleppo, Homs, etc., generally did not last, and since many of the organizers were Communists, the authorities usually banned the unions the moment they seemed to be acquiring wider influence. Frequently Communism was used as a pretext by the not-overly progressive-minded government to ban independent unions. It was only in 1936–37, at the time of the Popular-Front coalition in France, that trade unionism came gradually to be tolerated and recognized. The Association of Syrian Trade Unions, which had been formed in 1936, came out during the following year with a demand for a cut in working hours (an eighty-hour week was customary in many trades), for pensions or compensation for workers who had been dismissed, for banning child-labour, and the prohibition of the employment of foreign workers.

On the whole the Communists were more successful in penetrating the trade unions in Lebanon (where, since 1937, Mustafa al 'Arīs had headed the most important of them, the Beirut Printers' Union) than in Syria, where trade unionism was weaker on the whole, and where some of the more influential unions preserved their independence or their ties with parties other than the Communists. Communist action in the Levant trade unions between 1936 and 1939 was neither very spectacular nor efficient, but it paved the way for the party's successes after 1942. The party established the necessary cadres during the years preceding World War II, and the subsequent extension of its work was a matter only of favourable political conditions.

Among the Communist-"front" organizations, the Anti-Fascist League (originally "Congress"—Mu'tamar mukāfahat al fascistiyya) should be mentioned. It was founded in Beirut in 1938 and held its first big congress in the Lebanese capital in May, 1939. Its leader was the ubiquitous Antūn Thābit, lawyer and architect, the personification of "fellow-travelling." The Communist Party leaders appeared at the congress (e.g. Mustafa al 'Arīs, Farjalla Hilu, Khālid Bakdāsh), but sympathizers were also present, such as the parliamentary deputies Jubrān Twaini, Qāsim Khālid, Yūsuf 'Awwād, and others. Cables and messages of approval were received from leading Syrian and Lebanese personalities, including the leaders of the National Bloc (Lutfi al Haffār, Shukri Quwatli, Fā'iz al Khūri, Nazīm Qudsi, et al.), though not all of them proved to be such staunch anti-fascists after 1939.[20] The party press department stressed the great danger of Fascism in all its publications, but here, as everywhere else, there came the sudden, vertiginous somersault after the Nazi-Soviet Treaty of August, 1939.[21] *Sawt ash-Sha'ab* needed several weeks to adjust itself to the new line and to eliminate the old anti-fascist slogans, but the party was outlawed anyway on September 29, 1939, by the Daladier laws that had been adopted in France. The party executive went into hiding, but decided, of course, to continue its activities on a limited scale. The number of party members was at that time about 2000 each in Syria and Lebanon, but was reduced to half as the result of the sudden, and to many incomprehensible, changes in the party line. The authorities had, however, come to know the party leaders during the period of legality in 1936–39, and in December, 1939, most of the Communist chiefs, including Farjalla al Hilu, Bakdāsh, Rafīq Rida, and Mustafa al 'Arīs, were arrested.[22]

With this, party activities came to an end for some time. Under the

Vichy regime only sporadic leaflets of limited circulation were published, and they had no appreciable political effect. There is, moreover, some reason to assume that the Communist militants still at large were not much interested in making their views known. The Soviet alliance with Hitler was still in effect, and the party had no sympathy at all for the attempts of the Western democracies to defend themselves against the German and Italian onslaught in the Middle East. In fact, the Communist Party in the Levant opposed the successful invasion and overthrow of Vichy rule in Syria and Lebanon by the Allied forces in May, 1941. Only two months later, when Hitler attacked the Soviet Union, did it dawn upon them that the Allied invasion had not, as a matter of fact, been a case of "flagrant aggression" and war-mongering.

Chapter Eleven

Syria during World War II

I. STRONG GROWTH OF COMMUNIST PARTY

FREE FRENCH rule had been restored to the Levant in the summer of 1941, but the power behind it was merely a shadow of what it had been prior to 1939. The movement for Syrian and Lebanese independence received fresh impetus from the weakening of the French position; nor could the British representatives in the Levant be very accurately described (to put it mildly) as working for the strengthening of French influence in Lebanon and Syria. Consequently, France had gradually to give in to Lebanese and Syrian demands; there were anti-French riots in Lebanon in November, 1943, and a more widespread revolt in Syria in May–July, 1945, which, accompanied by British and Soviet pressure, resulted in the French evacuation of the two countries in 1945–46. The development of Communist policy in the Levant during 1941–48 must be visualized with this background in mind.

The Communist leaders were released from prison soon after the occupation of Syria and Lebanon by the Allies in the summer of 1941. In the autumn the Anti-Fascist League, headed by Antūn Thābit, was revived,[1] and from December of the same year *At-Tariq* (The Way), this group's paper, was published. The Communist newspaper *Sawt ash-Sha'ab* (The People's Voice) reappeared at about the same time.[2] Full-scale Communist activities got under way in the winter of 1941–42, but at that time the war in Europe still hung in the balance, and it was only in 1943, after the battle of Stalingrad and the defeat of the Axis in North Africa, that Communist propaganda found willing ears, and made progress in both Lebanon and Syria, especially the former.

The Communists underwent a national metamorphosis during the war years, and their programme became almost indistinguishable from that of other political groups, apart perhaps from the additional stress laid on friendly ties with the Soviet Union. Everyone in the Levant was in favour of friendship with Russia so soon as it became clear who was going to win the war. At the very beginning of the war, the party had voiced Socialist demands,[3] but during 1941–45 the main stress was, of course, on the "anti-fascist war effort" and the "just national demands of the Syrian and Lebanese people." A decision adopted by the party executive in May, 1943, read: "The party will work more than ever for the enlistment of all popular forces for national unity. . . . More than ever we shall strive for reviving the national traditions, to get our inspiration from our national history so that our nation may, once peace is restored, take its proper place in the world."[4]

Pro-Soviet sympathies reached their apogee when Russia (the very first country to do so) recognized Syrian and Lebanese independence in July, 1944, and when the Soviet ambassador, in his own car, smuggled the Syrian Prime Minister through the French cordon out of the country at the time of the 1945 crisis. The Communists took part in the independence movement, particularly after the end of the war. In 1943 and 1944 they had frequently advised the other groups to take a moderate line,[5] so that their national interests should not conflict with the anti-fascist war effort.

In particular, Communist progress in Lebanon was spectacular. New party branches were founded in Akar, Jabā'il, Kesrwan, Zahle, and other provincial centres, even in Baq'a and Jabal Druze. After the dissolution of the Comintern in the summer of 1943, the opinion had been voiced by party members that the establishment of separate Lebanese and Syrian parties would have a decidedly beneficial effect on the development of Communism in the Levant. (At the same time Jewish and Arab Communists split in Palestine.) After initial hesitations these suggestions were accepted by Khālid Bakdāsh, who provided the ideological justification in a long programmatic speech at the party Congress in Beirut in December, 1943.[6] Social and political conditions in the two countries were very different, Bakdāsh declared.

"(a) The national movement in Lebanon is less strongly developed than in Syria, its slogans and tactics are different. (b) Certain Lebanese circles are afraid of Syria and the other Arab countries. The imperialists and reactionaries are responsible for having created this fear. The establishment of a separate Lebanese Communist Party will make it possible, however, to reach these circles and to allay their fears. (c) Democracy is more deeply rooted in Lebanon than in Syria. In Syria the feudal landowners still continue to rule and want to limit the freedom of expression and association of the working class. (d) Separation will benefit the internal organization of both parties, and will make it possible to concentrate in future on definite, concrete objectives and will make it easier to adopt decisions swiftly. It will also bring about a broadening of the party organization and the influx of 'new blood.' This does not mean, however, that collaboration will cease altogether; close contact will be preserved between the two party executives. The party newspaper (printed and published in Beirut) will serve as the common organ of both parties until the Syrian Communists launch an organ of their own."[7]

At-Tarīq was an important instrument in Communist activities among the intelligentsia. This fortnightly soon became one of the best-edited magazines in the Arab East and greatly helped to win the party new friends and sympathizers.[8] The Stalin Peace Prize awarded to the journal in 1950 was well deserved from the Soviet point of view. The Twentieth-Century Publishing House in Beirut edited excerpts from Marx and Engels (*Communist Manifesto*), Lenin and Stalin, as well as Soviet and anti-Fascist writers (who at that time included, *horribile dictu*, Silone and Hemingway). There were, on the other hand, few if any contributions by local Communist writers on specific Middle Eastern problems.[9] The various "front" organizations were particularly successful among the intelligentsia in Lebanon, because they helped to rope in those individuals who were sympathetic to Communist aims but who were reluctant to join the party because they held official or important positions. One of the most successful types of activity was the arrangement of soirées, banquets, conferences, etc., at which the party invariably succeeded in producing as sponsor or guest speaker some prominent member of the government to lend prestige to the occasion.[10]

The trade-union field was not neglected in Lebanon. According to Communist claims there were about seventy trade unions by the end of the war (though only a minority of them on a country-wide basis), and the number of workers organized had reached about 30,000. All the more important unions (such as the power-plant workers' union, the drivers' and printers' union, building workers, etc.) were under Communist control. But in Syria the number of organized workers was only 18,000 to 19,000, and the Communists were less successful there in getting their members elected to the key positions. During the war there were comparatively few strikes (in order not to sabotage the war effort !), but during the second half of 1945, and particularly in 1946, the party-dominated unions headed a number of widespread strikes.[11]

2. THE PARTY LINE IN 1945

The first big test of Communist influence in the unions was precipitated by the elections to the first W.F.T.U. Congress in Paris in September, 1945. In Lebanon, Communist influence was paramount, and the delegation was headed by such well-known party leaders as Mustafa al 'Arīs (later to be elected a member of the W.F.T.U. executive), and Nikola Shāwi. The Lebanese government contributed a sizeable sum to financing the trip of this delegation. In Syria, on the other hand, there was opposition to Communist steam-roller tactics, and nineteen unions voted against the Communist list. As a result there were two delegations to represent Syria in Paris, but the W.F.T.U. executive recognized only the Communist group. Other post-war party activities included anti-Turkish protests (with the annexation of the Sandjak as pretext), protests against Zionism and the "Western Imperialists," and frequent clashes with Antūn Sa'ada's Syrian National Party. The fact that the French had agreed to cede the Sandjak in 1938–39 had been neither forgotten nor forgiven in Syria, and the Communist Party fully exploited nationalist complaints because they fitted in nicely with Soviet anti-Turkish policy after World War II. The party organized anti-Turkish student demonstrations,[12] and protested on the occasion of the visit of the Turkish Foreign Minister, Hassan Saka (August, 1945).

The party was anti-Zionist, as were all other Communist Parties, and its leaders, such as Mustafa al 'Arīs, Georges Hanna, Farjalla al Hilu, and others, collaborated with the other parties in demonstrations against Jewish Palestine on "Balfour Day" (November 2) and on similar occasions. Bevin's Palestine policy did not satisfy the party, so it was decided at a joint session of the two Communist Party executives that "the only solution is the abolition of the Mandate, the proclamation of Palestinian independence; it is necessary to stop Zionist immigration and to introduce national democratic self-government in Palestine."[13] When the Soviet Union, however, came out in favour of a Jewish state in Palestine, the Syrian and Lebanese parties had to modify their attitude too, which caused certain difficulties and had a temporarily detrimental effect on "fellow-travelling" organizations.[14]

The two parties did not, of course, differ from the other post-war Communist Parties in their attitude to "Western imperialism"; the reader will be spared the details of party propaganda in that field. In Middle Eastern politics King 'Abdullah of Jordan became their main whipping-boy. At their meeting in May, 1946, the two executives protested against the "Emir who has no right to represent his country," and criticized the Lebanese government for having sent delegates to his coronation.[15] They denounced the Arab League for its failures and for its giving in to foreign (Western) pressure to create "hostile blocs" in the Middle East. One of the main preoccupations of the Lebanese Communists was to protest (until 1947) against "British intrigues," and thereafter against "American attempts to draw Lebanon into the Western camp."

The frequent clashes between the Communists and Antūn Sa'ada's Syrian National Party are somewhat more difficult to understand. There were other pro- or semi-fascist parties in the Middle Eastern countries, and the Communists, on the whole, went along with them no less than with other parties, and sometimes even more. Perhaps the Lebanese Communists took their anti-fascism more seriously than their comrades in the other Arab countries[16]; however that may be, it is a fact that members of the two parties clashed almost every Friday and Sunday in the cities of the Lebanon, and on one such occasion Shartūni, an editor of *At-Tarīq*, was killed.

According to Communist reports, the number of party members in Lebanon had risen from 1500 in 1941 to 15,000 in 1946, and in Syria from 1500 to 8000 during the same period.[17] All these figures were exaggerated, especially those for 1946; 5000 for Lebanon and 3000 for Syria would appear to be closer to the truth. But it has to be added at once that these figures do not fully reflect Communist strength in the Levant. They refer only to the cadres, but there is a much larger periphery of sympathizers who are reluctant for one reason or other to join the party but are willing to support it in every other possible way. The party had participated in the Lebanese elections of 1943 without success. It took part again in the Syrian elections of 1947 after the president of the state had received the party leader and promised him full freedom of action. The Communists put up a moderately good showing in three districts, but did not succeed in getting a single member elected.[18]

Syrian and Lebanese Communists, especially the former, complained frequently during 1945–48 of being "persecuted" by the authorities and the other political parties. These accounts are, however, highly exaggerated if not altogether imaginary, apart perhaps from the fact that the Syrian police attempted for some time during 1946 to prevent the import of *Sawt ash-Sha'ab* (The People's Voice; printed in Beirut) into Syria. In a few cases party militants or leaders were brought to trial, as, for instance, Badr ad-Dīn as-Siba'i, a member of the party executive in Homs. But in all these cases the accused were acquitted and released at once.[19] Khālid Bakdāsh frequently declared (in order to remove all possible doubt) that the Communist Party in the Levant, just as everywhere else, was *not* a revolutionary one. "At the present time nobody among the Communists even thinks of building a Socialist society," he said; their only aim was to fight for full national independence and democracy, and this, after all, was the aim of all other parties, too. The situation in Lebanon was even more favourable. The Lebanese Communists served as go-between for the Beirut government, soliciting Soviet support for its demands in 1945–46, and the Beirut government preferred not to irritate Moscow by doing anything the local Communists would not like. There were occasional anti-Communist demonstrations of students in 1945–46, organized by Maronite groups (such as the Phalanges), against Communist teachers in Beirut, who had previously organized a protest movement in connection with anti-Communist measures taken by the Egyptian government at that time.

The official attitude towards the Communist Parties changed, however, when these began to adapt themselves to the new radicalism of the

Zhdanov line. The Soviet vote in favour of a Jewish state in Palestine brought this new trend to its first climax. In an anti-Communist demonstration in Damascus on November 29, 1947, three Communists were killed and more were wounded. The next day the party offices were closed by order of the Minister of the Interior; some of the party leaders were arrested and Communist demonstrations were banned. In Beirut a bomb exploded in the party offices. The Communists declared that this was a "Zionist-imperialist" provocation, but even this ingenious explanation did not help them very much. In January, 1948, the party was dissolved, some of its leaders (including Farjalla al Hilu) were arrested, and several of the "front" associations were requested to discontinue their work. These measures, however, were not carried out with much vigour, and both parties were able to continue their usual activities unmolested by the police, except when big demonstrations were organized in the cities.

3. NATIONALISM

During the war years party propaganda was based on emphasis of the "national character" of the Communist Party. "There is no contradiction whatsoever between nationalism and internationalism," Khālid Bakdāsh declared,[20] pointing to the lesson of the Soviet Union. The Soviet Union was undoubtedly internationalist, but the various Soviet peoples had preserved their national tradition and feeling and their culture. Nevertheless, the party leaders drew a deep breath of relief after the dissolution of the Comintern.[21] "This makes it impossible for hostile elements to describe the Communist Party as subservient to some outside power. On the other hand, it will make it easier to attract national elements to the party who agree, on the whole, with the party's principles on national liberation, but who did not join the party in the past because of its international ties."[22]

The social and economic demands of the party were exceedingly moderate. In his 1944 May Day speech, Khālid Bakdāsh declared that ". . . we have not demanded, do not demand now, and do not even contemplate socializing national capital and industry. On the contrary, we wish that both national capital and industry should make progress. We only want the improvement of the living conditions of the national [sic!] workers and democratic labour legislation to regulate labour relations between employers and employees. We promise the big landowners that we shall not nationalize their land. On the contrary, all we want is to help them by demanding irrigation and the mechanization of agriculture. All we want of them is that they should pity [!] the [small] peasant, and that an effort should be made to help get the peasant out of his present state of poverty, illiteracy, and disease. We promise the big merchants that we shall not demand the nationalization of their trade, and we only want them to put an end to speculation. We shall support the small merchants and demand a lightening of their big burden of taxes. They should also be given more credit."[23] The speaker emphatically denied the allegation spread by "the enemies of the Communists" that all these demands were mere slogans for outside consumption, and declared that all party members were educated in the spirit of his statement.

The party programme adopted by the 1943–44 Congress included the following points:

1. Syrian and Lebanese independence and a republican-democratic regime.
2. Closer economic relations between the Arab countries.
3. Revival of the national tradition in both Syria and Lebanon.
4. Social justice, increase in the standard of living, better education, and health services.[24]

Nikola Shāwi, elaborating on these points, wrote that national independence was the principal task. The necessity for closer co-operation with the Arab countries was obvious, since both Syria and Lebanon were in the area. But how may one explain the fact that even the term "socialism" itself did not appear in the party programme? He had an explanation for that, too: "The present party charter refers only to a certain historical stage, the period of the struggle for national liberation."[25]

Chapter Twelve

Syria and Lebanon since World War II

S YRIAN and Lebanese Communists could well be satisfied with their successes in 1948. The popular-front policy in the late 1930's had been modified to a national-front line. Party policy became gradually more and more "anti-imperialist" after 1945 and, although the "national-front" slogans were preserved, on the whole the party became more radical in its policy in accordance with the world-wide Zhdanov line of 1947–49. At that time the party stood, in theory, for the anti-imperialist unity of all parties (including the "national industrial *bourgeoisie*"), but it did not have enough latitude to pursue such a policy with any success. After Stalin's death there was another modification of the line; the anti-Western campaign continued unabated, but the party leaders were now once again ready to lean over backwards in order to collaborate with other parties.

I. ILLEGALITY

The Communist Party in Syria remained illegal from 1948 until the fall of Colonel Shishakli in February, 1954. But there seems to have existed some tacit understanding between the Syrian police and the Communist Party, and the Communists could, in fact, do as they liked, within certain reasonable limits. They were persecuted only when their publications printed particularly violent anti-government material or when their demonstrations got out of hand.

The history of Syria after the Palestine war was one of profound political shocks and frequent *coups d'état* engineered by the army. In March, 1949, Colonel Husni Az-Za'im overthrew the Damascus government and took stringent measures against the Communist Party after it had launched an all-out attack against him, the "American Slave,"[1] and had called the people "to combat the despotic decrees of Husni Za'īm."[2] But his rule lasted only until August, 1949; when a military counter-*coup* brought Colonel Hinnāwi to power, Za'īm was executed. All the political prisoners of the former regime, including the Communists, were released, and the Communists decided to participate in the elections scheduled for November, 1949. Bakdāsh again became the leader of a semi-legal party, and announced that he would run for election. This, however, seems to have been more than the government could take, and he was soon compelled to go underground again. (There was a farcical element in Bakdāsh's frequent jack-in-the-box public appearances, since there were standing orders to arrest him. He left and returned to the country at regular intervals, and his whereabouts were well known, of course.) On the eve of the 1949 elections Communist leaders were arrested (Najāt Qāsib Hasan and Dr. Nazwah Ja'afari), only to be released a few days later following student demonstrations.[3] The Communist Party used this opportunity, however, for a propaganda campaign against British "intrigues in the Middle East," "the criminal plans for a collective security charter," and so on. They also demanded that the licences given to the foreign oil companies be revoked. The party reached an election agreement with the People's Party, and advised its members to vote for candidates of this party for all offices not contested by the Communists themselves. This was probably the reason for the arrest of the Communist leaders, since the military clique wanted to use the Communists against the People's Party and to prevent such a bloc.[4]

In December, 1949, Colonel Hinnāwi's regime was overthrown by another army colonel, Adīb Shishakli, who ran the country from behind the scenes for the two following years, and ruled directly from December, 1951, until February, 1954. The years of 1950–51, therefore, showed relative democratic freedom in Syria, and the Communists could appear more or less openly, apart from occasional arrests which, however, did not seriously hinder their activities.[5] During June and July, 1950, large-scale demonstrations were organized by the party in most Syrian cities in order to express solidarity with the "North Korean people defending its independence and national unity" and to protest against the Three Power Declaration (of the United States, Britain, and France in May, 1950), which had stressed that Middle Eastern peace and stability were their common interest. These demonstrations resulted in several persons killed and wounded and more than 100 arrests by the police, and they induced the authorities to take more stringent measures against the party. What should be noted is that party propaganda became intensely violent during this period, and attempted deliberately to provoke clashes with the police; only very infrequently did its slogans voice social demands, call for strikes, etc. The main preoccupation of both the party and the new front organization (to be dealt with below) became the "struggle for peace." These were the tactics (to use Khālid Bakdāsh's own words) "of sound and fury." At the same time the party underwent a purge. Two leading Syrian Communists, Rashād 'Isa, a member of the party executive, and Najāt Qāsib Hasan, party secretary in the Damascus district, were charged with Titoism.[6] Several Lebanese militants were also expelled, and altogether about one dozen leaders were affected by a purge which, however, did not apparently weaken the party very much. The official reason given for the purge (reluctance to support the Soviet stand on Palestine) was almost certainly untrue, and it seems that personal rivalries between party leaders were the decisive factor. Some of the militants complained of the "regime of dictatorship in the party," as Khālid Bakdāsh[7] reported, speaking about "the uncovering and crushing of the Titoist-imperialist plot which has been built up for some time. . . . The Titoists, those cynical spies of imperialism, aimed at securing control of the central leadership of the party and of the regional leaderships, and destroying, liquidating, and changing the Communist Party into a nationalist, Titoist-*bourgeois* party. . . . Their show of tears over the alleged loss of democracy in the party was only hypocritical and intended to create an atmosphere of false, *bourgeois*, splintering democracy in the heart of the party and making it easier for the spies and traitors to carry out their activities of sabotage in an uncontrolled fashion."[8]

2. THE "PARTISANS OF PEACE" IN SYRIA

The peace movement had considerable success in Syria in 1950 and particularly in 1951; 60,000 signatures were reportedly collected in the country in the earlier year, and 265,000 in 1951. But it was not these figures (which cannot be checked, after all) that mattered, but the very high number of prominent personalities who signed the "Stockholm" appeal and openly identified themselves with a movement, the true character of which was no secret in the Middle East. Among the signers were a majority of the members of the Syrian parliament (including its president, Rushdi al Kihya), several former Prime Ministers and Ministers (including the then Minister for Education), most party leaders, and prominent intellectuals. When the Damascus government put some difficulties in the way of a "peace delegation" due to leave for the Berlin Communist Youth Festival in 1951, it was overruled by parliament. Rushdi al Kihya and other leaders of the People's Party claimed that "the participation of such delegations in these festivals is very useful indeed."[9]

The Syrian Partisans of Peace, the main Communist front in 1950–51, published a periodical, *As-Salām* (Peace), during 1951 and held a country-wide convention in Damascus in October, 1950. They also staged several demonstrations against imperialism on such occasions as the visit of General Brian Robertson, the officer commanding British forces in the Middle East. The president of the Syrian Partisans of Peace was Dr. Mustafa Amīn of Homs, and the editor of its paper was Ahmad Tālis. Other prominent leaders included Dr. Nazwah Ja'afari (Communist candidate for parliament and president of the Democratic Lawyers' Union), Sa'īd Tahsīn (President of the Artists' Association), Yūsuf Muslāli (President of the Syrian Democratic Youth), 'Abdul Majīd Jamal ad-Dīn (representative of the Association of Syrian Republican Students, another Communist front), and Shaikh Muhammed al Ashmar, representing the Damascus 'ulamā Islamic clergy. This list, which could be extended indefinitely, shows that a wide network of front organizations had come into being and that no profession was neglected. Representing the pro-Communist women was Mrs. Falk at-Tarzi, the sister of the director-general of the Syrian Ministry of Foreign Affairs.

Of those prominent figures who signed the various peace appeals (and we have left out the better-known "fellow-travellers," such as Dr. M. Dawalībi), the majority undoubtedly knew full well what they were doing and exploited the opportunity to express anti-Western views. From the Communist Party point of view, the big success of the peace movement was not, however, an unmixed blessing. "Certain comrades think that our support of the Partisans of Peace means that we are abandoning certain slogans of ours," said Khālid Bakdāsh; "this is a serious and disastrous error."[10]

"It may happen that a big feudal landowner supports the aims of the Partisans of Peace and signs the Stockholm appeal, for instance. Our comrades then think that they should keep silent about his deeds of bestial oppression against his fellaheen or that they should cease advocating the division of the feudalist's lands among the fellaheen, in order not to anger him. They are blackening the face of the party before the fellaheen and are damaging one of its most important slogans with them in order to appease a feudalist. This is entirely unacceptable, and there can be no compromise on this point." Bakdāsh went on to quote similar incidents involving "*bourgeois* industrialists," and concluded by saying that the organization of the working class, the principal and leading force in the democratic national revolution, should never be soft-pedalled in order to appease a member of the *bourgeoisie*, whoever he might be. Nevertheless, Bakdāsh's warnings were not taken to heart, and the "national *bourgeoisie*" continued to be appeased. Perhaps his warning was intended only to remind comrades that the party line should not be regarded as lasting and could be modified in the future.

After December, 1951, when Shishakli took over direct control, the Partisans of Peace found it more difficult to be openly active in Syria, and their leader, Dr. Mustafa Amīn, was imprisoned for some time. Meanwhile, it had been realized in Moscow that the peace movement was not an ideal instrument for the Middle East, or rather that a more militant and less pacifist framework should be found, which would succeed even more in the specific conditions of the Arab countries. The Arab Partisans of Peace found themselves, moreover, hampered by the Palestine issue; a consistent Partisan of Peace, taking his programme in earnest, would have to stand for peace in the Middle East, too, not only in the other parts of the world. But the Communists had no intention whatsoever of taking the initiative for peace between Arabs and Jews. It was decided, therefore, in the summer of 1953, to establish a new organization, the "Congress for the Defence of the Peoples of the Near and Middle East,"[11] which for the most part succeeded and took over the peace movement. In the programme of this new movement the stress was on anti-Westernism, not on the fight for peace. The Congress was convened in Beirut in December, 1953, and adopted a manifesto of fourteen points.[12] It was active in Syria, too, but on the whole it never attained anything like the high pitch of activity of 1951; the Communists now had other preoccupations.

3. TRADE UNIONS AND FELLAHEEN

The Syrian party was less successful in the trade-union field. It had succeeded in getting its representatives elected to most key positions at the time of the first W.F.T.U. Congress in 1945. But even then there had been a vociferous opposition, and the party's hold on the trade unions was broken in 1947–48. The Syrian Workers' Association, headed by Subhi al Khatīb, refused to join the I.C.F.T.U. after having left the W.F.T.U., but it was certainly not Communist dominated. In July, 1950, the Communists made another attempt to found a new trade-union organization, the Congress of Syrian Workers, with its magazine *Al Ālam*. But even a Communist leader had to admit that this was not really a new trade-union centre but rather "an attempt to restore unity between the existing unions, and it includes both workers which already belong to one of the unions, and unemployed, who are not organized in Syria. It also strengthens the solidarity between the various existing trade unions."[13] The lack of Communist activity in the trade-union field had been criticized in Khālid Bakdāsh's report of 1951:

"To date [our work] has been mainly confined to the better-paid elements and the rest have been almost entirely neglected. . . . It sometimes happens that our union comrades spend long hours in conferences and discussions or efforts with these elements [the non-Communist union leaders] without asking themselves whether these activities are reaching the masses of the workers. At the same time, some of our union comrades think they are spending too much time with the masses of terribly exploited workers, and there are even some who believe that this is not proper for union leaders. This happens, and we must frankly admit it. This must be changed."[14]

Up to 1950 the Syrian Communists had not been interested in the peasants, and were less active among them. There is less differentiation in land tenure in Syria than in most other Arab countries; in the main cereal-growing districts, however, large estates prevail and, as a result of the mechanization of agriculture in recent years, the trend towards polarization in land tenure has been increasingly felt. Successive Syrian governments have promised to limit landholdings, but the opposition of the feudal landowners has prevented any radical change. As a result, there has been some agrarian unrest in Syria (beginning in the summer of 1951 in the Homs and Hamma regions); the initiative in this movement was taken mainly by the Republican Socialist Party of Akram Hurāni and Michel 'Aflaq,[15] who demanded that the property of the landowners should be distributed among the peasants. Recently the Syrian Communist Party has also been active in this field, and has proposed that peasants organize in order to achieve their aims. The Communists proposed that the peasants should no longer continue to "work without payment" for the feudal landowners, and insist that they be given a larger share of the crops they had cultivated on the land belonging to the big landowners; they should demand lower taxes from the government, more schools and hospitals. "The revolutionary movement extended throughout the villages of Jazīra and the 'Alāwi mountain, the Hama and the Damascus districts. In this spontaneous struggle peasant committees have been established, which succeeded in many cases in achieving the aims of the peasants."[16]

Some of the peasant associations are now Communist dominated, such as the Jazīra committee, for example, which publishes its own newspaper; *Al Ard li'l fallāh* (Give the Land to the Fellah). Under Shishakli these organizations faced some difficulties and frequently had no legal status. But after the downfall of the Syrian dictator in February, 1954, they came out into the open, and voiced not only professional but also political demands. The Communist Party line on agrarian questions had been laid down in Khālid Bakdāsh's report of 1951: "We want to eliminate from the rural areas this class [of feudalists] who own wide expanses of land and exploit the toiling fellaheen on their lands, in most cases by share-cropping. Against this class we must and can marshal all the masses of the fellaheen. . . ."[17] The natural allies of the party in the countryside are the agricultural proletariat, the semi-proletarians, and those who have small plots of land. But the middle-class fellaheen, too, by virtue of their economic position, "are a great allied force in the struggle against feudalistic imperialism," and even the rich fellaheen, the rural *bourgeoisie*, can at least be neutralized because the struggle to put an end to imperialism and feudalism does not touch them directly or directly threaten their exploitation. "The confiscation of their lands is not an immediate objective of the working class, even after victory in its socialist revolution." But in 1954 the class-struggle-in-the-village theme was again played down.

4. COLLABORATION BETWEEN SYRIAN AND LEBANESE COMMUNISTS

It will be remembered that the Communist Parties of Syria and Lebanon had separated after the dissolution of the Comintern in the winter of 1943. They had continued, however, to co-ordinate their activities, and in December, 1950, collaboration became even closer, following the establishment of a common "high command," tantamount to an amalgamation of the leaderships of the two parties. In 1949, with the first *coups d'état* in Syria, there had been an attempt to transfer the executive of the Syrian party from Damascus, where it had comparatively few members and supporters, to the north (Aleppo). But working conditions for the executive became gradually more difficult, and in 1951 it was transferred to Beirut; inasmuch as the Syrian and Lebanese party executives had to guide, and to collaborate closely with, the Communist Parties of the other Arab countries, this could be done far more easily from Beirut than from Damascus. After the fall of Shishakli, Bakdāsh and other Communist leaders returned to Syria. Now they again appeared openly at meetings and demonstrations, and published periodicals and leaflets.[18] Their line in domestic policy again underwent certain modifications. In 1950–51 they had said that their job was to ". . . unmask the representatives of the upper *bourgeoisie*, i.e. the exposure of the rulers and the big *bourgeois* parties like the Populist Party and the Nationalist Party in Syria. . . . We must work constantly also to unmask groups and parties claiming to be 'socialist,' such as the Arab Socialist Party, the Islamic Socialist front, and Al Ba'ath in Syria, for through their seductive propaganda they constitute a danger to the growing democratic national movement against war and imperialism, feudalism and exploitation. They try to exploit the increasing popular orientation towards socialism, they especially destroy the effectiveness of our slogans of distribution of the lands of the feudalists and big landowners to the peasants. . . . They also try to prevent the growth of popular sympathy for the world-wide camp of peace and socialism led by the Soviet Union by calling for a so-called 'third force' or 'neutrality' between the two camps. This in effect leads to a breaking up of the wave of hatred and growing struggle, (*a*) against war and the aggressive schemes of the Anglo-American imperialists aiming at the occupation of our country, and (*b*) against the treason of our rulers."[19]

Under the Shishakli dictatorship, when opposition was illegal, the party had collaborated with the other opposition groups (in particular with the Syrian branch of the Moslem Brotherhood) in occasional demonstrations against the government. It had also co-operated with the right-wing People's Party in the northern regions of Syria, but relations with the left-wing groups had been far from friendly, apparently out of fear that these would steal some, and possibly much, of the Communist thunder with their own radical slogans. For obvious reasons they found it more convenient, and certainly less dangerous, to co-operate with right-wing elements on the basis of a neutralist foreign policy. This policy was somewhat modified after Shishakli's downfall.

The Syrian Communists, appearing as a "National Unity" bloc, were in a favoured position in the elections that took place in September, 1954. Their party had emerged more or less intact after the Shishakli dictatorship, whereas the other parties had considerable difficulties in reactivating their militants and members. The propaganda campaign of the Communists was better prepared and more intense than that of all other parties. Their leader, Khālid Bakdāsh, was elected in Damascus—the first Communist to become a member of an Arab parliament.[20] A Damascus newspaper called this "the most important event in the Middle East in the twentieth century"; this, of course, was slightly exaggerated, but it points to the impression made by the election. The other Communist candidates failed; among them were the head of the Communist trade-union federation in Damascus; Khalīl Harīri, also a trade-union leader who had been one of the heads of the "peace movement"; and Mustafa Halab, of Aleppo. But several right-wing nationalist candidates, campaigning on a sharply anti-Western platform (against a Middle Eastern defence pact and against American economic assistance), such as the ex-Nazi propagandist, Ma'arūf Dawalībi, and Khālid al 'Azm (both former Prime Ministers) were elected with Communist support. National-front tactics were used to perfection—and with handsome dividends for the Communists. Khālid Bakdāsh emerged as the most capable Arab Communist leader; the feudal politicians who had intended to use him as a mere tool were certainly no match for him. And he was ably assisted by a number of eager lieutenants, who made the Communists in Syria after 1954 the best organized political party.

5. STATUS OF LEGALITY IN LEBANON

After 1948 the Lebanese party became one of the strongest parties (and certainly the noisiest party) in the country.[21] Some of its leaders, notably Farjalla al Hilu, had been arrested at the time of the Palestine war, Nikola Shāwi was in hiding, and Mustafa al 'Arīs was arrested and released throughout 1949 with a fairly monotonous regularity. This, however, hardly impeded the activities of the party, which could safely rely on the inefficiency of the Lebanese police (and friends of the Communists in the police who would keep them informed about any action contemplated); they could be sure that public opinion and the majority of the newspapers would support them, just as they would every other opposition movement. The party used the trial against its trade-union boss, Mustafa al 'Arīs (in December, 1949), for a demonstration of strength; dozens of lawyers volunteered to defend him,[22] and in the end the majority of the accused were acquitted. Mustafa al 'Arīs and Nikola Shāwi (*in contumaciam*) were sentenced to one year in prison. This sentence again provoked many stormy demonstrations in Beirut, Tripoli, and other cities, which ended in clashes with the police, further casualties, new arrests, and a chain reaction of new demonstrations and new arrests.

Meanwhile there were new developments in foreign policy to be protested against: the treaty of friendship between Lebanon and the United States; and, later, the Korean war and the Three Power Declaration on the Middle East. There was not a week in 1950 without major demonstrations and clashes in the Lebanese cities, and in such centres as Beirut and Tripoli the Communists came to rule the streets. If the intention of the party was to attract public attention, it was undoubtedly successful; though in the long run these clashes became so regular and monotonous a feature of Beirut life that new ways and means had to be found to prevent a slackening of interest. The Communists had almost no competition in street demonstrations because in Lebanon, as in the other Arab countries, political parties in the Western sense do not exist, and the other political groups, whether backing the government or supporting the opposition, did not maintain a party apparatus capable of competing with the Communists. As a result, the Communist demonstrations were joined by hundreds, and occasionally thousands, of non-Communists who wanted to give expression to their dissatisfaction with the government of the day and the political and social regime in general, without identifying themselves with the Communist programme. Most of the Lebanese newspapers opposed police intervention in Communist demonstrations[23]; there were questions in parliament; and the governments, weak as they were, usually had to release the ringleaders a few days after their arrest in view of the combined pressure of women's delegations, new demonstrations, attacks in the press, further questions in parliament, etc. A short list of the major clashes early in 1950 will give a fair idea of the situation:

Beirut, January 12: Demonstrations against the 'Arīs trial.

Tripoli, January 19: Demonstrations against the 'Arīs trial; twenty-seven arrests.

Beirut, January 29: "Anti-imperialist" demonstrations; one dead, six wounded.

Tripoli, January 31: New demonstrations on the occasion of the funeral of the Beirut victims; three wounded, forty arrests.

Zahle, February 19: Demonstrations.
Beirut, March 12: Women's demonstration led by 'Arīs's wife.

During the second half of 1950 and in 1951, the peace propaganda by its very nature made a certain moderation obligatory in Communist tactics, and, though the Sunday demonstrations continued, they were on the whole less violent. Early in 1952 a major clash occurred between Armenian Communists and their opponents from the Tashnaks,[24] but this incident should be judged in the context of the particularly tense relations that exist within that community. Gradually party sympathizers lost interest, and the demonstrations attracted fewer and fewer participants; the fascination had worn off. A mere hundred party members demonstrated before the British Legation against the visit of General Brian Robertson. In Beirut there were fifty demonstrators on November 7, 1952, and twenty in Tripoli on the same date (the anniversary of the Bolshevik revolution).[25] Enthusiasm had petered out, and it was only in the summer of 1954 that the party regained some of its old momentum.

Nor were the Communists successful in the July, 1953, elections. Such well-known Communist candidates as Dr. Georges Hanna and Artin Maduyan lost their deposits, having polled less than 10 per cent. Emily Fāris Ibrahīm, the first and only woman candidate, and one of the heads of the Lebanese peace movement, fared no better in Zahle. Nor were matters any better even among the Armenians, where the Communists had found a wealthy non-Communist to run as their candidate; he was not elected.[26] It should be added, however, that Mustafa 'Arīs, the most popular Lebanese Communist, could not take part in the elections because of an order of arrest against him. On the other hand, the Communists had at their disposal a daily newspaper (*As-Sarkha*, The Call), several other dailies friendly to the Communist cause, as well as a number of periodicals.

The latest upsurge in Communist influence, in full spate at the time of writing, began in the spring of 1954. The Communists could now appear with neutralist slogans rather than the old intransigent line of demanding full identification with Soviet foreign policy. At the same time, popular discontent with the regime of corrupt bosses in the cities and of feudal landowners and their henchmen in the countryside reached a new height—especially after the (bloodless) "rosewater revolution" of September, 1952 (which had ousted the worst symbol of the system, Bishāra al Khūri, the President of Lebanon), had failed to effect any real changes in prevailing conditions. The Communists received much support from the students of the American University in Beirut, whose demonstrations and strikes compelled the authorities to close the university for some time early in 1954. Their only serious competitor on the left is Kāmil Jumbalāt and his Socialist Party; but Jumbalāt receives his main support from the villages of his Druze countrymen (who follow him in his role as the heir of a ruling family), and much less from left-wing elements in the cities.

6. THE "PARTISANS OF PEACE" IN LEBANON

The "peace movement" appeared in Lebanon even earlier than in the other Middle Eastern countries, and was fairly successful in collecting signatures from leading politicians, churchmen, and public figures in general.[27] A first appeal was published in April, 1949, and in the same month a Lebanese delegation, consisting exclusively of party members, took part in the Paris meeting of the Partisans of Peace. The propaganda campaign among non-party people got under way early in 1950, signatories among Lebanese politicians including Alfred Nacache (former President of the State), Sāmi as-Sulh, 'Abdullah Yāfi, Hamīd Frangieh, Gabriel al Murr, Pierre Jumāyil, as well as many other former and present prime ministers, ministers, parliamentary deputies, etc. Church dignitaries who signed included the Maronite Patriarch Arīda,[28] the Greek Orthodox Bishop, Elias Karama,[29] the Mufti of Baq'a, Archbishop Fotius al Khūri, et al. Other pillars of the local peace movement who took part in the Lebanese conference of the organization (in October, 1950) and in delegations to peace congresses abroad, included the president of the League of Women's Rights (a Communist organization headed by Mrs. Adma Galam), the president of the Lebanese Red Cross (Dr. Elias Bakalini), the presidents of the lawyers' organizations in North Lebanon and Beirut. Dr. Elias Shahīn, president of the Lebanese Democratic Youth (a "front" organization) doubled as president of the Lebanese Partisans of Peace, together with the indefatigable Antūn Thābit. There exist many other "front" organizations in Lebanon, some of long standing, others as mere subterfuges to evade government intervention. (The latter included, for instance, the National Congress, headed by Dr. Elias Idris, and the Lebanese Democratic Party in 1952.) Most of the other international organizations sponsored by the Cominform exist, or did exist, in Lebanon; e.g. the League for the Defence of Mother and Child, the Democratic Lawyers' Association, the Lebanese Students' Association, the Youth Commission for the Defence of Peace. It is not easy to evaluate the political importance of these groups, which frequently change their names but only rarely their constitution. They undoubtedly fulfilled a useful function by strengthening the ties between the party and its wide fringe of sympathizers among the intelligentsia, and by giving them limited assignments which fell short of the full loyalty demanded from party members.

7. COMMUNISM AND TRADE UNIONISM

The main instrument of the party among workers remained the Communist-dominated trade unions; that is, the "Federation of Trade Unions," which included the building workers', carpenters', and the printers' unions, and which is headed by Mustafa al 'Arīs.[30] There exist other trade unions as well, controlled either by the government or by individual Beirut bosses, such as Henry Phara'ūn, for example, a rich Beirut deputy and honorary president of the drivers' union. But the "official" trade unions have lost most of the little prestige they had, as they were "making no visible effort to help those most poorly paid and harassed by the continually rising cost of living, . . . the Communist-controlled unions, on the other hand, are constantly obtaining press publicity for their memoranda coupling the monopolizers and speculators on [sic] the people's food" with "criminal propaganda for a third world war," while the Iraq Petroleum Company is attacked as a "tyrannical company backed by the criminal imperialists, sucking the blood of the workers and people."[31] Another typical example of bracketing trade-union demands with the Cominform line is the memorandum forwarded by the "representatives of the workers' organizations in Tripoli"[32] to all candidates in the 1953 elections. They demanded, on the one hand, social insurance, labour legislation, medical help for workers, etc.; and on the other, opposition to the Point Four Agreement, opposition to any Middle Eastern defence scheme, etc.

The Lebanese Communist Party has again succeeded, after a temporary eclipse in 1946–50, in gaining a decisive influence over the country's trade unions by infiltrating a comparatively small number of militants (several dozens, 150–200 men at most) into the leadership of existing unions, and by founding new ones. Occasional articles in the party press hint at certain difficulties which, however, are not different from those experienced by most other Communist Parties in this field; a so-called "trade-union mentality" is prevalent among the cadres active in the unions. An additional difficulty arises from the fact that there is such a small number of "proletarian cadres" in the party; these cadres feel themselves to be representatives of the working class in the party. This, according to Khālid Bakdāsh, is a "wrong idea." They do not represent the workers in the party, but the party among the workers, because "the representative of the workers is the Communist party as a whole, for it is the party and vanguard of the working class."[33]

8. RELATIONS WITH OTHER LEBANESE PARTIES

Relations between the Lebanese Communists and other political parties in the country were different from those prevailing in Syria. In Lebanon the Communists were much stronger and did not need those political alliances which in Syria were a vital necessity for many years. In Lebanon, moreover, right-wing and Moslem extremists willing to collaborate with the Communists were not to be found. The Maronite organizations, such as the Phalange, were strongly combated by the Communists, who attacked them as "traitors and American hirelings." On the whole, the Communist Party, which stands for far closer collaboration and, if possible, union between Syria and Lebanon, opposes the separatist trends of the Maronites, who want Lebanese independence. Kāmil Jumbalāt's "Socialists" favour Lebanese neutralism and socialist reforms, but the Communists do not like hearing their own propaganda slogans voiced by other parties, and relations between these two groups have never been over-cordial.

The internal development of the Lebanese party in recent years has been comparatively uneventful. In 1949–50 some party leaders were purged and Farjalla al Hilu suffered temporary eclipse.[34] But the party as a whole passed through this crisis unscathed, and the main problem facing it now is the fact that it has a very great fringe of sympathizers but only a small number of cadres. Its leaders believe its "proletarian mass basis" to be inordinately weak; it still comes mainly from the intelligentsia.

Since the late 1930's it has been one of the assignments of the leaders of the Syrian and Lebanese party to co-ordinate the activities of other, weaker sister parties in the Middle East. Effective contact between Beirut and Moscow did not exist between 1938 and 1944, but Palestinian, Egyptian, and Iraqi Communists continued to regard the Beirut leadership as arbiters in their internal quarrels, and, after 1944, as their liaison officers with Moscow. This state of affairs was subsequently legalized, and the "peace movement," for instance, decided in 1951 to open its regional office for the Middle East in Beirut. In July–August, 1948, the Lebanese and Syrian Communists had taken the initiative in hammering out a common platform on Palestine, which should be binding for all Arab Communist Parties. In a common manifesto,[35] signed by the two Levant parties, the Iraqi Communist Party and the Palestine Arab League for National Liberation, they demanded that hostilities in Palestine should cease, that Arab refugees be returned, and an independent Arab state established according to the U.N. resolution of November, 1947. More recently, as a result of the "adverse conditions" prevailing in other Arab countries, the Lebanese capital has become even more important as the Communist centre for the Middle East.

9. THE PROSPECTS OF COMMUNISM IN SYRIA AND LEBANON

The Communist Party in Syria and Lebanon is now stronger than that in any other Middle Eastern country, and its prospects of rapid further growth are excellent, provided that they do not commit, or are not compelled to commit, major tactical mistakes. The instability of the political regimes in the two countries, the frequent changes of government and *coups d'état* (and the consequent weakening of the framework of the state), the incompetence of the ruling feudal groups in Syria and the plutocratic cliques (to quote the Chatham House review, *The World Today*) in Lebanon, which are leading their respective countries to slow but apparently sure disaster: these are some of the main factors which have made the Levant countries a favourable breeding-ground for Communism. At the same time, reform movements are weak, and the obstinate opposition of the ruling circles to any political or social change whatever makes radical change seem to be the only solution. The fact that the Levant states, and Lebanon in particular, are more advanced in many respects than the other Arab countries serves as a reminder that economic progress, higher living standards, or the establishment of more hospitals and schools do not automatically expedite the spread of Western ideas of human freedom and democracy. What these states need now more than anything else is good government by rulers who are not discredited by recurrent scandals involving corruption and nepotism. The West can supply material help, but it cannot provide these countries with a new *élite* that would be willing and able to give its homeland real and honest leadership. At the present time the government has remained the monopoly of certain vested economic interests— those least interested in social progress—while a considerable section of the intelligentsia belongs to the Communist Party or its "front" organizations, and the rest are, or have become, apathetic.

The leaders of the Syrian and Lebanese Communist Parties have shown a larger measure of political acumen than their colleagues at the helms of the other Middle Eastern parties. Their freedom of action has been very restricted, dependent, as every Communist Party, on instructions from abroad and the ever-changing politics of the Comintern and Cominform. But within that framework they have shown much adaptability to national exigencies and traditions. They have quoted the Koran and the Hadīth and made a wide use of Arab history and tradition. They have quarelled among themselves far less than have the Egyptian and Iraqi Communists, and they have in Khālid Bakdāsh a first-rate leader; that is, someone who exactly suits the demands of Moscow, who is not too independent to be dangerous and yet intelligent enough to be successful; an Arab Togliatti, in short.

The Communist programme in the period of World War II has been discussed above. In the era of radicalization (1946–50) the basic aims of the party were thus redefined by Bakdāsh:

"Our land and party are now in the phase of the democratic national liberation. Our goals in this phase can be summarized as:

(a) Putting an end to imperialist political and economic domination and to its agents.

(b) Liquidation of the remnants of feudalism in our country.

(c) Establishment of a popular democratic regime.

"Slogans in this phase: Peace, National Independence and Democracy. When this has been accomplished a new phase will begin, which will require:

(a) Strengthening of the popular democratic regime.

(b) Creation of conditions necessary for the realization of socialism in the country. . . .

"Our job during the present stage is to muster the broad masses and especially the workers and peasants. We must get them to embrace these slogans effectively and prepare for the struggle to the highest degree in order to realize them. To bring this about, the principal orientation of our efforts and activity must be towards isolating the nationalist *bourgeoisie* and putting an end to its influence among the people. . . ."[36]

This policy involved serious difficulties and was again modified to a certain extent in 1952—especially after Stalin's death. What was really meant by the demand, "to put an end to imperialist political and economic domination" in independent countries like Syria and Lebanon? The Communist leaders were at great pains to demonstrate that though the countries had become formally independent (this was their favourite example), imperialism still held them in a stranglehold by owning certain public utilities in Lebanese and Syrian cities. But it was depending too much on the gullibility of non-party people to expect them to believe that Lebanon and Syria were still dominated by the imperialists because certain British or American capitalists owned the trams in Beirut or the power-plant in some other city. Therefore, the Communist leaders usually fell back on their second line of propagandist defence, viz. even if the country has become independent, the agents of imperialism (the local *bourgeoisie*) are still ruling it, and the fight against imperialism has become the struggle against these agents. But this, in fact, meant that the main effort of the party should be the fight against the "national *bourgeoisie*" or all other parties, more or less, since after all, every non-Communist active in politics must be considered an imperialist agent. And this, of course, was something quite different from the new line (initiated by Mao Tse-tung) about the methods of the national revolution and the "new democracy"!

After Stalin's death there was a change in the Levant party tactics, in accordance with the general switch in Soviet foreign policy, and though, of course, not a single basic aim was dropped, the emphasis previously put on the fight against the internal enemy was toned down considerably, and the necessity of a popular alliance (including the national *bourgeoisie*) was again stressed. Talk about "strengthening a popular democratic regime" and "creating the conditions necessary for the realization of socialism in our country" was curbed or dropped altogether for the time being; the assumption was, apparently, that the present state of affairs in international politics was to last longer than Stalin had thought, that the day of reckoning was farther off, and that patriotic *bourgeois* elements should not be needlessly antagonized.[37] The chief internal problem of the two parties was considered by its leaders to be the lack of "proletarian mass basis." Bakdāsh stated in one of his reports that "nearly 75 per cent. of the activity of the party has been confined to petty *bourgeois* elements and selected workers," and this figure, according to first-hand reports, appears to be an understatement.

The historical explanation given was as follows:

"Owing to the circumstances of imperialist domination, feudal tyranny, and the weakness of the class struggle, it was natural that this noise [made by the party] should first attract those circles, referred to as 'enlightened,' from among the intellectuals, students, and certain enlightened workers. . . . But this attention to noisemaking and propaganda has continued for too long and has not been accompanied by the necessary effort to build solid foundations for the party among the workers and fellaheen. We are in danger of regarding the noise as an end in itself. . . ."[38]

The accusation that the general surroundings and atmosphere in which the Syrian and Lebanese parties work are not yet proletarian, but rather petty *bourgeois*, should be taken with a grain of salt. Bakdāsh undoubtedly knows that very few Communist Parties in the world, and certainly none on the other side of the Iron Curtain, are "proletarian" in character. Nor is it any longer fashionable to cling to such outmoded class beliefs; in the era of the revolution from above it is ideologically sufficient to be the party *for* the proletariat; there is no pressing need to be *of* the proletariat. What he wanted to stress (and he had to use, of course, Leninist terminology) was, most probably, that it would be dangerous for the party to become *exclusively* a party of the intelligentsia, and it is impossible to deny, in the specific conditions of Lebanon and Syria, that such a danger did in fact exist.[39] To make contact with workers and peasants and enlist support among them was, from the party's point of view, both possible and desirable in order to strengthen its political position, but it did not mean that "going to the workers" (or the peasants) was an end in itself; even at the present time, any dialectician can demonstrate that even without a workers' and peasants' mass basis, the Communist Party is still the vanguard of the working class and its only true representative, and that its policy is the only correct one, even if those who should be directly concerned do not yet realize it. A more detailed study of the ideological self-justification of Communist strategy in Syria and Lebanon according to the Leninist-

Stalinist categories (whatever its intrinsic interest) would be outside the scope of this survey.

Exact figures showing the social composition of the party have never been published. According to information which has become known about the composition of the higher echelons of the party (central committee, district secretaries of the party, etc.), it appears that lawyers are the leading group in the party to a degree which beats even the record of their colleagues in the parliaments and ministries of the French Third Republic (50–70 per cent.; this includes, of course, former lawyers and law students, who are now full-time party workers). After them come physicians, teachers, engineers, and merchants—the upper middle class being rather more strongly represented in the party leadership than in the lower echelons. At the same time, both the Syrian and the Lebanese parties have made a point of including at least one, if not two or three, workers or former workers in their leading institutions.

Notwithstanding the relative strength of Communism in Syria and Lebanon, a bid for power in the immediate future appears unlikely unless the general line of the Cominform should change. It is far more likely that the parties will attempt to consolidate their gains, gradually emerging as the strongest single political force in both countries, and effectively paralysing any attempt to establish a stable government. Short of a general world conflict, two situations can be imagined which would make Communist victory a possibility in the near future: one would be an unsuccessful war against Israel; the other, a complete disintegration of state power and a gradual transition to a condition of anarchy on the Mossadeq pattern.

PART SIX

IRAQ

Chapter Thirteen

Iraq before World War II

I. A GENERAL SURVEY

A BRITISH observer who visited Baghdad recently came to the
conclusion that the main reason for the lack of Communist success there was the fact that the Iraqi Communists were just as
inefficient as everyone else in Iraq. "Nevertheless, it seems likely that
the demand will ultimately create supply—and demand there certainly
is in every part of Iraq."[1] Iraq is *the* country of contrasts. It has five
times as much arable land as Egypt with only a quarter of Egypt's
population, and an abundant water supply from the two big rivers—
but the Iraqi peasant is as wretched as any in Asia. The polarization of
Iraqi land tenure is the highest in the Middle East, and perhaps the
highest in the world: 88 per cent. of the peasants own no more than
6·5 per cent. of the land, while the rest of the land is in the hands of the
state and about one thousand shaikhs—the very shaikhs who are the
pillars of society in Iraq and who control the parliament and the government. Iraq has a sizeable income from its oil production, but this has not
improved the lot of the vast majority of the people. Iraq is the most
nationalistic Arab country, and the one least tolerant of minorities; yet
it has more internal dissension than any other Arab country: the
Assyrians have been exterminated, most Jews chose to leave the country,
and the Iraqi army is fully occupied with keeping the Kurds in check;
the antagonism between the Sunni and Shi'i Moslems bedevils Iraqi
domestic policy. Nowhere else is the Communist Party so drastically
suppressed by police measures, and nowhere else in the Middle East has
it acquired more sympathizers. If the present reactionary regime
should collapse one day, the revolution will be more violent than anywhere else. Popular discontent is more intense in Iraq than in any other
Middle Eastern country.

In 1914 Iraq was a backward, out-of-the-way country even by

173

Turkish standards; service in Baghdad was dreaded by Turkish officials.[2]

"The level of enlightenment was low by any standards, gross superstition was rife, women were treated as inferior beings. Security was uncertain even in the towns, thanks to unpunished crime and the survival of bullying fanaticism, directed in bad times at the minorities. Malnutrition was the lot of four-fifths of the population. The infant mortality rate was among the highest in the world. Dominating all, lay the pervasive curse of poverty, removable only by fundamental changes in the whole territory's economy. Iraq in 1900 was a society of blighting shabbiness, low standards, and all the vices of the hungry and unsatisfied."

And then came World War I—and in its aftermath the British. They had some difficulty in imposing their rule, and Gertrude Bell wrote that making kings was more difficult work than she had believed. In 1920 both cities and tribes revolted against the new administration, and the suppression of this first demonstration of Iraqi nationalism took several months.[3] In the early 1920's the situation calmed down, although there was perennial strife in the tribal areas, and the delineation of the border in the Mosul area was to be, for many years to come, a matter of discord between Iraq and her neighbours. The British administrators were more efficient (and more paternal) than the Turks, who had cared little for the development of Iraq. The British built bridges and irrigation projects, fought the locusts, laid out railways and desert roads, and established a small army. In view of the small number of British officials on the spot, the yearly reports of the Mandatory government to the League of Nations were impressive documents. The Mandatory government had to find local supporters to maintain order, and it found them among the tribal *shaikhs*. One writer notes, "that they were in fact obliged to rely on the power of the landlords and shaikhs to a greater extent than the Ottoman government did."[4] Nevertheless, five-sixths of the cultivated land was state domain or collective tribal property when the British left in the early 1930's, and the distribution of the land among the shaikhs by the central government began in earnest after the country had attained independence.

The demand for full independence, *al istiqlāl al tām*, became more and more vociferous during the late 1920's. In 1930 the British, on the one hand, and the Iraqi king and government, on the other, agreed to abrogate the Mandate, and in 1932 Iraq became an independent state and a member of the League of Nations.

The country had made some progress since 1918, but even a friendly historian came to the conclusion that the Iraqi masses were not yet in any full sense citizens of the country—minorities and sects apart.

"The press was ill informed, irresponsible, rabidly partisan, crudely xenophobe. The demonstrations were organized easily and cheaply at any politicians' direction. The parties were mere cliques of personalities, without continuity and breadth of organization. Freedom of speech was allowed to extreme, rarely to moderate, views; violence or boycott awaited the exponent of any policy, however wise or sincere, if it seemed to fail in nationalist fervour. It was indeed doubtful whether one educated Iraqi in a hundred conceived society on truly democratic lines, or, given power, would have wished to organize it. Their nature was individualist and insubordinate; their tradition authoritarian, and the conditions in their society inimical to democracy."[5]

An Iraqi observer considers one of the main causes of the hopeless impotence of the moderate and liberal groups to be the absence of an important middle class. "This conservative policy of the Western powers has proved to be disastrous both to their gospel of democracy and to the stability of the newly created regimes in the Arab world."[6] The "new ideology which has captured the imagination of the masses, since it promises a brighter future, is Communism. It is true that these people have not grasped even the most elementary principles of these doctrines, but they have been assured by Communist propaganda that, in Marx's words, 'they have nothing to lose but their chains'."[7]

The complicated story of Iraqi policy after 1932 will be found in the history books. There were frequent changes of government—every six or seven months; but effective power always remained in the hands of a small clique of professional politicians representing the big landowners. They did everything they could to preserve the *status quo*, and with it the vested interests of the small ruling class; they did nothing, or next to nothing, to improve the miserable lot of the population. If tension increased, the only way they knew to let steam off was to incite the population against the minorities or "outside enemies": Britain and the Jews, Nejd and Persia, Christians and Kurds. The ministers and prime ministers of the 1920's and their supporters (such as Tawfīq as-Su'aidi, Jamīl Midfa'i and, above all, Nūri as-Sa'īd) have held power, with two or three short interruptions, for a whole generation; elections and parliamentary institutions have been a mere façade for their rule.

There were occasional demonstrations and local insurrections (some of them fairly widespread) against the government, such as the political strike of July, 1931, and the uprising in the middle Euphrates region in 1935, which caused some slight embarrassment to the rulers, but these were suppressed without much difficulty. (They were, incidentally, described by Communist sources as achievements of the party and its supporters, which was quite untrue.[8])

The first serious blow to the ruling group was the *coup d'état* of General Bakr Sidqi in 1936, which brought a different set of politicians to power for the first time. This reformist government (headed by Hikmat Sulaimān), though lasting for less than a year, played a very important role in the history of the spread of Socialist and Communist ideas in Iraq. The government of the *coup* was originally a coalition between army officers dissatisfied with corruption and incompetence in high places, politicians who had been offended by the government or had been left out of the cabinet, and a group of left-of-centre and liberal young intellectuals. The left-wing elements were dropped by General Bakr Sidqi and Hikmat Sulaimān without much ado as a result of right-wing pressure, and by the time the government fell (following Sidqi's assassination), little had remained of the original reformist zeal. Between 1937 and 1941 there were half a dozen more *coups d'état* without, however, any leftist or reformist colouring, culminating in the pro-Nazi uprising of Rashīd 'Ali in April, 1941. Generally speaking, Nazism and Fascism had made a strong impression and had gained many sympathizers in Iraq during the second half of the 1930's. This is mainly true of the army officer corps, but many high officials and politicians also visited Germany and Italy, and on their return helped to organize youth organizations on the pattern of the Hitler Youth and Fascist Balilla. Nūri Sa'īd, however, the main pillar of British influence in Iraq, did not desert his protectors in the critical weeks of 1941, and after the defeat of Rashīd 'Ali he again headed the Iraqi government for most of the (for Iraq) uneventful period of World War II.

2. THE FOUNDING OF IRAQI COMMUNISM

Historians will probably continue to argue about whether the Communist Party of Iraq was founded in 1932 or 1934,[9] but there is no basic disagreement about the fact that prior to 1936 the party had no influence whatsoever. There had been a "Marxist circle" in Nasireya (a city on the Euphrates nearer to Basra than to Baghdad) in the early 1930's, which decided in 1932 to form a political organization, which in its turn held a conference in Baghdad in 1934, transforming itself into the "Communist Party of Iraq." "This," says a Communist source, "was a turning-point in our national movement; the working class created its political party based on the idea of Marxism-Leninism. It led a vast demonstration under the slogan of 'Bread for the Hungry'."[10] Actually, there was no special reason for optimism. The new party had not been created by the working class, and even Marxist-Leninist ideology proved to be weaker than the personal antagonisms existing among the leading members of the group. Several weeks after the 1934 conference the "party" split into several diminutive factions, to be reunited, for a short period only, in 1940. Writing at a later date on the history of the party during that time, "Fahd," the first secretary of the party, said that the party was weak as a result of police persecutions and arrests, as well as from "weak leadership and the infiltration of destructive Trotskyite elements."[11] A weak leadership, unable to bring about the merger of the several dozen party members into one united group, was most probably the main reason for failure.

The ideological bone of contention between the small Communist factions was whether they should collaborate with the other left-wing liberal groups (called "Mensheviki" in the Communist press), which had come into being during the early 1930's and took a prominent part in the first stage of the Hikmat Sulaimān government. The "Ahāli" association, a group of young intellectuals (most of whom had just finished their studies either at Baghdad Law College, or in England or the United States), first made their views public in the winter of 1931–32. They proposed sweeping social reforms, but hoped to carry out their plans by parliamentary methods, without having to resort to violent revolution. They did not call for a class struggle, and recognized the value of the institutions of the family and of religion; they supported patriotism against nationalism, "the history of which was full of bloody tyranny and hypocrisy."[12]

The leading members of this association, who in turn established the "Baghdad group," a cultural centre, in 1934, were 'Abd al Fattāh Ibrahīm and Muhammad Hadīd, both of whom belonged to leading Iraqi families, and who had joined Socialist circles while studying abroad. They were joined by Kāmil al Jadarji and Ja'far Abu Timān, two somewhat older lawyers with liberal sympathies, who had a similar social background. There were differences of opinion between them as to whether or not a political party should be established; originally they had hesitated, and saw their main task as general cultural work among the intelligentsia (within the framework of the "Baghdad club," for example), or with the association to combat illiteracy. But in 1934–35 the group gradually became more radical and was joined by some Communists such as 'Abd al Qādir Isma'īl. It also established contacts with some of the older politicians who favoured reforms, such as Hikmat Sulaimān, who had been much impressed by the work of Kemal Ataturk in neighbouring Turkey. Hikmat Sulaimān, in his turn, contacted high army officers, more specifically Bakr Sidqi, the most outstanding of them. By the end of October, 1936, full agreement had been reached between the conspirators; the army revolted and entered Baghdad, the government was overthrown, and the first coalition supported by the liberal and left-of-centre forces in Iraq was installed.

This coalition had a heterogeneous character; few, if any, of its promises were carried out. The reformist elements were attacked as "Communists" by the right wing; such charges, when made by the representatives of the feudal clique in Iraq, mean no more than the accusation of "Trotskyism" when made by Communists; it is the stigmatic label pinned on all political enemies. This kind of propaganda has had the effect of making Communism popular, since, in the mind of the less sophisticated, Communism became synonymous with any attempt at social change. Bakr Sidqi and his prime minister, Hikmat Sulaimān, gave in to this pressure; the members of Ahāli had to resign from the cabinet in June, 1937, after the right wing had prevailed, and one of them, 'Abdul Qādir Isma'īl, was deported from Iraq, although he had been elected deputy to the parliament.[13]

The government of the *coup d'état* did not last much longer, and it was replaced by other army groups, which were supported by nationalist extremists and the feudal forces in the country. The reformists had to withdraw from politics until 1943–44, when political parties were again legalized. Kāmil Jadarji then founded the National Democratic Party, and became its president, with Muhammad Hadīd as his deputy (and later as its representative in Britain). 'Abd al Fattāh Ibrahīm, on the other hand, who had been the first to support the idea of a political Party in 1934, and who had left Ahāli in 1935 because it was not radical enough for him, reached an understanding with the Communists and founded the National Union Party, a Communist-front organization. The National Democrats occasionally collaborated with the Communists, and were undoubtedly infiltrated by them, but they did not consciously serve as a front organization.

The Communist movement was still very weak at the time of the 1936 *coup*. Its leaders, such as the lawyers Sharīf ash-Shaikh and Zakki Khairi, first opposed the new government, and not until the Comintern had given the green light (in January–February, 1937) did they come out in support of it. In Moscow there was much enthusiasm for this perfect Popular Front and National Liberation movement which had come to power in Baghdad: the support of all the progressive forces in Europe was promised, and exaggerated hopes were entertained.[14] Disillusionment was therefore all the stronger when the left-wing elements were sent packing, and some cynicism is now felt towards the reformist coalition of 1936–37.[15]

There was no modern industry in Iraq in the 1930's, apart from that of the oil-fields, which were then in their initial stage of development. Even in 1953 there were only 45,000 workers engaged in industrial undertakings of all types (and of these about 12,000 were in the oil industry). Out of these only 2000 were employed in modern industrial plants, while the vast majority were employed in small workshops. A few medieval guilds existed in Baghdad in the 1920's, but the first modern trade unions were organized only in 1928–29. First among these was the "society of artisans and factory workers" in 1928. In 1929 followed the Iraq Press Workers' Association, the Greengrocers' Association, the Taxi Drivers' Association, the National Club of Mechanical Engineers, the Barbers' Co-operative Association, and the Association of Artisans.[16] These unions were, however, closed by government order in 1931 because they had allegedly been active in politics. This was a highly unlikely charge, but it enabled the authorities to prevent any trade-union activities on a country-wide scale for more than ten years; only in 1943–44 was there a new beginning in that field. The

Communists were active to a limited extent among the Basra port workers, the tobacco workers of Baghdad, the workers in the oil-fields of Kirkuk, and the railway employees, but they did not succeed in getting a firm foothold anywhere at that time. They were even less successful among the peasants. We may assume that the peasants simply did not understand the complicated and dogmatic teachings of the agitators from the cities, who had not yet learned to reduce their agrarian programme to a few important, urgent, and generally intelligible demands.

Workers and peasants surely had every reason to revolt against the prevailing state of affairs, but they were potentially, rather than actually revolutionary classes. Their complaints were not conscious, except, perhaps, occasionally in their most immediate demands; they had not even developed a "trade-union conscience" (to use Lenin's phrase); and the Iraqi Communists, being divided among themselves, were not exactly the people to succeed under these difficult conditions. They were looking in vain for signs of a class struggle. But there were manifest conflicts to be found elsewhere. There was the conflict between the intelligentsia (and middle class in general) and the feudal landowners, the conflict between the nationalists and the British, and the conflict between the government and the national minorities, who were discriminated against and persecuted.

The Iraqi Communist Party was from the very beginning a students' party; when "Fahd" reconstituted the party in the early 1940's he once again relied on students, above all. "He thought that these students, the educated class in the country, would hold, in the future, key positions in the government, and through them the Communist Party would be able to achieve its aims. Most of the students were young, single, did not have to support families; full of nationalist fervour, they joined the party and spread its teaching among the workers without any difficulty."[17] There was an additional advantage in these conditions of illegality: many of the students came from leading families and, if arrested, could get off far more easily than, say, workers or low-ranking government employees. But among the intelligentsia and especially among the students, the pan-Arab nationalist and fascist organizations, such as the Futuwwa (led by Sāmi Shawkāt, who tried to import Mussolini's gospel of "living dangerously"), were far more successful during the 1930's. The Communists could never hope to gain the support of more than a small minority of the intelligentsia, so long as Nazi Germany and Fascist Italy seemed to be holding all the stakes in the future. Only after the post-1943 military defeats of the Axis was the majority of the intelligentsia ready to listen to the new ideas which had been preached until then by a few indefatigable voices.

There remained the minorities, and here, indeed, the party would have found a fertile field for its work. But there was no united party;

there were only small groups bitterly denouncing each other—so how could the Kurds and Assyrians, Jews and Armenians, suffering doubly from injustice and discrimination, possibly know which of the splinter groups was the true representative of the "great international camp of progress, peace, and socialism"?

The Communist movement, then, was extremely weak in Iraq during the late 1930's. Here and there discussion groups existed, but no party organization, no regular newspapers or magazines (apart from a few occasional typewritten proclamations). The Iraqi Communists had to work in more difficult conditions than their comrades in Syria and Lebanon; Communism had been outlawed in Iraq in 1938, although it had not been legal before that time. But unfavourable outward conditions could not explain the failure of the movement in Iraq. The early Iraqi Communists were all great ideologists, but there was no one with even a minimum knowledge of Communist organization and tactics. Only when "Fahd" returned to Iraq in 1939 did the movement get a leader who (though far from being a first-class organizer), possessed at least some knowledge and training in these fields. This does not mean that the return of "Fahd" was the big turning-point in the fortunes of the party; only after the suppression of the Rashīd 'Ali revolt and the first major defeats of the Axis did the conditions for successful Communist activities come into being.[18]

Chapter Fourteen

Iraq, 1939–49

I. IRAQ, 1939–47

WHEN World War II broke out in 1939 the Iraqi government severed diplomatic relations with Nazi Germany. This decision was not very enthusiastically received by wide sections of the public; it was certainly not supported by the officer corps. The pro-Western government of Nūri as-Sa'īd was compelled to resign early in 1940. One of its outstanding members, Rustum Haidar, the Minister of Finance, was assassinated. Anti-British feeling increased as a result of the Axis victories in Europe, and the Rashīd 'Ali government, which took over in July, 1940, became increasingly hostile to the Allied cause. Rashīd 'Ali himself, who had served in many previous cabinets, was not a Nazi, but he came to believe that Gemany and Italy were going to win the war, and that a pro-Axis orientation was, therefore, the obvious foreign policy for his country and dictated by national self-interest. Behind him, however, were the "four colonels" who, with short interruptions, had been ruling Iraq from behind the scenes since 1937, and there was no doubt about their ideological sympathies. On April 2, 1941, Rashīd 'Ali engineered a successful *coup* against the Taha Hāshimi government that had replaced his own only eight weeks earlier. The British attitude to Rashīd 'Ali was indicated by London's refusal to recognize the new regime. On April 29, Rashīd 'Ali (or rather the four colonels behind him) gave the army orders to oust the British from the air base at Habaniya, and a thirty days' war began, which ended with the defeat of the pro-Axis government and success for the British. Rashīd 'Ali had been in close contact with the Axis powers and received some help from them, but this assistance was insufficient. The pro-Axis revolt was apparently considered premature in both Berlin and Rome.

The attitude of the Iraqi Communists towards the Rashīd 'Ali *coup* was, on the whole, friendly. They had little sympathy for the fascist views of the colonels, but the decisive criterion was, at that time (as at so many important junctures of recent Middle Eastern history) the international question and not the domestic one. And from that point of view there were, indeed, many points of contact between the Communists and the "great national movement" (as it came to be called). Rashīd 'Ali opposed the British and wanted to expel them from their bases in the country; these were also the aims of the Communists. The Iraqi Communist stand reflected the Soviet attitude. Nowadays it is argued that the Soviet Union opposed the "fascist *coup*" of April, 1941.[1] But this was not what Moscow thought at that time, and, in any case, it did not prevent the Soviet Union from being the only country in the world to recognize the new regime. Tass, the Soviet news agency, published a statement in which it was reported that the Iraqi government had suggested establishing diplomatic relations with the U.S.S.R. at the end of 1940, but had proposed that the Soviet Union publish a declaration recognizing the independence of all the Arab countries. The Soviet government (it was then stated) did not think that it could make the establishment of diplomatic relations dependent on such a condition. On May 3 (four weeks after the Rashīd 'Ali *coup*) the Iraqi government proposed the unconditional establishment of relations, and this was accepted by the Soviet Union.[2] Non-Soviet historians of Russian foreign policy seem to agree that Russia's haste in recognizing the Rashīd 'Ali regime (when even formal recognition by the Axis powers was not granted!) can only be interpreted as a friendly gesture to Germany, although a long-term desire to curry favour with Arab nationalism may have played some part.[3]

The Iraqi Communists are in a more favourable position when they set about rewriting their history than many of their sister parties. They had no central party organ at that time, nor was there any central party organization. Whatever collaboration there was between them and the Rashīd 'Ali government (and they refuse to admit anything) was "unauthorized" and could not bind the party—for a party did not then exist. Elsewhere we have quoted the writings of a prominent Lebanese Communist, Ra'īf al Khūri (as well as leaflets of the Palestine Communist Party), who first came out against Rashīd 'Ali but later reversed their position. In Baghdad at that time there were a number of Communists who had already played, or were soon to play, an important role in this chapter of the movement's history. Among them Fuād Nāsir (who was later to become first party secretary in Jordan) and Nimr 'Uda[4] belonged to the entourage of the ex-Mufti of Jerusalem, who had been in the Iraqi capital since October, 1939, and who, under Rashīd 'Ali, was given a free hand in his anti-Allied propaganda. In a broadcast on May 9 he declared a holy war (Jihād) against Britain and asked all Moslems to participate in the struggle against the "greatest enemy of Islam."[5] Several leading Communists, among them George Mansūr (apparently the pseudonym of another refugee from Palestine), worked in Rashīd 'Ali's department of propaganda, which was headed by the well-known Iraqi fascist leader Sādiq Shinshil, who ten years later again collaborated with the Communists as one of the heads of the Istiqlāl Party; the historian of independent Iraq notes the active support given by the Communists to the Rashīd 'Ali regime, but adds that after the rout of the pro-fascist regime and Hitler's attack on Russia the Communists offered their co-operation to the British ambassador.[6] In conclusion, it must be said that the Iraqi Communists very wisely postponed the publication of their first official organ until after the Rashīd 'Ali revolt; the postponement subsequently saved them from serious inconvenience.[7]

Yūsuf Salmān Yūsuf (called "Fahd," the leopard), who returned in 1939 after a prolonged stay in Europe, was expected to set the Iraqi Communist Party on its feet. A native of Nasireya and a Christian, he was the only prominent Iraqi Communist leader with a proletarian background, and was, to boot, a self-made man.[8] "Fahd" remained something of a mystery man, and he certainly did nothing to dispel the wild and exaggerated notions about his movements outside Iraq and his contacts inside. According to the official version, he went to Paris in 1934 and later to Belgium. Subsequently he spent two years in the Soviet Union, married there, and was "trained by Dimitrov himself." But Malik Saif, the chief witness in the anti-Communist trial of 1947, and himself a member of the party's Central Committee, added that he was not too sure whether "Fahd" had ever been in the Soviet Union.[9]

However that may be, "Fahd" was the appointee of the Comintern for party leadership, and on his return he tried to found a Baghdad local committee as a first step towards the establishment of a party. But he encountered serious obstacles at the very beginning. Though political parties were still forbidden in the country, and Communist activities were theoretically punishable by penal servitude or death, the party became semi-legal after Hitler's attack on Russia, and all Communists were released from prison. However, outside of a small circle of intellectuals there was general indifference to party propaganda. Worse still, the party was beset by splits and unremitting internal dissension, and although the Syrian Communists did their very best to mediate between the various groups, they were unsuccessful.

"Fahd's" relations with the old-time Communist leaders, such as Zakki al Khairi and Sharīf ash-Shaikh, soon became strained. There was personal rivalry and there were differences of opinion on party tactics, mainly on the popular-front issue, which remained the main bone of contention in both Iraq and Egypt. In Egypt, however, the principal Communist group stood for a wide national front; the smaller factions opposed this "opportunist deviation." In Iraq, on the other hand, the

"Fahd" group stood for Simon-pure orthodoxy and doubted the wisdom of closer collaboration with non-Communists. The smaller Iraqi factions split away from "Fahd" because they wanted more attention paid to "front" organizations. "Fahd" allegedly went to Russia in 1945,[10] and notified his superiors there of the make-up of his Central Committee. Members were, apart from himself, Zakki Basīm, Husain Muhammad ash-Shabibi, Krikor Badrossian, 'Abid Tamir, Malik Saif, Mulla Sharīf, and Sāmi Nadir. All these were relative new-comers, and the old-timers, understandably offended, split away; the dispute became a matter of public knowledge when Sharīf ash-Shaikh and Zakki al Khairi[11] began to air their differences of opinion in semi-public leaflets and booklets. But this was by no means the only faction to secede. The Haqiqat (Truth) group, which published a magazine of the same name, charged "Fahd" with "infantile leftism" and dictatorial practices.[12] These charges referred, apparently, to the reluctance of "Fahd" to collaborate with other left-wing groups. However, to do him justice, "Fahd" revealed considerable elasticity in his magazine, *Ash-Sharara*. It would be difficult, for instance, to find any attack against the royal family in the party literature of the war years.

The chief split took place in 1942–43. The faction which later became the Iraqi Communist League (Ar-Rābita), under the leadership of 'Abdullah Mas'ūd, left "Fahd". Subsequently, Dahūd as-Sayigh became its most prominent exponent.[13] It had supporters among the students and in the army. The differences of opinion between these two groups cannot be explained merely as a matter of ideological quarrels; there was a bitter contest for the leadership of the movement, and personal antagonism played its part, too.

And yet, weak and internally split as the Iraqi Communist movement was, the whole political climate from 1943 onwards favoured its growth. The anti-Nazi alliance, victories on both the Eastern and Western fronts, and the decisive part played by the Soviet Union in this struggle, had aroused widespread pro-Soviet sympathies. Iraqi political life was paralysed at the same time, parties were not allowed to exist and, while elsewhere in the world blue-prints were being made for a better post-war world, Iraq seemed to be sinking farther into stagnation. In this atmosphere of ferment, bubbling up from below, there was a general trend towards the left; and, as successive governments had been telling the people for many years that "left," social and political reform, individual freedom, socialism, and communism were all synonymous, the various Communist and pro-Communist groups now cashed in on the situation.

In 1944 and 1945 the "Fahd" group convened its first Congresses and adopted a "National Charter," which will be treated in greater detail below. Establishing a mass political party now became a topical issue; it was not, in fact, the first attempt. Earlier in the war, in 1942,

"Fahd" and some of his associates had tried to found a Democratic Party; its programme had already been published in *Ash-Sharara*. But these projects apparently never got beyond the debating stage, and it was only in the spring of 1946, when the authorities again permitted the formation of political parties, that the Communist leaders came to think about the establishment of a legal front in addition to their illegal organization. The Communists' request to establish a National Liberation Party was rejected by the government of Tawfīq as-Su'aidi, but an Anti-Zionist League sponsored by the Communist Party was permitted to exist for some time. The Iraqi government later stated that it had intended at the time that the League should appear on behalf of the Jews of Iraq before the Anglo-American Inquiry Commission on Palestine. From the Communist point of view, anti-Zionist activity was not just a cover but a very urgent matter because of the strength of Zionist influence among Iraqi Jews. On the other hand, the party wanted to exploit this legal framework for Communist propaganda in general.[14]

The Communist movement was thus compelled to infiltrate the three left-wing parties which were founded in April, 1946. The one closest to them was the People's Party of 'Azīz Sharīf, a well-known Baghdad lawyer, who wrote a large number of pamphlets popularizing Communism. There were no major ideological differences between this group and the "Fahd" group, and the main stumbling-block for a full merger was, apparently, personal antagonism between 'Azīz Sharīf and "Fahd."[15] The People's Party merged during the second half of 1946 with another left-wing party, the National Unity Party, headed by 'Abd al Fattāh Ibrahīm, a member of the Ahāli in the early 1930's, who had left this group because it was not radical enough. Other prominent members of this group were Nazīm az-Zahāwi and Muhammad Mahdi al Jawahīri, a poet and the editor of a widely read weekly, *Ar-Ra'i al 'Am*, and subsequently the leader of the Iraqi Partisans of Peace.[16] When these parties merged (into the Popular Unity Party) it was decided that the new organization should adopt the political programme of the People's Party and the statutes of the National Unionists. *Al Watan* (The Fatherland) became the official organ of the party, but was suppressed, however, after a few months. The third leftist group in which the Communists revealed some interest was the largest of all, viz. Kāmil Jadarji's National Democratic Party, which continued the tradition of the Ahāli of the 1930's in a more radical vein. The leaders of this group were considered competitors rather than allies by the Communists, but there was a pro-Communist ("progressive") minority section in the party led by Kāmil Kasanji, another well-known Baghdad lawyer.

All these groups, as well as other discussion groups, newspapers, and magazines, all of them small, were organizations of the intelligentsia in Baghdad and a few provincial centres.[17] There were some stirrings in the trade-union field which could be observed among the tobacco workers in the capital, the port workers of Basra, and the workers in the oil-fields of Kirkuk. When the Baghdad tobacco workers' union decided to include some political demands of a progressive nature, the government insisted that the unions refrain from political activity.[18] Trade unions had been revived early in 1944, and among the stronger locals were to be found the Baghdad railway workers' (1500 workers), the tanners', and the woodworkers' unions (450 members each). At the time of the first convention of the W.F.T.U. in Paris in 1945, the existence of thirteen country-wide unions was reported, and early in 1947 a Communist source stated that 38,000 workers were organized in eighteen unions—all led by the Communist Party.[19] Labour conditions were extremely bad throughout the country. Wages were ridiculously low, in many cases there were no provisions for a yearly vacation, nor had the worker any claims to compensation in case of sickness or accident; workers frequently put in a twelve-hour or even longer day. Conditions were perhaps worst of all in Kirkuk, where unions had been banned altogether, and it was there in June, 1946, that the worst incident in the history of Iraqi labour relations took place. Police opened fire on a crowd of strikers; the number of dead was between five and sixteen (depending on the source), and there were about fifty wounded. The Communists were behind the Kirkuk strike, which was supported, nevertheless (and particularly after the bloodshed), by most other political parties—especially since a foreign company was involved. There were other big work stoppages in August and September, 1946. The railway workers went out on strike, and some days later the employees of the postal services struck when their union was dissolved. The printers struck in protest against the ban of twenty left-wing newspapers by the government; political sympathies and material interests went hand in hand for once.

The year 1946 was a stormy one in Iraq. The liberal government of Su'aidi, which had permitted the organization of the left-wing and pro-Communist factions, was replaced in June, 1946, by one led by Arshad al 'Umari, who had little sympathy for these groups. At the same time the Communists and pro-Communist groups intensified their activities, and there were mass demonstrations and clashes with the police which resulted in several fatalities.[20] 'Umari ordered the dissolution of the left-wing parties, the closing down of their newspapers, and the arrest of their leaders. Kāmil al Jadarji was given a one-year prison sentence and his newspaper was banned for one year, but the Court of Appeal quashed his sentence. 'Azīz Sharīf was also released. In another trial the leaders of the National Unity Party, Nazīm az-Zahāwi, 'Abdullah Mas'ūd, Sharīf ash-Shaikh (all three laywers by profession), and Mūsa ash-Shaikh Rādi (a Baghdad journalist) were accused of incitement in connection with the Baghdad and Kirkuk riots.[21] They, too, were released after a short period.

186

In November, 1946, the 'Umari government was replaced by a
coalition headed by Nūri as-Sa'īd, which in the beginning was believed
to be steering a more liberal course, and to be serving as an interim
government preparing elections. Muhammad Hadīd, Jadarji's lieuten-
ant, joined the new cabinet with this understanding, only to resign a
month later. The government of Nūri as-Sa'īd clamped down on the
Communists even before it came to power; Dahūd as-Sayigh, together with several members of the central committee of the group, had
been arrested. On January 18, 1947, a short while after the third Party
Congress, most of the members of the executive of the "Fahd" group
were surprised in session at the home of Ibrahīm Najīb Shumail, and
were arrested on the spot.

2. IRAQI COMMUNISM, 1947-48

Let us pause here for a moment to survey the internal state of the
Iraqi Communist movement in 1947-48. The National Charter of the
Iraqi Communist Party had been adopted by the party's Congress in
1945; it served as its political programme and platform for eight years.
"Fahd," who had apparently prepared it on his own, said in his ex-
planatory remarks that he had no experience in drafting programmes;
this, however, did not prevent him from producing a document
remarkably similar, even to the most minor details, *mirabile dictu*, to the
programmes of all the other Communist Parties in the world. We shall
therefore confine ourselves to those points which give the programme
its specifically Iraqi slant.

Chapter one of the programme was already somewhat outdated even
by the standards of 1945: "The Iraqi Communist Party is the party of
the working class. The Iraqi Communist Party was formed for the sake
of strengthening the working class." No mention is made of other
classes! "Fahd" goes on to say that the Iraqi working class faces a strong
enemy, to wit, international imperialism, and, in addition, pro-imperialist rulers at home who permit no parties, political organizations, meetings, etc. "The working class faces Nazi laws." All this compels the
party to organize itself as an illegal group, a "secret, struggling party
with a strong, iron discipline." "It believes in self-criticism based on
democratic centralism which can be applied in a way not conflicting
with the nature of underground work." But in fact all the important
decisions in conditions of underground work would have to be taken
by the party politburo or central committee, while a party conference,
as "Fahd" pointed out, would be convened only in the case of important political changes.[22] On this issue some of the party members
requested further information; this desire for information was probably
prompted by the authoritarian character of "Fahd", which was well
known to his comrades; "Fahd" seldom, if ever, thought it necessary to

consult his colleagues. It can, of course, be argued that in the prevailing conditions of illegality there was no other way of leading the party, and that if "Fahd" made mistakes one may well doubt whether they would have been corrected by consulting with his comrades in the politburo, who were in most respects lesser men.

A special section in the National Charter deals with the relations between the Communists and other parties and organizations. No Communist is allowed to work in any information or propaganda department of a foreign country, or in the police, or to maintain any contact with the government or the ministries, without the knowledge of the party. No member is allowed to join any other party or group, political or unpolitical, without permission of the Communist Party, and he is not allowed to remain in another party if the Communist Party has told him to leave it. Every member must avoid contacts with police agents as well as with Trotskyites and representatives of foreign countries. A party member must not leave his town without previously informing the party.[23] These and similar particular stipulations, some of which are undoubtedly unique in their content and formulation, were a result of the complicated relations existing between the Communists and the left-wing parties in Iraq, as well as being due to the fact that the Communist movement was still split.

The National Charter also provided for the establishment of Communist groups of Armenian and Kurdish origin (and, in the future, of Turkmen and Assyrian origin as well); they would establish separate party units "due to the differences in language and geographical conditions, and with the aim of expanding the revolutionary movement among the Kurds and Armenians."[24] The list of signatories to the National Charter clearly indicates that the party was still far from united. It included the branches of the Iraqi Kurdish and Iraqi Armenian parties, the Baghdad local committee and its branches, the three local committees in the southern districts, the committees that belonged directly to the central committee, the local committees, and the organizations represented at the first party Conference (in 1945), etc.

"Fahd" did not want to neglect any possibility of putting the party on a legal footing, and conditions in 1945 appeared propitious. A group of Baghdad lawyers, members or sympathizers with the party, was contacted, and agreement was reached about the formation of a legal organization, the People's Party (Hizb ash-Sha'ab).[25] The programme of the new party when announced did not differ from the National Charter in any important aspect. Communists also collaborated with the new party in another venture, a publishing house by the name of "Renaissance Letters."[26] Soon, however, differences of opinion arose. 'Azīz Sharīf, the moving spirit of the new legal party, toured Syria and met Khālid Bakdāsh in Damascus. On his return to Baghdad he announced a new policy for the People's Party, and proposed that the

Communist Party should give up its illegal status altogether and become a legal group within the framework of the new party. This caused a split in the ranks of the People's Party after "Fahd" had strongly criticized 'Azīz Sharīf's proposal in the party newspaper, *Al Qā'ida*. The People's Party was banned by the Iraqi government later, in 1946, and afterwards most of its members joined the Communist Party. As a result, "Fahd" was compelled to look for allies elsewhere, and that was why the National Liberation Party was established by the Communists.[27] Most rank-and-file Communists were asked to join this group, which became a clearing-house for the underground party; every active member of the National Liberation Party was asked to join the illegal party, too. The Communist leadership tried among other things to use the new framework for its activity in the rural regions (without much success), and for the organization of student committees, and of trade unions at the Baghdad post and telegraph office and the railway workshops and offices.

During all this time the Communist movement in Iraq continued to be internally divided, and although the "Fahd" faction was probably the largest section, its claims for supremacy were widely contested. The merger of most groups took place only in 1947, when "Fahd" was already under arrest; it appears likely that his absence expedited the merger. Among those groups which now united in an Iraqi Communist Party were, apart from "Fahd's" section, the majority of the People's Party, the "progressive" (Kasanji) faction of the National Democratic Party, as well as the National Revolutionary Committee. (This was a group headed by Zakki al Khairi and Sharīf ash-Shaikh which had split as the Haqiqat party from "Fahd's" section in the early 1940's.) It is not known for certain whether Dahūd as-Sayigh's group also joined; most of its leading members were at that time in prison. An attempt to mediate between "Fahd" and Dahūd as-Sayigh, which was undertaken by the leadership of the Syrian party, had failed only a few months before. The Kurdish section, which had split away in 1945, also reached a *modus vivendi* with the Iraqi party leadership in 1947, and almost complete unity was thus restored in the Communist camp.

There is no evidence for very active Soviet intervention in Iraqi party affairs at that period. "Fahd" was the man backed by Moscow, perhaps because he was the only one known there; probably he was the most capable leader of those available. But it may be assumed that Moscow was dismayed by the lack of unity and by "Fahd's" inability to bring about a merger. What material assistance the Iraqi Communists received was handled by the Armenian faction of the party; the agent for the distribution of Russian films in Iraq was apparently the contact man of the Embassy. Relations with the Syrian party were rather close up to 1947, the leaders of the two parties met frequently, and Iraqi Communists, who believed themselves persecuted by the police, often went to Syria for a few months. There were no relations whatsoever with the Egyptian movement; ties with Tudeh (the Persian Communists) were not as strong as might be assumed in view of their geographical proximity. Language difficulties were probably the main reason for the lack of permanent close contact.

Of the national branches of the party, three deserve mention. The differences of opinion which arose between the Kurdish faction and "Fahd" have been described in detail.[28] The leaders of this group were Khamza 'Abdullah, Dr. Ja'afar Muhammad Karīm, Sālih Rushdi, Rashīd 'Abdul Qādir, 'Awni Yūsuf, Ra'ūf Yūnis, Ibrahīm Ahmad—all of them lawyers. The differences between them and the "Fahd" group were settled in 1947. The Armenian section did not cause the party so many headaches. It numbered only a few dozen members,[29] and was headed by Krikor Badrossian, a member of the party's central committee. A musician by profession, he had arrived in Baghdad from Lebanon in 1937 and settled in the Iraqi capital. The Armenian section published two magazines, *Hamek* (The Basis) and *Banki Flakh*.

The Anti-Zionist League was founded by a group of Jewish party members[30] in 1945. Its aims, as defined in its paper (*Al 'Usba*, The League), were "to explain to the population the difference between a Jew and a Zionist and to work for the lessening of communal hatred." Its unofficial aims were to use this legal front for spreading Communist propaganda in general. All Jewish party members had to join the League; those who did not were charged with Zionist leanings. It is interesting to note that though there was always a Jew or two on the Central Committee of the party, the contact man of the League on this body was a non-Jew, Zakki Basīm. The League was banned by the Iraqi government in July, 1946.

As a result of the fact that most of the leading members of the Iraqi Communist movement and the majority of the militants were arrested and brought to trial in 1947-49, details have become known of the national and social composition of both the leading party organs and the rank and file. In 1946-47 about half of the members of the party's leading organs and much more than half of the militants belonged to ethnic and religious minorities. Since then the national breakdown of the party has changed. All but a few Jews have left Iraq, and there are now relatively far fewer Kurdish party members.

The predominant role of lawyers in the Iraqi Communist movement has already been mentioned; the list is too long to be quoted again. Among the members of the "Fahd" group's executive there was in 1946, however, a majority of teachers, among them Yehuda Ibrahīm Sādiq, Yasīn Hamūdi, and Malik Saif. "Fahd" himself and his brother Dahūd Salmān Yūsuf, an electrician, appear to have been the only members of the party leadership ever to have done physical work. After the arrest of the Central Committee, leadership passed for some time into the hands of Sason Shlomo Dalāl, a Jewish student, twenty-four years old at the time of his arrest in 1949. In subsequent trials about 40 per cent. of the defendants came from upper or middle-class families and the same proportion from lower middle-class homes.

3. THE HANGINGS OF FEBRUARY, 1949

The trial of the leading members of the Iraqi Communist Party, arrested in January, 1947, began in March of that year in a Baghdad magistrate's court, but the case was soon transferred to the Iraqi High Court. All of the accused gave evidence, but the most helpful prosecution witness was undoubtedly Malik Saif, a member of the party executive (and formerly a Moslem religious teacher), who has subsequently been charged by the party with having been a police spy all along. There can be no doubt that there were indeed police agents in the party leadership, but the case of Malik Saif appears to be somewhat more complicated. While under arrest, he wrote a letter to the director of the prison which recalls certain phenomena which we associate with political trials behind the Iron Curtain.[31] However that may be, the case against the Communist leadership was not based mainly on Malik Saif—it filled several lengthy volumes even without his testimony. One of the charges against them was Zionism. This point requires some elucidation, because the Zionist issue has, since then, come up frequently in the trials of Communists in the Middle East, and most recently in the trials of Egyptian Communists. The Iraqi Communists were among the staunchest opponents of Zionism and of the very idea of a Jewish state—up to the end of 1947. They had to adjust their line after the Gromyko and Zarapkin declarations (in the summer and autumn of 1947), which proclaimed Soviet support for a Jewish (and Arab) state in Palestine.[32] They never supported Zionism in so many words, but merely demanded that the U.N. resolution of November 29, 1947, should be implemented. In 1949, with the new "anti-cosmopolitan" switch in Soviet policy, Iraqi Communist propaganda again took on a distinctly anti-Israeli slant. The "Zionist" charge against the Communists was used by the Iraqi authorities in the hope of discrediting the Communists, and thus of marshalling public opinion against them. But this stratagem did not prove very successful, for the simple reason that Communist propaganda was quite clear and emphatic on its attitude to Palestine and Israel—and this attitude was very different indeed from what the authorities alleged it to be. The Communists were no less anti-Zionist in their own way than Nūri as-Sa'īd and his friends were in theirs.

The trial was quite eventful. Kāmil Kasanji, attorney for one of the principal defendants (and a leading "fellow-traveller" himself), was arrested on a charge of spreading Communist propaganda after he had concluded an impassioned plea for the defence; six other lawyers withdrew from the trial in protest. The sentences were pronounced in June, 1947. "Fahd" and two of his lieutenants were given the death penalty, sixteen others prison sentences of varying length, and seventeen defendants were acquitted. On June 26, Dahūd as-Sayigh and 'Abdul Amīr 'Abbās of the rival faction were sentenced to life imprisonment. There were many protests in the Arab countries and in Europe, especially against the death penalties—three weeks later the death sentences were commuted to life imprisonment.

Meanwhile "Fahd" continued to manage party affairs from within the prison walls. There was some rivalry between Yehuda Sādiq and Malik Saif, the two members of the Central Committee who had succeeded in evading arrest. "Fahd's" contact man with the party was Yehuda Sādiq, who had, however, to go underground outside of Baghdad, while Malik Saif was responsible for party affairs in the Iraqi capital. Malik Saif resented the fact that he was receiving his instructions at second-hand, and when "Fahd" later established contact with him, Sādiq, in his turn, was offended; there were personal explanations and counter-explanations, and in the end both Sādiq and Saif were arrested. Among those arrested with "Fahd" early in 1947 had been Sason Shlomo Dalāl, who was sentenced to one year in prison, and released in 1948. After his release from prison, Dalāl came to head the new ("third") Central Committee, which published a new party magazine and a few leaflets. This Central Committee lasted for about three months. A party member carrying leaflets from Baghdad to Basra was caught by the police, and this led to the arrest of the whole "third Central Committee," to a new trial, and eventually to the hanging of Shlomo Dalāl in June, 1949.

Meanwhile, "Fahd", ash-Shabibi, Zakki Muhammad Basīm, and Yehuda Ibrahīm Sādiq had been sentenced to death after a second trial, and the sentences were carried out in February, 1949. The new trial had taken place before a military court, and the public was far less interested in the case than it had been the previous year. The main charge against the accused this time was that they had continued to lead the party from prison and had thus been directly responsible for the revolt of January, 1948, when the Sālih Jābr government (which had just signed the Portsmouth Treaty with Britain) was overthrown.

This treaty had been intended to supersede the British-Iraqi Treaty of 1930, and it was an expression (in the words of the Iraqi Prime Minister) of the wish to live as free and equal allies and friends. This was not, however, what the other Iraqi politicians thought. They resented the fact that they had not been consulted, and also resented the establishment of a joint Iraqi-British defence board. Demonstrations against the government started on January 3, even before the text of the treaty had been made public. On January 16 the students went on strike; demonstrations continued throughout the week. There was a clash with the police on January 20 in which four demonstrators and seven policemen were killed. The main riots took place on January 27, when about thirty people (among them fifteen students) were killed, and about 300 wounded. On the same evening Sālih Jābr, the Prime Minister, handed in his resignation. The new government of Muhammad as-Sadr was more acceptable to the left (the Portsmouth Treaty was not confirmed); though Kāmil al Jadarji expressed his appreciation to the new prime minister, he did not join the government. The country slowly calmed down, though a major railway strike in March paralysed communications, and the Baghdad students, who supported the railwaymen, went out on a sympathy strike.

Both the Iraqi government and the Iraqi Communist Party seem to agree that the Communists played a leading part in the January, 1948, riots. Official party history now says that "in 1948 it headed the great national uprising of the people which abolished the treaty of Portsmouth and forced Sālih Jābr to resign."[33] Elsewhere we are told that a Co-operation Committee had been established on the eve of the uprising on the initiative of the Communist Party, and of the National Liberal Party, the Democratic Kurdish Party, the People's Party, the Zakki al Khairi=Sharīf ash-Shaikh faction, as well as the group of Kāmil Kasanji, took part in this organization."[34] The Iraqi government tends to accept this version and maintains that Kasanji was the head of the Co-operation Committee. The slogans given out by the committee were: "Cheaper bread and clothes!" "The Portsmouth Treaty must not be signed!" "For democracy, freedom, and liberty!" "Throw out the Sālih Jābr government!" "Dissolve Parliament!" "For new elections!"[35]

And yet, despite this remarkable unanimity, there is some reason to doubt whether the Communist Party was really the leading force in the January, 1948, uprisings. It would be more correct to see it as *one* of the factors which brought about the revolt. The extreme right-wing Istiqlāl Party was probably just as active as the Communists, and it was not, as yet, an ally of the Communists. In the riots which took place in such district centres as Arbil, Kerbela, and Nejef, the Communists had no influence at all. The main fact to be remembered is that the Sālih Jābr government, like all Iraqi governments, had no mass basis or support; there was widespread discontent for a great number of reasons, some of them economic, others relating to domestic and foreign policy, which all culminated in general opposition to the regime. This tension was bound sooner or later to lead to a major outbreak of violence. The Portsmouth Treaty was the immediate occasion, but it was certainly not the only reason for the explosion.

We have brought the story up to February, 1949, when the Communist leaders were hanged in Baghdad. The Communist movement in Iraq was now leaderless. But the official belief that it would be possible to stamp out Communism by mere repression proved to be mistaken; the ensuing lull in Communist activities lasted exactly one year. And then the party emerged once again, larger than ever. Now it had the additional advantage of being able to boast of martyrs who had given their lives in the struggle against an extremely reactionary regime that was bitterly hated by the great majority of the intelligentsia and by the politically conscious and active elements in the country generally. Up to 1948 the Communists in Iraq had had great difficulty in becoming a mass party and in being accepted as part of the national movement. After 1949 most of these obstacles had been removed—ironically enough by the very action of the government. The Baghdad government reported that everything was under control. Everything was indeed under control—on the surface. But below the surface Communism continued to make headway under conditions which were more difficult, perhaps, but which were in the long run more favourable to its success.

Chapter Fifteen

Iraq since 1949

---

1. COMMUNIST LEADERS IN PRISON

IN 1949, after the mass arrests and trials, the Communist Party was in full retreat. Most of its cadres were under arrest,[1] including all the members of the successive Central Committees. "Fahd" had established his first Central Committee in 1944, and had headed it up to his arrest early in 1947. Then came the second committee headed by Yehuda Sādiq and Malik Saif, and after their arrest the "third committee" led by Dalāl, who, in turn, was arrested in 1949. Between Dalāl's arrest and 1951 there were no fewer than four more Central Committees, most of them made up of men without experience and of little consequence. During 1949 *Al Qā'ida* appeared irregularly as a two-page sheet; only in 1950 was its regular publication resumed. Nor were the short-lived fourth, fifth, sixth, and seventh Central Committees successful in establishing a country-wide organization. The ties between the centre and the local branches continued to be extremely weak. After the arrest of the seventh Central Committee, Baha ud-Dīn Nūri came to head the eighth committee, which was more enterprising and successful than the preceding ones. But its members, too, were arrested by the authorities in a series of round-ups which started in May, 1953, and continued throughout the summer of that year.[2]

The party maintained its organization in prison and made of its stay there a virtual party seminary for the cadres, with daily courses in party history and ideology, with a library of its own, etc. The efforts of the authorities to break up the main group, which was concentrated in the Kut al Amara camp, were all in vain. Later attempts brought on a prisoners' hunger strike, resulting in the death of one Communist (Muhammad Sālih); and his death, in turn, provoked mass demonstrations in Baghdad in June, 1951. New attempts in June, 1953, to transfer part of the arrested Communists caused fresh riots, in the course of which seven of the prisoners were killed and twenty-three wounded. Again there were protest strikes (of the lawyers' association) and demonstrations in Baghdad, and the government was compelled to appoint an investigation commission. The situation got out of hand; the frequent clashes were not unlike those which took place at the same time in the North Korean P.O.W. camps in South Korea, where the Communists came to rule the camps and where each attempt to make any change or transfer resulted in riots and armed clashes. The number of those arrested and imprisoned varied from year to year. Many prisoners were released in 1951–52, but there were new arrests after the Baghdad revolt of November, 1952; the number of inmates of the prison camps had been over one thousand for most of the time since 1949. In November, 1953, a new amnesty was proclaimed, and at the same time a fairly large number of Communists declared their readiness to give up their Communist beliefs and to desist from any activity, thus conforming to the demands of the authorities.[3] This resulted in further releases.

Outside prison the party recovered from the losses suffered and made new progress in 1951–52, especially among the students, whose organization now came to be a Communist bulwark, just as a previous generation of Baghdad students had spear-headed the pro-fascist movement. Communist cells were established in the upper forms of the secondary schools and were uncovered even in the military academy (October, 1952).[4] Party activity among the intelligentsia, which actually, though not theoretically, remained the chief preoccupation of the Communists, was carried on principally in the Partisans of Peace, and other Communist-front organizations (about which more will be said below). There was a new, though more modest, upsurge in trade-union work and in propaganda among the peasants of southern and central Iraq. *Al Qā'ida* was widely, but not freely, circulated, and according to Communist sources its circulation was twice as high as that of the largest daily newspaper in the country.[5] Other Communist periodicals included the *Voice of Labour* (a trade-union journal launched in the spring of 1952), the *Voice of Students* (the mouthpiece of the Students' Congress), the *Voice of the Fellah* (all in Arabic), *Azadi* (the mouthpiece of the Kurdish section), a new periodical of the Communist Association for the Liberation of Women, and a daily newspaper of the Partisans of Peace, which was, however, banned after several weeks.

The smouldering opposition to the reactionary regime, which more or less equally affected all sections of the people, came to an open and spectacular climax in the Baghdad riots of November, 1952, which for a time threatened to overthrow the regime, and resulted in the establishment of military government. The Communist claim that their party prepared and headed this revolt (which subsequently spread to the district centres) is exaggerated, but it undoubtedly played a prominent part in the riots, which were spontaneous and came as the culmination of pent-up popular dissatisfaction with the regime. The revolt began with a strike of the students of the pharmacy school, who demanded a change in the examination system (a frequent cause of student demonstrations in both Iraq and Egypt). When the police intervened, other faculties joined the protest strike. Soon, the demonstrations took on a political character, and other elements joined them.[6] A more detailed survey of the events of November, 1952, cannot be given here, and it should suffice to point out that it revealed the weakness of the present regime in Iraq with the utmost clarity; it is a regime which has no mass support whatever and which has to rely, for effective aid, on two or three army divisions, at least one of which is permanently tied down in the Kurdish regions because of the latent danger of revolt there. It is unlikely that the Iraqi army will continue much longer to be a dependable instrument in the hands of this ruling group. Up to now it has been only the lack of co-ordination and the poor timing of the opposition's action which have prolonged the life of the present regime.

2. SPLITTING THE RANKS

The Iraqi party was given a new national programme early in 1953 (to replace the National Charter of 1945), which stressed that the aim of the party was the establishment of a Popular Democratic regime in Iraq following a revolution.[7] (Under the prevailing conditions the Communists could not very well envisage a *gradual* transition to such a regime, as they did in most other Asian countries.) More important than this platform, which was a copy of the standard programme adopted by all Communist Parties in dependent countries in 1951–52, was the new line on the "national democratic government," which had been decided upon at a session of the Central Committee of the party, following a report by the party's general secretary on the "Front of National Struggle Against Imperialism and War." Most interesting of all was the internal ideological discussion, which went on for almost four years and resulted in the expulsion of the Banner of Toilers faction in 1953.[8] This the Iraqi Communists called the "ideological, political, and organizational turning-point in our party."[9]

The new slogan of a national democratic government was thus defined by the party leadership: "A government within the framework of the existing system, which is not based on totally smashing the enemy but on forcing it to retreat; a government which makes a genuine stand against war plans and blocs and rearmament, abolishes the 1930 treaty [with Britain] and war bases in Iraq, works for the expulsion of the oil and other monopoly companies, and guarantees democratic liberties for the people. Our party has made it clear that it supports such a government while it takes national and democratic steps, but will criticize it for any hesitancy or compromise, not for the sake of weakening it but to strengthen it. The party does not stipulate its participation in such a government. It does fight to bring such a government to power through popular struggle led by a broad, united, militant national front."[10] In other words, the party would support a government coalition headed by Jadarji and the Istiqlāl, just as Tudeh had supported Mossadeq[11] with the intention of overthrowing him in due time.

It would be wrong to see the party split of 1953 solely as a result of the dispute on tactics to be applied. There was once again a struggle for the leadership of the party and there were personal antagonisms, and it is quite impossible to say which factor preceded the other, and which was decisive in the end. The majority accused the Banner of the Toilers faction of "right-wing opportunism," and said that it had learned how to handle this faction from the Soviet party's own struggle against the Bukharin opposition, and from the Polish party's action against Gomulka.[12]

According to the majority, it all boiled down to two basic differences of opinion: the Banner faction thought that the basis of the anti-imperialist front should be an alliance between the *workers and the intelligentsia*—whereas the majority believed that this alliance should be of *workers and peasants*. The majority also claimed that the Banner faction distinguished between the struggle for *national* liberation and the struggle for *social* liberation, and that the Bannerites wanted to stress the national struggle at the moment in order to attract wider sections of the population.

The majority said of itself, on the other hand, that it considered a dictatorship of the urban proletariat and the peasants to be necessary in order to put through the revolutionary measures which would ensure real national *and* social independence. The majority also accused the Bannerites (whom they called "right-wing opportunists") of being too anxious to compromise with other left-wing groups; thus the Bannerites refrained from attacking the royal family so as not to antagonize these groups.

The majority claimed, in its manifesto, that it "warned the democratic parties as early as 1946 not to be taken in by Nūri as-Sa'īd's tricks and not participate in the faked elections of that year.[13] Our party was the first to warn these circles and to urge them to oppose the Palestine war. Instead, they attacked the Soviet Union and the Communist Party [for their stand on the Palestine issue in 1947–48]. Nevertheless, our hand continues to be stretched out in friendship to these circles."[14] But, the majority added, it was not ready to compromise on this issue and to discontinue its fight for the sake of anti-imperialist unity. "During the revolt of October–November, 1952, the party did not intend to establish a popular democracy in Iraq. This attitude bears witness to the party's loyalty to the cause of establishing a [broad] national front."[15] What, then, do the Bannerites really want? They want (according to the majority) to give up the very idea of a popular revolt, and this at a time when the "masses have become convinced of the necessity of such a revolt, following the treason of the court and of the ruling circles."[16] The party majority, on the other hand, wants an uprising not in order to establish its own rule in the next stage of development, but in order to bring some Iraqi Mossadeq into power, and to compel him later on to carry out a more consistent anti-imperialist line than did the Persian Mossadeq.

Those parts of the party discussion which do make sense recall the differences of opinion between "Fahd" and his rivals, who split away in the early 1940's and who had also demanded a larger measure of willingness on the party's part to collaborate with other groups. The dispute about whether the alliance should be between workers and peasants or between workers and intelligentsia belonged to the realm of pure scholasticism and verbal hair-splitting, and it is difficult not to comment on this debate in a satirical vein. Both Communist groups were headed by intellectuals, mainly lawyers and students, and neither included peasants. The alliance between peasants and workers did not exist in Iraq, nor is it likely to come about in the near future. The Communist Party was a party of the intelligentsia, with some support from workers. These facts were known to both sides. But the Banner of the Toilers faction should, of course, have realized that Soviet theory was not to be revised on any account. The party majority, which had in theory so strongly condemned the stand of the "opportunist" faction, did not actually follow a course very different from the one proposed by the "rightists"—it was all a quarrel about words. Several weeks after the expulsion of the opportunist faction, the party majority came in fact to take, at least temporarily, a more "rightist" line than the Banner of the Toilers spokesmen had ever proposed. This was a result of the new line in Soviet and Cominform foreign policy, which made it necessary to compromise on social demands in order to rally as many sympathizers as possible within the framework of a broad national front. The error of the right-wingers was that they proposed the "correct line" too early —a misfortune which has befallen not a few Communist leaders in their party's history as a world movement. The party majority, on the other hand, was undoubtedly right in pointing to the fact that the Communists were now much stronger in relation to the other leftist groups (Kāmil al Jadarji, et al.) than they had been ten years earlier and that they had to make fewer compromises.[17]

The Partisans of Peace carried on a semi-legal existence in Iraq for about a year but had no outstanding successes. The prominent personalities of the movement were two poets, Muhammad Mahdi al Jawahīri and Muhammad Sālih al 'Ulum.[18] The latter published a book on the activities of the Partisans of Peace, and included some of his poems and a *fatwa* (religious edict) of Moslem religious dignitaries opposing the use of atomic weapons. Al Jawahīri, after his weekly magazine had been banned by the authorities, left the country for Egypt. Both he and al 'Ulum have been sentenced by the Iraqi authorities to short prison sentences for pro-Communist activities. The number of signatures collected in 1951 was said to be 20,000—less than in any other Arab country.

3. STUDENT AND WORKER ACTIVITY

More successful were the traditional "front" organizations among the lawyers, students, etc. The leading role of the students in all demonstrations since World War II has already been stressed. A students' strike, which affected all the institutions of higher learning in the capital, took place in February, 1952; the students were supported in this, as on many other occasions, by all the opposition parties. In March, 1953, another student strike, provoked by a quarrel between a teacher and a student at the elementary teachers' training college, led to political demonstrations and to a demand that martial law be abolished. The guiding forces behind these recurring student riots were the Communist Student Congress[19] and the Youth Federation, established in 1951. The contents of the Communist students' literature differ little from *Al Qā'ida*; it should be noted that despite police repression the Communist youth organizations succeeded in getting delegations to the Vienna Peace Congress in December, 1952, and to various other international "front" conferences in Europe during 1953–54.

Generally speaking, the higher forms of the secondary schools and the colleges have become the centre of Communist activities since the first big wave of arrests of party leaders in 1946–47. The students have always been the first to react to all important national and international events by strikes and demonstrations. They demonstrated on the anniversary of the January, 1948, riots, as well as on that of the November, 1952, uprising (each new riot creates at the same time a new anniversary to be celebrated!) against the visit of General Sir Brian Robertson, against French policy in North Africa, and in solidarity with the Basra workers—to give a few recent examples. The impression has been created that the high schools are 100 per cent. pro-Communist, which is incorrect; but it again shows how a minority can make its imprint on a big group and decisively influence its action. Arrested students were frequently acquitted because of their youth and their upper-class social origin, in contrast to other party members who received lengthy prison terms or worse[20]; it is not surprising, therefore, that the Communist leadership decided to use more and more students in the "agit-prop" departments. Nūri as-Sa'īd and other government leaders considered student unrest to be so important that they visited the teachers and school principals in person and admonished them to make a greater effort to combat "subversive influences." But these attempts were of little avail; nor were the charges against the students of favouring peace with Israel (which is tantamount to treason) very successful. There is good reason to doubt whether the student organizations made any such proposals in earnest.[21] Schools and colleges were frequently closed during 1953 and 1954, but the Communist hold on Iraqi youth was definitely strengthened.

The trade unions again showed signs of life during the second half of 1951; in December of that year several of their leaders were brought to trial, which in its turn provoked street demonstrations in Baghdad. It is extremely difficult to ascertain the extent of Communist penetration and domination in the trade-union fields, because any such activity is almost automatically suspect in Iraq. What has been proved is that the Communists were behind the tobacco workers' strike in Baghdad in September, 1953, which was renewed in December of that year. The main demand of the strikers was for recognition of their union. The same demand cropped up in the Basra oil-company workers' strike in December, 1953, which led to clashes with the police. There was growing militancy among the workers because of government reluctance to accept their demands, but trade-union organization is still weak in most places, and no country-wide organizations have come into being.

The abolition of martial law in the autumn of 1953 caused an up-surge in party activity, and the National Democratic Party, which had been out of politics for most of the period since 1947, again convened and elected Kāmil al Jadarji its president for another term. This was now the only left-of-centre party, and Communist infiltration became far more widespread than it had been in 1946. When the party organ, *Sawt al Ahāli*, reappeared in 1954, it conducted open propaganda for such "front" organizations as the Democratic Youth and the Partisans of Peace. It may be assumed that the leaders of this group, such as Jadarji and Muhammad Hadīd, knew full well what the real nature of the "front" organizations was. But now they had become far more hostile to the regime than they had been ten years earlier, and were ready for unlimited collaboration with the Communists. They even agreed (with Communist blessing) to enter a coalition with the right-wing extremist Istiqlāl party, who had been the friends of Rashīd 'Ali, and only four years earlier had been called "Fascists" in Communist and pro-Communist literature. The National Front received fourteen (out of 135) seats in the elections for the Iraqi parliament in the summer of 1954; in addition, the Popular Front received four.[22] The Communists supported both parties and *Al Qā'ida* was highly pleased with the results, which it called a great victory of the anti-fascist forces.[23] Several weeks later the Iraqi parliament was dissolved and the National Democratic Party banned. New elections in October brought Nūri as-Sa'īd a safe majority, and most candidates were returned unopposed since the parties had been dissolved.

4. THE PRESENT OUTLOOK

Of all the Arab countries Iraq arouses the strongest feeling of pessimism. Its economic potentialities are far greater than those of most other countries—its revenue from the oil companies reached £52 million in 1954, £75 million in 1955, and still rises. Yet there is no prospect in the near future of an increase in the standard of living of either the peasants or the majority of the urban population. After the arrest of its successive Central Committees in 1947–49, the Communist Party of Iraq was split internally, was completely disorganized, and had ceased to exist as a country-wide movement. Since that time the Iraqi regime has been one of scarcely veiled dictatorship and wholly re-actionary in its outlook; it has been neither able nor willing to carry out sweeping social and political reforms. Petty intrigues and feudal vested interests have prevailed over the urgent necessity to act for the benefit of the nation. As a result, the government has antagonized most of the population, including the entire middle class, which is now willing to make common cause with the Communist fronts in order to overthrow the hated autocracy. The parallel with Czarist Russia is uncomfortably obvious. At the time of writing, Communism in Iraq continues to be "under control"—but it will not remain so for many years, perhaps not even for many months. Nor will the strengthening of the army or the police preserve the regime indefinitely; even the best arms in the world are of no avail if the soldiers refuse to obey. The present regime is doomed; by clinging to power long enough it may make Communism the only alternative. The Iraqi Communists have revealed in the course of their history an unusual degree of incompetence and disunity, lack of purpose and direction, and a marked deficiency of political acumen and experience. But it looks as if they may mend their ways sooner than the rulers of the country. Their inefficiency has been the main safeguard of the West for a number of years—it would be unwise to expect it to remain so for ever.

PART SEVEN

TURKEY

Chapter Sixteen

Turkey and Russia

---

1. FRIENDSHIP BETWEEN KEMALIST TURKEY
AND SOVIET RUSSIA

TURKEY'S relations with Russia have been for many years the most pressing issue in its national policy, but Communism was never an important problem. There was a relatively strong Communist, or semi-Communist, movement in Turkey in the early 1920's, but the Kemalist reforms narrowly restricted the appeal of the party in subsequent years. Moscow preferred the friendship (or at least benevolent neutrality) of the new post-World War I Turkey to the support of a Turkish Communist Party; this lack of assistance undoubtedly further impeded the growth of such a party. When relations between the two countries deteriorated in the late 1930's, Soviet territorial designs, openly proclaimed in 1945–46, caused much resentment and hurt Turkish national feeling—still further hindering the development of a Turkish Communist Party. Elsewhere in the Middle East (and in Europe) lack of confidence among the ruling classes has given Communists their chance; whatever the Turkish middle class—which can look back on considerable achievements during the last thirty years—may lack, it is not confidence. Late in 1954 there was a certain change in Soviet policy towards Turkey; Kemal Ataturk was again proclaimed to be a great national hero in the Soviet press (though not in the *Soviet Encyclopedia*). But even if the relations between the two countries have been somewhat normalized, there are no indications of the growth of Communist influence in Turkey—outside a small circle of party stalwarts. The history of the Turkish Communist Party will be given in brief outline in the following pages. Its political importance hardly warrants a more detailed account at the present time.

The Turkish Communist Party is among the oldest in the Middle East. It was also the first to be made a member of the Comintern, at the second Congress in 1921. Its history, especially in its early stage, does not lack intrinsic interest, and in its subsequent phases we find instances of enthusiasm, idealism, and self-sacrifice, as well as of sordid intrigue, treason, and crime, just as in the histories of other Communist Parties. And yet the Turkish party has been and continues to be of far less political importance than any other Middle Eastern Communist Party. A short phase of hectic activity was followed by more than fifteen years of lethargy. A limited up-swing in the late 1930's (which continued up to 1946) came to an abrupt end following international events over which the Turkish Communist Party had no influence. Ironically enough, the first important and prolonged crisis in the history of the Turkish Communist Party came in the wake of very close collaboration between the Turkish and the Soviet governments, while the second crisis after World War II, on the contrary, was caused by the grave tension between the two countries.

The varied fortunes of the Turkish Communist Party can indeed be followed only against the background of Soviet-Turkish relations. Because of Turkey's proximity to the Soviet Union, and other specific historical circumstances, relations between the two countries had a direct impact. But a detailed description of Soviet-Turkish relations is outside the scope of this study; the subject has been fully dealt with elsewhere.[1]

Following the defeat of Turkey in World War I, large parts of the country were occupied by the Allied forces. The Sultan's government in Constantinople stood for complete surrender, but there were nationalist stirrings throughout the country, and when Greek forces landed in Smyrna in May, 1919, and proceeded to occupy Anatolia, Mustafa Kemal, who was Inspector-General of the Third Turkish Army, raised the banner of revolt in such centres of non-occupied Turkey as Samsun, Erzerum, Ankara, and Konia. National congresses were convened in Erzerum and Sivas in June–July, 1919, and the dismemberment of Turkey by the Allied powers was sharply opposed. A new parliament was elected the same autumn and convened in Ankara in January, 1920. It supported the national activist movement headed by Kemal, and in April of the same year Mustafa Kemal was chosen President of the Grand National Assembly. This followed the arrest of many other national leaders in Istanbul by the Allied forces, which proceeded to occupy the whole of Turkey. Two months later the Greeks, having been given the green light by the other powers, started a major offensive. The fighting continued into the second half of 1922, and after abortive peace talks and initial reverses, the Greeks were expelled from Asiatic Turkey.

In this war of liberation Soviet Russia was the first and principal ally of Kemalist Turkey. "It is no secret," Louis Fischer was told by Karakhan, then Soviet Deputy Foreign Minister, "that we helped Kemal with much cannon, money, arms, and military advice." In

March, 1921, a treaty of friendship was concluded between the two nations, and later the same year Mikhail Frunze, Trotsky's successor as Commissar for War, came to Ankara. Soviet-Turkish relations during the 1920's continued to be closer than those between Moscow and any other non-Communist country; there were frequent visits of Turkish statesmen to Russia, and vice versa, and also intensive trade relations. After the Montreux Conference on the future of the Dardanelles in 1936, there was a certain cooling off in the old friendship, but basically the ties between the two countries were not affected and remained as they had been up to the outbreak of World War II.

Soviet support for Mustafa Kemal was not, of course, unconditional, and Soviet spokesmen, especially in the very early days, frequently stressed their divergences of opinion.[2] Zinoviev, in his speech on the "tasks of the first Congress of the peoples of the East," said that Communists must not support Kemal in strengthening the power of the Sultan, "even if religious considerations would appear to make this imperative."[3] But, on the whole, Kemal's national revolution was considered to be sufficiently progressive (to use the latter-day jargon) to tip the scales in his favour when the Soviet government had to choose in 1921–22 between support for Kemal or for the Turkish Communist Party. Moscow came face-to-face with this dilemma quite suddenly and under rather dramatic circumstances.

One of the results of the 1908 *coup* of the Young Turks and the resultant new constitution was the emergence of a Socialist Party in Turkey. The first group came into existence in Salonika in 1909, where it was headed by Benaroi; most of its members were Greeks, Jews, and Bulgars. This organization decided to join the Second International, and participated in the elections to the first and second Turkish parliaments with some success. Among the foreign delegates who came to take part in its convention was the well-known German Socialist, Parvus. In 1912 a Turkish Socialist Federation was founded in Salonika, rather than in Istanbul—perhaps because the general climate was more conducive to the growth of the new organization outside the capital. Among the leaders and members of the new Socialist group there were by now native Turks, and in the years immediately preceding World War I the movement spread to Istanbul, Smyrna, and other centres of Asiatic Turkey. But this growth was not received with very great enthusiasm by the government of the day; one of the Socialist leaders, Ahmed Salim, is reported to have been murdered; another, Tawfik Nased, was forced to leave Turkey; and a third, Faik Hasib, was deported to inner Anatolia in a wave of repression in 1913–14. A fourth leader, Mustafa Subhi, fled to Russia in 1914 in order to escape from arrest in his homeland. During World War I he established contact with the Bolsheviks, and was active as a propagandist among Turkish prisoners of war in Russia. After the Russian Revolution he became head of the

Turkish section of the Central Bureau of the Eastern Peoples, a sub-division of the Peoples' Commissariat for Nationalities, headed by Stalin. Subhi took part in various international socialist meetings, such as the Petrograd Convention in December, 1918, and the first Congress of the Communist International in March, 1919, without, however, having the right to vote.[4]

Subhi edited *Yeni Dunya* (New World), first in the Crimea, later (in 1919–20) in Moscow, and eventually in Baku. Ismail Hakki became his successor as head of the Turkish section in the Commissariat of Nationalities, and he later represented his party at the second Congress of the Communist International.

Several days after the Baku Congress, Mustafa Subhi organized a meeting in the same city between members of the Turkish section in Russia and Communists from Turkey, headed by Hasis Mohammed, who had come to take part in the first Conference of the Peoples of the East. The aim of the meeting was to co-ordinate the activities of the various Communist groups and to create a unified Communist Party. This meeting is now regarded as the starting-point of the Turkish Communist Party.[5]

The delegates from Anatolia (two of whom were co-opted to the new party executive) had reported the existence in Turkey of a strong Communist movement, and of many local soviets, but their stories were not quite believed; Zinoviev had said that these soviets were "toys" but not real workers' councils,[6] and Pavlovitch, the main adviser of the party on Oriental affairs, spoke about "usurpers and hypocrites, veritable wolves in sheep's clothing."[7] The Comintern refused to collaborate with the "Angora Communist Party" (as the native Turkish Communist Party was called), and Mustafa Subhi and his comrades declared that the Angora Communist Party was merely the creation of some Turkish pashas who intended to deceive the toiling masses.

But the situation on the whole was extremely muddled, and in view of the breakdown in communications, in the aftermath of World War I, nobody knew exactly what was going on in Turkey at that time. Several Communist or near-Communist and Socialist groups were active; e.g. the Socialist Party, headed by Hilmi, and which was charged with reformism and opportunism by the more extreme elements. A Socialist Workers' Party, which was active mainly in Istanbul, had been founded by prisoners of war who had been in contact with Spartacist elements in Germany[8]; and a student group, affiliated with these Spartacists (as they sometimes called themselves), caused a one-day sensation by proposing Lenin's candidacy for the Nobel Peace Prize. In 1921 these groups sponsored a trade-union organization, the International Association of the Toilers, which consisted, however, mainly of Greek, Jewish, and Bulgarian members, and whose organ was a periodical in Greek.[9]

The most influential of all these groups was the Angora Communist Party (nicknamed the "Green Apple"), which was usually described by Communist sources with a vituperation not very different from that used thirty years later towards other "nationalist deviations" in Yugoslavia and elsewhere. The October Revolution had caused a wave of enthusiasm throughout the East, and in the conditions of anarchy which prevailed at that time in defeated Turkey, "soviets" of sorts may indeed have been established here and there. The application of Marxist theory in backward countries frequently produced strange results, and in view of subsequent events in Soviet Russia, the surprise and disgust of the Soviet experts in 1920–21 at native Turkish Communism was perhaps not quite justified.

Pavlovitch, in what appears to be one of the earliest descriptions of native Communist activities in Turkey, charges the party named "Unity and Progress" (the "Young Turks") with having usurped the name and the programme of the Communist Party and having established a Central Committee in Ankara. He also accuses them of persecuting the followers of the real Communist Party of Mustafa Subhi.[10] The man who prepared the "pseudo-Communist, pan-Turk, and pan-Islamic programme" of the "Green Apple" was said to be Kar Ali Bek, a former assistant minister for supply and a Young Turk. He was called by his friends the "Turkish Marx," because he had been the first to use historical materialism in re-evaluating the history of Turkey. Kar Ali Bek favoured the nationalization of banks and of large-scale commerce, but recognized the right of private property. He did not oppose religion, and he "does not belong to those who believe in the final triumph of Communism, nor is he convinced that the contrary will happen. Such an approach is in his opinion a fruitless, theoretical preoccupation."[11]

The main charge against the Angora Communist Party was that it put the national ideal above the Communist one. One of its leaders expressly stated that Turkish Communism was merely "an instrument to serve the welfare of the Turkish nation and the strengthening of its power."[12] National collectivism was thus regarded as the way towards unity: "Collectivism has become a necessity, but it is a programme for the present which can be changed or improved upon tomorrow. But nationalism is unchangeable. . . . National unity is the only and the dearest ideal of man; Bolsheviks do not preach the opposite; on the contrary, they consciously maintain the same position. . . . Communism is no final aim for the Turks, but a means; the ideal is the unity of the Turkish nation, the golden apple." Soviet observers were particularly angry about the allegation that the "Russians were compelled to give up part of the teaching of Karl Marx," and that consequently Bolshevism could not be transplanted to Turkey but that Marxism should rather be adapted to Turkish conditions. "Possibly we shall have to adopt an even more radical social system than Communism, but we cannot simply take over systems worked out by other nations in different conditions; Turkey is not Russia and the Turks are not Russians."[13] In view of the fact that the Soviet leaders were attempting to proselytize not just for Communism in general but for the Russian brand, the writer felt that Bolshevism, the "terrible typhoon" from the north, should be categorically rejected.

The "Green Apple" movement existed for about three years, and had considerable influence among the Green Armies which were part of Kemal's forces in the fight against the Greeks. Headed by Hakki Behic, Edhem, and Hikmet, these large-scale partisan groups were of some importance during the early stage of the fighting. But with the consolidation of military power in the hands of Kemal, he decided to dissolve the Green Armies. It was proposed to Edhem, the partisan leader, that he accompany a Turkish mission to Russia; he refused this offer; his army was attacked and defeated by the government forces, after which he fled to the Greeks.[14] Initially Soviet observers regarded the Green Army favourably, later they were disappointed and came to see its commanders simply as bandits; Mikhail Frunze called Edhem an "adventurer and demagogue *par excellence.*" Only on the occasion of the thirtieth anniversary of the murder of the leaders of the Turkish Communists was a more favourable view again taken retrospectively. Relations with Turkey had meanwhile deteriorated, and much of the early history also came to be rewritten.

Meanwhile Mustafa Subhi continued his organizing work in Baku, and published a series of Marxist classics and popular leaflets for distribution in Turkey.[15] As the executive committee of the party was cut off in Baku from events at home, it was decided in the winter of 1920–21 to transfer its seat to Turkey; apparently the political atmosphere in Turkey was then considered to be suitable for such a move. Subhi and sixteen other Communist leaders left Baku and set out for Ankara by way of the Black Sea coast. However, the receptions arranged were not at all friendly. In Erzerum and other cities there were demonstrations against them, and when they reached Trebizond they were arrested by the local authorities and killed by drowning in the sea. A contemporary Communist report[16] maintains that the mayor of the Trebizond municipality and the head of the local "security office" had organized the murders, and that the local Soviet representative was threatened with lynching when he tried to intervene. "Among the demonstrators there were unenlightened people, bought by the *bourgeoisie.* They attacked our comrades and attempted to tear them to pieces. On the way nobody was ready to sell them bread or fodder for their horses. And the government, the real culprit, intended to appear to be defending our comrades!" According to Pavlovitch, the "hate of the Turkish nationalists for the Communists had reached a new paroxysm" following the revolt by Ehmed Pasha (Edhem) on the Greek-Turkish front a few days before the arrival of Mustafa Subhi and his comrades.

The leaders of the Turkish Communist Party were killed on January 28, 1921, but more than two months passed before the news was published. On March 16 a friendship pact between the Soviet Union and Turkey was signed in Moscow, seven weeks after the murder of Subhi and his comrades. Only a fortnight later, on April 2, Tevada's letter was sent to Pavlovitch, and there is some reason to assume that the publication was intentionally delayed in order not to spoil the effect of the pact and create an unfavourable public reaction in Russia.[17] The Soviet leaders had already decided by that time (though the murder of the Turkish Communists was, of course, a heavy blow) that it was more important for them to establish friendly relations with Kemal's regime than to put all their money on such a doubtful horse as Turkish Communism. The Soviet Commissar for Foreign Affairs requested details about the fate of the Turkish comrades,[18] only to be told that they might have perished in a sea accident; but some time after the agreement had been signed the Angora government promised to release the Turkish Communists in prison and to hand over for trial "those guilty of the killing of Mustafa Subhi."[19] Relations between the two governments were hardly affected by the Trebizond affair; it was thirty years later, when relations between Moscow and Ankara had very much deteriorated, that the fact of the murder of Subhi and his comrades was again prominently mentioned in Soviet propaganda.[20]

After the Trebizond disaster new attempts were made to establish a Turkish Communist Party by means of the merger of the Istanbul Socialist Workers' Party and an Ankara group. In 1922 the new united party held its meeting, the first Communist Congress, only to be banned again the same October. The charge brought against the organizers of the congress was that they had invited delegates from abroad though they had known that this was forbidden.[21] The new party saw its main task to be trade-union work; it founded new trade unions on the basis of the programme of the Profintern, and attempted to take over already existing non-Communist trade unions. It succeeded in organizing a local trade-union congress in Mersin in October, 1922, and during the subsequent year it convened a meeting of representatives of nineteen trade unions which were dominated by the Communist Party.[22] Meanwhile, in 1923–24 the Communist Party again resumed its political activities, profiting from a relaxation in the general political atmosphere, and in 1925 the second party conference was convened. But following the promulgation of the new law for the "stabilization of state security" (in March, 1925) the party again became illegal, and in August, 1925, most of its leaders were arrested. From that date on the Turkish Communist Party has remained illegal.[23]

But activity in the trade unions continued. The sections dominated by the Communists included the ammunition workers of Ankara,
the railway employees at Eskeshir, and some groups of Ismir spinners.
The party also infiltrated with some success the semi-official General
Workers' Association; "Communists who were not known to be party
members were elected as executive members, and the Kemalist agents
were eliminated," it is reported.[24] And at the same time the Profintern
organ declared that the Turkish trade unions were now entirely free
from the influence of the government (à la Subatov in 1902–03 in
Czarist Russia), and the main protagonist of the "yellow trade unions,"
Dr. Rafik Bey, had been defeated.[25] As a rule, such sanguine reports
were, however, greatly exaggerated, and by the time these lines were
published in Russia very little had remained of either the Communist
Party in Turkey or its trade unions. The consolidation of Kemalism,
even more than the ban on the party, had provoked a crisis among the
party militants; some were of the opinion that the capitalist-statist
trend would become anti-imperialist in due time, and therefore should
not be opposed. Others, on the other hand, "lost their presence of
mind as the result of government terror," and took refuge in what one
spokesman called "heroic individual acts," which seem to have been
terrorist acts.[26] But such "ultra-left sectarianism" was not less sharply
denounced in Moscow than the "right-wing opportunism" of compromising with Kemalism; Kemalists should be branded as traitors to
the revolution because they had made a *rapprochement* with the "*com-
prador bourgeoisie*" (that part of the colonial *bourgeoisie* which collabor-
ates with "foreign imperialists"). This development, said the party
spokesman,[27] was perhaps inevitable; "the capitalists were backed by
the army, and the Communist Party on the other hand was weak and
taking only its very first steps." It would be interesting to know to what
extent this opinion on the "treason" of Kemalism was shared by the
Soviet leaders; the impression is that the Soviet leaders took an altogether different view. The late 1920's and the 1930's were a period of
the almost total eclipse of the Turkish Communists. This was reflected
inter alia in their dwindling representation at Comintern meetings. At
the fifth Comintern Congress the Turks still had two delegates. There
was only one at the sixth Congress in 1928, and there was no Turkish
representative at all at the seventh Congress in 1935, nor was reference
even made to the existence of a Turkish party.

At the same time cultural and economic relations between the two
countries were strengthened[28]; even the reports of the Turkish Communist Party about the alleged murder of some of its leading members
in prison were only perfunctorily mentioned in the Comintern publications, and hardly mentioned at all in the Soviet press. Kemal Ataturk
was believed by the Soviet leaders to be a neutral, who should not be
irritated in an otherwise hostile world; even if latter-day Soviet his-

toriography takes a different view, the main charges for the worsening of Soviet-Turkish relations are brought against his successors rather than against him. In November, 1954, following another somersault in Soviet foreign policy, Kemal again became a "national hero" for *Pravda*.

The Communist Party in Turkey was handicapped by the conditions of authoritarian rule, and perhaps even more by the fact that Kemalism was based less on terror than other contemporary dictatorships, and rather more on genuine political support. There were many reasons for complaint by the urban workers, and even more by the peasants of Anatolia. However, the Communist groups which existed in the late 1920's and 1930's contained a number of poets, but hardly a peasant and few workers. The party, or rather its remnants, during the 1930's were beset by internal splits; only in 1937–38 was an attempt again made to reorganize the party.

At that time a new party central executive was elected, the moving spirit of which was reported to be Hikmet Kivilcim. The party organ *Orak Chekitch* (Sickle and Hammer), first published in 1930, began to appear regularly for a time, and efforts were made to enlist "fellow-travellers" within the framework of a popular-front campaign. But this attempt, too, was nipped in the bud by the authorities; in the trial which attracted most attention in 1938, the poet Nazim Hikmet and the writer Kemal Tahir were given long prison sentences.[29]

2. END OF THE FRIENDSHIP

The traditional friendship between Moscow and the Kemalist regime came to an end in 1939. Looking backwards for the factors which brought about this change, one can only underscore the statement of a Turkish writer: "The change was not brought about by a shift in Turkey's own policy but by the forces of world politics."[30] In the summer of 1939, when Turkey had entered an alliance with the Western democracies, Russia had expressed satisfaction with this development. But later that year a non-aggression pact was signed between Russia and Nazi Germany, and Moscow's interests in the Near East changed overnight. When the Turkish Foreign Minister came to Moscow in September, 1939, he was asked by the Soviet representatives to dissociate himself from the Western powers in order to maintain absolute neutrality. The conversations concerning a pact of mutual assistance broke down, and relations began to deteriorate, though Molotov denied in one of his speeches in October, 1939, that the Soviets had demanded the cession of the provinces of Kars and Ardahan and certain privileges in the Straits. During 1940–41 the issue of the Straits was more than once the subject of negotiations between Nazi and Soviet statesmen, and what the Turks learned subsequently about Soviet designs did not please them at all. After Hitler's invasion in

June, 1941, the Soviet attitude towards Turkey again changed completely. Formerly Ankara had been blamed for *not* preserving complete neutrality; now it was gradually accused of "objectively" serving the interests of Nazi Germany by staying neutral.

The main reason for the deterioration of relations was not, however, the changing Soviet military and political objectives, but the shift in the balance of power. Russia had been for centuries the arch-enemy of Turkey, and if the tension decreased so dramatically after 1917 this was primarily because the new Russia was weak and unable (and, at least in the early period, unwilling) to pursue the traditional aims of Russian imperialism. Turkey had no reason to be afraid of Russia in the 1920's and early 1930's, but the situation changed radically in the late 1930's, when the Soviet Union again became one of the leading military powers and returned, in its foreign policy, to the old pattern of territorial expansion. This development had a profound effect on Turkish domestic policy; and open Soviet attacks, such as the charge of the attempt to "drive a wedge between Germany and Russia" and criticism of the internal regime,[31] did not contribute to creating friendlier feelings in Turkey. Moreover, Soviet charges gradually became more violent, especially after the battle of Stalingrad, and they estranged by clumsy personal attacks those very people, like the publicist Yalcin, who had not entirely given up the idea of Soviet-Turkish friendship. Another cause of such friction was the attempt on the life of von Papen in February, 1942; several Macedonian Communists and two Soviet citizens were brought to court in the course of the Ankara trial.[32]

In the early phase of the war, Communist activities in Turkey were sporadic and un-coordinated. The party, in accord with the Comintern line, was in favour of a *rapprochement* with the West in 1938–39, but in favour of neutralism and a loosening of the ties with the West in 1939–41, and against Turkish neutrality after June 21, 1941. These somersaults, which were all too obviously conditioned by the interests of a foreign power, were hardly likely to win any sympathizers, but after Stalingrad the general climate of opinion in Turkey became somewhat more favourable. Communist groups again resumed their activities in the larger cities and industrial centres; in 1943 several dozen Communists were arrested and brought to trial. A Communist cell consisting of five officers headed by Omar Ilmas and two sergeants was discovered in the Kars military district; according to the bill of indictment they had engaged in espionage; they were executed in 1943. In the same year a Communist-front organization called "Union of Progressive Youth" (later "Young Progressive Turks") came into existence, and in 1944 five of its members were brought to trial.[33] Little is known about the court proceedings against them, which were held behind closed doors, but it seems that the members of this organization appeared as "antifascists," and not as Communists, before the judges. Also arrested in

1944 was the Communist leader Hikmet Kivilcim and the Communist trade-union leader Lachat Fuat, who was given an eight-year sentence. Official secrecy about these trials and the tendency to attribute Communist activities to all left-wing and socialist groups; and, on the other hand, the Communist tactic of creating "anti-fascist fronts" together contributed to obfuscating the issue. It cannot be doubted, however, that the Communists profited from the inability of official sources to distinguish between home-grown reformist, or even revolutionary, trends and activities undertaken on behalf of a foreign power. This made the Communist Party for a time the rallying-point of left-wing and liberal trends, especially among students. Among the legal newspapers, only *Tan* gave support to Soviet demands; and it was destroyed, together with a number of Soviet bookshops, in 1945, in the wake of a mass demonstration.

3. COMMUNISM IN TURKEY, 1945-55

A new lift was given to Communist activities in 1946, as the result of the abolition of the old party law, which had given a virtual monopoly to the state party of Kemal Ataturk and Ismet Inonu. New parties were founded at once, and the Communists sponsored one, and possibly two, of them: the Socialist Party of Workers and Peasants, and the Socialist Party of Turkey, led by Esad Adil Mustecabi. This interlude lasted, however, only up to December, 1946, when the leader of the new legal party, Dr. Shefik Husni Degmer, was arrested, and the party dissolved.[34] At the same time several trade unions, which had been sponsored by the Communists, were also banned.

The main emphasis of Turkish Communist propaganda shifted in 1950 (when there was a new relaxation in political life) to open and veiled anti-American propaganda: "Instead of sugar, they give us American tanks; instead of butter, the fascist government offers the Turkish people American guns. . . . There is only one way to save the people from imperialist subjugation and cruel exploitation, and that is to tear up the American-Turkish agreement."[35]

Anti-American and anti-Western propaganda, however, stood but little chance in view of the tension in Soviet-Turkish relations after World War II. In March, 1945, Russia had indicated that it was not prepared to renew the Russo-Turkish Treaty of Friendship on the old terms unless Russia was given bases in the straits, and unless territorial adjustments were made. In face of a flat Turkish refusal to comply with these demands, they were made public, and it was proposed that "historic injustices" should now be remedied and the "southern territories of Georgia" be restored, as well as the parts of the Soviet Armenian Republic under Turkish rule. At the same time the claim for control of the straits was pressed, and the Turks asked themselves what would remain of their country and its independence if the Soviet territorial demands were accepted. In this situation, because of the clear danger of aggression, the alliance with America appeared to most, if not all, Turks as the only logical step to be taken; and Communist propaganda against increasing military expenses and receiving American aid fell on barren ground.

For the same reason the Partisans of Peace had no outstanding successes in Turkey, though for some time, in 1950–51, Communist activity was concentrated on the collection of signatures for the "Stockholm Appeal." The Turkish "friends of peace" started their activity in July–August, 1950; their association was headed by Dr. Bahiga Boran, an American-educated professor of sociology at Ankara University; its general secretary was Adnan Jamgil, a journalist and former lecturer in philosophy in Ankara. They denied emphatically "allegations with regard to contacts with Communist Parties abroad,"[36] but the authorities decided to bring them to trial, and seven of their leaders were found guilty and given prison sentences in January, 1951. The magazine of the Partisans of Peace, *Baris Yolu* (The Way to Peace) continued to appear illegally and, according to Communist sources, was sent to 10,000 addresses.[37] The Communist Party had more success in the establishment of another front—the one which worked for the release of Nazim Hikmet, the poet, who had been in prison since 1938. Hikmet was released from prison after declaring a hunger strike in April, 1950. He escaped from Turkey in June, 1951,[38] and was given a very cordial reception in Moscow. The party had previously collected signatures among the intelligentsia demanding the release of Hikmet, and even several months after his flight from Turkey the police found circles of Communist sympathizers named after him.

The most comprehensive insight into Communist activities in Turkey in recent years was offered by the "trial of the 167," which began in Istanbul in October, 1953.[39] These arrests had been made following the seizure of, in October, 1951, Professor Sevim Tari, the main contact between the present centre of the Communist Party in Paris and its cells in Turkey.[40] Among the accused were 43 workers, 34 students, 35 officials, 21 artisans, as well as several physicians, 2 army officers, and 8 unemployed, a fact noted by the Soviet press, which said that the accused were merely "progressive patriots who opposed the project to make the country a basis of foreign aggressive armies."[41] But the public prosecutor, apparently no progressive, took a different view and charged the group with collaboration with Moslem extremists and right-wing reactionary groups in an attempt to provoke unrest in the countryside. The well-known right-wing extremist, Facil Kisakurek, editor of *Buyuk Dogu*, was named as their contact with this camp, while Saidi Kurdi (Nursi), the head of an Islamic extremist organization (Nurculuk), was mentioned as liaison officer with the Kurds, among whom the party was said to have tried to foment ethnic and religious resentment against the Turks.[42] Among the leaders, Dr. Shefik Husni Degmer, the physician who had headed the Socialist Party in 1946, was again named in first place, but Zeki Bashtimer, who escaped the police in 1946, appeared to have been the party's "grey eminence." Bashtimer had been head of one of the sections of the archives of the Turkish parliament for many years, and gave up his post when he founded the Ankara branch of the Socialist Party in 1946. Intellectuals prevailed, generally speaking, in the party leadership. Apart from Mihri Belli and Sevim Tari, university professors who had acted as contact men with the Paris centre, they included the army captain, Abdul Kader Demirkan, a lecturer in the officers' school of Kuleli.[43]

After Stalin's death, in accordance with the new line of Soviet foreign policy, the Turkish government was told by Moscow that the territorial demands for the cession of Kars, Ardahan and Artwin had been squashed, but relations between the two countries did not improve very much owing to the deep-rooted conviction in Turkey that ultimate Soviet aims had not changed.

The second economic revolution, which began in 1949–50, has, above all, affected the Turkish countryside. The Communists had always faced serious difficulties in gaining a foothold in the countryside; "How many enemies we had to combat within the party: sectarians, worshippers of spontaneity in the peasant movement, 'Bonapartists,' liquidators, anti-peasant deviators, and so on," reports a Communist source.[44] The agrarian reforms of recent years and the mechanization of agriculture made it easier for the Communists to reach the countryside. On the other hand, it was extremely difficult for them to run down the social system in their propaganda at the very time when Turkish agriculture was expanding at a faster rate than Soviet agriculture. A similar situation existed in industry. After 1951 the Turkish government had gradually permitted the formation of trade unions, and there were even a few strikes. But the opportunity to infiltrate these trade unions was scotched by the possibility of the development of a free trade-union movement. Viewed from abroad there is some reason for concern that the present economic expansion, accompanied by inflation, may intensify the trend towards economic inequality and provoke social unrest if it is not subjected to a certain amount of control. Another source of peril is that the government may continue to identify all left-wing, reformist, socialist, and even liberal movements with "Communism." But on the whole it seems that Communism stands less chance in Turkey than in any other nation of the Middle East. Turkey is the area which has made the most rapid economic progress, and it is the country, on the other hand, most directly threatened by the Soviet Union. Communism is not now considered in Turkey to be an issue which can be separated from Turkish-Soviet relations in general.

PART EIGHT

COMMUNISM AND THE MINORITIES

Chapter Seventeen

Minorities

I. THE KURDS

NATIONAL minorities have everywhere been given much attention by Communist Parties, and they played an important part in the early history of Middle Eastern Communism. Twenty or even ten years ago it would have been necessary to devote extensive space to the role of the ethnic and religious minorities in most of the left-wing movements: the Syrian and Lebanese parties were founded by Armenians. Jews, Greeks, and other foreigners constituted the bulk of the Egyptian factions up to 1947–48, and at one time between 70 and 80 per cent. of the Iraqi party's membership consisted of minority groups.

But in 1956 the situation had radically changed—many of the Armenians had gone to Soviet Armenia, most of the Jews emigrated to Israel, and those who remained (as well as other foreigners) find it difficult and frequently impossible to be active in an atmosphere of rabid nationalism which all too often turns into xenophobia.

Only the Kurds continue to attract the interest of Communist policy makers, although on the surface everything has been quiet in Kurdistan for a number of years.

An analysis of the growth of Communist influence among the Kurds reveals the success of "Popular-front" tactics in political, social, and economic conditions reminiscent of the atmosphere of Kipling's India: turbulent tribes on the North-west Frontier, local intrigues and power politics, highway robbery, and the charge of a light cavalry brigade.

The Kurds are one of the oldest peoples in the Middle East; most of them were, and many still are, nomad herdsmen. Yet though tribal organization has remained the basic characteristic of Kurdish social and political life, there has been (quite apart from the forcible measures taken by the Turks) an unmistakable trend towards agricultural settlement and urbanization. With the growth of the oil industry in the Mosul area, Kurdish labourers came to work at the oil-fields, while an urban Kurdish middle class developed at Sulaimanya and the other Kurdish centres in Iraq. The area populated by them extends from Eastern Turkey through Northern Iraq to Western Persia. Kurdish nationalists claim that 8 million or more Kurds live in that area, but the total seems to be nearer to 3–4 million. In Turkey there are about $1\frac{1}{2}$ million, in Iran more than 1 million, most of the rest in Iraq (where they constitute about 15 per cent. of the total population), some in Syria, and 60,000–80,000 in the Soviet republics of Armenia and Azerbaidjan.

Up to the early nineteenth century the Kurds had their own principality, a vassal state of the Sultan in Constantinople. At the time of the disintegration of Turkish power, on the eve of World War I, when the various minorities in the Ottoman empire came to press their claims, the Kurds, too, for the first time, rose up in revolt. This was in 1909; only a year after that the first nationalist Kurdish party, Heiwa (The Hope), was founded.[1] At the time of the peace treaties in 1919 the Allies played with the idea of establishing an autonomous state of Kurdistan as part of Turkey, and there was, in fact, a clause in the Treaty of Sèvres calling for its establishment. But this, like so many other provisions of these peace treaties, was never realized. Following the settlement of territorial disputes between Turkey, Iraq, and Persia in the early 1920's, most of the Kurds were split between these three countries; their history between the two world wars is studded with revolts against their new masters—against the Turks in 1925, 1928–30, and 1937–38; against the Iraqi authorities throughout the early 1920's, and again in 1930–32; and against the Persian central government throughout the 1920's and in 1932. Again and again the governments concerned had to send military expeditions to suppress the revolts, frequently with great losses to both sides, but only in Turkey was a serious attempt made to find a more lasting settlement. The Turkish government declared the Kurds "Mountain Turks," provided work for them in near-by cities, and settled them as farmers, hoping thus to put an end to their nomadic existence. In Iraq and Persia, on the other hand, government control in the Kurdish areas was never firmly established, and relations between the central government and the chieftains of the tribes oscillated between appeasement and punitive military actions. In these Kurdish revolts of the 1920's and 1930's[2] there was no sign whatsoever of Russian inspiration. Turkish and Soviet newspapers, in fact, charged the British with responsibility for the Kurdish revolt in 1927, although a Kurdish source[3] subsequently claimed that the decision to revolt had been taken at an all-Kurdish congress at Agri Dag. Kurdish revolts can only partly be regarded as "evidence of a conscious and active feeling of Kurdish unity and nationalism or even of an overwhelming desire for statehood."[4] It may be supposed that the opposition of the tribes to a sedentary mode of life, especially in the dismal conditions prevailing in Iraq and Persia (exploitation in the local industrial centres, or misery and dependence on landowners in agriculture), was the most decisive factor in the revolts already mentioned and those which were to follow. The religious aspect cannot be disregarded either; most of the Kurdish upheavals were headed by religious leaders[5]—the revolt of 1909 was headed by Shaikh Sa'īd; the anti-Turkish revolt of 1925 by the head of a Dervish Order, the Nakshabandri; the Iraqi revolt in the 1930's was headed by the brothers Shaikh Ahmad Barazāni and Mulla Mustafa Barazāni; and the head of the "Independent Republic" in 1945–46 was a Qādi (judge of a Mohammedan court), Qādi Muhammad.

All this does not imply that the complaints about national discrimination and even persecution were unjustified. The lack of tolerance towards minorities, worse in Iraq than in the other Arab countries, caused even moderate leaders, "collaborators" as they were called by the more radical Kurds, to protest. "The administration in Iraq is very bad, the spirit of rabid nationalism has been growing and has reached an all-time high among the Arabs. This has caused the Kurds to think about the necessity for defending their independence and to desire a separate homeland."[6] Though the Kurdish language had officially equal status with Arabic in the districts populated by Kurds, it was claimed that this, like so many other laws, was not observed in practice. There were 200 schools in Iraqi Kurdistan, but Kurdish was the language of tuition in only half of them. In all the public libraries of Iraq there were only 141 books in Kurdish.[7]

Of the two political parties among the Kurds, Heiwa was the older, but Khoiboun (Independence) soon became the more important. It had been founded in Syria in 1927 by members of the 'Ali Badr Khān family, the heroes of Kurdish history in the nineteenth century. The line taken by that organization has always been one of not offending anyone. It justified Russian policy, but declared at the same time that the Kurds were good friends of the West; it was in favour of close relations with the Baghdad government; it successively declared its loyalty to the Paul Reynaud government, Vichy, General de Gaulle, and the British.[8] Khoiboun accepted the Popular Front programme of the Mahabad republic in 1945–46, but at the same time continued its alliance with Tashnak, the very strongly anti-Soviet Armenian party. The main assignment of Khoiboun appears to have been to make the Kurdish views known abroad; for the last twenty years it has been responsible for most of the Kurdish propaganda outside Kurdistan. In Paris Dr. Kamouran Al Badr Khān, the son of the founder, has been publishing the *Bulletin du Centre des Études Kurdes*, which after 1948 received a distinct pro-Soviet slant. Khoiboun was, in short, a propaganda centre rather than a political party.

When World War II broke out, the most active of the Iraqi Kurdish tribes, the Barazāni, and their leaders Shaikh Ahmad and Mulla Mustafa had been exiled for some years from their traditional tribal pastures to Sulaimanya. But after the collapse of 1941 the power of the Baghdad government had not been effectively restored in the outlying areas and it even distributed arms to Kurdish tribes for reasons which have never been fully elucidated to this day.

In 1943 Mulla Mustafa Barazāni, who had escaped from Sulaimanya with many of his followers, again headed a revolt. He was joined by Kurdish officers as well as Kurdish government employees. But this time the Iraqi government took no immediate action. Apparently it lacked the military forces required for another expedition. In addition, though this was perhaps only a minor factor, severe criticism of its treatment of the Kurds was voiced in parliament.[9] Many deputies noted that the government had broken its promises to the tribes, and had deported them to an area in which there was no livelihood for them. Almost all speakers, furthermore, complained about corruption in the local administration and the absence of reforms. After some further prodding in parliament a general amnesty was proclaimed for the Barazāni tribe in April, 1945. But the news had hardly reached the Kurdish region and the Barazāni tribe was again up in arms. In a government counter-attack, Kurdish villages were bombed and destroyed, and in October, 1945, Mulla Mustafa was forced to cross into Iran. The immediate reasons for this revolt were given in a speech in the Iraqi parliament by Majīd Mustafa, one of the moderate Kurd leaders: "The situation in the northern region was said to be especially bad; the inhabitants lacked food and clothing as the result of the war. The government had distributed sugar, but nothing else, and irritated the local people by detaining some leaders of the youth, charging them with 'preoccupation with Kurdish affairs'."[10]

The Kurds in the Soviet Union, residing almost exclusively in Armenia and Azerbaidjan, were completely cut off from the Middle Eastern Kurds until World War II. They were, in effect, neglected, especially by the Armenians, who were strongly reprimanded by the Soviet government for "letting national animosities interfere with their Kurdish policy." The Kurdish peasants were not even organized in the Kolkhoz. But the Soviet government apparently did not consider at all their political potentialities, and did not want to appear as a "Kurdish power" in Middle Eastern politics.

Meanwhile, however, important events had taken place in Persia. With the occupation of Persia by the Allies in 1941, the central government's rule had ceased altogether. The Persian Kurds found themselves mainly in the Soviet zone of occupation, and large stores of arms fell into their hands in the district centres, such as Mahabad and Urmia. The Soviet occupation authorities, realizing at last the possibilities inherent in the situation, appeared as the protectors of the Kurds; in view of the attitude of the Sa'adabad powers and the lack of interest (if not worse) of the West towards Kurdish national aspirations, this was not too difficult a task. In 1942 a number of Kurdish leaders from Persia had been invited to come to Baku. In 1944 the chief of Soviet propaganda in Persia, the press attaché of the Teheran Embassy, Daniil Kommissarov, came to head the Soviet consulate at Rezayeh, where he established close contact with the local leaders, especially Qādi Muhammad.[11] A Kurdish-Soviet Friendship Society was established in Mahabad, and a periodical in Kurdish, edited under Soviet auspices, was founded.

At the same time, internal political organization among the Kurds made rapid progress. The old political groups were in a process of disintegration, but new forces appeared on the scene. There had been a Kurdish section of the Iraqi Communist Party in the late 1930's, but with the many splits of that period it did not last, although there were many Kurds among the leadership and rank and file of the party. According to some sources about 35–40 per cent. of the members of the Iraqi party were Kurds in 1946–47.

In 1943 a new political party was founded in Mahabad, the Kommala Ziani Kurd (Kurdish Youth Committee). The leaders of this group, who hailed mainly from the urban intelligentsia, were not so very young, nor were their followers, but they placed themselves in opposition to the established leadership. Eighteen months later they established, together with the left wing of the Heiwa party (led by Khamza 'Abdullah, 'Awni Yūsuf, and Dr. Ja'afar Muhammad 'Abdul Karīm, and a group of Kurdish Communists), a popular front, Ruskari Kurd (The Kurdish Epoch).

A Soviet historian comments thus on the political development during that period: "In the Kurdish national movement, too, the leading role passed from the feudal and *bourgeois* leadership into the hands of the Kurdish Democratic Party,[12] which was a party alliance of different classes in which, however, the Kurdish workers played an important role. This party entered into an alliance with the Communist Party of Iraq, and thus made a beginning towards a *rapprochement* between Kurds and Arabs. The basic content of the national liberation movement was the demand to abolish the slave treaty (with Britain) of 1930."[13] This appraisal of the events of 1944–46 is not without interest, in showing what should have happened according to Stalinist dogma, but it does not altogether tally with the events themselves. The Kurdish Democratic Party, the force behind the independence movement and the Mahabad Republic, was an alliance between some representatives of the urban intelligentsia and the more radical tribes, in particular, the Barazāni. The Kurdish "proletariat," insofar as it existed, lived in places such as Mosul, which remained outside the sphere of the independence movement. Nor is it true that the Kurdish independence movement saw its main tasks as establishing close relations with the Arabs and in protesting against the 1930 treaty. It was interested in Kurdish independence and little else.

In fact, the Iraqi Communist Party strongly attacked Ruskari Kurd and the Kurdish Communist Party supporting it, calling the latter "apostles of division." They were accused of "separatist tendencies" because they should have found their place within the Iraqi party, which had a Kurdish section with its own newspaper.[14] The Iraqi Communists rejected the assertion of the Kurdish Communists that each people needs its own Communist Party, because "such splits only weaken the anti-imperialist struggle." Nor did they accept the idea of an independent Kurdish state made up of Turkish, Iraqi, and Persian Kurdistans. Were not the Persian Kurds satisfied with home rule within the present borders of Persia? In a second article, published the following month, the Iraqi party organ strongly criticized the assumption of the Kurdish Communists that progressive Arabs did not reveal any interest in the difficulties of the Kurds, and that the realization of Arab ideals in Iraq would hardly benefit the Kurds. It asserted that the tasks of Iraqi and Kurdish Communists were largely identical: the struggle against poverty and disease, against the exploitation of the fellah, the exploitation of the national resources, and so on. The paper concluded by saying that the Kurdish question was part of the larger Iraqi question,[15] and that the liberation of Iraq would bring liberation of the Kurds and the other national minorities.

But the Kurdish Communists were not convinced.[16] What was wrong with establishing a "United Front"?[17] Did not the programme of the new "front" include national self-determination for the Kurds; the fight for the liberation of Iraq from the influence of imperialism and reactionary governments; the demand for administrative independence in Iraq; the demand for social reforms and democratic freedom? Was not the Iraqi Communist Party (or rather the Qā'ida group) to be charged with lack of consistency? Originally they had told the Kurdish Communists to go ahead and establish a "national front." They had even helped to formulate the programme of the "front" and published it in their paper (*Azadi*). But the party having taken root among the masses, the Baghdad Communists all of a sudden declared that it was a mistake to maintain a separate Communist Party. The Communist Party in Iraqi Kurdistan, to give it, for once, its full name, did not contain only Kurds, it numbered also Arabs, Turkmens, and Assyrians among its members. It formed part of the general Communist movement in Iraq, of which Al Qā'ida was the largest group—but not the only one. The whole Communist camp was split between "opportunists" and "loyalists," and Al Qā'ida was no exception to that rule.[18] The Kurdish Communists concluded their polemic by pointing out that the Kurdish people could not be asked to forgo its right to unity and national self-determination; their aims could only gradually be achieved, and the destruction of imperialism and the grant of administrative independence to Iraqi Kurdistan were the first stages towards that aim. The members of the national front fought for the general cause of the Kurds, in Turkey and Persia as well as in Iraq. Did not the Iraqis, too, work for the "liberation of Palestine"?[19]

During the second half of 1946 the Kurdish Communists left Ruskari Kurd nevertheless, and what remained of the latter changed its name, as already mentioned, to Barti Demokrati Kurd. But this "national front" continued to collaborate with the Communists, and there is some reason to assume that the Kurdish Communists left the front, not as a result of the Baghdad charges of "opportunism," but rather in order to make it a more efficient instrument of directing non-Communist groups by remote control, and at the same time to make it seem a "safer" group in the eyes of the authorities, a stratagem which, incidentally, succeeded.[20]

Again, the scene shifts to Persia, where important events had meanwhile taken place. The Kommala (the Committee of Kurdish Youth) in Mahabad had been founded in August, 1943, but it was a semi-secret society and it decided to come into the open only in April, 1945.[21] It was at this time, too, that Qādi Muhammad was accepted as a member of the party. Archibald Roosevelt, Jr., one of the five Westerners who visited the Mahabad Republic during its existence, reports that the Kommala leaders had originally decided not to admit Qādi Muhammad, fearing that, because of his strong and authoritarian character and also because of the deference which they themselves had been accustomed since childhood to show him, he would eventually dominate the party and end its democratic character. And this was indeed what happened.[22] According to all the evidence available, the appointment of Qādi Muhammad had been made under Soviet pressure after three other tribal leaders had politely rejected a similar offer. But there is some reason to believe that the left-wing elements of the Kommala became convinced in the end that they alone would not be able to rally Kurdish opinion for a movement of national liberation, and that a national leader was needed. They needed Qādi Muhammad, just as Muhammad later needed the Barazāni to defend the Kurdish Republic; or, to choose another recent Middle Eastern example, just as the Cairo junta needed General Naguīb for its *coup d'état* in July, 1952.

On September 12, 1945, Captain Namazaliev, Soviet town commandant in Minandaob, summoned the chiefs of the important Kurd tribes, together with Qādi Muhammad and Saif Qādi (his brother and commander of the local gendarmerie), to Tabriz, ostensibly to see the Soviet consul. When they arrived the bewildered Kurds were suddenly told to proceed to the railway station, where they were hustled on to a train and taken to Baku. For three days they lived in a villa outside the town, and were entertained with tours, the theatre, and the opera. On the fourth day they were ushered in to see Baghirov, the President of the Azerbaijan S.S.R., who harangued them regarding the wrongs they had suffered under Reza Shah, and said that the Soviet government would help the new Democratic Party, which was dedicated to freedom for the oppressed and which he strongly urged them to join. He condemned both the Tudeh Party, which he characterized as a group of ineffective trouble-makers, and the Kommala, which, he said, was started in Iraq under the auspices of British Intelligence, and was nothing but an instrument of British imperialism. Then, after being warned not to say anything about the trip, the Kurds were put on the train to Tabriz, where they were loaded into Red Army vehicles and driven off to their homes.[23]

Several days later, at a meeting of notables and tribal leaders, the Democratic Party of Kurdistan was founded. The aims of the new movement, as laid down in a manifesto, included:

1. Self-government in the administration of Kurdish local affairs and autonomy within the limits of the Persian state.
2. The Kurdish language to be used in education and to become the official language in administrative affairs.
3. Immediate election of the provincial council of Kurdistan.
4. All state officials to be of local origin.
5. A single law for both peasants and notables.
6. A special effort to establish unity and complete fraternity with the people of Azerbaijan.
7. The improvement of the moral and economic state of the Kurdish people through the exploitation of Kurdistan's many natural resources, the progress of agriculture and commerce, and the development of hygiene and education.

It is interesting to note that a contemporary Soviet account believed points 1, 2, and 5 of the manifesto to be the most important and did not mention the rest.[24]

On October 11, 1945, Mulla Mustafa Barazāni, whose exploits in Iraq we have already reported, crossed the border into Persia with several hundred fighters of his tribe, to escape from a pursuing Iraqi army force. With him were several of the leaders of the Iraqi Democratic Party (Ruskari Kurd), and several Kurdish officers, deserters from the Iraqi army, who had been excluded from the Iraqi amnesty previously mentioned. The stage was now set for the establishment of the Kurdish republic. Five days after the surrender of the Persian government garrison to the local Democratic Azerbaidjani forces, Qādi Muhammad proclaimed the establishment of a "Kurdish People's Government" in Mahabad (December 15, 1945). During the second half of January, 1946, a parliament of thirteen was assembled, undoubtedly one of the smallest in history, and Qādi Muhammad was elected president of a Kurdish Republic of about one million inhabitants.

The story of the Mahabad Republic was comparatively uneventful on the domestic front; it was less than a "Popular Democracy," and a Soviet source notes that in contrast to Azerbaijan no agrarian reform was carried out in Kurdistan.[25] This is not surprising in view of the fact that the members of the government belonged to the old ruling classes and that the villages were run by their old landlords and tribal leaders. They were backed up by a gendarmerie locally recruited but commanded by officers from Mahabad in Soviet uniforms.

According to the evidence of the same observer, Kurdistan was to outside appearance free from Soviet agents. There were few if any political prisoners, and only one or two cases of political assassination. Outside broadcasts could be listened to in the streets of Mahabad; the net result was to make the regime popular at least among the citizens of Mahabad, who enjoyed their respite from the exactions and oppression they considered to be characteristic of the central Persian government.[26] In the cultural field the new government saw its main task as publishing school text-books and newspapers in Kurdish. On the whole, it would appear, therefore, that the Soviets were satisfied with the existence of a strongly pro-Russian government and did not want to press for any major changes, at least during the initial stage of the Kurdish Republic. Qādi Muhammad was not slow to adapt himself to the official Communist jargon in his speeches, but even thus it appeared that he was interested in Kurdish independence more than in anything else. It is doubtful whether he would have entered Soviet historiography as the "most distinguished Kurdish national leader" had he lived longer.

Several interesting differences between the programme of the Mahabad Republic and those of the Kurdish Democratic Party in Persia and its sister party in Iraq should be noted. Qādi Muhammad was in favour of Kurdish autonomy within the Persian state. The Iraqi Kurdish Party, on the other hand, demanded a federative Iraqi state, but freedom for the Kurds in their foreign policy, too. They also demanded the nationalization of all natural resources—while preserving ownership of the land—economic development, and an increase in the standard of living, as well as separation of the "Church" from the "State." This last demand is of particular interest, because in the Mahabad Republic the national movement and the party were headed by the clergy. The reason for this divergence was, in all probability, that among the Iraqi Kurds, and especially among the urban middle class who constituted the mainstay of Ruskari Kurd, the religious dignitaries were less influential.

There was, inevitably, some friction between the Kurdish Republic and the central authorities in Teheran, but considerably less than in the republic's relations with the Azerbaijani Communist Democrats in Tabriz. This apparent paradox can easily be explained. Between the Kurds and Teheran there were hardly any bones of contention, apart, perhaps, from a few local clashes in May and June, 1946. But both Tabriz and Mahabad claimed a comparatively large area west of Lake Urmia, and the Soviets had frequently to intervene as peace-makers. In April, 1946, a Treaty of Friendship and Alliance between Tabriz and Mahabad was signed. This, however, did not lead towards a lasting improvement between the two regimes, and there was the feeling in Mahabad that "the Kurds had progressed from the condition of a minority in the Persian state to that of a minority in an Azerbaijani Turkish state."[27] In the end, Qādi Muhammad even went to Teheran to complain to the central government about the encroachment of the Tabriz regime! But his time was running out fast. After the Soviet evacuation of Azerbaidjan, the Teheran government proceeded to re-establish its authority in the northern regions. Azerbaijan fell without any opposition worth mentioning, and the turn of Kurdistan came soon after. Meanwhile, Qādi Muhammad had arranged for elections, and he announced, without apparently realizing how much the situation had changed, that, though he was perfectly loyal to the central (Persian) government, no troops were to enter the republic during the election period. But Teheran by now cared little about formalities, and an army column proceeding from Tabriz entered Kurdistan in mid-December. There was no fighting, and relations between the Persian army commanders and the government of Qādi Muhammad were excellent in the beginning. But soon the members of the Mahabad government were arrested. According to one source, Qādi Muhammad was arrested in Mahabad, while according to another he went to the capital to express his loyalty to the central government and was arrested there, after having been received by the Persian Prime Minister. Qādi Muhammad and several members of his government were executed in March, 1947. Some of the tribal chiefs were executed, too, and all outward signs of Kurdish independence were destroyed. What were the reasons for the defeat of the Kurdish Republic—without, in fact, any resistance? The traditional tribal enmities were one of the main causes. When the Russians appointed Qādi Muhammad to head the republic, they antagonized automatically other leading Kurdish personalities. When Qādi Muhammad used the Barazāni tribe as his main military force, he antagonized other tribes. Moreover, there was much friction between the Barazāni and Qādi Muhammad during the second half of 1946. Kurdish patriotism did not prevail over petty traditional jealousies. Another contributory factor was the discontent of many tribes that had lost the markets for their products as the result of the establishment of the state, and whose economic position had deteriorated. And lastly, the urban intelligentsia, the main driving force in the national movement, did not see eye to eye with the tribal leaders. Everything that Marx and Engels had said about the weakness of peasant movements came true—and many of the Kurds were not even peasants but nomads. The Russians, who had promised much help, did not provide any, and in the end Qādi Muhammad was betrayed by all.

The aftermath of the Mahabad Republic can be summarized very briefly. Mulla Mustafa Barazāni and his warriors fought their way back to Iraq, but, harassed by Iraqi government forces, they had to leave the country again and crossed into the Soviet Union in June–July, 1947. Some of his aides were executed in the summer of 1947 by the Iraqi authorities, thereby provoking another small-scale revolt, headed by Mulla Mustafa's nephew, Muhammad Khālid, in October, 1947.

In the same year the Turkish press complained about Kurdish collaboration with the fanatical Moslem circles in Eastern Turkey, while the Syrian press reported in January, 1948, an all-Kurdish congress to prepare another big revolt; if, indeed, this meeting did take place, it cannot have been of great importance. A member of the Kurdish propaganda centre, Muhammad Ilmi Bey, representing the Kurdish Democratic Party, contacted the heads of several delegations at the U.N. at this time, requesting their help on behalf of the Kurds. Other reports during 1948–49 announced the establishment of a new Kurdish people's government on Soviet soil and a return of the Barazānis in the near future. But nothing came of these plans, and in June, 1949, Shaikh Mahmūd, one of the Kurdish rebel leaders, admitted defeat in a letter to the Baghdad government, and requested the appointment of a governor in Sulaimanya, which had been held by his forces up to that date. After some delay the Baghdad government sent a representative, and the Minister of the Interior promised, as several of his predecessors had promised, to do something for the final settlement of the Barazānis.[28] At the same time, another amnesty for ninety-seven leading Barazānis (excluding, however, Mulla Mustafa) was proclaimed.

The Kurdish revolt, to all intents and purposes, was over then, and the Kurdish national movement ceased to exist, apart from the sporadic activities of a few propagandists outside Kurdistan. But there is little reason to doubt the reports that pictures of Qādi Muhammad and Stalin still hang, or have been hanging, in many a Kurdish home.[29] Neither the Baghdad nor the Teheran governments have been able to establish full authority in the Barazāni, Sulaimanya, and Mahabad area, and the Kurds there can do very much what they like—apart from proclaiming independent republics. At the same time, Mulla Mustafa and his men in the Soviet Caucasus are undoubtedly held in reserve for future action. One of the reasons for the defeat of the Mahabad Republic was the lack of capable cadres; it can be taken for granted that a future attempt will not fail for the same reason. Whether massive Soviet help will be given in future to the Kurdish independence movement mainly depends, admittedly, on the international situation. However, as long as the Middle Eastern governments concerned refuse to compromise with the Kurdish movement for independence and national autonomy, as long as the West prefers to take an attitude of studied disregard towards the Kurdish movement, its orientation towards the Soviet Union will probably continue. Iraqi and Persian intransigence towards the Kurds, coupled with the lack of stable and efficient central government, makes a new Communist-led upsurge of the Kurdish national movement in the not too distant future a likely prospect.

2. THE ARMENIANS

Pro-Russian sentiments among Armenians in the Middle East (as elsewhere) are pronounced, but of more recent origin than is generally supposed. The Czarist government used to deport many of the troublesome Armenians from the Caucasus, and to incite the various peoples of the Caucasus to fight each other; this diplomacy of divide and conquer resulted in repeated and bloody massacres of Azerbaijani Turks, Armenians, and Georgians. Generally speaking, however, the Armenians were not more discriminated against than the other nationalities, and they could reach influential positions in all walks of Russian life, including politics (e.g. Prime Minister Loris Melikov). The government which had come into existence in Erevan, the Armenian capital, after the Russian Revolution of 1917 was far from being Communist; it was headed by the Dashnak Party, and it was overthrown only after more or less co-ordinated pressure and military attacks by Turks and Soviet Russians. Moreover, in 1920 the Soviet government ceded to Mustafa Kemal the Kars and Ardahan districts, making its later claims to be the protector of the Armenians appear in a somewhat peculiar light. On the other hand, there was a strong workers' movement among the Armenians even prior to World War I. Shaumyan, Spandaryan, and Knunyants were among the leading Bolsheviki of their time. In the 1920's the percentage of Communist Party members among the Armenians was considerably higher than among Great Russians. There have been, and still are, Armenian members of the Soviet Politburo (Mikoyan), Armenian army marshals (Bagramyan), etc. In Turkey many thousands of Armenians had been killed, while in Russia they had received a republic of their own, however small and dependent. There is no reason to doubt that the Soviet Union represented for many Armenians the lesser evil—and this by a wide margin. Armenian pro-Sovietism must, therefore, be viewed against the background of their implacable hostility towards Turkey.

The largest Middle Eastern community of Armenians was in Syria and Lebanon (180,000). There were 100,000 Armenians in Persia; 30,000 in Egypt; and 15,000 in Iraq. The influence of the Armenians in the Syrian and Lebanese Communist Party was, therefore, the strongest by far; in Iraq it was much weaker, and in Egypt hardly felt at all. Ohannes Agbashian, the leader of the Armenian section of the Lebanese Communist Party, was also editor of the Armenian Communist newspaper *Yogvurti Tsai* (Voice of the People). In the 1950's Artin Maduyan became one of Bakdāsh's most trusted lieutenants. In Iraq *Banki Felah* was the organ of the Armenian section which, however, according to reliable reports, numbered only some dozen members. There has been no Armenian Communist newspaper in Palestine (Israel), and no regular publication in Egypt.

The Communist groups in Syria and Lebanon were very much weakened, and many local branches ceased to exist altogether, as the result of the Soviet repatriation policy in 1946–48. This decision of the Moscow Politburo in November, 1945, was obviously intended to intensify the war of nerves against Turkey and to give additional stress to the Soviet territorial demands for Kars and Ardahan. All in all, slightly more than 100,000 Armenians[30] entered Russia during 1946–48, and only a few hundred thereafter; in 1950 repatriation was discontinued altogether. The repatriates were mainly pro-Soviet elements; Dashnak was hardly interested. As a result, relatively few Armenian Communists have remained in the Middle East. What has been preserved is the dependence of large parts of the Armenian Church on the "Armenian Pope," the Catholikos in Etchmiadzin, near Erivan.

3. THE CHRISTIAN ORTHODOX CHURCHES

There used to be close ties between the Christian Orthodox Churches in the Middle East and their traditional "protector," Russia. This, of course, has no direct connection with the activities of the Communist Parties in the Middle East, but it is not purely accidental either that most of the Arab Communist leaders in Palestine are, or were, Greek Orthodox; "Fahd," the leader of the Iraqi Communists, was a Christian, as is Nikola Shāwi, editor of *Sawt ash-Sha'ab* in Lebanon, among others. The attitude of the Orthodox community towards Russia has, on the whole, been a favourable one, and some of the more amenable clergymen, including the very highest, have received material help from Moscow. Yet, largely owing to the refusal of the Moscow Patriarchate to recognize the Constantinople Patriarch as *primus inter pares* of the four Patriarchates in the Middle East, Constantinople is no friend of the Soviets; Alexandria had been rather friendly in 1944–45, but cooled down subsequently; and Jerusalem is neutral, though willing enough to accept Soviet support. Only the fourth Patriarch, Alexander III Tahan of Antiochia, has been staunchly pro-Soviet. His attitude has been rewarded, and his Patriarchate has been allowed for several years to maintain a mission in Moscow and to arrange regular prayers in a

Moscow church.[31] Alexander Tahan has frequently been in Moscow since World War II, and an interview after one of these visits gives a fairly typical example of his political outlook:

"Our ties with Russia have existed ever since our Church came into being, and they will continue whatever regime prevails in Russia. . . . The Catholic Church, headed by the Pope, fights us everywhere in our villages, towns, and organizations, in Syria, Lebanon, and elsewhere. It relies in this struggle on the Western powers. In these conditions we had no alternative but to put an end to our isolation. I did this as head of the Orthodox Church, which has sister Churches in Russia and elsewhere; together we shall be able to resist the enemies and defend ourselves against their intrigues. 'To resist' means to withstand the onslaught of the hostile groups which rely on the powers calling themselves 'democratic.' . . . I asked the Moscow Patriarch, the strongest of all, for spiritual and material help. . . . It is alleged that Communism is against religion, but the victory of religion in Russia points to the contrary."[32]

It should be mentioned here that the Russian Church frequently exploits the resentment of the lower Arab clergy against the Greeks who hold the higher positions. Alexander Tahan is the only Arab among the high dignitaries of the Orthodox Church.

4. THE JEWS, ASSYRIANS, AND OTHERS

Jews have played a prominent part in the Communist movement in the Middle East. They have been in leading positions in the Egyptian party, as well as in Iraq (Dalāl and Yehuda Ibrahim Sādiq), though they have never played an important role in the strongest section, the Levant Communist movement. During the last ten years, however, the situation has radically changed, as the result of the emigration of many Jews to Palestine, because of the emergence of native cadres in Egypt, and in view of the fact that it has become very difficult, if not impossible, for Jews to be active in the Arab countries.

Some importance should be attributed to the Assyrians (mainly in the Communist Parties of Persia and Iraq), the Greeks, and Italians (in Egypt), and other minorities. But these were numerically too weak to be of great political consequence. In the first stage of the history of Communism in the Middle East the great majority of members belonged to such minorities. This is, perhaps, not surprising if one considers that the middle class and the intelligentsia in the Middle Eastern countries are, at or least have been up to very recently, predominantly foreign. If, for instance, about 25 per cent. of the members of the Iraqi Communist Party in 1946–47 were reported to be Jews, it has to be remembered that this was approximately the percentage of Jews among the urban middle class.

Nonetheless, national complaints and demands, especially in regard to Armenians and Jews, cannot be disregarded altogether; these and other minorities have felt persecution and injustice more acutely than the majority, and have been more ready to fight for what they believed to be an internationalist creed which would put an end to national injustice once and for all.

Chapter Eighteen

Partners for a National Front

FOR more than ten years now the Middle East has been a success-ful experimental field for Communist-front organizations of various kinds. "Communists scorn to conceal their real intentions," runs one of the concluding sentences of the *Communist Manifesto*. Latter-day events have proved Marx mistaken: the lesson of twenty-five years of Communist history (1918–43) in the Middle East has been that very little can be achieved by open statements of intentions. And the lessons of the ten subsequent years show beyond the shadow of a doubt, that concealing one's intention does pay. Communist collabora-tion with other political parties and movements began in the late 1920's when the party line was to collaborate with the left wing of national movements, such as the Wafd in Egypt or the Istiqlāl Party in Palestine. But this co-operation could not be fruitful because there were no strong socialist or left-wing democratic movements in any of the Arab countries, nor are there any now. The political allies which the Com-munists have found in recent years came from quite different quarters: the extreme right-wing and fanatical religious camp, such as the Moslem Brotherhood and Ahmad Husain's "Socialist" party in Egypt, the Istiqlāl in Iraq, and other groups elsewhere. Each particular tie of this kind could probably be explained as a freak, an interesting phenomenon but nevertheless atypical. But the fact that such collaboration has not been restricted to one particular country but has taken place everywhere in the Middle East makes generalization and the drawing of certain con-clusions imperative. It cannot be pure coincidence that the main proponents of Fascism in Egypt, Syria, or Iraq co-operate nowadays with the Communists in the framework of sundry national, anti-imperialist, and "peace" fronts.

I. THE MOSLEM BROTHERHOOD

(a) *The Origins of the Moslem Brotherhood*

Best known among these groups in the West was the Moslem Brotherhood, but its notoriety is largely due to news reports of attempted assassinations of political enemies (admittedly a prominent feature of Brotherhood activities), rather than to investigations into its political and social motivations.

The Moslem Brotherhood was founded in Isma'ilia in the Suez Canal Zone in April, 1929, by a young teacher, Hasan al Banna'. In the late 1920's and the early 1930's several such Moslem youth organizations were launched throughout the Middle East, but only the Ikhwān lasted. Al Banna' was only twenty-three years old when he engaged on this venture; he served as a teacher of the Arabic language and Moslem religion, and excelled as a spellbinder of the masses and especially of the youth. A devout Moslem, he set a pattern for his followers in his modest way of life; a nickname of later years, "Shaikh Rasputin," would appear to belong to the realm of political calumny.

The basic idea of the Brotherhood, that both private and public life should be remodelled according to the teachings of Islam, fell on fertile ground in the Egypt of the 1930's.[1] There was growing dissatisfaction with both the traditional parties and the Wafd; for the peasants (among whom no Egyptian party had ever got, or had ever tried to get, a firm foothold) the idea of reforms had, of course, a strong attraction. At the same time, the pronounced xenophobic trend, far surpassing anything known up to that date in Egypt, was a major asset of the movement and very much in line with the prevalent state of mind and the emotional exigencies of the urban masses. Hasan al Banna' established close relations with 'Ali Māhir, Prime Minister in 1939, and with the Palace; he received financial assistance which was used to launch various economic enterprises, such as factories, big shops, etc.

The Brotherhood bitterly fought the Wafd, its main competitor as a mass movement, but when this party came to power in 1942 al Banna' and Mustafa Nahhās, Wafd leader and Prime Minister, reached a working agreement which lasted almost up to the end of the war. Early in 1942 Hasan al Banna' promised Mustafa Nahhās to discontinue his pro-Axis propaganda and was subsequently released from prison. (He had been arrested in May, 1941.) It would appear that on the whole this undertaking was kept by the leadership of the Brotherhood. Some of the leading personalities of the Brotherhood entered government service, notably the Ministry for Social Affairs, and were given virtually a free hand to organize branches in the villages throughout the countries, thus exploiting their official status. In 1946–47 Hasan al Banna' switched his political support several times; first he backed the anti-Wafdist government of Isma'īl Sidqi, but after the Bevin-Sidqi pact (which never came into force) he joined the opposition headed by the Wafd. Soon, however, new disputes arose between these two main forces in Egyptian politics. The Wafd left wing, which had been greatly strengthened immediately after World War II, regarded the Brotherhood as a reactionary movement to be combatted, while some of the Wafdist right-wingers, such as Fuād Sarāg ad-Dīn, saw it, on the contrary, as a useful counterweight to both Socialist and Communist ideas.[2] However, owing to the authoritarian structure of the movement, only the "Supreme Guide" and the executive knew the full truth about these political manœuvres, the rank and file was hardly ever informed and remained unspoiled by the intricacies of political horse-trading and power politics.

In 1946–47 the Brotherhood reached the summit of its influence; according to one of its leaders, the number of members was then 2·5 million.[3] The fighting units of the movement were given military training for the impending struggle in Palestine, and police and government offices received instructions not to hinder the Brotherhood in collecting arms. This followed an agreement between Hasan al Banna' and Haj Amīn al Husaini, the ex-Mufti of Jerusalem; collaboration between these two leaders had begun in the late 1930's when the Mufti had assisted al Banna' to get the support of influential circles which had originally hesitated in backing such a "plebeian" organization. Military camps were established at El Arish in the Sinai and in the western desert by the Brotherhood units, which later participated in the Palestine campaign without, however, greatly influencing its outcome.[4]

When the units of the Brotherhood returned to Egypt they did what armed units in similar situations have done time and again—they revolted against the powers that be. The fate of Hasan al Banna' was similar to that of Codreanu, the leader of the Rumanian "Iron Guard," a movement whose ideology and history offers some striking parallels; King Farouk, too, was exiled in the end, just as his Rumanian cousin had been. The Sa'adist-Liberal government in power in 1948 had originally supported the Brotherhood, but after the defeat in Palestine, and in the general atmosphere of dissatisfaction, it came to regard the Ikhwān as a formidable danger; the leaders of the movement had apparently decided to turn their arms against the government. It has never been proved whether Hasan al Banna' really intended, as was argued at a later occasion,[5] to take over state power at a predetermined date, killing most of the leaders of the day, proclaiming a republic, and having himself elected caliph. But there can hardly be any doubt that even if zero hour had not been fixed, the whole political atmosphere made such a development at least a possibility. In November and early December a number of serious terroristic outrages were committed by the fighting units of the Brotherhood; several foreign-language newspaper offices were blown up, and the commander of Cairo police killed. In this situation the Prime Minister, Mahmūd Nukrāshi, banned the Brotherhood on

December 8. Hundreds of the party leaders and militants were arrested and held in the concentration camps of Tur and Huckstep, together with Jews and Communists.[6] However, the Brotherhood's campaign of terror continued unabated, and several days later the Prime Minister himself was killed. His successor, Ibrahīm 'Abdul Hādi, now took severe measures to suppress the Brotherhood, and the murder of Hasan al Banna' in February, 1949, would not appear to be entirely unconnected with these steps. This counter-terror was temporarily successful, and the Brotherhood terrorist campaign ceased.

In October, 1950, however, after the Wafdist government once again had come to power, the demand for ending the ban on the Brotherhood was renewed, and government coalition and opposition soon competed in requesting the release of the last arrested of the movement and the return of the property of the Brotherhood that had been seized in 1950. In May, 1951, the ban was lifted on condition that Ikhwān political activities would be subject to certain limitations and that the semimilitary activities would have to be discontinued altogether. But the Brotherhood spokesmen proclaimed at once that they would not heed these warnings. In October, 1951, the new Supreme Guide of the movement was elected. The lack of a leader had very much impaired activities after the murder of al Banna'. But the new Supreme Guide, Hasan al Hudaibi, a former judge of the Court of Appeal, was quite unlike al Banna'; an eminently respectable and conservative citizen, who was even received by King Farouk in audience after his election, he utterly lacked the mass appeal and the enthusiasm of al Banna', especially the latter's zest for social reform. His election was a blow to Sālih Ashmāwi, who had been the deputy leader of the movement since the death of Hasan al Banna', and who was far more radical in both his national and his social demands. Around Ashmāwi and his magazine Ad-Da'wa (The Appeal) an opposition group crystallized, and the struggle between Ashmāwi and the official leadership seriously weakened the activities of the Brotherhood up to the time of its dissolution in 1954.

The political line taken by al Hudaibi was one of "safety first," and he was criticized not only by the Brotherhood opposition but by extremist circles outside it. Owing apparently to al Hudaibi's reticence, the movement was not officially engaged in the events which led to "Black Saturday" in January, 1952. But the Brotherhood had been instrumental in establishing fighting units for the struggle against the British in the Canal Zone, and the Cairo members of the movement had joined the Bulak Nizām (the auxiliary police) in their demonstrations. After "Black Saturday," Hudaibi collaborated with 'Ali Māhir, who was appointed Prime Minister, but he was much more reserved in his attitude towards Hilāli, who replaced 'Ali Māhir in March, 1952. Under the pressure of the radical wing of the Ikhwān, al Hudaibi, in a memorandum, demanded that a time-limit should be set for talks with the British.

The group of officers who carried out the *coup d'état* in July, 1952, and deposed Farouk included a number of Brotherhood members (notably Colonel Rashad Muhanna) and sympathizers; one of the members of the Brotherhood executive became a minister in the new government (Shaikh Hassan al Baqūri). But it cannot be said that the Ikhwān and its leaders knew about the army initiative or participated in the *coup*.[7] However, several weeks after the revolt the Brotherhood executive gave up its attitude of studied reserve and declared that in the interests of Egypt it would "guard and protect" the military movement. But the radical reforms, especially the agrarian reforms, were not after the liking of al Hudaibi and the conservative leadership; at one time, in October, 1952, it was reported that al Hudaibi had resigned, or been forced to resign, and that leadership had passed into the hands of Sālih Ashmāwi and 'Abdur-Rahmān al Banna', the son of the first Supreme Guide. Al Hudaibi was said to have emphasized the pan-Islamic character of the Brotherhood and its ties with other countries, whereas Ashmāwi and his friends wanted to make the movement an Egyptian political party—and a radical one at that.[8] But by this time the initial reformist zest of the junta had already cooled considerably after having encountered unforeseen obstacles, and in the end al Hudaibi was restored to the Supreme Guideship.

Relations between the Brotherhood and the new regime remained excellent, at least on the surface; members of the junta came to visit the Ikhwān clubs, and appeared, together with Ikhwān members, in public meetings and demonstrations. When the political parties were dissolved in January, 1953, this move did not affect the Brotherhood, which was recognized by the authorities as a "non-political organization." (It was resolved, however, at the same time to discontinue the activities of the political department of the Brotherhood.) But in fact there was much dissension between the officers and the heads of the Ikhwān, who demanded an Islamic constitution, not "Western reforms."[9] In foreign policy the Brotherhood opposed talks with the British on evacuation, repeatedly stating that a "people's war" should be preferred to negotiations. At the same time there were serious differences of opinion within the leadership of the movement; the Ashmāwi group continued to attack al Hudaibi and the other conservative leaders for not actively participating in the reform work of the "Liberation Movement." The elections for the 1953 conference of the Brotherhood brought a strengthening of the radical opposition; Shaikh Farghalli, the head of the organization in the Canal Zone, and Hasan al Banna's son were both elected to the executive of the Ikhwān.[10] Several leading members of the Brotherhood, including the Mufti of the Moslem Brotherhood, were ousted during a new internal crisis of November and December, 1953; in January,

1954, after further quarrels and attacks upon the government, the junta dissolved the Brotherhood and arrested 400 of its leaders. Three months later, however, the Brotherhood was again permitted to resume its activities; Colonel Nāsir did not yet feel himself strong enough for a decisive contest, but his hand was soon to be forced.

On October 26, 1954, while he was speaking in Alexandria, an attempt on the life of Colonel 'Abdul Nāsir was made by Mahmūd 'Abdul Latīf, a member of the Brotherhood; Nāsir escaped unhurt. Mass arrests of the Brotherhood followed; the junta announced that a general massacre of its members and their military supporters had been planned. From prison some of the Brotherhood leaders suggested terms on which peace should be restored between the government and the Brotherhood (the demand was made that further arrests cease in exchange for a promise that the Ikhwān would dissolve its secret military organization). But the junta, apparently believing that the clash was unavoidable, resolved to continue the purge, which affected also Brotherhood sympathizers in the army, navy, and air force—and General Naguīb. On December 5 the Brotherhood was officially declared dissolved, and on the same day seven of its main leaders were condemned to be hanged. (The death sentence imposed on the Supreme Guide was later commuted to life imprisonment.) Some militants escaped to Syria, where they attempted to launch a protest movement against the policy of the Cairo junta. Meanwhile, however, their organization was broken up, and although some underground cells were undoubtedly not uncovered, the Brotherhood as such ceased to exist.

During the last phase of its existence, collaboration between the Ikhwān and the Egyptian Communists had been fairly close. An agreement had been reached in July, 1954, between the two movements to co-operate in distributing leaflets. (The Brotherhood newspaper ceased to appear in July, 1954, and Sayyid Qutub published instead a series of leaflets.) Agreement to this effect was reached at a meeting between a Communist representative, Muhammad 'Abdul Mun'im Tamām, who was in charge of the Agitprop department of the Egyptian Communist Party, and Brotherhood leaders. At a subsequent meeting, also in July, 1954, another Communist leader, "Nāsir," discussed with his Brotherhood contacts the feasibility of armed demonstrations against the junta.[11] The Brotherhood representatives proposed a two-point common platform: (a) the cessation of the negotiations with Britain and the renewal of the armed fight, and (b) the abolition of military law and "all the laws opposed to freedom." This was accepted by the Communists, who demanded, however, a more concrete and specific programme of action. At a third meeting, when Tamām again represented the Communists, it was resolved to go slow on opposition activities in the army, because these would become known at once to the junta. There were apparently differences of opinion among the Brotherhood chieftains with regard to the desirability of an armed demonstration, but after further talks in Alexandria between Yūsuf Tala'at, the head of the Ikhwān secret branch, and the Supreme Guide, it was resolved to publish leaflets in favour of the demonstration and in collaboration with the Communists. The Brotherhood and the Communists also used an illegal broadcasting station in common,[12] and there were further revelations of co-operation following the arrest in December, 1954, of an Egyptian journalist who had allegedly served as liaison officer between the Brotherhood and the Communists.

The change in attitude of the Brotherhood towards Communists, and vice versa, from extreme hostility in 1945–46 to close co-operation in 1953–54, should be seen against the background of common opposition to "Western influences" and of the attempt by the junta to Westernize (or rather modernize) the country. No ideological affinity was needed to cement that common front; in documents published at the time of the Cairo trials of leaders of the Brotherhood it was occasionally argued by them that the Communists were no serious rivals, and that they could be easily eliminated once the Ikhwān were victorious in their fight.

In fact, the very opposite proved true, and not a few members of the Ikhwān went over to the Communists because the latter had a clearer political programme, and emerged, generally speaking, as the stronger political factor in view of their much larger experience in underground work and organization. The leaders of the Brotherhood who refused to take the Communists seriously as a factor of equal political importance under conditions of illegality, and who thought it would be easy to get rid of them in due time, proved to be no match for the Communists.

(b) Their Creed

Both the ideology and the practice of the Moslem Brotherhood changed considerably during the years of its existence. The founder of the movement was undoubtedly a radical, however vague his social programme, whereas his successor was a conservative. Hasan al Banna' was a socialist in the same sense as the leaders of the Rumanian Iron Guard. His was a national socialism minus the class struggle. Al Hudaibi, on the other hand, thought social reforms were largely unnecessary, and believed that all problems could be solved without taking refuge in new-fangled Western ideas and slogans, merely by adhering closely to the prescriptions of Islam.

The ideology of the Brotherhood goes back to the fundamentalist teachings of Muhammad Ibn 'Abdul Wahāb in the eighteenth century; it does not have much in common with the attempts made in nineteenth-century Egypt by leaders like Muhammad 'Abduh to reform Islam by adapting it to the modern world. The fanaticism of the Wahabites was fundamentalism pure and simple: a return to the Koran and the elimination of all relaxations of religious discipline which have appeared in the course of time. It meant that the study of the Koran, prayer, and the observation of fasts were again to become the centre of human activity, and that puritanism in daily life was to be restored and all luxuries, including the consuming of spirits and tobacco, were to be banned. Life was again to become as simple and pure as it had been in the time of the Prophet; the only problem, of course, was, how to apply these teachings to city life in the twentieth century.

In a similar way the "restoration of morality" was again to be the central issue in the eyes of the Brotherhood. "The only solution is a reform of morals," al Hudaibi stressed time and again, and when asked how the religious precepts of Islam could be adapted to modern conditions, he occasionally provided even details[13]: "Foreign journalists have told me that there are two Islamic laws incompatible with present-day conditions: the one which demands that the hand of the thief should be chopped off, and the other banning interest on money. I have replied that we should by no means renounce these laws. Before announcing this precept, Islam had already assured the livelihood of everybody and nobody was compelled to steal. If somebody steals nevertheless, without necessity, his hand should be chopped off. But if he has not enough to live on and steals for this reason, his hand should not be chopped off. As for taking interest, I understand that there are German and British economists who favour banning interest because they believe it to be the main reason for the deterioration of economic conditions in the world. Islam has preceded them by fourteen centuries. But apart from the two points nobody has been able to find anything in the prescriptions of Islam which contradicts the conditions of modern life."

There happens to be an interesting parallel between the Moslem Brotherhood's opposition to taking interest (which, however, in practice is watered down and mostly disregarded) and the attitude of many right-wing "socialist" movements in Europe, including the early socialist phase of Nazism in Germany. But there are many more stumbling-blocks—the position of women in Islamic society is one of them. When asked whether he approved of women being active in political life and social affairs, the Supreme Guide replied that the "natural place of a woman was in her home." If, however, having fulfilled her duties at home she wished to serve society, there was nothing in Islam to prevent her from doing so, provided this was done under conditions "compatible with her dignity and honour." As an illustration he mentioned that one of his daughters was a lecturer in Cairo University and the other was studying medicine. It should be noted, on the other hand, that the lower echelons of the Moslem Brotherhood have been far less tolerant, and there were frequent clashes between Ikhwān adherents among the students and Wafdist or Communists on the issue of women students in the university.

The organizational structure of the Brotherhood resembled the set-up of the fascist and authoritarian parties in Europe, but there were certain changes after the death of Hasan al Banna'; important decisions were later made by the executive as a whole (*Maktab al Irshād al 'Aām*) rather than by the Supreme Guide. The *Fuehrerprinzip* was largely relinquished. This, however, was caused mainly by the absence of a strong personality as leader and not by any process of democratization. In the lifetime of Hasan al Banna' the members of the executive were appointed by the Supreme Guide, not elected, but after his death, and as a result of the many splits, the holders of nearly all important assignments in the movement were elected. Apart from the Brotherhood executive there were sub-committees dealing with financial, foreign, social, religious, and propaganda affairs; a special department dealt with student affairs, and there was an intelligence service. The semi-military storm-troops of the Brotherhood, Al Gawāla, were headed by a ten-member command; the basic units consist of five members who receive military training from ex-police and army officers. From these military units small groups for special (mostly terrorist) actions, the Fadayān, were recruited.

The outstanding features of the ideology of the Brotherhood were its vagueness and the considerable contrast between the articles of belief and the practice of the Ikhwān. Their doctrine was the Koran, and they wanted to put society on an Islamic basis. This, they believed, would not be difficult at all, since Islam was a system of positive law and ". . . all religions can accept the criminal, civil, commercial, or international law of Islam. It conforms more to the spirit of Christianity and Judaism than does the French law [in use in Egypt] which stems from the Roman heathen and is of materialistic rather than of Christian inspiration."[14] Why should a minority object to being ruled by Islamic law so long as it enjoys full freedom of conscience and religious service? But, in fact, the attitude of the Ikhwān towards the non-Moslem has been ambivalent. The leaders of the movement have occasionally stressed the necessity of a common struggle for national liberation, and demanded religious tolerance[15]; but in fact both Coptic churches and Jewish synagogues were frequently attacked by Brotherhood units in 1944–46 and again during the riots of 1952–53, and the attitude of the rank and file towards the religious minorities has been on the whole very hostile. The most intricate point of Brotherhood ideology was perhaps their attempt to co-ordinate Islamic unity and Egyptian nationalism. Hasan al Banna' defined *wataniyya* (patriotism) as love of "this country, populated by Moslems," and the wish to liberate it from the yoke of the foreign intruders.[16] But there is an important difference between this idea of patriotism and the Western notion shared by other Egyptian parties. According to the latter the frontiers of the fatherland are geographic; according to the Ikhwān', the fatherland is where Moslems live. *Qaumiyya* (nationalism) means, according to al Banna', the preservation of the traditional values, such as readiness to engage on a holy war for the ideals of Islam. The Ikhwān opposed a return to the national ideals of the pre-Islamic period (such as in Turkey), and the theories of racial superiority (such as prevailed in Germany and Italy). As a "pan" movement the Brotherhood could not accept the existence of separate Moslem states, inasmuch as its final aim is the establishment of one great Moslem fatherland. But this will be achieved only with final victory, according to Hasan al Banna'.

The Ikhwān favoured a theocratic state; this demand brought them into conflict with all democratic parties and with the military regime, which does not accept this tenet. Occasionally their leaders have attempted to explain away this demand or have argued that the dispute was based on a misunderstanding; Sayyid Qutub, for instance, has stated that the Ikhwān have never demanded that the affairs of state should be entrusted only to beturbaned shaikhs: "We need neither shaikhs nor turbans; Islam has no clergy which is to be charged with these responsibilities. It is enough that the Sharī'a, the Moslem law, is applied, to give the state an Islamic character."[17] But in effect the religious leaders would become the supreme authorities for the application of Sharī'a, and on this issue the propagandists of the Brotherhood have had very little to offer by way of refutation. The only major argument used by them was that Pakistan, a country larger than Egypt, has adopted an Islamic constitution that makes the study of the Koran obligatory, and prohibits the consumption of alcohol, games of hazard, prostitution, and the taking of interest between Moslem nations. "Egypt should follow the Pakistani example and even go further."[18]

The social programme, or what goes under that name, has perhaps been most succinctly presented in one of the Brotherhood booklets (*How Do We Speak to the Public*, 1946): "One man said to our leader Hasan al Banna', 'Your call will not help if you do not build hospitals to heal our sick.' Said al Banna', 'Do you believe that physical recovery will solve the other problems?' Said the man, 'No, you have to build schools, too, in order to educate the people.' Said al Banna', 'Do you believe that the country will achieve independence if we do this?' Said the man, 'No, you have to establish banks for providing loans and credit, too.' Replied al Banna', 'Will this promote the country's independence?' Said the man, 'What will help more?' Replied al Banna', 'There is only one way, the way of the Prophet, to propagate Islam and the congregation of all believers. After this, there comes the struggle for the realization of our teachings. There is no other way.'"[19] These inanities were fairly typical of the level and the content of Brotherhood propaganda.

Under Hasan al Banna' the "fight for social justice" was frequently stressed; so was the need to restrict real-estate holdings. But in fact the Ikhwān leadership made no serious attempt to promote agrarian reform. Their slogan among the workers was "Egyptians, do not strike in Egyptian factories," and the leadership of the Ikhwān was frequently accused by left-wing groups of organizing bodies of strike-breakers. On the other hand, the Brotherhood permitted and encouraged strikes in factories owned by foreigners, Copts, or Jews.

Under Hasan al Hudaibi the conservative element was further strengthened, and the Supreme Guide declared that there was no need whatsoever for social security schemes because the Islamic provision of *Zakāt* (according to which the rich have to contribute one-fifth of their money to help the poor) was fully sufficient.[20] Al Hudaibi opposed even the moderate projects of agrarian reforms proposed by the army government in 1952, and suggested that 500 rather than 200 feddans should be the upper limit. However, his stand was hotly contested by the more radical group, and *Ad-Da'wa* published strong attacks against the feudal regime, which had flourished under Farouk, when it had been possible for the feudal landowner "to kill a peasant like a dog, because he was his slave, and the government had no right to intervene."[21] These differences of opinion reflected undoubtedly the mixed social composition of the Brotherhood; the rank and file consisted mainly of the poor in the cities and fellaheen in the countryside. The militants were mainly students, government employees (of the lower echelons), and teachers. Among the leadership, on the other hand, the *bourgeois*, conservative, and respectable element prevailed; Hasan al Hudaibi was the typical *bien pensant* representative of these circles, who believed that the Brotherhood could be used to prevent the spread of socialist ideas. The activists, on the contrary, said, with some justification, that with such a policy the Ikhwān would never have become a mass organization. The conservative leadership of the Brotherhood when hard pressed by the extremists has always preferred to intensify its nationalist propaganda campaign and to play down social demands. The underlying suggestion was that little damage would be done to those who have a vital interest in the preservation of the *status quo* if the masses were given a chance to let off steam in attacks against foreigners. Whereas by acceding to social demands lasting damage might be caused to the interests of the feudals and the rich in the cities. The short-sightedness of such a policy need not be elaborated here. The "anti-imperialist" attitude taken by the same group of leaders stems from the same source. Al Hudaibi emphasized more than once that the Communist danger in, and to, Egypt was a mere invention of British propaganda,[22] and the Supreme Guide has repeatedly attacked "American economic, social, and cultural infiltration into Egypt."[23]

In fact, the Ikhwān served already at that time as an ideal recruiting ground for the Communist Party, and the reasons are not difficult to divine.[24] Leninism-Stalinism does not appear to be a highly sophisticated political theory in the eyes of most Western observers, but for many members of the Ikhwān, especially students and the militants, it was a revelation, a far more convincing ideology than al Banna's mystifications. The Communists aver that they fight, after all, for the same, or almost the same, aims as the Brotherhood. The Ikhwān fights against imperialism—so do the Communists. The Ikhwān combats social injustice—and so do the Communists. The Communists state, in fact, that they are the more radical and consistent fighters for the "national aspirations"; the leadership of the Brotherhood was frequently accused by extremists of corruption, having allegedly received money from the British against a promise to sabotage the anti-British struggle, etc.[25] The Communists have an even stronger case against the social programme of the Brotherhood: Zakāt, they say, is an excellent idea. But who has ever heard of rich men paying it as they should? And if they do not pay voluntarily, should enforced change of the social system not be envisaged? Ideologically, then, the Brotherhood were not serious competitors of the Communists; politically they acted as involuntary pacemakers for the party. In foreign policy this was all too obvious, but it was not very different on the domestic scene either. The Ikhwān were incapable of ruling the country, but they were powerful enough to sabotage effective rule for years.

2. AHMAD HUSAIN'S "SOCIALISTS": THE PRECURSORS OF "MILITARY SOCIALISM"

The development of Ahmad Husain's Socialist Party in Egypt during the last twenty years reflects perhaps better than any other illustration the vacillations of extremist Arab politicians between pro-Fascist and pro-Communist orientations. Ahmad Husain, then a young lawyer, started his career in the early 1930's in the Wafd, as practically every politician in Egypt did. In 1933 he launched a new group (gāmi'a) by the name of "Young Egypt" (Misr al Fatah), which in 1938 became a political party.[26] Among his collaborators were several of his more activist contemporaries, mainly students and young graduates, such as Fathi Ridwān. Both the semi-military organization of storm-troops ("greenshirts") and the ideology of the party were copied from the Fascist and Nazi originals: the restoration of the old glory of Egypt, the establishment of a great empire, a corporative economic system, the stress put on the two main principles: faith and action. The storm-troopers had another ten commandments to fulfil, such as to speak only Egyptian [sic], to buy Egyptian products, etc.[27]

The main preoccupation of this party in the 1930's were brawls with the Wafd and with other parties, and the trips of Ahmad Husain and other leaders to their Mecca—Rome. On such an occasion he declared that Young Egypt was to establish a party with a new spirit: "All the youth, including the king, is with us. We are infinitely nearer to Rome and Berlin than to Paris and London. We do not think it possible to talk about dictatorship in Italy and Germany—Hitler and Mussolini have the full support of their peoples, and they are the reason and the life of their peoples (*'la ragione e la vita dei loro populi'*). Italy and Germany are today in Europe the only true democracies, all the others are parliamentary plutocracies. . . ."[28]

Ahmad Husain said that, like Mussolini, he wished to fight for social justice and had come, therefore, to study the Fascist *Carta del Lavoro*. Relations between Egypt (ruled by Misr al Fatah) and the great Italian empire would, of course, be closer than with any other foreign country. After his return to Egypt he expressed his admiration for Italy and Germany, and denounced the "crusade of the so-called democracies against the 'dictatorships'; there have been, after all, such democratic regimes before Hitler and Mussolini came to power, but all they did manage was to spread disorder and chaos, to let the people vegetate in misery, unable to combat unemployment, while the dictatorships have brought both order and prosperity."[29]

When World War II broke out Ahmad Husain, being afraid that his party would be banned by the government, declared that he would stand by Britain till final victory, in order to lay the foundations of a glorious future for Egypt.[30] But the party continued to receive assistance from Rome and Berlin, and its followers demonstrated against the Western Allies and for a speedy Axis victory. They sabotaged the Allied war effort by various means, attacked British and Dominion soldiers in the streets of Cairo and Alexandria, and organized the assassination of pro-Allied Egyptian statesmen, such as the Prime Minister, Ahmad Māhir.

Ahmad Husain and several other leaders were arrested after more evidence of their activities on behalf of Rome and Berlin had become known; when they were released from prison in the autumn of 1944 the party, though still in existence, had largely lost its *raison d'être*; the old ideas had become unfashionable with the downfall of Fascism and Nazism. The main attraction of the regimes established by Hitler and Mussolini had not been, after all, their new and striking ideas but rather their power, and once this power had vanished very little sympathy was left among the supporters of Misr al Fatah. The years of 1945–47 were years of suspense for Ahmad Husain and his friends. Already in 1945, a few months after the end of the war, we find articles favourable to the Soviet Union and Communism in *Misr al Fatah* (October 17 and December 26, 1945, for instance), but Ahmad Husain was yet ready to give the West a chance. He went to the United States, and there published a book on the Arab war effort, in which he demonstrated how important the help given by the Arabs to the cause of the Allies had really been, and how they had always supported the Western ideals of democracy and liberty.

But Western democracy had little to offer to Ahmad Husain and his friends. They made an effort to understand it, but somehow it did not appeal to them. It lacked colour and enthusiasm; it did not do spectacular things; it had no power, or at least did not demonstrate any. Ahmad Husain believed for a time that the Labour government in Britain was doing a very good job, and that democratic socialism in general was the movement of the future. But he soon realized his mistake; how could democratic socialism possibly appeal to people in the East? And when Ahmad Husain made his comeback in Egyptian politics in July, 1949, the word "socialism" was mentioned many times—but it was not the socialism of the democratic brand. His reorientation to a new totalitarianism had been almost completed by 1948, and it was a symptomatic process, not one affecting only him. Fathi Ridwān, at present Egyptian Minister for Propaganda, had co-founded Young Egypt but later seceded and joined one of the traditional parties and found his way at the same time to the Communist "peace movement," and there were many more in this generation of young intellectuals who transferred their sympathies in a similar way from Rome and Berlin to the East.

Ahmad Husain's new programme stressed the "socialist" character of his party—and at the same time its independence of socialism abroad—demanded British evacuation, proposed a transition to a socialist regime by peaceful means, and changed the name of his party to "Egyptian Socialist and Democratic" Party.[31]

The foreign political orientation of the old-new party was defined in one of its first plenary meetings: "In view of the pressure exerted on Egypt to give in to Israel and Jordan, there is no other way but to sign a pact of friendship with the Soviet Union."[32] The argument may have been deficient in logic, but the intention was clear.

With the increase in tension in 1950–51 the new party became again a factor to be reckoned with, and it took an important place in the "anti-imperialist struggle." In the 1950 elections the party had succeeded in electing only a single deputy (Ibrahīm Shukri), but its influence in the Cairo streets was considerably greater than that. Though no support was forthcoming any more from Rome and Berlin, the party disposed of certain property and again organized its storm-troops. Collaboration with the "peace movement" became close and relations even intimate. At a meeting called by Ahmad Husain in August, 1951, Yūsuf Hilmi, president of the Egyptian Partisans of Peace, was one of the main speakers, although only a few years had passed since the Communists had called Ahmad Husain a "fascist agent." The leader of the "Socialists" declared on that occasion that the rich had sold out Egypt and had not followed up the struggle of liberation in 1919; all treaties with Britain and the United States should be cancelled.[33] Again, several weeks later, the Socialists forwarded their demands to parliament. All political prisoners should be released, the political police, which had been created by imperialism, should be disbanded. Ahmad Husain was brought to court for lese-majesty, but was released after praising Farouk and explaining that his anti-monarchism was directed against nobody in particular.

The confidence of Ahmad Husain and his friends rose considerably in the hectic weeks of autumn and winter of 1951–52; they had again become part of the national movement, and the most radical part at that. They were respected by both the Wafd and the Communists, and the Moslem Brotherhood gladly collaborated with them. Their members headed most demonstrations in the large cities, and organized the partisan units fighting the British in the Canal Zone. Only yesterday Husain had been an outcast; now he could deliver to the government an ultimatum—within fifteen days the real war against England would have to begin.[34] "We as Socialists fight for the liberation of the people and cannot agree with the government policy." And Ibrāhīm Shukri reiterated the party's pro-Soviet orientation: "Why does the government not sign a pact of friendship with the Soviet Union? Why does it not recognize China?"[35] Ahmad Husain informed the press that ten thousand party members had enlisted for fighting in the Katā'ib (Phalanges) in the Canal Zone, which was, of course, a gross exaggeration. But there is little doubt that the Socialists took indeed a prominent part in these units, whereas both the Communists and the Moslem Brotherhood were not over-active in that field.

At the same time Ahmad Husain continued to publish his periodical *Ishtirākiyya* (Socialism). This now was a unique brand of socialism, which can be compared only with the early writings of Adolf Hitler in the *Voelkischer Beobachter* of 1921 and 1922. Incitement to kill all foreigners, together with anti-feudalist slogans, an anti-Jewish hate campaign, threats against the "Western plutocrats," demands for agrarian reform, and defence of religion and the interests of the holy fatherland. The paper was frequently suppressed by the authorities, and Ahmad Husain consequently came out in favour of unrestrained freedom of the press; he accused the government of sabotaging partisan warfare in the Canal area. After having visited the theatre of war, he stated that the government had not assisted the fighters at all, and that these had to buy weapons with their own money.

After the riots of "Black Saturday," Ahmad Husain was arrested and his party dissolved. There have been conflicting versions of his part in these events. According to the indictment he was seen in a jeep among the rioters, who set fire on that day to many houses, shops, and cinemas owned by foreigners and Jews, and had fled to the Polish Legation in Cairo when the riots had been suppressed by the army. According to his own description, he had been ill at home on this day.[36] The authorities appear not to have been particularly interested in finding out the truth; Ahmad Husain's trial lasted for several months, and was discontinued after the military junta had come to power later in 1952, though the bill of indictment was never withdrawn.

There is no doubt about Ahmad Husain's important part in the preparation of the events on "Black Saturday." His party headquarters planned the demonstrations and he was allegedly in contact with foreign Communist representatives in Cairo. (In connection with this affair, the Egyptian government demanded the recall of the Polish diplomatic representative.) This does not mean that Ahmad Husain and his friends had any clear idea of what to do on the "Black Saturday"—certainly there was no serious attempt made to overthrow the government. The impression gained is that it was intended to stage a great "anti-imperialist" demonstration which somehow got out of hand, and caused the downfall of the Wafdist government. This, from the Communist point of view, was highly undesirable, because under this regime they had been given almost full freedom of action, and poor Ahmad Husain was now again branded, for a few weeks at least, an enemy *agent provocateur*. (He was forgiven a year later, and during 1954 he appeared frequently in the Cairo courts as counsel for the defence in the trials of leading Communists.)

In November, 1952, Ahmad Husain had been released from prison, and a few days later was again elected president of his party. Once more he had to adjust himself and his party to the new conditions created by the army *coup*; a number of articles published in the party press while he was in prison had already foreshadowed the shift to socialist-radicalism in propaganda. When the army ousted 'Ali Māhir (its own candidate for Prime Minister in September, 1952), *Al Ishtirākiyya* welcomed this decision, "'Ali Māhir must not rule—because he is a Pasha, not a man of the people."[37] At the same time the party demanded the nationalization of public services, not only in the capital but throughout the whole country.[38] And the new party programme provided, not only for the liberation of the Nile Valley and the union of all Arab countries, but also a maximum limit of 50 feddan for all landowners (according to the army law, 200 feddans).[39] When the political parties were dissolved in 1953, the Socialists disappeared together with the rest, to wait for better times and a more favourable regime to renew their activities.

It would be a mistake to consider Ahmad Husain a mere adventurer, a Levantine "sword for hire," a man without political convictions, ready to serve any master. According to all the evidence, he is a man of strong convictions, and hardly a person in Egypt found anything reprehensible in his close collaboration with Fascism in the 1930's and with Communism in the 1950's. He is, in more than one respect, the most consistent of all Egyptian extremist politicians. Many sympathized with him, though few were willing to join him because his party was not respectable enough, just as German right-wingers sneered at the demagogue

Hitler up to the end of the 1920's. But Ahmad Husain's alliance with the Communists was not just a tactical move; it was a real communion of interests, if not of souls, which brought the two parties together in the most perfect example until now of a popular front, Middle Eastern style. This united front did not bring victory to any of its partners, but merely hastened the downfall of the parliamentary regime under which these groups had thrived. This in its turn produced mutual recriminations, but at the same time new common interests appeared, and, above all, the common struggle for the overthrow of the military regime in which not only the Communists and the Socialists but also remnants of the Wafd and the other parties and the Moslem Brotherhood were, for obvious reasons, vitally interested during 1952–55.

Political observers who apply categories of right and left only towards Fascism and Communism will have some difficulty in explaining what may appear to them as the riddle of Ahmad Husain. It is, in fact, one of the most common phenomena in the Middle East. On the basis of disbelief in democracy—the one factor which has remained constant throughout the years—political figures and whole parties have switched their allegiance from one totalitarian system to the other, because the differences between Communism and Fascism, important as they are, are less weighty than those between them and democracy.

3. TURKEY

Since the end of World War II, more specifically since the ascension of the Democrats to power in May, 1950, there has been an Islamic revival in Turkey. Kemal Ataturk's reforms, and secularization in general, had been less profound than frequently assumed; they had not yet grown deep roots and had hardly affected life in the countryside or the more backward sections of the population in the cities, especially the provincial towns.[40] In the wake of this revival a number of extremist and reactionary groups, such as the Tijanis, the Mevlevis, the Kadiris, and other orders and Dervish brotherhoods, have again become active. Periodicals, like *Buyuk Dogu* (Great Orient; "boulevard Fascism with religious colouring matter") and others, have been published, demonstrations against the existing regime and its vestiges have been made, attempts on the life of republican leaders have been carried out (including one on Ahmed Yalman, editor of the well-known daily *Vatan*.)

In the beginning the two leading Turkish parties revealed a large measure of tolerance not only *vis-à-vis* the Islamic revival but also to its more sinister concomitants. There was even some competition between them in exploiting it to get the votes of the rural electorate. But as early as the summer of 1951 it was realized by some sections of the public, especially the students and parts of the intelligentsia, that the obscurantist and semi-Fascist groups of the right, if allowed to exploit the backwardness of the masses, would soon become a major danger to the very existence of Turkish democracy. Pilavoglu, the leader of the Tijani himself, was reported to be not a believing Moslem, but he exploited unscrupulously the darkest instincts of the masses to promote his ambitions; and Facil Kisakurek, the editor of *Buyuk Dogu*, was reported to be a similar type. "The problem has become serious," wrote *Hurriyet;* "the existence of the bearded Tijanis must be ended immediately if Turkey is to live in freedom and independence." And the daily *Zafer* said (what was at that time undoubtedly a shot in the dark): "Is it not possible to see a connection between the smuggling of Nazim Hikmet[41] behind the Iron Curtain and the proclamations issued by the Tijanis and their line of action?"[42] Only two years later more tangible facts of these suspected ties became public knowledge.

There are important differences between the ideology of the Tijanis and the Buyuk Dogu, for instance. The articles of faith of the former are very similar to those of the Moslem Brotherhood; they are fanatical pan-Islamists and oppose Turkish nationalism. The Buyuk Dogu, on the other hand, are Turkish monarchists and clericalists, and the attempt to unite incompatible elements has brought them into difficulties not unlike those experienced by the *Action Française vis-à-vis* the Catholic Church. What they have in common is, apart from anti-Semitism, the opposition to a secular way of life and Western ideas of freedom and democracy.

After the attempt on the life of Ahmed Yalman in November, 1952, wider circles of the public awoke to the danger. The assailant, it appeared, was a member of the reactionary group Bak Dogu and of the Islamic Democratic Party (another extremist front organization). A number of members of the Baktashi, a Dervish order, had already been arrested, including their head, Siri Baba Galina, an Egyptian citizen. In January and February, 1953, a number of other leading right-wing extremists were arrested, including Kisakurek of the Buyuk Dogu (the periodical was closed); Atilhan, the head of the Democratic Islamic Party; Yuksel, editor of *Serden Gecti*; Bagislayic of *Buyuk Cihat*, and several others. The Turkish authorities were particularly interested in the financial backers of the many semi-Fascist and right-wing extremist journals in Istanbul and the provinces,[43] whose sales were extremely restricted and which had to rely on outside help. This was the occasion when it was first revealed that money transfers from Egypt and Persia, which had originated in all probability in an Iron Curtain country, were used to back Turkish reactionaries.

The Turkish authorities were helped in their investigations by the internal dissension within the extremist camp; Atilhan, for instance, the head of the Islamic Party, had formerly been a member of Buyuk Dogu, but later left this organization and founded his own group. He was now ready to provide evidence against his former boss, Kisakurek. At the same time various nationalist associations had attempted to infiltrate, with some success, all Turkish parties, which proceeded now to purge themselves of these elements, who included members of parliament. Student and journalist associations opened a counter-offensive which moved the authorities to prevent the convention of a pan-Islamic meeting which had been called by Nuri Demirag, and to discontinue the publication of official advertisements in the publications of these groups. In July, 1953, as the result of this pressure, a new law for national defence was adopted, according to which "the exploitation of religion for partisan and political purposes" was forbidden in both public and private meetings.[44] At the same time the Nationalist Party was dissolved; this had been one of the main public bodies infiltrated by the reactionary groups, and the organizers of the attempts on the life of Yalman were brought to trial.

Turkish public opinion and the press had always spoken of the "twin dangers" of Communism and the reactionary groups. The underlying assumption was that these organizations intended to undermine the unity of the nation and of Turkey as a modern state—to reduce it to the state of Egypt or Persia. In recent years, as the result of the trials against the leaders of these groups, and mainly the trial of the "167" (Communists) in Ankara (October, 1953), disturbing revelations have been made with regard to the contacts of such groups as the Tijanis and Buyuk Dogu with the Communists. The suspicions of Communist collaboration with these groups have at least partly been proved true. Such co-operation, needless to say, never occurred on the popular level, and a rank-and-file Turkish Communist or Tijani would have thought the very idea utterly absurd. But in the given conditions there was no need at all for such popular-front co-operation, and the activity of a few well-chosen people in key positions in the right-wing organizations, coupled with financial assistance, was enough to strengthen them and to damage the regime. It should not be forgotten that Communism in Turkey has very few roots, and that the open Soviet territorial demands voiced in 1945 had made Communism impossible in the country. But the roots of Islamic extremism went back many centuries, and even if the country had undergone profound changes since the turn of the century, the spirit of Islam continued to permeate many spheres of life, and not only in the countryside. The revival of Islam is therefore thought by some observers to be a perfectly natural phenomenon, and it surely need not degenerate into the Moslem Brotherhood or Fadayān Islam type of xenophobia and obscurantism. But there can be little doubt that such a development offers excellent opportunities for an unscrupulous third party to pervert the spirit of the religious revival and to exploit it for its own ends.

4. SYRIA

The Islamic Socialist Front in Syria offers an interesting parallel to both the Moslem Brotherhood and Ahmad Husain's "Socialism." This Front is the Syrian branch of the Moslem Brotherhood, but in view of the different conditions prevailing in Syria the emphasis of its activities has always been on extreme nationalism rather than on preaching religious fanaticism. The history of the Syrian Brotherhood goes back to the 1930's, but it gained political importance only in the late 1940's. Like most other parties, the Brotherhood was banned after Colonel Husni Az-Za'īm's *coup d'état* in 1949, but it reappeared in the 1949 elections after the downfall of Colonel Za'īm's regime. In its programme there were several radical demands, such as distribution of land to the landless, and alleviation of the taxes of the poor. The Front opposed merger with Iraq because it wanted to preserve the republican regime; at the same time it demanded strengthening of the ties with all Islamic countries. In domestic policy it stood for theocracy and a constitution based on the Koran, and its views were rather similar to those of the Egyptian Brotherhood.[45] In the elections it put up a list only in the capital, Damascus, and emerged there as the strongest party. Several of its leaders, such as Ma'arūf Dawalībi, were moreover elected on the list of other parties.

Soon thereafter, in the summer of 1950, the Islamic Socialists engaged on a concentrated anti-Western campaign. Shaikh Mustafa As-Siba'i complained in parliament about "tremendous Anglo-American pressure" on the Arab League. In a great demonstration in May, 1950, the following resolution was adopted: "The Syrian people demands that the Arab League should stand up against the Anglo-American pressure and adopt an Eastern [Soviet] orientation if this pressure should continue."[46] This demonstration ended with ovations to Stalin and the shouting of slogans to the effect that Islam be decreed the state religion. In a press conference several days later the following replies were given by Shaikh Mustafa as Siba'i to questions of journalists:

Question: Is your orientation towards Russia only the result of Anglo-American pressure or do you intend to collaborate with Russia, also, in case this pressure ceases?

Reply: We shall fight the West regardless whether its pressure continues or not; we shall co-operate with the Russians and ask them for help.

Question: What do you think about the Western defence schemes for the Middle East?

Reply: We shall fight the West with acts not words.

Question: What is your attitude towards Islamistan or the project of an Islamic-Catholic bloc to fight Communism?

Reply: Previously I was a supporter of the idea of a Catholic-Islamic bloc to fight Communism. But I have changed my mind because I have realized that this project is intended to serve the interests of imperialism, not the Arabs.

We shall welcome the idea of Islamistan on condition that it is not directed against the Soviet Union.[47]

Subsequently Muhammad Mubārak, another leader of the Front and one of its representatives in parliament, was asked for a short definition of the ideology of his party; he replied that the "Islamic Socialist Front is a Marxist drink in a Moslem cup."[48] But the widest publicity was given to the statements of Ma'arūf Dawalībi, another leader of the Front, who was at that time Minister of Commerce. Dawalībi was no great friend of the Western democracies; World War II he had spent working for Nazi propaganda in Berlin as a political secretary of the ex-Mufti of Jerusalem, Haj Amīn al Husaini. After the defeat of Germany he fled to Paris and hid from Allied police searching for him in connection with charges of war crimes. This appears not to have strengthened his friendly feelings towards the West, and soon after his return to Syria he became the leading exponent of a pro-Soviet orientation. In an interview with the Egyptian daily *Al Misri*, he declared that the Arab countries would prefer to become a Soviet republic rather than a Jewish state following American pressure. How could the Arab world become part of a Jewish state? Well, American diplomatic representatives had stressed the necessity of peace between the Arab states and Israel as a prerequisite for peace and stability in the Middle East—and was this not tantamount to establishing an American colony in the Middle East? There was only one way to prevent a new war, namely the signing of a non-aggression pact with the Soviet Union.

Dawalībi's call was warmly supported by the Front, and a few days later a member of this organization made a bomb attack on the American Legation in Damascus. At the same time close relations between the Front and the Syrian peace movement were established. All the leading personalities of the Front signed the Communist "peace" appeal and helped to collect signatures. Dawalībi became in addition one of the sponsors of the Moscow Economic Conference under the auspices of the "peace movement." One of the Damascus 'Ulamā, Shaikh Muhammad al-Ashmar, a former gang leader in the Palestine revolt of 1936–39, went to Moscow and China as a guest of the "peace movement" and became on his return the head of the Syrian peace movement.[49]

In 1951–52 the political importance and influence of the Front declined somewhat in connection with internal dissension among its leaders, mainly between the more conservative 'Ulamā and the more radical lay component of the Front. Under the Shishakli dictatorship the Front was suppressed, but after Shishakli's overthrow it appeared again on the political scene with the ubiquitous Dawalībi serving for some time as Minister for National Defence.

5. IRAQ

The Istiqlāl (Independence) Party in Iraq offers another illustration of the gradual transition of a fascist party to a pro-Communist attitude after the defeat of Nazi Germany. The history of this party goes back to the Muthanna Club, a pan-Islamic society, founded in Baghdad in 1935, "dominated by a few ultra-nationalists who had outspoken totalitarian ideas."[50] Their totalitarian ideology was best expounded by Sāmi Shawkāt, one of their members who wrote variations on Mussolini's theme of *vivere pericoloso*. The Muthanna Club was one of the main forces in the pro-Nazi *coup d'état* of Rashīd 'Ali in April–May, 1941, and several of its members joined his cabinet.

With the suppression of the Rashīd 'Ali revolt most of its members were arrested; some fled to Nazi-occupied Europe. The remnants of this clique established themselves as the Istiqlāl Party in April, 1946, under the leadership of Muhammad Mahdi Kubbah (a former vice-president of the Muthanna Club) and Sādiq Shinshil, director of propaganda under Rashīd 'Ali. The fascist myth was dead, and there were no more trips to Berlin and Nuremberg and no financial assistance; the main difference between this and the other Iraqi parties was its strong anti-Western attitude. Another ideological ingredient which had remained useful was an anti-Jewish programme on a racial basis.[51]

The party had a handful of deputies in the Iraqi parliament and was part of the opposition to the pro-Western government that ruled Iraq after the end of World War II. Its foreign political orientation was clearly defined in its annual conference in November, 1950, when M. Kubbah said that close association with one of the powers had always damaged the Arab cause. Neutralism was therefore the logical policy for the Arab countries, and the Egyptian decision not to support the West on the Korea issue was therefore highly commended. A *modus vivendi* could perhaps be attained with the West on condition that the Western Allies should atone for the evil they had done the Arabs, especially in Palestine. But even then the Arabs should promise the West only armed neutrality; the Arab states would refrain from attacking the West.

The leaders of the Istiqlāl did not yet take part in the "peace campaign" of 1950–51, nor did they participate in the first attempt to establish a neutralist popular front in March, 1951. But during the same summer the first talks between them and the pro-Communist groups occurred, and, as a result, in October, 1951, a common statement, signed by the Istiqlāl, Muhammad Reza Ash-Shabībi (one of the heads of the "peace" movement), and the leftist National Democrats, was published inveighling against the Anglo-Iraqi agreement and any project for the establishment of a Western defence scheme in the Middle East. This collaboration was extended to street fighting in the November riots of 1952, which caused the temporary dissolution of political parties and the establishment of military rule. Most of the Istiqlāl leaders, such as Sādiq Shinshil, Fā'ik al Samara'i, and Isma'īl Ghānim, together with the heads of the pro-Communist and leftist parties, were among those arrested as responsible for the riots.

Only in the autumn of 1953, when the state of siege was abolished, were the activities of the party renewed on a larger scale. At the same time, at the yearly conference of the party (accompanied by a major purge affecting several of its main branches outside Baghdad), Kubbah reiterated the demand for a "third bloc" in world politics, to consist of the Arab states and their friends.

When elections were again fixed for the summer of 1954, the Istiqlāl decided to renew the alliance ("national front") with the National Democrats of Kāmil al Jadarji on the following basis[52]: rejection of any American help; neutrality between the two world blocs; nationalization of oil resources and industry; the right of workers to strike; abolition of the 1930 treaty between Iraq and Britain; changes in the constitution; solidarity with the other Arab countries in their struggle against imperialism; and finally, "a solution of the Palestine problem without imperialist mediation."

This alliance with the pro-Communist forces[53] meant that the pendulum had swung to the other extreme so far as the Istiqlāl was concerned. In the middle 1930's they had attacked the mildly reformist Hikmat Sulaimān government, exploiting the Communist bogy to the full and generally appearing as implacable foes of Communism, when the only real "danger" in Iraq was one of social reforms. Twenty years later, when Communism was infinitely stronger in the country and Iraqi security in grave and permanent danger, the Istiqlāl resolved to collaborate with yesterday's enemies, thus demonstrating that their early anti-Communism had merely been a tactical move, and that there were no insurmountable differences between them and the Communists on the ideological level to prevent close co-operation.

6. SUMMARY

The Moslem Brotherhood and the Iraqi Istiqlāl, Ma'arūf Dawalībi and Ahmad Husain, the Tijanis and Shaikh al-Ashmar—it is a list by no means complete.[54] We have mentioned only some of the more extreme revelations of affinity between totalitarian movements and their supporters in the Middle East. But even if Ahmad Husain, Dawalībi, or the Istiqlāl are extreme cases, even if the majority of the politically active elements in their own countries did not follow them all the way from Fascism to pro-Communism, they are in more than one respect typical of the whole climate of opinion among the *élite* in these countries. This climate of opinion in the Middle East of the late 1930's was vaguely pro-Fascist just as it is now vaguely pro-Communist.[55] This does not mean that all the main tenets of totalitarian ideology were or are accepted by most of the people. But there was and is a conviction that Fascism (and Communism), apart from certain excesses, has somehow a good kernel, that it fills people with enthusiasm and rejuvenates nations, that it gets things done, and that, in short, the future belongs to these dynamic movements.

The common denominator, to sum up, is Middle Eastern disbelief in the feasibility and desirability of democracy. What should not be disregarded, moreover, is the similarity in the social base of both totalitarian movements—in the Middle East, at least. Communism in the Middle East is not a revolutionary workers' and peasants' party, but a movement of the intelligentsia and the urban lower middle class. So was Fascism. Hence the strong power of attraction, offered by both totalitarian regimes, of an elevated social status for the intelligentsia—far exceeding what could be offered not only by the Middle Eastern states but also by the West. If the class interest of the intelligentsia in the Middle East was to be regarded as one of the decisive factors, Soviet society of 1955 was certainly not acting as a deterrent. And Soviet power is, of course, incomparably greater. Fascism, especially the Italian brand, had revealed a more benevolent attitude towards religion, but Russia, too, has discontinued the more offensive anti-religious practices. And, anyway, for a large segment, probably the majority of the intelligentsia, religion is no longer the decisive issue.

Among the collaborators with Communism there are great differences. On one hand, we have the "Zealots" (to use Toynbee's nomenclature), reactionary groups, the Moslem Brotherhood and the Tijanis, who refuse to take cognizance of anything new and who wish to escape to the past; and, on the other hand, the "Herodians" like Ahmad Husain and Dawalībi, who wish to combat the West by imitating it. Political leaders such as Ahmad Husain and Dawalībi appear now (February, 1956) to have been merely precursors of a general trend which has subsequently assumed far larger proportions and political importance: the alliance between Communism and extreme Arab nationalism. And there are many in between these extremes. The latter are, as a rule, fully conscious collaborators with the Communists, while the former will indignantly deny any such charges; their assistance is frequently both unsolicited and unconscious. For all that, it is not a less effective factor in today's Middle Eastern politics.

Chapter Nineteen

Russia re-enters the Middle East

THE year 1955 will enter history, it now appears, as the year when Russia re-emerged as a major Middle Eastern power. When the heads of the "Big Four" convened in Geneva in July, 1955, the Middle East did not even figure on their agenda. But several weeks later it had already become the main area of a new cold war. The Soviet political offensive in the Middle East may have taken some Western statesmen unawares, but it certainly did not come altogether suddenly and surprisingly—there had been many signs to foreshadow it. And some observers remarked that the only remarkable thing about this Soviet drive was that it came relatively late in the day. It might as well have been launched in 1951–52, in the days of Mossadiq in Persia and the "Black Saturday" in Egypt. This delay shows, if anything, what has been known for some time—that the Soviet policy of expansion is coupled with a great measure of caution.

After World War II, Soviet policy had been for some years to keep aloof from Middle Eastern affairs; its attitude had been one of studious unconcern. As a result, not a few Western observers have tended to forget that this apparent unconcern could not be more than a transient phenomenon in view of the geographical proximity of the Middle East to Russia and the traditional Russian interest in the Middle East. It has been too easily forgotten that throughout the nineteenth century, and even earlier, the Near and Middle East had been Russia's main sphere of interest and expansion; that the "Oriental question" had been one of the main bones of contention between the powers for more than 150 years. It was Russian policy then, as it is now, to launch or strengthen anti-Turkish movements in the peripheral areas. It was to that end that Baron von Thonus (Mr. Daniel Solod's first forerunner in Egypt) was sent to Cairo by Catherine II. (The end of his mission was unfortunate —he was strangled in prison on the orders of Ibrahīm Pasha, who deeply

260

regretted the sudden death of the Russian consul in an official communique the next day.) Trenchant observations on Russia's Oriental policy were made (from opposed vantage-points) by Karl Marx and Friedrich Engels in their articles on the Crimean War and in Dostoyevsky's *Diary of a Writer*. Marx, in particular, noted the incessant territorial progress made by Russia since Peter the Great, and stated that Russia was superior to the West in tenacity and in the application of clever political stratagems.

After 1917, the Bolshevik leaders renounced Czarist imperialism; in subsequent years, too, when the original anti-imperialist zest had long disappeared, the Middle East continued to be of little interest to Moscow in view of its reduced political importance and the absence of a strong Communist or nationalist revolutionary movement in that part of the world. In the wake of World War II attempts were made to gain a foothold, such as the demand for the cession of several Turkish provinces (and pressure on Turkey in general), and Soviet reluctance to evacuate its positions in Northern Persia.

It is difficult to say in retrospect whether the Russian retreat from the Middle East in 1946 was merely a tactical response to Western pressure or whether it was a policy. There can be no doubt that Soviet absence from the Middle East paid handsome dividends in 1949–52: Soviet and Communist propagandists could point to the stark contrast between Moscow's policy of "hands off" and Western imperialist attempts to "organize" the area, to draw the various countries into all kinds of suspect "defence" blocs. These Western activities tended to fan smouldering anti-Western resentment and to antagonize most of the Arabs, who were psychologically quite unprepared; the Soviet danger was in their eyes some mythical invention, or perhaps a clever stratagem of American and European "imperialists" desirous of perpetuating their rule in the Middle East. As a result, Soviet prestige grew.

These developments were undoubtedly highly agreeable to Moscow; but prestige is only something in the nature of a prerequisite in international politics—it helped Moscow up to a point, but no farther. It did not prevent, for instance, the Turko-Iraqi alliance in January–February, 1955, which subsequently, as the result of the adhesion of Persia, Pakistan, and Britain, became the famous "Northern Tier." The emergence of this defensive alliance was viewed in Moscow with far greater concern than was realized in the West at that time; it appears quite clearly in retrospect that Moscow realized at this time that a more active Soviet policy would be needed from then on in the Middle East. Prestige alone would not be enough to promote Soviet interests in that part of the world. It was, as subsequently emerged, the turning-point in Soviet Middle Eastern policy. *Izvestia* published on April 17, 1955, a statement of the Soviet Ministry of Foreign Affairs on the Middle Eastern situation, which was not given much attention at the time, though it announced in effect the change in Soviet Middle Eastern policy. It began with a statement that "the situation in the Middle East had greatly deteriorated of late," and ended with the declaration that the Soviet Union would do everything to develop closer relations with the countries of the Middle East ("in the interests of peace," to be sure).

The Soviet Middle Eastern offensive was foreshadowed in another field little remarked at the time by Western observers—the revival of Soviet Middle Eastern studies and the important revaluations undertaken at the same time. The study of the contemporary East had virtually come to a standstill as the result of the purge of the 1930's and had not been revived throughout the 1940's. It was only in the winter of 1954–55 that fresh impetus was given to Soviet Oriental studies. After a break of eighteen years Soviet Eastern experts were again given a magazine of their own (*Sovietskoye Vostokovedenie*, the first issue appeared by coincidence in April, 1955—the very same month the Foreign Ministry statement on the Middle East was published). There was a sudden flood of new books and studies, and the official party bi-weekly, *Communist*, as yet dissatisfied, called in May, 1955, for a fresh upsurge in the field, for more attention, more and better books, and fresh Oriental experts. This revival was anything but academic: it only reflected the growing Soviet interest in the Middle East. It was more than just the publication of so many new books or periodicals: it coincided with a far-reaching tactical revaluation of some of the Middle Eastern governments.

Changing Soviet comment on Egypt may serve as an illustration. In 1954 the leading Soviet Egyptian expert, L. N. Vatolina, had characterized the Naguīb-Nāsir regime as "madly reactionary, terrorist, anti-democratic, demagogic," etc.[1] One year later, in another work by the Soviet Academy of Science on the peoples of Africa,[2] the Anglo-Egyptian Treaty of July, 1954, was defined as "contrary to the national interests of Egypt and the other Arab countries." The Egyptian government was again attacked for its undemocratic character and, it was stated rather ominously, "the Egyptian toilers would as yet have to fight many a struggle up to the victory of real democracy." Communist criticism became even more violent following the execution of Moslem Brotherhood leaders and the arrest of Communist militants in Egypt throughout the winter of 1954–55. But in late spring and early summer of 1955 this attitude was radically modified. In June the Cairo leaders were already praised by Moscow radio for their stand against Western defence pacts and for neutralism; in early July they were commended for the support given to the Sudan, "which played an important part in the liberation of the Sudanese people." Colonel Nāsir received a pat on the back for, "dressed in the simple uniform of a lieutenant-colonel, he had contributed a great deal to the success of Bandung, supporting the principle of peaceful coexistence."[3] The same Soviet source soon thereafter even more emphatically stated that "both Egypt and the Soviet Union stand squarely on the platform of peace and oppose the policy of aggression. Common to them is the deep desire to live in peace. . . ."[4] The change in the Soviet position came not, of course, as the result of the realization in Moscow that some grievous ideological mistake had been committed *vis-à-vis* Egypt. The new line was the outcome of a more elastic approach on the one hand, the endeavour to activate Soviet policy in the Middle East and, lastly, the fact that certain common interests between Moscow and Cairo had, in fact, emerged. Syria could have served as an alternative jumping-board for the Middle East; Syrian Communists had considerable, if indirect, influence on Syrian foreign policy at the time. But Syria is not a central factor in Middle Eastern politics, and thus Egypt was chosen. Ideologically, this *rapprochement* presented no particular difficulty for Moscow; Stalin and his disciples have carried out more difficult manœuvres in their time.

Soviet emissaries found in Cairo a political climate highly propitious to their plans. The Cairo leaders deeply resented the fact that they had lost their predominant status in the Arab world, following the transfer of the centre of political and military gravity in the direction of the "Northern Tier." To lead a Great Power policy has been the one constant urge among Cairo policy-makers; Soviet assistance in their eyes offered the double chance of regaining supremacy in the Arab League and making Egypt a leading African power. Soviet leaders were hardly much concerned about the motivation of the Egyptian junta. Way back in the 1920's and the early 1930's, Comintern officials had warned against the *bourgeois* nationalist movements in Asia and Africa, who wanted close relations with the Soviet Union in order to play out the West against the Soviet Union and vice versa, thus strengthening their own position. But the international situation had changed during the past thirty years, the Soviet Union had grown in strength and experience, and were gladly prepared to take upon themselves that calculated risk. Few if any political leaders have ever succeeded in getting the better of Moscow in a deal; it appeared unlikely, to put it mildly, that Gamal Abdul Nāsir and his colleagues would succeed where more sophisticated and experienced statesmen had failed. Lastly, it has to be recalled that certain striking affinities exist between the Communist regime and other twentieth-century dictatorships, and that they are closer to each other than to the democracies; there is a surprising similarity between the anti-Western propaganda of the Soviet Union, Nazi Germany, and present-day Egypt.[5] This, too, may have contributed to a certain extent to a *rapprochement* between the two regimes.

The new Soviet line in the Middle East has been reflected, since spring, 1955, in increased political, economic, and cultural activity in that part of the world. Soviet "cultural missions" and sports clubs (mainly footballers and weight-lifters) toured Egypt, Syria, and the Lebanon. Among the Arab delegations to the U.S.S.R., the Syrian parliamentary group (July, 1955), as well as a Syrian scientists' mission and an Arab woman delegation, should be mentioned. Hassan al Baqūri, Egyptian Minister of Waqfs, visited China, and Fathi Ridwān, Egyptian Minister of Communications (at one time co-founder of the Fascist "Misr-al-Fatah") went to Hungary and Czechoslovakia. Soviet and Chinese Moslem pilgrims came to Mecca in July and visited Al Azhar in Cairo. The Orthodox Patriarch of Antiochia, Alexander III, went to Moscow, with several other Syrian and Lebanese bishops, on another good-will tour. But Alexander Tahan had been known as a friend of the Soviet Union for many years, whereas Christoforos II, Patriarch of Alexandria and all Egypt, who also went to Moscow in the summer of 1955, had not been known previously as a sympathizer. All this—and the list could be prolonged—does not perhaps add to much in comparison with Soviet activities in Europe. But, then, it has to be recalled that the Middle East had been neglected by the Communist bloc in previous years, and there was something of a novelty in all these visits.

The state of affairs in the economic field has given rise to various misconceptions. There has been a Soviet trade drive in the Middle East of late, but its scope has been limited and its political impact restricted. Eastern bloc imports from the Middle East (including Greece and Yugoslavia) increased in 1954 by about 56 per cent. over 1953, while exports to the Middle East increased by about 26 per cent. However, a closer scrutiny of the figures shows that in comparison with 1953 the increase was far less marked (24 per cent. for exports and 10 per cent. for imports). It shows also that trade relations with Greece and Persia had developed at a swifter pace than with the Arab states, who were the main object of Soviet wooing. The Soviet bloc took in the autumn of 1955 about 16–20 per cent. of the Egyptian cotton exports, which was considerably more than the 1953–54 average (9 per cent.), but not much more than what the Communist countries had taken back in 1952–53 (16 per cent.). The situation in this field has, however, changed as a result of the arms deal with the Soviet bloc; it is reported that in consequence Egypt had to distrain most of its cotton and rice crops for the coming few years. Czechoslovakia and Hungary have made great efforts to get larger slices of the Egyptian market, and the Soviet pavilion has made much impression at successive Damascus fairs. Egypt has trade agreements with most satellite countries, including a tripartite agreement with Rumania and the U.S.S.R., according to which the latter supplied petroleum products at prices 15 per cent. below the world market. Egypt also has a new trade agreement with Communist China, and negotiations between several Arab states and other Eastern-bloc countries are pending. Significant for the political character of these trade relations is the fact that almost all Middle Eastern countries can show at the present an export surplus in their trade with the Communist bloc.

It would be wrong, on the other hand, to compare the Soviet trade offensive with the German drive in the Balkans in the late thirties. Communist possibilities are more restricted: the Soviet Union cannot offer a wide range of finished products, and it needs fewer raw materials. Its underlying aim is, according to all evidence, to gain maximum political advantage as the result of minimum economic investment. The trade drive is mainly directed by political not economic considerations, and trade relations are therefore frequently artificial. No attempt has been made so far to gain a monopoly for the Soviet Union (as the Germans did in the Balkans), but rather to attain some commanding positions by a few well-chosen investments.

The same goes for the offers to give the Arab countries economic aid and equipment and building material to cover their needs in all aspects of economic development. This should include the $250 million project of the Aswan Dam, a plan which has intrigued Egyptian rulers for more than a generation. It is difficult to comment on these reports, be it only for the fact that no details have become known so far, apart from those which have emanated from Middle Eastern capitals (as yet unconfirmed by Moscow), and which have therefore to be taken with due caution. It is a well-known fact that Soviet industry is now in the throes of a second technological revolution demanding enormous investments. It is no secret either that Soviet industry at this time has been unable to give all the help needed by China, and it is therefore unlikely that it can undertake and carry out major new obligations elsewhere. The assistance promised to the Middle Eastern countries would appear to be, therefore, of psychological rather than material importance; it strengthens, for instance, the bargaining position of the Egyptian government *vis-à-vis* the World Bank and the West in general.[6] For this alone, admittedly, the Egyptian government has reason to be grateful to Moscow.

But, on the whole, it is difficult not to regard trade relations (just as the new cultural and religious ties) as minor developments, sideshows to the main events which are taking place on the political scene. The negotiations leading to the arms deal with the Soviet bloc had apparently taken place in Cairo in July, 1955, and according to some reports they were initiated by the Soviet Union. D. P. Shepilov, editor-in-chief of *Pravda* and since recently a prominent figure in Soviet foreign policy, came to Cairo to take part in the celebrations of Liberation, and declared on that occasion that "the sentiments of the Soviet people are wholly on the side of the Egyptian people's aspirations" (Tass cable, July 29, 1955). Several days later it was officially announced that Colonel Nāsir had been invited by the Soviet government to visit the U.S.S.R. In late August, rumours about a Communist-Egyptian arms deal began to spread, and provoked comment from Mr. Dulles.[7] The Israeli Minister to Moscow, when asking for information, was told that these reports were inventions and that no negotiations were in train, that the U.S.S.R. had not even considered selling arms. But there was an ominous postscript: the Soviet Union, he was given to understand, regarded the sale of arms needed for the defence of the purchasing state or for internal security measures as a normal commercial transaction. By the end of September the news of the arms deal could no more be kept secret; it was first revealed by Gamal Salem, a member of the Cairo junta, on a trip to India, and subsequently confirmed by the Egyptian government. Soviet press and radio tried to play down for some time these "exaggerated reports," stating that there was no ground for Western anxiety. In view of the evident concern in the West, this approach was, however, discontinued after some days, and *Pravda* carried on October 2, 1955, a short official statement. There it was reiterated that "each state has the legitimate right to look after its defence and to buy weapons for its defence requirements from other states on the usual commercial terms." Elsewhere the Soviet press published attacks against the West from Arab Eastern sources, according to which the U.S., Britain, and France were criticized for not having supplied more arms to the Arab states and for having stipulated all kinds of "conditions," viz. the demand for guarantees that the arms supplied would not be used for aggressive aims.

According to the evidence available, Soviet leaders had some misgivings as to the impression their policy would make in the West. The fact that Czechoslovakia, not the Soviet Union, was chosen to carry out the "commercial transaction" points to that. The statements of Arab leaders were, as a rule, reported in full in the Soviet press—but the anti-Israeli attacks were usually censored. And the anti-Western polemics on Middle Eastern issues in the Soviet press ceased on the eve of the second Geneva conference; there was no wish to shelve a new policy that had been so successful, but there was no desire either to have the Soviet Middle Eastern offensive made the subject of close international scrutiny.

All other developments in Soviet-Middle Eastern relations since early October, 1955, have been of lesser importance in comparison; Moscow's denial that it had offered arms to Israel was a matter of routine. The Middle Eastern situation being what it is, it was sufficient to supply arms to *one* of the rival camps in order to promote Soviet interests in the area; arms supply to both sides would have created complications and raised unnecessary suspicions of foul play. Persia's adhesion, in mid-October, 1955, to the Turko-Iraqi Pact provoked emphatic and dire, if unspecified, threats in Moscow, and the governments belonging to the defence pact were described as the "lickspittle of the colonizers." As a counterweight, Soviet activities in other countries were stepped up: diplomatic relations with Saudi Arabia were re-established, the Soviet-Yemen pact of 1927 was renewed, and negotiations for diplomatic contacts with the Sudan and Libya were started, arms were offered to Syria and Saudia—all during the second half of October, 1955.

Soviet policies in the Middle East have been successful of late and Soviet designs in that area rather transparent. Nevertheless there were, in the beginning of the Soviet offensive at least, several conflicting versions offered by Western observers to explain the motives and the background of the Soviet political offensive. It transpired only gradually that far from removing the danger of local wars, the Geneva conference (of July, 1955) had actually increased them; once it had emerged that a global war was ruled out by both sides, it became far less dangerous than before for interested parties to engage in local conflicts. The Communist leaders have apparently drawn the obvious conclusions from this new situation. But part of Western public opinion continued to believe that the "spirit of Geneva" meant that the Communist world had given up the idea of promoting Communism and Soviet interests by force outside the present frontiers.

It was argued by others that the recent Soviet moves in the Middle East had come merely as a reaction to Western defence schemes in that part of the world, that it was a defensive rather than an offensive action. It may be true that the establishment of the "Northern Tier" hastened the Soviet drive in the Middle East; but it is extremely unlikely that Moscow would have "neglected," in any case, the Middle East in its global plans much longer. If the Soviet arms supply to Egypt and the other recent moves was a defensive action, it would follow that the Soviet leaders may be ready to join the Western powers in their endeavour to maintain peace and stability in the Middle East—to sign, for instance, a declaration guaranteeing the *status quo*. This, however, seems unrealistic; Soviet diplomats may of course prefer not to close altogether the door to diplomatic negotiations with the West, scheduled to remove the "Northern Tier"—while maintaining the Soviet positions. Basically, however, Russia has nothing to gain and much to lose from the preservation of the *status quo* in the Middle East. The assistance to Egypt is given at present for the very same reason that Israel was supported in 1948—that it appears to be the one political factor most likely to upset the political balance in the Middle East, most likely to produce conditions of anarchy.

Another fairly widespread misconception was the assumption that ideological considerations are somehow involved inasmuch as the Soviet Union is concerned. But Soviet policy in the Middle East is almost entirely free from short-range ideological motivation, is power politics pure and simple. If we disregard for a moment the propaganda slogans, it would appear that the Soviet policy-makers like one Middle Eastern country as much as another. But they like even more conditions conducive to the spread of Communism and Soviet influence. Such conditions come to exist (as the experience of the last forty years has shown) mainly in the wake of a war, when state machinery is weakened—and not only in the state that lost the war. Stalin in his last book reiterated the thesis of the "inevitable armed conflicts" within the Western camps. His heirs would be less than faithful to the teachings of Lenin if they failed to exploit such a promising situation as the Arab-Israeli conflict. Russia has no vested interest in the victory of Egypt in a possible war despite the assistance rendered; one can imagine, on the contrary, that the conditions for the growth of Communism in a defeated Egypt or Syria would be better than in an Israel which has lost a war. Be that as it may, whatever the outcome, if Egypt should prevail in the arms race against Israel it will be owing to Soviet help, and Soviet prestige will increase enormously. If Egypt should be defeated for a second time, Communism (and thus indirectly the Soviet Union) will again be the main beneficiary. It is—heads I win, tails you lose.

Soviet penetration in the Middle East offers great prospects, but there are, at present, certain limitations to it. Soviet actions in the Middle East tend to jeopardize to a considerable extent the "climate of confidence" which Soviet diplomats have created with so much effort in Europe. Soviet policy-makers appear to be perfectly ready to accept this risk, and they are disinclined to give up what must appear to them a most promising line of action. But it is possible that in the face of Western pressure Soviet action would become more cautious; little may change in substance, but the openly hostile character to the West of these actions would probably be somewhat concealed.

Basically, however, all signs point to the fact that the present Soviet policy in the Middle East will be continued. Even if it should not come to a local war, Russia's alignment with Egypt, and to a lesser degree with Syria and Saudia, is highly important for Moscow because it may disrupt Western defence schemes. These pacts may be the prototype of a new form of alliance in specific Middle Eastern style. True enough, neither the local Communists nor the democratic liberal elements figure in this "popular front from above." But the political effect may well be similar. When the European Socialist movement tried to counter Communist attempts to subvert their parties during the "Popular Front," they had at least some experience and an organization to operate with. Middle Eastern leaders have neither this experience of Communist theory and practice nor a political organization to compete with their present allies. What they have by way of ideological equipment is woefully insufficient to compete with the vast appeal of Communism in backward areas. The Egyptian leaders may be perfectly honest in their protestations that they will get Communist arms, not ideas. But the very idea that they will be able to get the one without the other points to either megalomania or an extraordinary degree of *naïveté*, absence of experience, or lack of political imagination—and perhaps both. There are historical reasons for all this, and Soviet foreign policy has astutely exploited it. Egypt and Syria have become in their blueprints the "weakest link" in the non-Communist chaim. It would be difficult to deny the validity of this assumption.

It remains to be seen how the Soviet Middle Eastern drive will affect the prospects of Communism in that area. The minimum Soviet aim is, of course, the neutralization of the Middle East. But in countries in which this aim has already been attained, the Communists press for more than that, for the creation of a "united national front" which, under Communist guidance, is eventually to become the leading force in a "Popular Democracy," Middle Eastern style. We have it on the authority of a well-known Soviet expert for Middle Eastern affairs that Communist activities have been most successful so far in Syria and Lebanon.[8] According to the same source, the struggle of the Arab Communists against the "*bourgeois*" (i.e. non-Communist) parties for the domination of the "national front" should not be too difficult because the "national *bourgeoisie* in the Arab countries is relatively weak and has developed slowly under conditions of foreign capitalist rule." Communist chances are even better in Syria than in the Lebanon, where the many ethnic and religious divisions and the *esprit de clan* make it extremely difficult for a political party to attract all sections of the population. As for Egypt, it is unlikely that the Soviet leaders will jeopardize their collaboration with the Cairo junta by open support for the comparatively weak and disunited Communist movement in that country. In the long run, however, efforts will undoubtedly be made to put this collaboration on a broader and more satisfactory basis (from Moscow's point of view). This should not be too difficult in view of the favourable political climate created by official Egyptian propaganda over a long period. There is no such hope for co-operation on the part of the Iraqi and Jordanian governments. In these countries the Communists are encouraged to lead the opposition against the powers-that-be, and, generally speaking, to make as much trouble as possible for the governments of Baghdad and Amman in collaboration with right-wing extremist groups (viz. the widespread and effective demonstrations in Jordan in December, 1955). Communism in Israel appears to have been written off by Moscow for the time being.

The main difficulty of Communist strategy in the Middle East at the present time is one of timing, not of tactics. The Communists in Syria, for instance, may conceivably be able, in the not too distant future, to attain power via a "National Front." But the premature emergence of a Middle Eastern "Popular Democracy" would probably act as a deterrent in other Arab countries, and may be considered, for this reason, undesirable until further notice.

Meanwhile the West will continue to face an uphill task: How to persuade the peoples of the Middle East, and especially their political *élites*, that they can attain industrialization (including socialist planning if they want to) and modernization without resorting to totalitarianism. Generous economic help on a far wider scale than hitherto would be a prerequisite for success. But even more important is a reorientation in the political field, tantamount to a fairly radical breach with the past.

Chapter Twenty

Conclusions

IT is possible to discern four different periods in the history of Middle Eastern Communism. In 1919–20 the first Communist groups came into being in Turkey, Palestine, and Egypt. But their efforts were doomed from the outset; the Communists of that era put themselves into deliberate and radical opposition not only to the governments of the day, but also to all political, religious, and social institutions and traditions. They wanted to create proletarian mass parties in countries without an industrial proletariat. They launched a frontal attack against Islam at a time when its hold on the masses was as strong as ever.

By 1923 it was obvious that these attempts had failed. The Communist Parties in Turkey and Egypt ceased to exist, the party in Palestine lingered on precariously without any hope of gaining mass support. It was only in the middle 1930's that a break was made with the "radical" past. This break came as a concomitant of the popular-front tactics of the Comintern in Europe and America; but it was the line which came to stay in the Middle East, with certain important modifications (such as the change to a "national," or "anti-imperialist" front, etc.). By now all the radical-socialist demands were dropped, as was the enmity to Islam, and the unwillingness to collaborate with other parties. In countries such as Syria and Iraq, Communist Parties grew during that period and attained (in the Levant, at least), a certain importance. Their main competitors at that time were the semi-Fascist groups whose power of attraction was often greater than their own.

It was World War II which brought the great upsurge in Middle Eastern Communism. Two of the reasons for this growth in influence were the emergence of the Soviet Union as one of the two great world powers, and the downfall of Nazi Germany and Fascist Italy. It is true that World War II also brought economic, and especially industrial, progress to the Middle East, and the consequent emergence of stronger workers' organizations than had existed previously. But it was not the class struggle which gave Communism its main impetus, but rather a general feeling that the Middle East was at last beginning to stir after so many years of stagnation. Communist Parties made considerable progress in Egypt and Palestine, in the Levant and Iraq, and even in Turkey. The social group most closely connected with Communism in all these countries was the intelligentsia. Although there prevailed a feeling among them that things were in motion, the intelligentsia had not attained full political emancipation anywhere in the Middle East.

The fourth period began almost immediately after World War II with the deterioration in the relations between the Arab countries and the West. The popular front of 1935–37 was now continued as an "anti-imperialist" front in which there was room for all "honest patriots without distinction of class, political, or religious convictions." The Middle East became the testing-ground *par excellence* for all kinds of Communist-front organizations.[1]

Achievements in Turkey and Israel were less spectacular, for several reasons. There was no serious agrarian problem in either country; their Westernization (or modernization) had gone very far; the politically active *élite* in both countries was, on the whole, more mature; and, last but not least, Russia had been directly threatening Turkey's independence, on the one hand, and had launched a campaign against "cosmopolitans" in Russia and the satellites on the other, which, though discontinued after Stalin's death, was not easily forgotten in Israel. But if there was stability in Turkey and Israel, the political, social, and spiritual crisis in the Arab world had grown rapidly since World War I, and in the vacuum created as the result of the breakdown of tradition, Communism rushed in as one of the strongest political competitors for leadership.

The sources of Communist strength are manifold. The decay of Islamic society and its values, together with the absence of liberal and democratic-socialist forces (for which there was little room in the specific conditions of the Middle East), made Communist success easier than it was in Europe, where it had to face political and spiritual competition. Resistance to Communism was confined to retrograde forces, vested interests, and certain religious dignitaries, but there was no opposition to Communism among the intelligentsia. Such opposition could have been based only on the defence of freedom and the liberty of the individual, but freedom and liberty were lacking in the Middle East, and where they had existed they were not so highly valued.

Proletarian exclusiveness had been outmoded for many years in Soviet practice, and if one wanted to prove that class interests are really so important in history, one could choose no better example than the peculiar fascination which Soviet society exercises on the intelligentsia, or the "working intelligentsia" or the managerial class (in its widest sense), in the Middle East. The turn of events in the Soviet Union and the satellite countries has shown them that in the Soviet world the technical intelligentsia is one of the most privileged classes, and that its privileges are likely to continue, if not actually to increase, in the future. Nevertheless, it is extremely doubtful whether such considerations of class interest were really decisive for the political orientation of most of the intelligentsia. What can be taken for granted is that from a class angle there was certainly nothing to repel the intelligentsia.

"They are to be the masters, teachers, builders, makers of the new country, and the new man; they will be lavishly equipped with all the facilities that can promote their work; rather than foreign bodies in their old communities they will be the centres around which a new community crystallizes; the more comprehensive the new structure grows, the higher will be their place on the pyramid of functions that they themselves have to organize and to populate with their pupils and assistants. . . . There is no limit to the glory that is to come to them. The sociology of the 'expert' centres in his concern for his professional career; this is the greatest danger, even in democracy. As Walter Rathenau used to say, 'there are no experts, there are only people with vested interests.' Whatever people in democracy would have to give up if they submitted to totalitarianism, as experts they would gain professional standing and income."[2]

Elsewhere we have drawn attention to academic unemployment in the Middle Eastern countries, notably Egypt, and a similar situation can be discerned in other Asian countries. On the whole, however, it must be said that the Arab states have succeeded in absorbing a larger part of the intelligentsia (and in higher posts, too) than most other Asian countries. Communist support in Cairo and Beirut, in the old city of Jerusalem, and in Baghdad often comes from well-to-do lawyers and physicians; they may be *déclassé* and spiritually "strangers in their own country," but they are certainly not so socially, and their "economic" roots are fairly firm.[3] It should be noted, incidentally, that as far back as 1928 the leadership of the Comintern recognized this tendency of intellectual cadres to predominate, and said in one of its resolutions that, "an important if not predominant part of the Party ranks [are recruited] in the first stage of the movement from the petty *bourgeoisie*, and in particular from the revolutionary-inclined intelligentsia, very frequently students."[4] The implication was, apparently, that in the second and later stages of the development, leadership would pass to other hands. But exactly the opposite has happened. The Communist leaders have drawn the necessary conclusions in practice, if not in theory, and have adjusted their policy and propaganda for the consumption of the intelligentsia. The West has suggested various gradual reforms such as "Point Four," which may bring economic relief to the masses and may be welcomed by them in accordance with their interests, but they are hardly apt to catch the imagination of the key group, the intelligentsia. The Communists, on the other hand, turn almost exclusively towards the intelligentsia. "A programme of seizing political power followed by prolonged industrialization, economic planning, recasting of the social structure, realignment of a country's international situation in favour of the U.S.S.R.—these are considerations of the type which can attract intellectuals only."[5]

There is, of course, in all this, as repeatedly has been pointed out, a considerable element of self-deception. This privileged Soviet *élite*, whose position seems so enviable to impoverished Middle Eastern and Latin-American intellectuals and civil servants, is hag-ridden with fears and repressions inconceivable elsewhere. But this dark side of the moon is invisible to people living in a "pre-revolutionary" society, where the restrictions and proscriptions of an efficient totalitarian state can hardly be imagined.[6]

In European countries such as France and Italy a *secessio plebis* has given the Communists a real proletarian mass basis. Elsewhere, the Communists have appeared in the role of a national party spearheading the fight against outside rulers (as in Yugoslavia or Indo-China), or have headed and exploited agrarian revolts for their own purposes. But in the Middle East and South-east Asia, in view of the absence of an urban proletariat or agrarian unrest, the Communists have become the party of the intelligentsia *par excellence*. This has been noted by Sjahrir, the leader of the Indonesian Socialists; given the still strongly surviving heritage of a "feudalist" authoritarian mentality among many Indonesians, he believes that his grounds for these fears are very real. The Communists were able to exploit this authoritarian heritage by building a powerful party along authoritarian lines. The Communist leaders themselves, he says, exemplify the effect of this (totalitarian) heritage: "Most of them come from the old aristocratic families and a paternalistic authoritarianism is ingrained in them."[7] The same phenomenon has been noted by Masani in India, who found that Communist propaganda was more successful among the well-to-do managers, educators, scientists, etc., than among the workers and peasants. This led him to the conclusion that it was not poverty or starvation which were the main causes for the spread of Communism, but rather psychological and emotional factors; the psychological and emotional vacuum created by the decay of traditional religion, the latter being in the process of replacement by some new religion of materialism.[8]

The situation in the Middle East is highly illuminating in this respect, too: the main pro-Communist spokesman in Egypt is one of the ten biggest landowners in the country. All prominent Arab Communist leaders in Syria, Lebanon, Israel, and Jordan (with one exception) hail from well-to-do families. In Turkey the party has won, relatively speaking, many followers among poets, but very few among industrial workers. The militants of the Iraqi party are almost exclusively intellectuals. Recent events have shown that the Tudeh party in Persia has many well-wishers among the army officers, but hardly any among the non-commissioned officers and privates. In Israel the Communist Party obtained a lower percentage in the Histadrut (trade-union) elections than in the parliamentary elections.[9]

Communism in the Middle East has functioned widely as a movement of middle-class revolt against feudal rule. But this does not mean that the intelligentsia, having attained its political emancipation, will automatically cease to be Communist. It has no liberal and democratic tradition, it is authoritarian with a vengeance, and is perhaps the most perfect specimen now extant of "totalitarian democracy" (in Dr. Talmon's sense of the phrase). It probably believes in the essential goodness of the fellaheen and workers, but it also thinks them utterly incapable of managing their own affairs; the masses will need the tutelage of the enlightened vanguard for many, many years. In the meantime a revolution will have to take place, and they see no better theory of "revolution from above" than Communism. Is it another link in the chain of the *trahison des clercs*? They can claim, of course, that one cannot betray what one has never possessed. Their Western values have never been more than skin deep. And why blame the intelligentsia? Democracy and basic human rights presuppose certain emotional characteristics; they are not intrinsic needs of the intellect. The impact of Communism as a technique for modernizing the Middle East, of overcoming its present backwardness in the shortest possible time, is therefore of the greatest importance. Capitalism was identical with imperialist rule, and democracy was something the imperialist powers allegedly practised at home. Democracy was not a militant creed, nor very attractive to them, and it did not provide the answers to many specifically Asiatic questions. Democracy could not inspire the masses, and it did not give firm spiritual support to the *élite*. It could not promise a much better life in the immediate future, nor could it put on a spectacular show in which everybody was to be told just what to do—whereas Communism had all the force of a secular religion—in Asia even more so than in Europe.

Nationalism in the Middle East is not a force opposed to Communism. On the contrary, at the present time it has paved the way for and has collaborated with it. Communism, more often than not (like nineteenth-century liberalism in Europe) had grown up together with nationalism, and for many years a conflict between the two was not even considered possible.[10] The meaning of nationalism had been very clear under foreign rule: it was independence, home rule, and the evacuation of foreign forces. But once independence had been achieved, cynicism and disillusionment took over and the general state of mind was one of:

"Que l'indépendance était belle sous l'impérialisme."

What was the content of the new nationalism? As acute an observer as Mr. Nehru said he did not know what it was. What common ideals and traditions, what common history, culture, and myths, did the new nations of the Middle East possess? Were they nations at all or were the few common ties that they did have (which transcended present political frontiers), based on religious and pan-Islamic notions rather than on the idea of a nation state? And was not each state actually made up of two or more nations, because only a very small minority took part in public life, with the vast majority illiterate and utterly apathetic to what was going on in the capital? Disraeli had spoken of the two nations of nineteenth-century England, but was not the abyss immensely wider in twentieth-century Egypt or Iraq, for instance? Asian nationalism has been pictured as a "huge and often uncontrolled source of energy, not often clearly formulated either in ideological slogans or in concrete economic and political programmes. It is, rather a huge emotional reservoir which can be tapped and used for good or ill, depending on the kind of leadership which captures it."[11]

Developments in the Middle East have been even less promising than in South-east Asia, though most of the Middle Eastern countries attained independence at an earlier date. There is more stability and political maturity in South-east Asia, and though it would certainly be premature to say that democracy has succeeded in establishing itself in such countries as India, Ceylon, or Indonesia, it cannot be said about them, as one has to say about the Arab countries of the Middle East or Persia, that it has already failed.

The numerical strength of Communist Parties in the Middle East may not appear impressive to the American or Western European observer.

Egypt	. .	7000–8000
Israel	. .	4000–5000
Lebanon	.	8000–10,000
Syria	. .	10,000
Jordan	.	1000–2000
Iraq .	.	3000–5000
Sudan	.	1000–1500
Turkey	.	3000

It may be argued that the Communist Parties in Holland and Belgium have more than 30,000 members each, and in Austria there are even 60,000. All these countries are less populous than Egypt, and not much bigger than Syria or Iraq. Nevertheless, Communism in Belgium, Holland, and even Austria is a negligible quantity. Such comparisons are utterly misleading: Austria may have far more Communists than the whole Middle East, and yet the Austrian Communists can never compete with the two main parties in that country, the Social Democrats and the Christian Social (the Austrian People's) Party, who have party structures which are more loosely knit but much larger than the Communist cadre. The decisive issue in the Middle East is that no party in Syria and Lebanon, for instance, apart from the Communists, has more than 10,000 militants. The situation should be compared with the state of affairs in under-developed countries where political parties have not existed or are only very feebly developed.[12] A comparison with Russia in 1917 would be more to the point: party membership in Russia on January 1, 1917, was 23,600 and it reached, a year later, after the Bolsheviki had attained state power, only 115,000 in a country of 160 million. Which shows that in most Middle Eastern countries the Communist Party has, relatively speaking, far more members than it had in Russia on the eve of the Revolution.

The decisive test, however, is not in figures—above a certain essential minimum, of course—but elsewhere. How strongly rooted is the power of the state? Has the Communist Party any serious rivals on the left, or elsewhere? Would it be sufficient to take over a few urban centres? How many sympathizers does the party have, how strong are its "front" organizations? The replies to these (and several other) pertinent questions would obviously differ greatly if we compared the situation in some Western European country with the state of affairs in a Middle Eastern state (apart from Turkey and Israel)—or even with the situation in Russia in 1917.

Local differences make generalizations difficult, of course, if not impossible. The need for a change is very strongly felt in Iraq, the country with the most reactionary government, where anti-Westernism has for several years been submerged but remained violent. This is also the country which is geographically closest to the Soviet Union. However, the arrest of the party leaders, and more important the inability of the local Communists to unite and build a strong party, make it impossible to predict exactly what would happen if the present regime in Baghdad were to break down. In Lebanon, on the other hand, the Communist Party is already the strongest numerically, and in Syria it may soon become the leading force under a popular-front regime. But the presence of democratic institutions (however imperfect), on the one hand, and the communal division, on the other, make it much more difficult for the party to make headway in Lebanon. In Egypt, the chances of Communism have greatly improved, in the long-range view, as the result of the policy followed by the Cairo junta. It recalls events in Italy between the two world wars; but Mussolini's heritage was the emergence of the strongest Communist Party in western Europe. Israel and Turkey appear very nearly hopeless at the present time from the Communist point of view; the governments there not being discredited at all and political maturity at too high a level. A pro-Arab Western policy in the Middle East may gradually force Israel to follow a neutralist line in foreign policy, but it would hardly affect the internal balance of strength in the country. An Arab-Israeli war, whatever its outcome, would greatly expedite the growth of Communism in the Arab states and perhaps even produce one or two "popular-democratic" regimes. Only a very rapid deterioration in the economic and political situation in Turkey (or the Western world in general) could produce similar results in Turkey.

Seen in isolation, a bid for power by the Communist Party of one of more of the Arab states in a possible coming crisis would appear to stand certain chances of success. But it is impossible, to be sure, to see events in any one country in isolation. The decisive criterion for whether such an attempt would be made or not is of course the general world situation and the general line of policy followed by Moscow. It is of course conceivable that in a state of anarchy a local Communist Party might decide to go ahead without waiting for the green light to be given by Moscow. But if Tudeh did not try it in 1951–52 in a country adjacent to the Soviet Union, where the most ideally anarchic conditions existed and where local success was virtually certain, it is not likely to happen elsewhere *against* the wish of the central leadership. What, then, were Soviet intentions with regard to the Middle East in the summer of 1955?[13]

Here we face conflicting trends and interests. On a short-term view the Soviet policy of studiously avoiding any involvement in Middle Eastern affairs, of staying out—in contradiction to Western policy, which is trying to "organize the area"—was undoubtedly promising. In view of the process of internal decomposition in the Arab countries, the hostility between them and Israel which may lead to a local war, the resentment towards the West, and the justified assumption that a trend towards union and progress (which is dangerous from the Soviet point of view) is least likely to take place in the Middle East, Moscow had much to gain by letting the Middle East stew in its own juice.

But this was profitable only up to a certain point, and from that point onwards the policy of non-intervention was not likely to bear fruit.* It is not impossible, of course, that Communist Parties may come to power in the Arab states within the framework of popular fronts in certain circumstances, but this possibility is far from being likely at the present time. Such a development may occur as the result of a further shift in the international balance of power, as a result of growing Soviet might and the gradual weakening of Western influence in the Middle East. But historical experience has shown that without active outside intervention, the local Communist Parties may never get the impetus necessary to attain state power. Such intervention, whatever form it

*Recent Soviet activities in the Middle East are dealt with in greater detail in Chapter Nineteen of the present study.

may take, would be easier in the Middle East than in Europe; in Europe the borders between East and West have been frozen for several years, and no decisive change is believed likely to take place under present conditions. Most of the Middle Eastern countries, on the other hand, are "undefined" and do not belong to the Western camp; they therefore constitute a vacuum between West and East which will hardly be tolerated in today's world. This does not mean that such attempts would not provoke Western counter-action and that they would not lead to a new war. What should be emphasized is that the Middle East is likely to become one of the main areas of conflict between West and East—as a result of its weakness and its refusal to take its place on the side of one of the two camps.

We face similar conflicting trends in the role of the Communist Parties. Their task in the age of "revolution from above" is definitely not to engage in a "leftist deviation," i.e. to try their luck in a revolution. Strategically speaking, their assignment is that of a fifth column which is not to strike before the other four are on the march—however strong the fifth column may be, and even if it were able to cope with the task alone. But, on the other hand, an entirely new situation may be created as the result of a prolonged atomic stalemate. In such a situation the Soviet Union may not be able to assist other Communist Parties to gain power, and the dilemma would be of either permitting these parties to try their luck alone in favourable conditions, or to give up the idea of the further spread of Communism for a lengthy period. Provided disastrous mistakes are not committed by the West in the Middle East, such a development is by far the likeliest, but it is rather difficult to know whether this dilemma, with all its implications, is already fully realized in Moscow, as well as by the leadership of the local Communist Parties. What can be safely predicted is that it will not be too difficult for Soviet foreign policy to achieve its minimum target: to neutralize the Middle Eastern countries, except Turkey and Israel. (The future foreign political orientation of Israel depends upon Western rather than Israeli policy.) This is comparatively easy, because public opinion in the Arab countries is strongly in favour of neutralism, and the governments are almost without exception very much dependent on public opinion in their foreign policies. They are doubly dependent because they do not want to give in to public opinion in domestic policy, which would imply carrying out political and social reforms, and they vitally need a popular neutralist foreign policy as a safety-valve.

But even among the rulers, support of the West is not very strong. There have been, and are now, a few politicians here and there genuinely in favour of an alliance with the West. But these are few and far between, and they do not remain, as a rule, for more than a few months or, at most, for a few years in power; and where everything depends on the personality of one leader, whether his name is 'Ali Razmara or Adīb Shishakli or *Al Majali*, where a single pistol shot may make all the difference in policy, stable rule cannot be expected. But the pro-Western elements are a minority, anyway, and the rest believe that the community of interests with the West is not big enough to warrant support and close relations. The big landowners, of course, would lose their privileges under Communist rule, but they are not too sure whether they would preserve them in the case of a closer association with the West. Perhaps they are right from their point of view: they do not fit into the usual categories of either Western democracy or "Eastern dictatorship," and their interests tally neither with Capitalism nor with Communism, and certainly not with democratic socialism. They are at least as likely candidates for a third bloc, as, say, some of the French neutralists. Of the others, most take Middle Eastern security for granted, and though they may occasionally be ready to admit that the Middle Eastern countries alone are not able to defend this part of the world against outside attack, they agree on the following two basic assumptions: (*a*) that the Communist bloc would be in favour of peaceful co-existence if only "Western imperialism" would get out of the area, and (*b*) in the unlikely case of Communist aggression the West will help to defend the Middle East, anyway.[14]

A dispassionate review of the political trends in the Middle East appears to show that the question of whether or not these countries will become Communist has not yet been decided. But it would also tend to show that there is no reason for undue optimism for the West. It will depend only partly upon events in the Middle East itself, and even if the West were to be wiser politically than it is now in its present dealings in the Middle East, it is doubtful whether this would decisively influence the course of events in the Middle East. It would merely create the prerequisites for success, but no more than that. For the West can give money, can supply agricultural machinery and even jets and tanks, but it cannot provide what is needed most: a competent native *élite* with a high degree of political maturity. There is little sense in closing one's eyes to the reality; the absence of such a group is the main source of the permanent Middle Eastern crisis—so far as it depends at all on these countries themselves. At the time of writing (and for some years past) some Arab countries have been moving slowly but steadily towards Communism. It is not the growth of Communist Parties in itself that is the most spectacular feature of this development (though this is certainly quite important in itself), but rather the utter inability of the ruling classes to give their countries moderately efficient governments, to promote social and economic progress (however slow), and to create a minimal atmosphere of hopefulness instead of the present climate of despair. Conditions conducive to the growth of Communism are also quite favourable in Iraq and Jordan, even though political repression has forced the Communists underground in those countries. This has put the damper on news of Communist influence in Iraq and Jordan, but it has certainly not prevented the spread of this influence itself. If these extremely reactionary regimes should be overthrown (and there is little doubt that this will happen sooner or later), the Communists are likely to emerge as one of the leading forces in the two countries if not *the* leading force. A state of suspense prevails in Egypt, which is the largest and politically the most important country by far. An underground popular front consisting of the remnants of the Moslem Brotherhood, the Wafd (not yet regenerated but continuing its fatal tradition of 1950–52), and the Communists would appear to be the only, but disastrous, alternative to the present regime. But a weak junta, which is vague and wavering about domestic policy, which is gradually forced to adopt the policy of its foes in order to out-manœuvre them, which involves Egypt in military adventures instead of carrying out a programme of domestic reform—such a government is likely to be no less disastrous. The outcome of the struggle in Egypt depends on whether the military junta (which, apart from its *fascist* elements, also contains reformists) will be able to make its own policy and on how much it will be dependent on the demagogic slogans of its foes. There is at least a possibility of reforms on Kemalist lines in Egypt, though the chances of success have very much diminished of late.

The situation in Turkey and Israel is altogether different from the conditions prevailing in the Arab countries; nothing which could possibly happen there would affect developments in the Arab countries. An Arab victory over Israel or an Israeli victory over the Arab states would change little in the trends outlined above; it might, of course, hasten the process of disintegration. Peace between Israel and the Arab countries would be a very welcome stabilizing factor, but it is unlikely in the near future.

What, then, remains to be done by the West? We have stressed time and again that the possibilities of action are fairly limited. The key is in the hands of the native Arab *élites*. It is quite true, as an Indonesian prime minister stated in Delhi recently to great applause, Asian affairs are no longer settled in London and Paris. What remains to be seen is whether the new rulers of the Middle East and South-east Asia will be able in the future to prevent Asian affairs from being decided in Moscow and Peking.

The development of a political awareness of the nature of the Communist threat among the nations of Asia is, indeed, as vital a condition for containing Communism as is the creation of a military counter-weight: "The point is that we have no more specific Western interests to defend in Asia and no wish to draw the Asian neutrals to our side for such a purpose. Our only aim is to prevent the further advance of Communism, and for that it will be perfectly sufficient if the Asian neutrals are ready to defend their own cause."[15]

But will they be ready to defend their own cause? Will they be able to distinguish between social reform and progress and totalitarianism? The Turks will defend their independence because they feel the danger at close quarters; the Arab governments question the very existence of danger. Some of these countries are ruled by extremely reactionary regimes which see their main task to be the prevention of social progress. All reform movements have been branded "Communistic" in these countries, and there is hardly any reason for surprise that for them the Soviet Union and the Communist Party have become the symbol of social justice and progress. It is almost hopeless to try to convince citizens of these countries that they are likely to loose human freedom and basic liberties under Communism; they can hardly be afraid of losing what they do not have, anyway.

The obvious course of action for the West would therefore be to support the forces of reform against the reactionary powers who are leading their countries towards catastrophe. Many opportunities have been let slip by Western policy in that field. But it would be unjust not to admit that serious difficulties have to be faced. In some countries these forces of reform do not exist at all, and in others they are as yet too weak to constitute an alternative to the present regime. Elsewhere, these forces have taken up a very critical or hostile stand towards the West, and have created some specific Middle Eastern brand of "left-wing" Fascism (Egypt) or merely produced anarchy (Syria). Nevertheless, there is no good reason to accept the defeatist conclusion that the West has to continue backing the reactionary forces up to the bitter end—because there is no alternative. In some countries there *is* an alternative, and elsewhere the West can contribute much towards its creation.

We are not pretending to advise Western statesmen. Many excellent suggestions have been made in the last few years by experts on under-developed countries, and a vast new literature on the subject has grown up. The major problem at this time is not the lack of good advice, but rather the gulf between the policy which most people agree should be followed and what is actually done in practice.

Ten, or even five, years ago it was almost unanimously believed in the West that economic and technical assistance was the most efficient way of stemming the flood of Communism in backward countries. It is most interesting to note that many people who very much resent the teachings of Karl Marx suddenly became fervent believers in historical materialism, and saw economic progress as the key to the whole situation—contrary to the Communists' own view! By now it has been realized by the most concerned that "economic development doesn't necessarily make nice people."[16] Nor does it create believers in the principles of Western democracy. Lebanon, the least backward of the

Arab countries, is also the one with the strongest Communist Party, and the areas of India with the highest degree of literacy are also those most affected by the spread of Communism. This does not mean, needless to say, that economic and social progress automatically leads towards Communism, but it certainly does mean that in the process of development these countries are more likely to be affected (at least temporarily) than before. Which clearly shows that the appeal of Communism is far wider and more complex than is believed by the economic determinists.

Communism has never found a favourable breeding-ground in very poor countries unaffected by outside influence. Nor do very poor people resent their poverty so long as their fellow citizens share their lot. This has been observed, among others, by Marx, who wrote that a house may be big or small—so long as the neighbouring houses are also small, it satisfies all social demands. But if a palace is built next to it, the small house becomes a wretched shack in the eyes of its owners, who will thenceforward feel dissatisfied, uncomfortable, and oppressed.[17] The Egyptian fellah and the Syrian worker feel their poverty acutely since they have seen that a far higher standard of living is possible. The Arab intellectual feels it even more strongly because he knows even better than the other classes what life can be like in a more developed society. It is at this point that the competition starts—between Communism, which promises to work wonders, and the West, which promises slow progress or nothing at all. Actually, political propaganda apart, economic progress has not been a Communist monopoly. The classical example of Soviet propaganda for the consumption of Middle Eastern countries is the development of the Central Asian republics during the past twenty years. If we compare these results in Central Asia with the state of affairs in countries which have been stagnating (such as Persia or some of the Arab countries), this may appear very impressive indeed. If we compare achievements there with the headway made by Turkey (where consumption of electric current, production of cement, and grain crops have doubled in the course of three to four years, to give only a few examples), the thesis of Communist superiority becomes rather difficult to maintain. But most of the Middle Eastern countries have *not* made such progress, and, even more important, there is no upward trend in sight. Great development schemes have been planned in Iraq, and the means are available to implement them; nevertheless, the living standard of the majority of the population has not risen, nor is it likely to rise in the next few years, which may be decisive years for the future of the Middle East.

We all know by now that there is no facile correlation between economic and political progress, and the point need not be laboured here. The Middle East is a world in urgent need of a universal message, and this goes, *a fortiori*, for the Middle Eastern intelligentsia. The West has been offering technical aid and Point Four loans, while Communism offers a new creed. To paraphrase the late Joseph Schumpeter, technical aid is a poor substitute for the holy grail. Communism's power of attraction as a quasi-religious creed should never be underrated, and it is nowhere so strong as it is in backward countries such as those of the Middle East. In the Soviet Union everybody has a first-hand opportunity of comparing ideals with realities; one can see for oneself how much social justice and freedom there are in the Soviet and satellite societies. In the countries of the West, much information on Soviet realities is also available, and Leninism has a tough time standing up to competition in the free market of ideas and ideologies. But the intelligentsia of the Middle East gets Leninism pure and unalloyed, and next to nothing is known about Soviet conditions; anyway, the *idea* is the important criterion. They want to receive Leninism as if it had not yet been tried anywhere in the world.

This is not a book about the appeal of Communism in underdeveloped countries in general. But we have had to return to that subject time and again. If rapid economic development were the main attraction it would still be a formidable threat, but the example of Turkey (and to a lesser degree of other countries) should suffice to show that there is another way. But the religious and ethical elements in Communism have been of far greater importance, and must be so at a time when the quest for a universal faith is stronger than ever, with traditional religion sterile and losing appeal. Any attempt to understand the power of attraction of Communism in the Middle East which disregards the very existence of its moral concepts and the sources of its religious fervour and ideals is doomed from the outset. But this also goes for all under-developed countries and is not an observation specific to the Middle East. What is specific to the Middle Eastern situation is the decline of Islam. We stated at the beginning of this study that for the majority of the intelligentsia of the Arab countries, Islam has ceased to be a living force, and a detailed investigation of whether Islam was aiding or arresting the growth of Communism would be a question of a certain speculative interest but of little practical importance—so far as the intelligentsia is concerned. Islam is more important for the masses in the Arab countries, but the authoritarian character of Islamic society, in its state of disintegration even more than in its early stages, makes an easy transition to the Communist ideology a possibility, and in some cases a probability. Traditional Islamic autocracy rests—as Professor Bernard Lewis has pointed out[18]—on three pillars: bureaucracy, the army, and the religious hierarchy. And it is quite true that in this pattern only the third factor, the religious hierarchy, need be changed in order to prepare the way for a Communist state.[19]

Successful resistance to Communism is possible on the basis of a society which is either very developed, or is untouched by what is commonly called civilization. Unfortunately, most Middle Eastern countries are very far from being modern societies, and even farther from achieving the internal balance—but they have proceeded too far from the primitive state to put the clock back. A rational exposition of the mistaken basic tenets of Communism presupposes fairly extensive philosophical, psychological, and historical studies of such questions as the nature of man, the will to power, social progress, and kindred subjects, which to the intelligentsia of these countries appear highly abstract if not altogether irrelevant. We shall come to that, they say, but first things first. What we need now, they explain, is economic development to overcome backwardness; later we shall cope with the nature of man. By then, one fears, it will be too late; not perhaps from the point of view of the astronomer's time-scale, but certainly for the social scientist and for the ordinary mortal, who are concerned with the present and the foreseeable future. Nevertheless, it would be wrong to end this study on an entirely pessimistic note. Mob rule and xenophobia in the Middle East have been stressed more than once in the course of this study, the sort of referendum and recall which follows the pattern of Cairo's "Black Saturday" and repeated attempts at political assassination. Everything now depends on whether these Middle Eastern countries will be able (in a far shorter period) to make the social, political, and economic progress made by the West in a hundred years—and how much time has remained for such vital experimenting. It depends on whether the men will be found to head this immense task, and whether the masses will co-operate; whether the inner strength can be found for an effort unparalleled in many centuries of Middle Eastern history.

There is no manifest destiny, no inevitable development; man is shaping his own history in the Middle East not less than anywhere else. And the greatest authority for historical materialism wrote that "history does nothing, possesses no enormous wealth, fights no battles. It is rather man, the real living man who does everything, possesses, fights. It is not 'History,' as if she were a person apart, that uses men as means to work out her purposes, but history itself is nothing but the activity of men pursuing their purposes." It is an observation to be kept in mind by all concerned.

APPENDICES

Appendix I

Marxism, Leninism and the Middle East

THE *obiter dicta* of the classics of Marxism-Leninism on the Middle East have never been systematically collected and analysed. This is a really interesting task for the historian. What is more difficult and what shall be attempted here is to find out how much Marx's, Engels's, or Lenin's specific opinions on Oriental economy, society, and politics have, in fact, influenced the Communist leaders—and those who led the leaders—in the Middle East. It seems that in recent years such influence, if there really was any, must have been very small. But it cannot be denied that in the past, not only Marxism-Leninism in general, but its specific views on the East as well, have been carefully scrutinized by the Communist leadership, and we may therefore allow ourselves a short digression from our main theme at this point.

Marx and Engels wrote many articles on the "Eastern question" at the time of the Crimean War. Marx's basic position on that issue is very well known: he considered the Czarist regime to be the chief enemy of the European revolution. But he regarded democratic pan-Slavism and the "fanatic Slavic nationality" as no less a danger, and frequently pointed to the great territorial acquisitions of Russia and its expansionist trends in general. He always hoped for Turkish victories over the Russians, and frequently over-estimated the strength of the latter.[1] Marx and Engels regarded the Russian advance in the direction of the Straits and "Czarigrad" (Constantinople) as one of the basic aims of Russian foreign policy, one of the stepping-stones to an even higher purpose: viz. world domination. "The policy of Russia is changeless. Its methods, its tactics, its manœuvres may change, but the polar star of its policy—world domination—is a fixed star." It is interesting to note that even Marx, the dialectician, could reach the conclusion that there was something changeless in the world. We are not concerned here, however, with the attitude taken up by Marx and Engels towards the events of the day but with some more fundamental observations made by them. Describing the situation of the Greek Christians of "Turkey" (which, it should be remembered, was in those days synonymous with the whole Near and Middle East), he correctly appreciated how difficult the disestablishment of Islam would be in the East: ". . . if you abolish their subjection to the Koran by civil emancipation, you cancel, at the same time, their subjection to the clergy, and provoke a revolution in their social, political, and religious relations. . . . If you supplant the Koran by a civil code, you must occidentalize the entire structure of Byzantine society."

Islamic xenophobia was no sensationally new phenomenon for Marx: "The Koran and the Mussulman legislation emanating from it reduce the geography and ethnography of the various peoples to the simple convenient distinction of two nations and of two countries; the Faithful and the Infidel. The Infidel is 'harby,' i.e., the enemy. Islamism proscribes the nation to the Infidels, postulating a state of permanent hostility between the Mussulman and the unbeliever." It should be added that Marx had the Islam of the sixteenth century in mind, of course, and not the allegedly golden days of Andalusia. Marx actually provided an apologia for Western imperialism: "As the Koran treats all foreigners as foes, nobody will dare to present himself in a Mussulman country without having taken his precautions. The first European merchants, therefore, who risked the chances of commerce with such a people, contrived to secure themselves an exceptional treatment and privileges originally personal, but afterwards extended to their whole nation. Hence the origin of capitulations."[2] We find in Marx little of the guilt-feeling of latter-day non-Marxist Westerners.[3] What Marx said about the mob in the great cities of the Near East (which in "every important *coup d'état* has to be won over by bribes and flattery") may serve as an epitaph to more recent events in the Middle East: "Certainly there will be, sooner or later, an absolute necessity for freeing one of the finest parts of this continent from the rule of a mob, compared with which the mob of Imperial Rome was an assemblage of sages and heroes."[4]

The question of landed property came up prominently in the exchange of letters between Marx and Engels; both regarded it "as the key to the whole Orient."[5] Replying to a letter of Marx, Engels wrote that it was also the key to the political and theological history of the East; but could one explain the fact that the Orientals did not even have feudal land tenure? Engels thought that this depended mainly upon the climate and geographical conditions (deserts, etc.). Artificial irrigation was the first and basic condition for agriculture, and had to be administered by the communal authorities, the provincial or the central government. "Government in the East always had only three departments: Finance (i.e. robbing the inhabitants of the country); War (i.e. robbing citizens of one's own and other countries); and Public Works (concern for 'reproduction')." Engels saw that the main lesson to be learned from history was that whole areas then in a state of desolation were formerly cultivated, and this as the result of a breakdown in irrigation following upon a war. A single war depopulated a whole country for centuries and put an end to its civilization. Engels agreed with Marx that the decisive element in the "Muhammadan revolution" was the destruction of South Arabian trade by Muhammad. The history of Muhammad was seen by him as a "Bedouin reaction against the degenerating fellaheen, whose religion too was on a very low level, where a cult of nature had been mixed with Jewish and Christian elements."

Marx, in his reply, drew attention to the centralization of all public works in the East and the decentralization of the rest of life.[6] This explains, in Marx's view, the static character of life in Asia, despite all the movement on the political surface. Nobody has succeeded in answering so far the questions raised by Marx and Engels—if such a reply is really possible. There were some factual mistakes in the very wording of the questions: the form of landownership was radically different from that prevalent in Europe; but economic historians did not yet have details about it in the mid-nineteenth century. The very attempt to find in the economic facts (in this instance reduced to geographic conditions) the reply to the underlying causes of Eastern history is, of course, a case of over-simplification. But the question had to be asked, and, even though they did not provide a conclusive answer to such all-embracing problems, Marx and Engels were just about the first to attempt to find it and, despite some of their doctrinaire pupils, the impulse given by them has been a fruitful one.[7]

In their later work Marx and Engels only rarely found occasion to comment on Near and Middle Eastern issues; they believed that the social order which had been preserved in that part of the world (or had been preserved until very recently and was now disintegrating) belonged to what they called the Asian society and social system. Their remarks on nomads and the origins of nomadic invasions, later elaborated at greater length by Karl Kautsky,[8] are of no particular relevance here. Their basic idea with regard to the East was that the East, in its development, would have to pass through the same social and economic stages (*Formationen*), as the West had. This prediction caused serious headaches to twentieth-century Marxists who tried to analyse the present state of affairs in the East, and to classify it; and who naturally encountered serious difficulties when they made comparisons with the West. Another, even more disputed issue, became the question of whether any stage of development could be skipped by the East, and the problem of how capitalism could be made to work on Communist initiative, and under Communist supervision. But these quarrels almost exclusively affected the Far East, where strong Communist Parties existed, some of which attained power in the course of time, and not the Near and Middle East, where the parties struggled for their very existence and for whom all this was a matter of things to come.

It is interesting to note that Engels, in some of his later letters and articles, did correctly predict (in general outline) certain events which were to take place three and four decades later. "Disorder welds the Turks together," he wrote in 1890.[9] "The indestructible common soldier, the son of the imperturbable Turkish peasant, found precisely in this disorder an opportunity to repair the damage done by the corrupt pashas." And elsewhere he wrote to his party comrade Bracke, "You'll be surprised by the Turks!" He added, in explanation, that an Oriental society based on a healthy peasantry would be able to sustain incredible setbacks; it had only to overthrow its corrupt ruling class in order to be able to stand up against Russia.[10] He defended himself and Marx against the accusation of pro-Turkish partisanship: "Of course we are not enthusiastic about any of these two systems which are now fighting each other on the fields of battle of Bulgaria and Armenia. Both are old despotisms which are in flat contradiction to the spirit of the times."[11] And yet, on other occasions, he pointed out that if the overlords of the Porte would only be ousted, new men could work wonders with the Turkish army. But was there any chance of the capitalist mode of production prevailing in Turkey and of the country, generally speaking, being modernized? Engels did not think so even in 1890; in actual fact, the Turkish, like any other Oriental domination, is incompatible with a capitalist economy; the surplus value extorted is not safe from the hands of the greedy satraps and pashas. The elementary basis of *bourgeois* acquisition is lacking: the security of the person and property of the trader.[12] This opinion was shared by all of the more important pupils of Engels; e.g. Otto Bauer and Karl Renner, who occasionally tried to find an explanation for the fact that the Turkish state, though partly modernized, had not been based on the capitalist mode of production.[13] Otto Bauer was one of the first to ponder the dynamics of economic revolutions in the Orient, and noted what he called a current in two directions: the nationalism of the Westernized landowners, officers, state employees, and intellectuals, and the wish to establish a nation-state or at least to achieve national autonomy; and, on the other hand, the democratic movements rising in revolt against the destructive influence of European capital investment, the mass basis of which was made up of the peasantry and the lower middle class, and which, in the absence of political organization, not infrequently resulted in terrorism and the emergence of robber gangs. One of the possibilities in this situation was the expulsion of the big landowners and the emergence of a strong peasant class owning the land; another was the expropriation of the peasants by the landowners, who would exploit the prevailing religious law and create a landless agricultural proletariat. Hence the all-embracing importance of agrarian reform in the Near East.[14] Marx considered news about socialism in the East to be a curiosity (to use his own words), in the same category with the story of the traveller from China who had reported socialist influences in China: "If our European reactionaries on their impending flight will eventually reach the Chinese wall and knock at the doors of the refuge of arch-reaction and conservativism, who knows whether they shall not see the sign: 'République Chinoise. Liberté, Egalité, Fraternité'? "[15] But this, of course, was a mere joke in 1850; the revolution was expected to prevail in the industrial countries of the West and not in the backward East. And if Lenin, more than sixty years later, wrote an article headed, "About Backward Europe and Progressive Asia" (1913), which came to be quoted in our time as proof (together with two or three other examples) that he had correctly assumed that Communism would first prevail in Asia, it should be added at once that Lenin saw this as a paradox. At the same time he noted, to be sure, the effect of the Russian revolution of 1905 on many Asian countries, and also the fact that the middle class was still joining forces with the proletariat against the revolution in Asia, while in Europe the proletariat had become the only progressive class. It was only after the revolution that he spoke about the "hundreds of millions of Asians who were now ceasing to be objects of colonial exploitation and becoming active participants in the decisions on the fate of the world." In one of his very last articles, in 1923, Lenin wrote: "The outcome of the struggle depends in the last resort on the fact that Russia, India, and China, etc., constitute the vast majority of mankind. And just that majority is being drawn, with unusual rapidity in recent years, into the struggle for its liberation, which means that there cannot be the slightest doubt as to the final outcome of the world struggle."[16] To the same period belongs one of Stalin's articles, headed: "Do Not Forget the East!" in which he wrote that, "He who wants the victory of socialism must not forget about the East."[17]

But such writings remained the exception, even during the 1920's, and if towards the end of that period Asian affairs came more to the fore, the discussions almost exclusively concerned the tactics to be followed in China by the party. Stalin and the other party leaders never bothered unduly about the Middle East, and the elaboration of theses in accordance with the exigencies of the times and Soviet foreign policy was left to the lower echelons of the Comintern hierarchy. The key-note had been given by Lenin himself at the second Congress of the Comintern: the necessity to assist *bourgeois* democratic movements of liberation, the temporary alliance with the *bourgeois* democracy of the colonies and backward countries. But at the same time the peasantry should be assisted against the big landowners and against all signs and relics of feudalism. The Indian delegate, Roy, in contrast to Lenin, made a distinction between the *bourgeois* national movements in the backward countries (which intended to achieve their political aims within the framework of the existing social order) and the struggle of the peasants against every form of exploitation. Roy demanded that this, the latter movement, should not be sacrificed, even temporarily, to an alliance with *bourgeois* elements which could only be temporary.[18]

Lenin stood for an alliance in the colonial and dependent countries because not only the proletariat but all the inhabitants (apart from an insignificant percentage of collaborators with foreign imperialism) were suffering twofold oppression and exploitation. This "bloc" policy of entering alliances with the (*bourgeois*) national movement was followed (despite much left-wing criticism) up to the defeat of the Communist Party in China in 1927. At the Sixth Congress of the Comintern a new modification of the line in the colonies and dependent countries was undertaken and important revisions inserted: it was then stated that it was necessary to reject the formation of any kind of bloc between the Communist Party and the national reformist opposition in these countries; complete political independence should be preserved, and a relentless struggle should be waged against *bourgeois* nationalism. Temporary agreements and the co-ordination of separate activities in connection with definite anti-imperialist demonstrations were permissible in the future too. But the stress this time was not on the *alliance*, but on the *dissociation* of the Communists, both politically and organizationally, from all the petty *bourgeois* parties.[19]

This trend became even more pronounced after 1928, and Communists everywhere in Asia accused the respective national movements of their countries of betrayal, of selling out to the imperialists, and so on. But with another change in the world situation, some time after Hitler's rise to power in Germany, the line in the East was modified too, and at the Seventh Congress of the Comintern new slogans were proclaimed: "In the colonial and semi-colonial countries the work for the creation of an anti-imperialist front is the main task of the Communists." Now the Communist Parties were again ordered to collaborate with the "national reformist elements" and even actively to participate in the movements headed by them, and to appear together with them "on the basis of a concrete anti-imperialist platform."[20] This was tantamount, in practice, to putting most of the revolutionary class demands of the party (including, sometimes, even the demand for agrarian reform) into cold storage for the duration, and subordinating everything else to the movement for national liberation.

This was, in barest outline, the development of the general Comintern line for the backward countries. But what did it all mean in relation to the Middle East? No authoritative statements of principle on the Middle East have been made for many years by Soviet and Communist leaders. There was relatively much more interest in Middle Eastern affairs in Russia during the 1920's and early 1930's than there is now. At that time, when there were no Communist Parties worth speaking of, many books and articles were published on the "revolutionary movement" in that part of the world, and there were special magazines dedicated to this very subject (*Novi Vostok, Revoliutsioni Vostok* (New East, Revolutionary East). At the present time, on the other hand, very little official interest is revealed, there are no periodicals dealing with Near or Middle Eastern problems, articles on these topics are few and far between. We do not profess to know the reason for this lack of official interest. One of the reasons may be the lack of experts,[21] and another the assumption, perhaps not incorrect, that events in South-east Asia would be decisive and that the Middle East would follow, in the end, in the footsteps of India and Indonesia. There has been a revival in Soviet Orientalist literature in 1955. See Chapter Nineteen of the present book. (February, 1956.)

However that may be, it remains only to be noted that today the Communist blueprints for the Middle East are practically identical with the programmes for all other under-developed countries. The programme of the Egyptian Democratic Movement for National Liberation (the equivalent of the Communist Party) is not much different from the programme of the Indian Communist Party, and the platform of the Israeli party reads like a translation of the Japanese programme, or vice versa. They all call for the "establishment of a popular front which will be an alliance between workers, peasants, lower and middle class, and the democratic intelligentsia."[22] In some cases the provisions for the alliance are even more far-reaching: the industrial *bourgeoisie* is included too, because the interests of the local factory owners are opposed to those of the foreign imperialists.[23] Tactically, the patriotic anti-imperialist front is not radically different from the various united and popular fronts of the 1930's. But the aim is entirely different. The target of the popular front was to combat fascism, but "final salvation this [popular front] government cannot bring. It is not in a position to overthrow the class rule of the exploiters, and for this reason cannot finally remove the danger of fascist counter-revolution."[24] The "national, anti-imperialist front," on the other hand, may well serve as a stepping-stone towards the establishment of a regime *à la* Arbenz or Mossadeq, and perhaps even go further than that.

According to official historiography, this new theory of the "New Democracy" is an invention of Mao Tse-tung in the 1930's. But in fact other Asian Communist Parties had been moving in the same direction independently, before the theoretical justification was provided by the Chinese leader. In no Asian country, Japan excepted, was there an industrial proletariat numerically strong enough to head a successful revolutionary movement. The only theoretical alternative, according to orthodox Marxism, was therefore to give up the struggle for a social revolution and to wait until such a revolutionary leadership would emerge. Then along came Mao Tse-tung and taught that revolution could be carried out on the basis of the "united front of all revolutionary classes," workers, peasants, petty *bourgeois*, "including even such capitalists as oppose feudalism and foreign imperialism." But did not all revolts based on peasants fail in the past because of the lack of discipline and cohesion? Well, said Mao Tse-tung, the peasants could be educated to cohesion and discipline and become no less devoted to the cause of Communism than industrial workers. In the Middle East there has been no large-scale peasant movement and in several countries feudalism has been gradually disappearing, and the party had not been able to enlist mass support among the fellaheen. But if it were possible to educate the peasant to discipline and cohesion, contrary to what Marx, Engels, and Lenin had been teaching, why should it be impossible to find similar support among the "democratic intelligentsia?" The parties would also need a mass basis, of course, but this problem could be solved easily once the necessary cadres were available.

Several other differences should be noted. The United and Popular Front was an alliance between the Communist and Socialist and Democratic Parties against the common enemy. In the Arab East there are no socialist and few democratic parties. The patriotic anti-imperialist front one finds there is not an alliance with democratic parties, but with groups whose attitude towards democracy is for the most part hardly more positive than that of the Communists themselves. The Moslem Brotherhood, the Istiqlāl Party in Iraq, and other Communist allies in the anti-imperialist front could not be called "democratic" even by the wildest stretch of imagination. But they are "objectively progressive," according to Moscow (whatever their "subjective" ideologies and intentions), because they fight the West. Everything else in the present situation is subordinated to this struggle. Just as the Communists refrained from openly attacking the Socialist leaders during the era of the popular front, so do they abstain from criticizing the right-wing, semifascist or fanatically Moslem organizations.[25] For there is one, and only one, criterion so far as they are concerned; a given party may be socialist and democratic, and yet be considered an enemy if it is not sufficiently anti-Western. Another group may be reactionary, obscurantist, fascist —and yet an ally, if it takes part in the "anti-imperialist struggle." The decisive criterion is not the class character of the party, nor its social and economic programme, nor its general stand on domestic issues—but only its foreign political orientation, its attitude towards West and East.

The programmes of the Communist Parties in the Middle East also deal with what would happen if the "anti-imperialist forces headed by the Communist Party" would take over the reins of power. But this part of the programme hardly differs from what all other Communist Parties in the world now say on that subject—and from what has actually been done in the "Popular Democracies." In fact, there are no plans for attaining state power in the near future, and the chances, at the present time, of establishing "national liberation armies" in the Middle East are not as good as they are in most other Asiatic countries, and this is so for a variety of reasons. Soviet policy seems to be aimed at neutralizing the Middle East (just as all other countries outside North America), and to assume that gradual Communist domination in the Middle East will be assured in the more distant future as a result of a shift in the balance of power—but not as the result of a revolution from below.

Marxism, which was originally the theory of proletarian revolution in the most highly developed industrial countries, has thus been made in our time (in its post-Leninist stage) the practice of revolution in the backward countries. The realization of this fact does not in the least affect the historical importance of Marxism; Columbus is no less important because we happen to know that he really wanted to find a new route to India. Nor does this weaken the political force of Marxism. Most of the countries in the world are backward, and should Communism prevail in all or most of them, it would stand a fair chance of conquering the West. The historical reasons for the changes undergone by the appeal and application of Marxism, over a period of one hundred years, have been frequently analysed and need not be recapitulated here in detail; the capitalist countries have changed out of all recognition since the days of Marx. They have not become socialist, but we may well doubt whether most of the old definitions of capitalism used by Marx still apply to them. In fact, the situation in the under-developed countries now is in many respects more similar to what Marx and Engels observed in Western Europe at that time; it is *there* that capitalism has failed (or has not been tried at all). It can be argued that capitalism has never been given a chance there—just as it is frequently said that Marxism has never been given a chance because it came to be practised in a backward country first.

However that may be, the transference of the theory of Marxism from the advanced, industrial countries to the backward parts of the world has not been accompanied by a change in Leninist doctrine. The fact that the appeal of Marxism-Leninism is greater in the under-developed countries, has been discovered by trial and error; it is not the result of any dialectical analysis. To this very day it is not reflected in Marxist-Leninist theory.[26] Mao Tse-tung has contributed something very important to Leninism, but it is a tactical not an ideological contribution. He has shown that the Communists do not need an urban mass basis to be victorious in a given country. This came not as the result of theoretical speculation, as already pointed out, but as a practical necessity.

In the Middle East, the more activist Communist leaders engaged on similar ventures, though with a lesser measure of success. Khālid Bakdāsh made interesting experiments in winning religious support by going much further in this direction than other Communist leaders elsewhere in the world. When it became obvious that there was more sympathy for the Communists among the intelligentsia than among the working class, Bakdāsh saw nothing reprehensible in letting the Communists become a party of the intelligentsia, without, of course, neglecting the "mass basis" of the party. The Kurds made a brave attempt to establish a "popular democracy" in the conditions of a semi-nomadic society, which was even more backward than Yunan. But these and other attempts, many of them successful, have not culminated, as we said, in ideological changes. Leninism is taught now just as it was thirty years ago, though the divergence between theory and practice has become rather greater than that between Euclidean and non-Euclidean geometry. The adepts of Leninism are first taught one thing, and on graduation something quite different; when they become active, they are given to understand that, according to Mao, practice is the decisive criterion, and that in practice almost everything is different from theory.

This is somewhat surprising, since the doctrine of Leninism could be changed, after all, without giving up too much of its dogma. It could be argued, for instance, that the proletariat, and the dictatorship of the proletariat, is not an end in itself, but merely the means, the means of abolishing all classes and of establishing a classless society. In countries where the proletariat does not exist or is too weak to fulfil its "historic function," a coalition led by the revolutionary intelligentsia could take its place. Such a modification of doctrine would not affect its kernel, viz. the theory of the classless society. Nevertheless, such an attempt has not yet been made, and Communist theory continues to lag behind Communist practice. There may be various reasons for this, which cannot be examined here in detail. One is undoubtedly the fact that theory is no longer what it was for the leading Communists a generation ago. It may be an exaggeration to say that it is not made much of now, because some basic aims and assumptions have certainly remained axiomatic, and no one in his right mind among the Soviet, Chinese, and satellite leaders would dare to express any doubts about them. But if theory and practice clash there is no such urgent impulse, as there was thirty years ago, to find ideological justification for the course adopted in face of new situations or emergencies. Ideologically there have been no important changes in Marxism-Lenism for many years. There are additional reasons, to be sure. The party is monolithic and its theory should be monolithic, too. Any ideological changes, it is feared, rightly or wrongly, may shake the whole edifice.

The practical conclusions which have been drawn by the Communist leaders with regard to their policy in the "colonial and dependent" countries (including most of the Middle East) are obvious and can easily be summarized. Power can be attained everywhere, provided the necessary cadres exist. The subjective factor is decisive, not "objective conditions"; the cadres, indeed, decide everything. They may be exclusively of the intelligentsia (student movements) or intellectuals heading an agrarian movement, or nomad tribes, or a partisan movement in a war against a foreign invader, and so on. This vanguard has to exploit *all conflicts*, national and social, and to weaken the existing regime. It may use all slogans likely to strengthen its appeal, all tactics likely to promote its influence and bring it nearer to power, for "all ways lead towards Communism" (Molotov). Total principles have thus been replaced by the total *absence of principles up to the moment of reaching power*. It is not relations and conditions of production which are decisive, but the *human factor*: a strong will, singleness of purpose, lack of moral scruples, the belief in historical materialism—and readiness to act as if historical materialism was altogether wrong.

Splits in Palestine Communism, 1938-49

<hr>

AS a result of the Arab rebellion in 1936–39 the contact between the Jewish and Arab branches of the party had been severed and the activities of many came to a standstill. The Jerusalem branch was the first to resume activities in 1938, and in collaboration with several Tel-Aviv[1] militants it published for a time *Kol Ha'am*, the central party newspaper. But there were ideological or at least far-reaching tactical differences of opinion between this group, the "Jewish Section" as it was called, and the Party Executive; the Party Executive, which also continued to exist, decided to dissolve the "Jewish Section," and the latter's mainstay, its Jerusalem branch, in December, 1939. The "Jewish Section" refused, however, to comply, arguing that the last party executive had been appointed almost ten years previously, that no party congress had been convened since then, and that the present executive was therefore illegal. The "Jewish Section" decided to convene a congress of its own (the so-called "Eight-party Conference" in the summer of 1940), and starting from October, 1940, to publish a magazine of its own (*Emet*, Truth), thus bringing the split, which had hardly been a secret, into the open.[2] The main differences between the two groups have already been pointed out: the "Jewish Section" had second thoughts about the Arab revolt of 1936–39 and collaboration with the ex-Mufti, it did not welcome the "White Paper" enthusiastically, and believed the party could and should be active within the left-wing Zionist parties. During 1939 and up to the late summer of 1940 negotiations between the two groups had taken place which proved to be abortive. When the first issue of *Emet* was published in the autumn of 1940, the executive opened an all-out campaign against the rebels: "Provocators at work ... a small group of the scum of the working class has committed a shameful crime and a mean provocation."[3] Thus was the public informed about the split. The "Jewish Section," which had been educated in the same school, did not hesitate to reply in the same vein: "Liquidationists . . . why don't you mention the Mufti in your articles?"[4] New fuel was added to the fire when *Emet* protested in the spring of 1941 against the slogan then given out by the *Executive* ("Immediate peace with Hitler"), and said that this was a gross falsification of the Comintern line. It is not certain at all whether the Executive did wrongly interpret the Comintern, but both groups continued for many weeks to quarrel about the correct interpretation of Moscow's attitude. After the Germans invaded Russia fresh impetus was given to unity talks, but almost a year was to pass until the merger was effected. *Emet* was, on the whole, more interested in unity than the party Executive, which had been greatly strengthened under the new conditions of legality. In the end the "Jewish Section" was dissolved and its members returned to the Executive, which had meanwhile adopted some of their demands (such as dropping the slogan of "Independence for Palestine," the demand of the Arab nationalists). The new unity did not last very long, and a new crisis occurred in the summer of 1943, when Mūsa and his Arab aids tried to take up an outspoken pro-Arab and anti-Jewish line again. The Jewish militants protested, and in retaliation the Haifa and Tel-Aviv branches were declared to be dissolved and Shmuel Mikunis and Pnina Feinhaus were expelled from the party Executive.[5] But Mikunis and his friends did not give up the struggle, and constituted themselves as the "real Communist Party of Palestine."

The weeks following July, 1943, heralded a period of unprecedented confusion. Apart from the one major split, there were several minor ones. The situation on the Arab side was comparatively easy, because the Mūsa group did not continue to exist for long and the League for National Liberation emerged as the semi-official Communist agency. On the Jewish side, however, about half a dozen splinter groups continued to exist for some time, and it was only in 1944 that their number was again reduced to two: (1) the official Communist Party of Mikunis, Wilner, and others, and (2) the Communist Educational Association (later Communist Association, and still later Hebrew Communists). This latter group, headed by Kalman Gelberd and two Moscow-trained stalwarts, Simha Zabri and Meir Slonim, had started as an extreme pro-Arab group willing to collaborate with Mūsa even after the 1943 split. After a few months, however, following a sudden and somewhat mysterious somersault, they appeared on the political scene with a programme which was sympathetic to Zionism. The subsequent history of the Hebrew Communists is not lacking in intrinsic interest, but does not belong to the main stream of Israeli Communism, difficult enough to follow as it is. The Hebrews, as they came to be called, had greater influence than the Mikunis group among academic youth and the younger generation in general; but the party apparatus remained in the hands of the bureaucracy, and this proved decisive in the long run. The Hebrews favoured "national independence" for the Jews in Palestine (which for all practical purposes was identical with Zionism). The Cominform could apparently not make up its mind for some time which group it should recognize, and up to 1948 both the Mikunis wing and the Hebrews sent their delegations to the satellite countries. In 1948, however, pressure was exerted to end this state of affairs, and at the time of the merger with the Arab League for National Liberation, the Hebrews, too, rejoined the Communist Party and were given representation on the party's Central Committee. They continued, however, to quarrel with the Mikunis group and had apparently for some time played with the idea of establishing a common front with the "Fighters for the Freedom for Israel" (the Stern gang). All the leading Hebrew members were again expelled early in 1949 under rather dramatic circumstances—after an attempted bank robbery in Tel-Aviv by a member of this circle in the best Caucasian tradition of financing party activities by "direct action." Some have subsequently joined MAPAM, the pro-Soviet Zionist United Workers' Party, while the appetite of others for practical politics appears to have been saturated, and they disappeared altogether from the political scene.

Appendix III

Bibliographical Note

I. GENERAL

THE main sources for the 1920's and 1930's are the Soviet periodicals *Novi Vostok* (New East) and *Revoliutsioni Vostok* (Revolutionary East). Articles of interest will also be found in *Communist International* (1919–43) and *Inprecorr* (the weekly organ of the Comintern, the German edition being the fullest), as well as the periodicals of the Red Trade Union International (*Profintern*). In 1932–33 the Sredasbiuro (Central Asian Bureau) of the Central Committee of the Communist Party of the U.S.S.R. published *Na Zarubeshnom Vostoke* in Tashkent. Occasional articles of interest are to be found in *Revoliutsiya i Natsionalnosti.*

There exist no such sources for events in later years; all the more important resolutions of Middle Eastern Communist Parties during the last decade have been published in *Al Ittihād* (Haifa, 1944—). The various publications of the World Federation of Trade Unions and the Communist Peace Movement contain details about trade unions controlled by Communists and the local associations of the Partisans of Peace.

All the important documents for the 1920's and comments from a non-Communist point of view will be found in *Revue du Monde Musulman*, and more especially *ibid.*, vol. 52 (1922): "Le Bolchevisme et l'Islam hors de Russie."

Elias Hurwicz, *Die Orientpolitik der Dritten Internationale* (1922); and Aurelio Palmieri, *La Politica Asiatica dei Bolscevichi* (1924), deal only with the very first stirrings of Comintern action in the East. There is no comprehensive account for the later period.

Communism in the Near East, a supplement to *The Strategy and Tactics of World Communism* (Washington, D.C., 1949), edited by Sidney Glazer, is a thirty-six-page survey of Communist activities, mainly during the period of World War II. Aharon Cohen, *The Arab*

Workers' Movement (Hebrew, Tel-Aviv, 1947), deals chiefly with Communist activities in the trade-union field in 1944–46 in the Arab countries. *Moyen Orient*, published in Paris in 1949–50, includes articles of interest for the late 1940's.

Early Soviet studies, apart from the periodicals mentioned above, include: M. P. Pavlovitch, *Sobranie Sotchinenya*, vols. 1–3, 5–7; and V. A. Gurko-Kryashin, *Arabski Vostok i Imperialism* (1926). There are two more recent works of a general character: V. B. Lutski, *Arabskie Stranie* (1947); and I. A. Genin, *Strani Arabskovo Vostoka* (1948). The most recent comprehensive work is *Noveishaya Istoria stram Sarubeshnovo Vostoka*, vol. 1, 1918–29 (Moscow, 1954). *Activités Communistes au Moyen Orient* (Centre de Documentation et de Synthese, Paris, 1954), is a privately published quarterly survey, very detailed and somewhat indiscriminate.

2. SYRIA AND LEBANON

The early period is covered from a Communist point of view in P. V. Kitaigorodski, *Syria v ogne vosstanie* (1925); and V. Lutski, *Natsionalnaya Revoliutsiya 1925–27 g v Syrii* (in *Trudi pervoi sessii Arabistov*, 1935, 1937). Also the same author's *Arabskie Strani* (1947).

The main source is *Sawt ash-Sha'ab*, 1937, the organ of the Syrian and Lebanese Communist Party up to 1948. Since then *Nidā ash-Sha'ab* has become the mouthpiece of the party, and *As-Sarkha* and other legal or semi-legal journals in Beirut and Tripoli have expressed the Lebanese party point of view. *At Tarīq* (Beirut, 1942—) has served the Anti-fascist League, Friendship with the Soviet Union, the Peace Movement, and various other "front" organizations.

Among the many legal and illegal publications of the two parties, all in Arabic, the following merit mention:

> Khālid Bakdāsh: *The Arabs and the Spanish Civil War*, 1937; *What happens in Al Jazīra*, 1937; *The Arab Communists and the National Movement*, 1937; *Communism and Nationalism*, 1944; *Report to the Party Congress*, 1944; *Report to the Party Central Command*, 1951.

Nikola Shāwi: *The Resolutions of the Party Congress*, 1944.

Books by Dr. George Hanna, Professor Kāmil Ayāt, and other pro-Communist writers cannot always be taken as an official expression of the party line. The same goes, incidentally, for the publications of Fathi ar-Rāmla in Cairo and 'Azīz Sharīf in Baghdad. These men were undoubtedly connected with the party, but they did not serve, just as their Levantine counterparts, as the mouthpiece of the party. They specialized in the production of "Marxist" literature of a more general character.

Other books or booklets by Khālid Bakdāsh deal with Soviet-Arab relations, the national problem (apart from the one mentioned above), the struggle for peace and against imperialism, etc. More recently *At-Talī'a* (1954—) and *Al Nur* have become the mouthpieces of the Syrian Communists.

3. JORDAN

The (illegal) mouthpiece of the Jordan Communist Party is *Al Muqāwama ash-Sha'biyya* (People's Revolt), 1950. *Al Ittihād* (Haifa) frequently reprints articles from this source.

The only early study known to the present writer is M. Axelrod; "Transjordania," in *Novi Vostok*, vols. 26 and 27. Axelrod visited the Middle East as a representative of various Soviet trade agencies, and became later a frequent contributor to that journal on the lesser-known Arab countries.

4. EGYPT

Soviet literature on that subject includes: I. D. Levin, *Yegipet* (1937); L. N. Vatolina, *Sovremeni Yegipet* (1949). Both are mainly based on secondary sources.

There have been many dozens of Communist magazines and newspapers in Egypt reflecting the internal division of the movement, some of them legal, up to 1947, all illegal after that date. Only the more important will be listed here: *Al Fagr al Gadīd* (The New Dawn), 1945–46. *At-Talī'a* (Vanguard), originally the organ of the pro-Communist Wafdist association of university graduates. *Al Magalla al Gadīda* (1943–44) was the mouthpiece of the Trotskyite faction. *Ad-Damīr* (The Conscience) and *Al Ahd al Gadīd* (The New Epoch, 1945–56) expressed the view of the main faction in Egyptian Communism, destined for trade-union consumption. Appealing to a wider public was *Al Gamāhir* (Masses), a weekly edited by the same faction (1947–48). This was followed during the period of the "national front" by *Al Malāyīn* (Millions, 1950–52), and the organ of the Egyptian Peace Movement, *Al Katib*, edited by Sā'ad Kāmil. Magazines published by other factions in 1950–51 include *Sawt al Prolitariūn* (The Voice of the Proletariat) and *Al Kader ash-Shuyu' īyya* (The Communist Cadre). M.D.L.N. published in French: *Nouvelles Egyptiennes* (1949) and *Bulletin d'études et d'information sur l'Egypte et le Sudan* (1951–53), both in Paris. *Democratie Nouvelle* was published by the Fagr al Gadīd section.

Several non-Communist newspapers and magazines followed fairly closely the Communist Party line during different periods. These include *Sawt al Umma* (The Voice of the Nation; Wafdist) in 1945–46, and *Ruz al Yūsuf* (Independent, 1950–52), as well as *Al Gumhūr al Misri* (Wafdist, Independent).

Fathi ar-Rāmla published a semi-legal magazine, *Al Mu'arrada* (The Opposition), during the second half of 1952. Illegal magazines published under the Naguïb-Gamāl 'Abdul Nāsir regime include, in addition to *Al Malāyīn* and *Al Katīb* (already mentioned), *Al Gabha* (Front), organ of the United Democratic Front (U.D.F.) and *Al Wāgib*. The Paris organ of the M.D.L.N. changed its name to *Nouvelles d'Egypte*. A rival Communist group (N.H.S.M.) published in 1952–53 *Al Muqāwama* (Resistance).

Many Communist booklets were published in 1945–46, but comparatively few thereafter. Some of the more important are: Sādiq Sa'ad, *Mushkilāt al Fallāh* (Problem of the Fellah; Cairo, 1946); 'Omar Rushdi, *Wataniyyatuna* (Our Nationalism; Cairo, 1946); Fathi ar-Rāmla, *Al hadāf al Ishtirākiyya* (The Socialist Aims; Cairo, 1946), and *At-tarīq ila 'l'Istiqlāl* (The Way to Independence); Mansūr al Rudbān, *Al Fāshīyya fi'l Misr* (Fascism in Egypt; Cairo, 1946). Fathi ar-Rāmla and his friends have also written on the "Crimes of Egyptian Capitalism," the "Woman Question," etc. The main document of the more recent period is the programme of the M.D.L.N. (1950–51), published also in French, *Programme du Mouvement Démocratique de libération Nationale*.

5. SUDAN

Umdurmān, published in Cairo in 1945–46, was the organ of the Communist students from Sudan. An excellent short survey of left-wing influence in the Sudanese national movement is contained in Gabriel Baer, "The Future of the Sudan" (in Hebrew) in *Be'ayot*, April, 1946. On the Sudan Graduates' Congress and the history of the national movement in general, see Makki 'Abbās, *The Sudan Question* (1952); 'Asad Halīm's, *Qadiyyatu-us-Sudān* (The Sudan Question; Cairo) is a treatise written by an Egyptian Communist; S. R. Smirnov's, *Vosstanie Mahdistov v Sudane* (The Revolt of the Mahdiites in the Sudan; Moscow, 1950) is concerned with one particular chapter of the history of the country, but brings political developments up to 1949.

Among the present publications of the Sudanese Communists and their "national fronts," *At-Talī'a* (Vanguard), the organ of the Communist-dominated Sudanese Trade Union Federation, and *Al Gabha* (The Front) should be listed. A hectographed news-sheet in English, *Sudan Review*, was published in 1952–53.

6. PALESTINE: ISRAEL

All the important documents of party history are contained in *Forois* (Forward; in Yiddish, 1926–32); *Ha'or* (The Light; in Hebrew, 1930–34; the issues published thereafter do not reflect the official party point of view); and *Kol Ha'am* (The Voice of the People; in Hebrew, 1937). Originally a monthly, *Kol Ha'am* is now a daily newspaper. The programme of the Israeli Communist Party (*For a People's Democracy in Israel*) was published in 1952.

The Arab weekly of the Israeli Communist Party, *Al Ittihād* (Union, 1944, with an interval in 1948), was preceded by *Ila'l Amān*, which was published irregularly between 1928 and 1932, and *Sawt ash-Sha'ab* at even larger intervals between 1935 and 1942.

Both Jewish and Arab Communists have published a large number of books and booklets dealing with topics of the day, but there is not a single study on Communist history in Palestine. There exist, however, four collections of documents of Communist history (no author, no date) covering the period of 1924–42, published by non-Communist sources. In addition, G. S. Israeli, *M.O.P.S., P.C.P.—MAKI*—the history of the Communist Party in Israel, 1919–53 (in Hebrew; Tel-Aviv, 1953, 224 pp.)—is a heavily documented history written by a non-Communist. M. Alexander, in *Commentary*, August, 1952, and April, 1953, reviews Communist activities in 1951–53. An article by Martin Ebon on Communist tactics in Palestine (*Middle East Journal*, 1948) deals with events in 1946–48. *Al Ittihād* published several issues in English during 1945–47, and *Kol Ha'am* appeared for some time in German (1941–48) as *Volksstimme*.

For Communist deviationist groups: *Emet*, 1940–41, and *Ahdut*, 1945–48.

7. PERSIA

On the early history of the Persian Communist Party, see Ossetrov in *Novyi Vostok*, vol. 1, and various notes in vols. 2 and 3 of the same journal. On the situation in the 1920's, see two undated booklets in Persian, *Kongreye Dovome Firgeye Kommuniste Iran* and *Beyanieye Firgeye Kommuniste Iran*. About the emergence of Tudeh, see Ihasan Tabari, *Beresye . . .* ("An Investigation into the Conditions of Development, Growth and Struggle of the Tudeh Party"), in *Mardom* (Teheran; May–June, 1947). Tabari was editor-in-chief of *Mardom*, the ideological journal of Tudeh. Also see I. Eskandari, "Histoire du parti Toudeh," in *Moyen Orient* (Paris; 1949–50). A recent Soviet study on the Communist movement in Persia is A. V. Bashkirov, *Rabotchieye i profsoyusnoye Dvishenye v Irane* (Moscow, 1949). All the aforementioned have been written from an official Communist point of view. George Lenczovski (*Russia and the West in Iran*) gives a good survey of Tudeh activities in the 1940's.

8. IRAQ

A short survey of the development of the Communist movement in Iraq up to 1937 is given in R. Vitol, "Gosudarstvenni Perevorot v

Irake" in *Revoliutsioni Vostok*, vol. 1, 1937. For the later period (1941–48) the main sources are the two publications of the Iraqi government mentioned above: the *Secret Compilation* (6 vols., 1949–50) and the *Trial of the Communists in Iraq* (1 vol.), both in Arabic. *Ash-Sharara* (The Spark), the first illegal party organ, was published in 1941–43 and occasionally thereafter. *Al Qā'ida* (The Basis) began publication in 1943 and continues to appear. (There were lengthy intervals between issues in 1948–49, at the time of the arrests.) Other Communist publications (periodicals) in 1945–46 include *Ila'l Amām* (Forwards) and *Al 'Ummāl* (The Workers), the latter the organ of the faction of Dahūd as-Sayigh. *Azadi* (Liberty) and *Shursh* (Revolution) were the organs of the Kurdish sections in 1945–47. The former has been published sporadically also in later years. *Al 'Usba* (The League) was the organ of the Jewish Anti-Zionist League in 1945–46. Many semi-authoritative, short-lived periodicals, legal and semi-legal, were published in 1944–46, too many for enumeration. Publications of Communist-front organizations after 1949 include, apart from those mentioned in the text, *Al 'Aqīda* (Faith), the mouthpiece of the Iraqi Partisans of Peace, closed by the authorities in November, 1951; and *Wahdat u'l 'Amal* (Workers' Unity), a trade-union paper. Books and leaflets published by leading Communists include: 'Abdul Fattāh Ibrahīm, *The Unity of the Democratic Movement* (in Arabic, 1946), and *Problems of Supply* (1946). 'Azīz Sharīf's many books include *The British Imperialist Policy in the Middle East* (1946), *The National Movement in Syria and Lebanon* (1945), *Oil and the War* (1946), all in Arabic. Together with his comrade and colleague, Tawfīq Munīr, he wrote *The Speech from the Throne* (in Arabic; 1946). Other books and booklets published by the Ba'ath publishing house (by the Communist Party and 'Azīz Sharīf) were *Fascism—the Enemy of the Peoples*; international topics of 1943–46; *The Teacher* (a symposium dealing with the situation and the problems of the Iraqi teachers), etc.

Documents reflecting recent developments within the party are to be found in *Al Qā'ida* for 1953–54. They include the report of the secretary-general of the party (*The Front of National Struggle against Imperialism and War*), the new programme of the party, and *The Differences of Opinion between Us and the Opportunists of the Faction "Banner of the Toilers" of the Palace.*

9. TURKEY

The first four volumes of *Novi Vostok* contain some material on the early history of Turkish Communism. The period of the civil war is described in Halidé Edib, *The Turkish Ordeal* (New York, 1928), and *Voprossi Istorii*, vol. 9 (1951); the episode of the "Green Apple" in *Kommunisticheski International*, vol. 17 (1921); and in M. Pavlovitch,

Revoliutsionnaya Turtsiya (1921). The subsequent fortunes of the Turkish Communists in the 1920's are the subject of "Yoldshu: Ot Revoliutsii k kontr-revoliutsii" (*Novi Vostok*, vols. 16 and 17); Gurko-Kryashin, "Vozniknovenie natsionalnoi osvoboditelnoi dvishenii v Turtsii" (*Novi Vostok*, vols. 23 and 24); A. Melnik, *Respublikanskaya Turtsiya* (1927); M. Pavlovitch, Gurko-Kryashin, *et al.*, *Turtsiya v borbe na Nesavissimost* (1925). The leading authority today on Turkey is B. Dantsig, one of the few survivors of the contributors of *Novi Vostok* in the 1920's: *Turtsiya* (1940 and 1949, Voyenisdat, Moscow). The latter edition includes on pp. 215–58 a survey of the history of Turkish Communism.

The central illegal organ of the Turkish Communists, *Orak Cekic* (Sickle and Hammer) has been published at irregular intervals since the early 1930's. Publications by Communist-front organizations include *Baris Yolu* (The Way of Peace). More readily available are the publications of the Young Turkish Progressives, with their headquarters in Paris. The recollections of a leading Turkish Communist ("Ustyungel") have been published in *Novi Mir*, vol. 9 (1951).

Notes

CHAPTER ONE, PAGES 3–27

[1] "Islam and Communism in the Middle East," *Contemporary Review*, Feb., 1953.

[2] Majīd Khaddūri, "The Role of the Military in Middle East Politics," *American Political Science Review*, June, 1953.

[3] Manfred Halpern, "The Implications of Communism for Islam," *Muslim World*, Jan., 1953.

[4] Khālid Bakdāsh, "The Communists and the Arab National Movement" (in Arabic), Damascus-Beirut, 1937.

[5] E. A. Speiser, *Middle East Journal*, Spring, 1953.

[6] Quoted by H. Kohn, *Geschichte der nationalen Bewegung im Orient*.

[7] W. Thomson and H. Kohn, *Nationalism in the Middle East*, 1952.

[8] Kāmil Jumbalāt, *Kul Shai'*, Beirut, Sept. 9, 1950.

[9] Many of the Egyptian Pashas had French and English wives.

[10] H. Kohn, *Nationalism in the Middle East*.

[11] The Egyptian chronicler, al Cabarti, quoted in H. A. R. Gibb and Bowen, *Islamic Society and the West*, vol. 1.

[12] The military regime in Egypt has had great difficulties in carrying out many of its reforms, not because of opposition, but because of the lack of spontaneous interest and the absence of collaboration on the part of the fellaheen and urban masses.

[13] A. Hourani in an interesting article in *International Affairs* (London), 1953, takes a different view and says that "the essence of imperialism is to be found in a moral relationship, that of power and powerlessness" and that consequently Arab resentment has to be understood against this background. This explanation is somewhat unsatisfying: the relationship of power and powerlessness is no exclusive feature of imperialism—and the Middle Eastern countries had been occupied by foreign powers for many centuries prior to the seventy years of British rule.

[14] Most illuminating in this context is perhaps the case of Syrian and Lebanese anti-imperialism. Since 1945 there have been no grounds for contention between these two countries and the Western powers. Nevertheless, the anti-French propaganda has simply been replaced by opposition to the West in general.

[15] Occasionally this explanation has been adopted by Western observers, too. Cf. Robert Montagne, "Reflexions sur la violence en pays d'Islam," *Preuves*, Aug., 1954. The same argument is frequently used by Arab authors. Cf. M. Rifa'at, *Middle East Journal*, 1952, p. 256: "The

terroristic methods used by the former Hagana, the Stern gang, and the IZL in Palestine, both before and after World War II, opened the eyes of the Arabs to the effectiveness of such methods. The creation of Israel has contributed to that effusion of religious militant enthusiasm so prevalent among peoples."

[16] Thoughtful observers have noted that the religious and social taboos and, as a consequence, the utter impossibility of such extramural activities as, for example, raiding coed's dormitories, are directing all the students' energies in the Moslem countries into the single channel of politics. When student politics were curbed under Naguīb and Gamāl 'Abdul Nāsir, the Egyptian press began to complain, after a few months, about the many cases of bad behaviour and misconduct by students in the streets and public places. Cf. 'Ali Amīn in *Al Akhbār*, July 19, 1954, on the "demoralization of youth."

[17] In 1937, 7500 holders of school certificates and 3500 with university degrees in Egypt could not find jobs, and in 1942, at a time of full employment, there was still a total of 10,000 academic unemployed. (O. Holloway, "University Students of the Middle East," *Royal Central Asian Journal*, Jan., 1951.) The academic proletariat has not decreased in number since then. The Egyptian press reported in 1953 that graduates of the medical faculties could not find work despite the urgent need for medical care and supervision in the country.

[18] This explains, among other things, the high frequency of Christians in the Arab national movement, especially in its earlier phases.

[19] A. J. M. Craig, "Egyptian Students," *Middle East Journal*, 1953.

[20] C. Worth Howard, "Education in Egypt of Today," *Nationalism in the Middle East*, 1952.

[21] *Ad-Da'wa* (the organ of the extremist wing of the Moslem Brotherhood), Sept., 1952.

[22] *Al Misri*, Jan. 6, 1953. In November, 1951, nine out of twelve "Brotherhood" candidates were elected in the department of trade, eight out of fifteen in the veterinary faculty, and eleven out of thirteen in the faculty of natural science. Most of their competitors at these elections at Fuād I University were Communists. (*New York Times*, Dec. 1, 1951.)

[23] A. J. M. Craig, *loc. cit.*

[24] Quoted in "Youth and Politics in the Near East," *World Today*, Mar., 1951.

[25] There have been, and presumably still are, some Communist students in the Turkish universities, but, on the whole, Communism has never been considered a problem in Turkish academic life. On the other hand, the stratum of the politically conscious and mature is considerably wider in Turkey than in the Arab countries, and the political importance of the students is consequently smaller. In the Hebrew University, Jerusalem, Communists have never polled more than 10 per cent., and that in favourable conditions of very low attendance—the result of a lack of interest in politics which almost equals conditions in British or American universities.

[26] The Asian countries offer much material for the extension and validation of the thesis of Dr. E. Fromm.

[27] Pierre Rondot, "Parliamentary Regime in the Middle East," *Middle Eastern Affairs*, Aug.–Sept., 1953.

[28] Rondot, *loc. cit.*

[29] "Intelligentsia," it may be necessary to add, is not synonymous with intelligence; more often than not it includes a majority of semi-intellectuals. *Intelligentsia as a social group is here meant, of course.*

[30] Rondot, *loc. cit.*

[31] E. E. Abouchdid, *Thirty Years of Lebanon and Syria.*

[32] Khaddūri, *loc. cit.*

[33] Anwar as-Sādat, a member of the Cairo junta and editor of its central newspaper, wrote, several months after the rise to power of the new regime in Egypt, that Hitler had been a great patriot who always worked for the good of his people and whose merits would be acknowledged in due time (in an interview with the weekly *Al Musawwar*). The then Minister of Health, Nūr ad-dīn Taraf, expressed a similar opinion.

[34] A. Hourani writes that "the new regimes in Egypt and Syria rest on a combination of army officers and officials (who have mastered the technique of modern administration) and educated nationalists." ("The Decline of the West in the Middle East," *International Affairs*, 1953.) Events have proved Hourani somewhat over-optimistic, both with regard to the alliance between the officers and other social groups and the "mastering of the techniques of modern administration."

[35] *Al Ahrām*, Sept. 4, 1952.

[36] This, of course, does not preclude ups and downs in the last years, too, including such disquieting events as the jailing of the leading opposition journalists in November–December, 1954.

[37] *Review of Economic Conditions in the Middle East*, 1949–50, and the subsequent yearly supplements to the *World Economic Reports*.

[38] About the political implications of the polarization of land tenure more will be found below.

[39] *Review of Economic Conditions in the Middle East, loc. cit.*

CHAPTER TWO, PAGES 31–41

[1] R. Palme Dutt, *World News and Views*, Jan. 5 and 9, 1952. The *Great Soviet Encyclopedia* mentions the Egyptian Communist Party in one place (vol. 15), but elsewhere omits it from the full list of all Communist Parties (vol. 23, published Oct., 1953).

[2] It should be noted in passing that Marx and Engels did not take an over-sanguine view of the stirrings of the Egyptian national movement. At the time of the 'Arabi *coup*, Engels, in a letter, warned Bernstein against too-outspoken support for this movement: "From Ireland to Russia, from Turkey to Egypt it is the main role of the peasant to be exploited. The repudiation of the debts of the Khedive (as a political demand) is all very well, but what then? And we Western European Socialists should not let ourselves be trapped as easily as the Egyptian Fellah. . . ." (Karl Marx and Friedrich Engels, *Sotchinenya*, vol. 27 (Moscow, 1935).)

[3] J. M. Landau, *Parliament and Parties in Egypt* (Tel-Aviv, 1953).

[4] I. D. Levin, *Yegipet* (1937); also L. N. Vatolina, *Sovremenyi Yegipet* (1949).

[5] He was later deported from Egypt by the government, but was allowed to re-enter after a protest campaign in the British press, mainly in the *Daily Herald*. The Rosenthal family has maintained close contact with the revolutionary movement in Egypt. Charlotte Rosenthal was among the leaders of the Communist Party arrested in June, 1925, and as these lines are written the Egyptian press reports that Mary Rosenthal has been given a five-year prison sentence in a Cairo trial against the "United National Front." (*Al Ahrām*, Sept. 2, 1954.)

[6] *Jahrbuch fuer Politik, Wirtschaft, Arbeiterbewegung*, 1923–25. There are, however, conflicting figures even in the various volumes of the *Jahrbuch*, edited by the Comintern in Hamburg. Avigdor in *Revolyutsionni Vostok*, vol. 6 (1934), reports 2000 members for 1922.

[7] Levin, *loc. cit.*

[8] The manifesto is dated December 22, 1921. It was published in the *Labour Monthly* of March, 1922.

[9] All these unions were strongly nationalistic, and the strike movement mentioned above was almost exclusively directed against factories and enterprises owned by foreigners.

[10] In view of the dearth of cadres in the early days, the members of the central committee of the party also doubled as leaders of the trade unions which had joined the Profintern in 1922.

[11] This figure, which is given in both Communist and some non-Communist publications, is very much exaggerated.

[12] A correspondent in the *Labour Monthly* (May, 1928) said that the Confederation of Trade Unions, which had been until 1923–24 under Communist leadership, was "on the way of becoming a real mass movement."

[13] Some details about the trial are found in the *Egyptian Gazette*, July–Oct., 1924.

[14] Crossley, "Egypt at the Crossroads," *Labour Monthly*, Jan., 1926; also Avigdor, *loc. cit.*, and *Egyptian Gazette*, June, 1925. *Al Musawwar*, Dec. 24, 1954, published the pictures of the defendants in the 1925 trial.

[15] It is an interesting though unfortunate fact that the early history of the Egyptian Communist Party appears not to be very well known in Communist circles. The only recent authoritative (but extremely short) review is the report delivered by Hasan 'Abdur-Rahmān to the economic council of the W.F.T.U. on the occasion of its Berlin conference in 1951 (published in *Novoye Vremya*, Feb., 1952). But this survey is not based on contemporary Communist sources but on the book (in French) of a non-Communist, Zakki Badawi, quoted *supra*, which is not always exact in its data. The Soviet journals of the 1920's, specializing in Eastern affairs, and also the Comintern organs, published relatively few articles and little news on Egypt—obviously for want of reliable news. Only after 1925 (when Soviet trade representatives appeared in Cairo for some years) were there occasional articles which appeared signed "Avigdor" in the Communist press, date-lined Cairo. But on the whole the British

Communist press was more detailed and more reliable on Communism in Egypt during the 1920's, and for many years thereafter.

[16] Willi Muenzenberg, *Solidaritaet* (1930). This organization is reported to have renewed its activity in 1931, when the water-drawers at Assiut went on strike.

[17] Al Gritly, "The Structure of Modern Industry in Egypt," *L'Egypte Contemporaine*, 1947.

[18] Individual Egyptian Communists have contributed to our understanding of the Egyptian village. In this context the books of Fathi ar-Rāmla on the life of the fellah should be mentioned.

[19] Stalin, *Sotchinenya*, vol. 7 ("The Political Tasks of the University of the Peoples of the East").

[20] Theses on the revolutionary movement in the colonies and semi-colonies. (1928.)

[21] Theses of the Agitprop department of the Executive Committee of the Comintern on the occasion of the fifteenth anniversary of the foundation of the Comintern (Mar., 1934).

[22] Violet Conolly, *Soviet Trade* (1935). George Kirk (*The Middle East in the War*) says that Semenyuk tried to propagate Communism for nearly three years while selling cheese at a loss.

[23] *Inprecorr*, May 29, 1931.

[24] *Ibid.*, vol. 29, 1929.

[25] *Al Ahrām*, Jan. 10, 1935, quoted by Badawi, "Problèmes du travail. . . ."

[26] Kāmil, a journalist who had been a teacher, was arrested in 1938 for having published a leaflet in which he demanded that the government "should distribute bread to the poor." His group published in 1944-45 *Al Magalla al Gadīda*. It was strongly attacked by the Egyptian Stalinists. Cf. Fathi ar-Rāmla, *Hal inharafat Rūsia?* (1945; "Did Russia Deviate?").

[27] An official Soviet source stated in 1950 that the British were fully justified in staying in Egypt and keeping their army there during the war. "Despite the protests of the Egyptians and even the active opposition of some elements in Egypt. . . . Only enemies of democracy or madmen can argue that the action of the British government [in Egypt] was tantamount to aggression." "Falsifikatori Istorii" in *Vneshnaya Politika Sovietskovo Soyusa, 1948 god* (1950).

CHAPTER THREE, PAGES 42-51

[1] Abbreviation of *Mouvement Egyptien de Libération Nationalé*; the French expressions will be used; most of the party discussions were held in French at that time.

[2] "The Spark" (*Ash-Sharara*, in Arabic).

[3] Iskra had 22 per cent. intellectuals, 22 per cent. students, and 40 per cent. foreign residents in Egypt, according to its own statement.

[4] The Marxist League was a faction which split away from M.E.L.N. in the summer of 1946, at the time of the arrests carried out by the Sidqi regime. It was accused of "liquidationism" by the M.E.L.N. majority.

[5] The Sulaimān faction was expelled after it had demanded, in a session of the Central Committee early in 1948, that the existence of factions in the M.D.L.N. should be legalized.

[6] Towards a Bolshevik Organization, The Voice of the Opposition, and the "Adéliéns" (followers of 'Ādil, a member of the central committee); all three were united in the demand that the party should be mainly active among the workers and declared that "centralism" in party life was tantamount to fascism. Personal factors played a great role in all these splits.

[7] Iskra had more sympathizers but fewer members than M.E.L.N.

[8] "O.R." stood for *Ouvriers révolutionnaires*. The two smaller groups, Towards a Bolshevik Organization and The Voice of the Opposition, united. N.H.S.M. was the only faction to continue to exist, under various names, for a number of years.

[9] *Al Muqāwama* (Resistance) and *Kifakh al 'Ummāl* (Workers' Struggle). *Al Muqāwama* changed hands and became subsequently (in 1952–53) the organ of one of the factions of the H.S.M. (Egyptian Communist Party).

[10] Hatāta, a young physician, joined the Communists in 1945. Kāmil 'Abdul Halīm is a poet and leading member of the peace movement.

[11] "Of the many rival groups which profess Marxism, that which seems to have emerged as the most powerful movement is the M.D.L.N. . . . It seems to have inspired the peace campaign in Egypt, paved the way for the growth of the trade unions, and has big influence among the peasants." Idris Cox in *World News and Views*, Aug. 30, 1952. The writer had later to retract this part of his article.

[12] He was arrested in 1954 and given a seven-year sentence (*Bourse Egyptienne*, Dec. 30, 1954).

[13] In order not to over-complicate the picture, only the major groups have been mentioned here. Smaller organizations, such as HASHAM (initials of Al Haraka ash-Shuyu'iyya al Misrīyya, Egyptian Communist movement) or DALCHIN (Dimukratiūn sha'abiyūn, Popular Democrats) have not been mentioned at all, nor was the Trotskyite movement in Egypt.

[14] Idris Cox, *loc. cit.* In Egypt all Communist fronts published statements welcoming the "glorious army movement." Typical is the following appeal of the General Confederation of Trade Unions: "The people's army has realized the hopes of all citizens. . . . We proclaim without any hesitation that the army movement is an expression of our suffering and our hopes, etc." This was signed by members of the Central Committee of the M.D.L.N., such as Anwar Makkār and others. A French translation of this and similar documents appears in *Bulletin d'études sur l'Egypte et le Sudan*, edited by the M.D.L.N., Aug., 1952.

[15] He was given a five-year sentence in a trial of some Communists in August, 1954, while his brother Abdur-Rahīm Sidqi received three years. Mustafa Kamāl Sidqi is the husband of Tahīyya Cariuca, one of Egypt's most famous dancers, who appeared at the Bucharest Peace Festival in 1953.

[16] *Al Akhbār*, Nov. 14, 1952. *Bourse Egyptienne* (Nov. 14, 1952) reported 400 founding members of the new party "representing all provinces." Al Bindari could not make up his mind whether to call his party "Progressive," "Popular Democratic," or "National Liberation Party."

[17] Al Bindari in *Al Misri*, Sept. 25, 1952.

[18] *Mu'ārada*, Sept., 1952. Also the reports of the proceedings of the Egyptian Supreme Court (State Council) in November, 1952, when Fathi ar-Ramla protested against the refusal to legalize his party.

[19] It has not been clearly established to this day whether the Communists (and if so, what group) were behind the Kafar ad-Dawar riots. Later it became in Communist literature a "demonstration of anti-working-class policy" and "ferocious repression by the reactionary regime of Naguīb." But at the time of these incidents, M.D.L.N. bulletins reported that in Kafar ad-Dawar imperialist elements had instigated a vile plot against the popular movement of the army, a movement which should be supported by all class-conscious and patriotic workers. The trade-union leaders published an appeal in *Al Misri*, Aug. 10, 1952, warning against *agents provocateurs*. A French translation was published in the *Bulletin d'études*, vol. 17 (1952), of M.D.L.N.

[20] Palme Dutt in *Daily Worker*, Oct. 27, 1952. Idris Cox, who had relied on the Egyptian Communists, had to apologize: "My [previous] article failed to give a correct political assessment of the role of the Naguīb regime . . . it tended to present it as a progressive force." (*World News and Views*, Nov. 15, 1952.) About Soviet reactions to Naguīb, see below.

[21] Both were arrested and given prison sentences in September, 1954. Saif an-Nāsir is the son of a Wafdist ex-minister who had organized pro-Communist student groups in 1953-54.

[22] One trial affected twenty-four members of M.D.L.N. and its fronts, and included Muhammad Shata, a member of its central committee, and Dr. Sharīf Hatāta, as well as Albert Arye and Naomi Kanael, charged with having served as liaison officers with Communists abroad. Altogether, 252 Communists were brought to trial during the first six months of 1954, and about 100 during the second half of that year.

[23] *The Times* ("Weekly Review"), London, Sept. 23, 1954.

[24] These were the main defendants in the M.D.L.N. trial of December, 1954. Rifā'i was the secretary-general of the movement, 'Amr and Hasan 'Abdur-Rahmān have headed the trade-union work of the party and represented M.D.L.N. frequently at international Communist congresses. Fādil was the Cairo Communist student leader, while Badri was in charge of the Partisans of Peace and other "fronts" in Alexandria. Most of the other Communist leaders of 1944-54, mentioned above, were arrested and given prison sentences in a series of trials in September to December, 1954. The defendants included Muhammad Shata; Ahmad Taha Ahmad, a trade-union organizer and journalist; Zakki Murād, a young Sudanese lawyer and leading party organizer; and Yūsuf Hilmi (who recanted to some extent in prison). The oldest among this new generation of Communist leaders, Shata and Muhammad 'Ali 'Amr, are not yet forty. Most of them were members of the famous "students and

316

workers council" in Cairo early in 1946; most were arrested after the events of the Black Saturday in Cairo in January, 1952. The intellectuals among them, i.e. the majority, took a leading part in various "front" organizations and headed delegations to the international congresses of these groups. There was one woman among them, Naomi Kanael, a non-Egyptian who had married Kāmil 'Abdul Halīm, the poet and peace movement secretary—who is not to be confused with Ibrahīm 'Abdul Halīm, who edited the party organs *Al Malāyīn* and *Al Maidān*, and who headed the Egyptian delegation to the Communist Youth Festival in Berlin in 1950.

CHAPTER FOUR, PAGES 52–62

[1] Al Mudrik was an old trade unionist who favoured the "politicizing" of the unions. Later he headed a splinter group outside the main trend of the Egyptian Communist movement. Nahoum was deported to Italy by the Sidqi government, while the two others remained members of the executive of the pro-Communist "Congress" up to its dissolution.

[2] *Ad-Damīr* (Conscience), Sept. 26, 1945. The Workers' Committee for National Liberation was founded a fortnight later, on October 8, 1945. It became, in February, 1946, the National Committee of Students and Workers, and it disintegrated after a few weeks' existence. Attempts made by the M.D.L.N. to revive the "Committee" in the summer of 1946 were unsuccessful.

[3] Hasan 'Abdur-Rahmān in *Novoye Vremya*, vol. 3 (1952).

[4] The Congress of Workers' Unions, the Alexandria workers' congress, and an organization uniting employees of commercial establishments.

[5] This is one of the strongest unions in Egypt. Muhammad Ibrahīm Zain ad-Dīn had taken part as an observer in the Paris Conference of 1945, and the Communists had apparently expected that he would join their group.

[6] The appeal of the former was published as a leaflet early in August, 1952. The statement of the latter was published in *Al Misri*, Aug. 10, 1952.

[7] Quoted in F. Lagache, "Les journées de février, 1946," *Moyen Orient*, Feb., 1950.

[8] *Ibid.*

[9] Leaflet, Feb. 21, 1951.

[10] *Students versus Colonialism*, vol. 2 (1952). This is an English-language bulletin of the I.U.S., the Communist International Students' Federation, published in Prague.

[11] One of the Egyptian women delegates to the Vienna Congress, after her return published a very unfavourable series of articles on the situation of Moslems behind the Iron Curtain.

[12] *Al Gamāhīr*, Jan. 25, 1948.

[13] *Ibid.*, Nov. 23, 1947.

[14] *Bulletin d'études*, etc., published by M.D.L.N., No. 17, Aug., 1952, p. 5.

[15] Hankey was at the time British ambassador in Cairo. Quoted from the November, 1953, issue of the M.D.L.N. bulletin: "What Does the Present Regime Mean for the Working Class and the People in General?"

[16] *Programme du Mouvement Démocratique de Libération Nationale* (1951), translated here from the French text.

CHAPTER FIVE, PAGES 63-69

[1] The Sudan Movement for National Liberation (the French initials are M.S.L.N.).

[2] Its name was subsequently changed to *Common Struggle*.

[3] Galāl ad-Dīn al Hamamsi, *What Is Happening in the Sudan?* (in Arabic; Cairo, 1945). The Communist line is given in Asad Halīm, *Qadiyyat Sudān* (The Sudan Question), Cairo, 1946. For the subsequent period, see Qāsim Amīn, *The Sudan Agreement in the Balance* (Khartoum, 1953). Qāsim Amīn, a Communist chief, is a leader of the railwaymen's executive board.

[4] *Umdurmān*, Jan. 1, 1946.

[5] Zakki Murād, a young Sudanese lawyer, had permanently settled in the Egyptian capital and apparently represented the S.M.N.L. interests there.

[6] *Allies for Freedom* (London, 1954).

[7] *Al Misri*, May 13, 1952. Sa'id Fādil was replaced as general secretary by Ash-Shāfi Ahmad Ash-Shaikh at the annual session of the Federation in January, 1953 (*Al Ahrām*, Jan. 15, 1953). The real leader of the Federation (and the S.M.N.L.) is believed to be A. M. Bashir, who was in Europe in 1952-53.

[8] For a correction of the original Communist line for the support of Naguīb, see the S.M.N.L. "Manifesto" in Arabic (Khartoum), Apr., 1953.

[9] *Al Ahrām*, Nov. 1, 1953. According to this law, promulgated in October, 1953, Communist (and Fascist) activity was made an offence punishable by one year in prison. Among the Communist organizations listed, all the major "fronts" were included.

[10] One Communist candidate was returned for one of the five seats reserved for university graduates. The secretary-general of the group is Ahmad Sulaimān, a lawyer; its organ is *As-Sahrā*.

[11] Back in 1947-48 Al Azhari was attacked as a "fascist" by the Communists. Cf. *Al Gamāhīr*, Nov. 23, 1947: "Isma'īl al Azhari has joined the fascist front of Misr al Fatah and the Moslem Brotherhood." But meanwhile both Misr al Fatah and the Moslem Brotherhood became the allies of the Communists in the National Front.

[12] For the first Northern Province peasant congress in Atbara, cf. *Al Gabha* (Khartoum), August, 1952. A summary of the proceedings of the Congress and the "Ten Point Demands" is contained in *Sudan Review*, bulletin 5, a mimeographed Communist news-sheet in English. The issue, as a whole, has been reviewed from an official Communist point of view

in "The Peasant Movement in Sudan" in *For a Lasting Peace, For a People's Democracy* (the Cominform journal), July 3, 1953.

The executive of the Gazira union was originally in the hands of Independents, but was infiltrated by the Communists in 1952-53.

CHAPTER SIX, PAGES 73-85

[1] *From the Foundation Conference* (in Hebrew; Jerusalem, 1920). A full account of the early history of the Communist Party in Palestine is given in *The History of the Communist Party in Israel* (in Hebrew), by G. Israeli (Tel-Aviv: *Am Oved*, 1953). Pp. 15-73.

[2] "The Communist Movement in Palestine," Part I (in Yiddish); *Der Funk* (Warsaw, 1930). This is the only official attempt to write the history of the party. The second part has apparently never been published.

[3] *Davar* (daily newspaper), Tel-Aviv, May 25, 1952. Obituaries for Gershon Dua, mistakenly reported to have been killed in a Polish prison, were published in Communist periodicals in several countries in September, 1926.

[4] "The Communist Movement in Palestine," *op. cit.*, p. 16.

[5] *Workers' Thought* (Yiddish), May, 1923.

[6] "The Communist Movement in Palestine," *op. cit.*

[7] The main documents for the Afula incident are the leaflets of the Haifa and Jaffa branches of the Communist Party, dated Nov. 29 and Dec., 1924; the article "Afula" in *Working Class* (Yiddish), Jerusalem, 1924; *Ha'aretz* (Hebrew daily newspaper), Tel-Aviv, Nov. and Dec., 1924; and the "Communist Movement in Palestine," *op. cit.*, p. 39.

[8] *Working Class* (Yiddish), Dec., 1925.

[9] "Open Letter of the Communist Party to All Members of the Achdut Avodah" (the leading Zionist Socialist group), Oct. 25, 1926.

[10] Memorandum presented by the "Jewish Workers' Council" (leaflet), June 28, 1928.

[11] Memorandum of the Palestine Communist Party, dated June 2, 1928. The whole incident is described in *Forward* (Yiddish), nos. 8 and 9, July and Aug., 1928. *Forward*, the monthly illegal organ of the Palestine Communist Party, was first published in 1926 and continued to appear until 1931.

[12] *G'dud Haavodah* (Hebrew; Tel-Aviv, 1930), pp. 196-205; *Our Struggle* (Yiddish), Apr., 1925, p. 6; *Class Struggle* (Yiddish), June, 1925, p. 3.

[13] *Forward* (Yiddish), Mar., 1931. The letter written by Elkind is dated December 18, 1930. "Via Nova" was dissolved when Elkind and most of the other members were arrested during the great purge of 1936-38. Nothing is known of their fate.

[14] Open Letter of the First Groups Leaving for Biro Bidjan" (Hebrew), Aug. 17, 1932.

[15] "The Agrarian Question" (Hebrew), published by the General Council of the Communist Party, February, 1929; also *Forward*, Mar., 1929.

[16] "Reply to Those who Slander Us" (Hebrew), 1928. *The Workers' Way* (Hebrew), Feb., 1928.

[17] *The Lesson of the Petach Tiqva Events* (Hebrew), by Z. Berman, Jan., 1928. Berman was a Communist leader.

[18] *Inprecorr*, Oct. 10, 1935.

[19] *Forward* (Yiddish), May 19, 1929.

[20] *Ibid.* For the old slogans, see *Forward* (Yiddish), July, 1928.

[21] *Danger—Provocateurs!* (Yiddish), Aug., 1929.

[22] "Everyone who incites others by word or deed to riots is a criminal, a traitor, an enemy of the people." Leaflet dated August 19, 1929.

[23] *The Bloodshed and the Working Class* (Hebrew), Sept., 1929.

[24] The local party organ said that the *Rote Fahne* article was "very much mistaken," cf. *The Communist Word* (Yiddish), 1929.

[25] *The Workers' Way* (Yiddish), Oct., 1929.

[26] *Forward* (Yiddish), Dec. 25, 1929.

[27] *The Arab Revolutionary Movement and the Tasks of the Proletariat*, Oct., 1929.

[28] *Ibid.*, Oct., 1929; also *Forward*, vol. 24 (1929).

[29] *Forward*, vol. 25 (Dec., 1929).

[30] *Ibid.*

[31] *Inprecorr*, vol. 7, No. 5.

CHAPTER SEVEN, PAGES 86–103

[1] *Forward* (Yiddish), Feb. 27, 1930.

[2] *Ibid.*

[3] *Forward*, Jan. 26, 1930.

[4] *Ibid.*

[5] *Crossroads* (Hebrew), published by the Young Communist League of Palestine, 1930, p. 9.

[6] Among them were all the party leaders of the 1930's, such as "Mūsa," Sidqi Najāti, and Meir Slonim. Some of the graduates of the Comintern school subsequently left the party or were expelled, like Būlos Farah, who was one of its main pillars during the late 1930's. One of them, 'Abdul Ghani al Karmi, now represents the Hashemite Kingdom of Jordan in Madrid; most of the rest now live in Israel and Jordan.

[7] *Ha'or* was edited by M. Stein, a Tel-Aviv lawyer, and M. Z. Colton. Colton left the country in the early 1930's and disappeared in the Russian purge. Stein remained in Palestine but strayed from the party line, and although *Ha'or* continued to appear even after 1935, it no longer expressed the party view after that year.

[8] *Forward*, vol. 41 (June, 1931).

[9] The date of the Comintern directive is October 26, 1930.

[10] Various leaflets issued by the party executive between 1932 and 1934, especially the one published on the eve of the Jewish Purim holiday, 1934.

[11] "Down with Zionist Provocation," a Communist Party executive appeal.

[12] *Ibid.*

[13] *Appeal to Arab Youth*, Communist Party Executive, Nov., 1931. Also the (Arabic) leaflets on the occasion of the second anniversary of the 1929 riots, Aug., 1931.

[14] Leaflet issued by the party executive, June, 1932. The anniversary had been transferred from August to June in view of the execution of three rioters on June 17, 1930.

[15] *Ha'or*, Dec. 24, 1931.

[16] The Murison-Trusted report on the riots was published on January 4, 1934, as a supplement to the *Palestine Gazette*.

[17] *Survey of International Affairs*, 1934 (London: Royal Institute of International Affairs).

[18] *Ibid.*

[19] Hamdi Husaini ceased to collaborate with the Communists (or to be a member of the party) during the 1936–39 riots, but again renewed his ties with the Communist Party during World War II. The leader of Istiqlāl, 'Awni 'Abdul Hādi, is at the time of this writing, Jordan ambassador to Egypt.

[20] Letter to the party cadre, Apr. 5, 1933.

[21] *On the Present Political Situation* (Yiddish), Oct., 1933.

[22] *The Beginning of the Revolutionary Crisis* (Hebrew), Oct., 1933.

[23] *Ha'or*, Dec. 31, 1933.

[24] Z. Colton in *Ha'or*, July 4, 1933.

[25] M. Hashomroni, "Nationalism and Socialism," *Ha'or*, Nov. 26, 1931.

[26] G. Yacovson, *Ha'or*, Dec. 24, 1931.

[27] *Ibid.*

[28] S. Harussi, *Ha'or*, July 18, 1930.

[29] *Kol Ha'am* (People's Voice; in Hebrew), Aug., 1940.

[30] Leaflet of the Young Communist League (in Hebrew), June, 1932.

[31] Leaflet of the Jerusalem branch of the Young Communist League (in Hebrew), May 22, 1934.

[32] Leaflet issued by the Central Committee (in Hebrew), June 24, 1933.

[33] Leaflet by the Jerusalem branch of the Young Communist League (in Hebrew), May 22, 1934.

[34] A. Lerner in *Ha'or*, Aug. 17, 1933.

[35] N. Yacovson, *Ha'or*, Nov. 17, 1933.

[36] A. Lerner, *loc. cit.*

[37] *Who is Responsible for the Jewish Blood Shed in This Country?* (in Hebrew), Aug., 1936.

[38] *Kol Ha'am*, Dec., 1938.

[39] *Ibid.*, Nov., 1939.

[40] *Kol Hano'ar* (magazine of the Communist Youth League), May 1, 1941.

[41] *Ibid.*

[42] Leaflet published by the Central Committee (in Hebrew), Mar., 1942.

[43] *Ibid.*

[44] Party executive leaflet, Nov., 1935.

[45] It is not known whether Fuād Nāsir was by that time already a party member or only a sympathizer. He is now secretary-general of the Jordan Communist Party. Nimr 'Uda later participated in the Rashīd 'Ali *coup* in Baghdad. He was expelled from the Communist Party in 1951.

[46] *Ten Days of the Heroic Struggle of the Arab People* (in Hebrew), May, 1936.

[47] *Seven Weeks to the Liberation War* (in Hebrew), June, 1936.

[48] *What Has Happened and What Caused All That*, June, 1936.

[49] "Tajar" was reportedly a pseudonym of A. Liebling, "Yosef" of Ridwān al Hilu. *Rundschau*, Apr. 5, 1935.

[50] *Ha'or*, Dec. 7, 1936, and Jan. 7, 1937.

[51] *Ibid.*, Dec. 7, 1936.

[52] "Memorandum to the Comintern," Sept., 1939. There was no official Communist Party at that time, the "Jewish Section" being one of the two active Communist groups.

[53] *The Policy of the Party with Regard to the Arab National Movement*, Aug., 1941.

[54] *Rundschau* (the Comintern organ in German; Basel), vol. 29 (1936).

[55] Leaflet, *Revolutionary Bands Fighting for the Political and Social Liberation of the Workers in Palestine, South Syria* (in Arabic), Haifa, Aug. 26, 1936.

[56] Leaflet issued by the party executive, Mar., 1937.

[57] *Tableaux from the Bludan Conference* (in Hebrew), Sept., 1937.

[58] *Kol Ha'am* (in Hebrew), Nov., 1937.

[59] *Ibid.*, vol. 18 (1938).

[60] *Protocol of the Meeting Between the Representatives of the "Jewish Section," the Jerusalem Branch, and the Party Executive*, Nov., 1939.

[61] "Memorandum to the Comintern," Sept., 1939.

[62] Leaflet issued by the party executive, Aug., 1937.

[63] *Kol Ha'am*, vol. 1, No. 1 (Aug., 1937).

[64] *Ibid.*, vol. 1, No. 4 (Dec., 1937).

[65] *Ibid.*, Aug., 1938.

[66] *The Communist Party Executive on the Dissolution of the "Jewish Section"* (in Hebrew), Dec., 1939.

[67] "After the Publication of the White Paper" (in Hebrew). A leaflet issued on May 26, 1939, by K.P.P. (the "Jewish Section").

[68] *Kol Ha'am*, vol. 4, No. 3 (Mar., 1940).

[69] The Palestine Communists did have a somewhat amateurish intelligence service in the early 1930's. Its exploits are of little importance in this context.

CHAPTER EIGHT, PAGES 104–119

[1] There were differences of opinion about the interpretation of German-Russian relations between the party executive and the "Jewish Section," about which more will be said below.

[2] "The First of August," leaflet issued by K.P.P. (the "Jewish Section").

[3] A. Rossi, *Les Communistes français pendant la drôle de guerre.*

[4] *Kol Ha'am*, special edition, Aug., 1939.

[5] Leaflet of the "Jewish Section," Sept., 1939.

[6] Leaflet issued by the party executive, Oct., 1939. See also "Report on the Discussions between the Members of the Executive and the 'Jewish Section,'" Nov., 1939 (in stencil).

[7] "The Reply of the Secretariat of the 'Jewish Section' to the Cadre," Apr., 1940.

[8] *Kol Ha'am*, June, 1940.

[9] *Ibid.*, Aug., 1940 (this editorial, for a change, was written in Yiddish).

[10] *Ibid.*, Dec., 1940.

[11] *Ibid.*, Dec., 1940.

[12] February, 1940. The party executive organ, *Kol Ha'am*, and the rest of the propaganda material between September, 1939, and June, 1940, were published in stencil. (The party printing press appears to have been seized by the Mandatory police.) Between June, 1940, and April, 1941, all literature issued by the party executive was in print, but the last issue of *Kol Ha'am* prior to Hitler's attack on Russia was again in stencil. The "Jewish Section" issued, 'in addition to leaflets,' the periodical *Dapey Spartacus* (Spartacus Letters), some in print, others in stencil. Apart from these central publications there were anti-war leaflets in stencil put out by party branches, in Haifa bay and elsewhere. The Haifa branch of the party, which had seceded from the "executive" but did not want to join the "Jewish Section" either, published a newspaper of its own, *Ha'nitzotz* (The Spark) in the winter of 1940. Dating and placing the various leaflets issued in that period of internal splits is a highly complicated task, equalled only by the state of affairs in Egypt, where there were more splits initiated by even smaller groups of people.

[13] *Kol Ha'am*, Dec., 1940.

[14] The party executive was accused by its political enemies, and occasionally by rival factions within the party, of having been in contact with Nazi agents during the rebellion of 1936–9. Detailed proof for these accusations has not been given.

[15] *Kol Ha'am*, Apr., 1941.

[16] Leaflet in Arabic. Hebrew translation in *Kol Ha'am*, May, 1941.

[17] The Syrian and Iraqi Communists supported Rashīd 'Ali.

[18] Leaflet in Arabic, June, 1941.

[19] Leaflet signed by "League of Communist Soldiers," May 1, 1941.

[20] *Kol Ha'am* (German edition), May, 1941.

[21] *Ibid.*, May, 1941.

[22] Party Executive leaflet, June 26, 1941.

[23] *Emet* (Truth), June 30, 1941.

[24] *Kol Ha'am*, Aug., 1941.

[25] Party Executive leaflet, Oct., 1941.

[26] Details about these arrests in *Kol Ha'am*, July, 1941, and a leaflet "Save the Great Democratic Fighter Ridwan al Hilu Who Is in Mortal Danger, Just as Dimitrov was in the Hands of Goering" (July, 1941). In 1952 it was established, however, by the party, that Ridwan al Hilu had been "a spy and provocateur" all along.

[27] "Thesis on the Party Policy and its Present Tasks," 1943.

[28] These Communist activities caused much bitterness among the Jewish soldiers, and the head of the "Association of Communist Soldiers" was summoned before an ex-soldiers' court of honour after his discharge from the army to defend himself against charges of informing against fellow-soldiers.

[29] The editors were Jabra Nikola and 'Arif al Asūni. The former, despite several deviationist blots on his record, continues to be a staff member of *Al Ittihād*, the Arab Communist weekly in Haifa at the time of writing. The other is now a staff member of the Jerusalem (Old City) daily *Filastīn*.

[30] Shanīr later became party secretary of the Jaffa district, and during World War II became party expert on trade-union questions. Others who went to Moscow were Būlos Farah (afterwards expelled from the party), 'Ali Abdul Hālik (killed in the Spanish Civil War), Hasan Yahia Abu 'Aisha, and Zuhdi Baidas.

[31] Both Mūsa and his rivals continued to publish separate editions of *Kol Ha'am* for some time after May, 1943.

[32] A young teacher from Haifa, now one of the leaders of the Israeli Communist Party, and a member of Parliament. This leaflet (in Arabic) is dated May 29, 1943.

[33] Emil Tūma, a Cambridge-educated intellectual coming from a wealthy Haifa family, was the editor of *Al Ittihād* under the Mandate. He was undoubtedly the most gifted of all the Arab Communist leaders, but was relieved of all party functions in 1949 in view of his opposition to Soviet support of the partition of Palestine. Though remaining a member of the party, he has not been readmitted to its leadership up to the time of writing.

[34] Such as Nādi ash Sha'ab (People's Club) in Haifa, or the Rābitat al Muthaqqafīn headed by Mūsa Dajāni.

[35] British censorship in Palestine had forbidden the mention of the Mufti's name. On these visits, *vide Al Wahda*, Jerusalem, Nov. 10, 1947.

[36] *Al Ittihād*, June 23, 1946.

[37] Leaflet issued on October 17, 1947.

[38] *Kol Ha'am*, May 11, 1944.

[39] *Ibid.*

[40] "The Way to Liberation" (in Hebrew), Meir Vilner's theses for the Eighth Party Congress, 1946.

[41] *Kol Ha'am*, Oct. 13, 1947.

[42] *Ibid.*, Oct. 16, 1947. (The party organ had by now become a daily newspaper.)

[43] *Ibid.*, Sept. 17, 1949.

[44] *Ibid.*, Dec. 20, 1949.

[45] M. Alexander, "Israel's Communists," *Commentary*, Aug., 1952; and "Israel's Left Reels to the Shock of Prague," *ibid.*, Apr., 1953.

[46] Their percentage in Nazareth fell to 43 per cent. in 1951, and to 38 per cent. in 1954, but they remained by far the largest party.

[47] Dr. Sneh, a member of a right-wing Zionist Party up to 1947, joined MAPAM only in that year. An excellent orator and accomplished

journalist, he was at one time (prior to 1946) chief of the Hagana (the Jewish para-military underground).

[48] Ironically enough, Oren was a member of the Sneh wing of the party, and was arrested in Prague on his way back from a meeting of some Cominform front in Berlin.

[49] The MAPAM minorities, Ahdut Avoda and Poale Zion, who oppose close collaboration with the Communists, split away in August, 1954. The leaders of the minorities also take part in such fronts as the "peace movements."

[50] This is one of the few facts which has been statistically proved. The Communists received in the elections to the Histadrut (the General Federation of Jewish Labour) a lower percentage of votes than in the elections for Parliament. The percentage of Communist votes in such key unions as the metal workers and builders was lower than 5 per cent.

CHAPTER NINE, PAGES 123–133

[1] *Al Mikhmāz* (in Arabic), May 12, 1946. One of the first front organizations in Jordan was Rābitat al Muthaqqafīn (League of Intellectuals), founded in 1947. Its leader, 'Abdur-Rahmān Bey Tamal, was arrested in May, 1948. (*An-Nasir*, Amman, May 4, 1948.)

[2] Fuād Nāsir, born in 1910, a Christian Arab by origin, was an armed-gang leader during the 1936–39 riots in the Jerusalem-Hebron-Jericho triangle. He was in Baghdad at the time of the Rashīd 'Ali revolt, returned to Palestine early in 1943, and was detained for some time. He became one of the leaders of the League for National Liberation (the Communist Party), and switched his stand late in 1947 from support for the Mufti to acceptance of Soviet policy in Palestine. Nāsir was arrested in July, 1948, by the Egyptian authorities for distributing leaflets in occupied Palestine, but later was released. Illegally active in Jordan, as secretary-general of the party, he was arrested in Amman in December, 1951, and given a ten-year prison sentence. Rushdi Shahīn, born in Nablus in 1916, was one of the secretaries of the League for National Liberation during World War II.

[3] *The Arab World* (Chicago), 1953.

[4] *Al Muqāwama*, Dec., 1949.

[5] This trade union had been founded by Sāmi Taha (who was later killed by political adversaries) in Haifa under the British Mandate.

[6] In a speech in London in May, 1949.

[7] Among them Mūsa and other militants in Nablus; others were arrested in Bethlehem and Bet Sahūr (*Filastīn*, Oct. 1, 1949).

[8] *Al Ittihād* (Haifa), Mar. 12, 1950 (quoting *Al Muqāwama*).

[9] Jordanian censorship prevented the publication of reports about that incident. But *Al Muqāwama* (May, 1950), as well as the daily paper *An-Nahda*, carried accounts.

[10] *Al Ittihād* (Haifa), May, 1950, quoting *Al Muqāwama*.

[11] Twelve Jerusalem Communists were brought to trial in February, 1950 (*Filastīn*, Feb. 16, 1951).

[12] *Al Muqāwama*, May, 1951. Two months later the same paper wrote that this had been a "leftist deviation" and that "the party had been led astray by opportunists who had lost contact with the masses."

[13] Originally the party had appeared with eight candidates in five electoral districts: Mahmūd Mutlaq (a lawyer) in Amman, Dr. 'Abdul Majīd Abu Hajla and Rushdi Shahīn in Nablus, Dr. 'Abdur-Rahīm Bādr and 'Isa Shākir in Jerusalem, Ahmad 'Ali 'Arikāt in Jerusalem, Dr. Nasri Musallim in Bethlehem, and 'Isa al Madanas in Karak. However, of these, four were in prison (Shahīn, Badr, 'Arikāt, and Madanas). Five of the candidates, including Shākir and Musallim, who were not in prison, gave up their candidacy at the last moment, and only Rushdi Shahīn, Dr. 'Abdul Majīd Abu Hajla, and Mahmūd Mutlaq stood for election.

[14] Details in *Al Muqāwama*, June and July, 1951.

[15] *The New Dawn* was published in Amman by Hasan Sa'īd an-Nabūlsi.

[16] A. Bandak had been the editor of the Communist periodical *Al Mikhmāz* under the British Mandate.

[17] Dr. Zayā Dīn, Dr. Abdur-Rahīm Badr, Mahmūd Mutlaq (a lawyer), and Hasan an-Nabūlsi were elected members of the World Peace Movement Council at the Bucharest session, according to *Al Hawādith*, July 7, 1953. The editor of *Al Hawādith*, Muhammad Abu Shalabiyya, was also arrested at this time but released on bail.

[18] They were Jābir Husain Jābir, Sālim Iliās Mitri, and Iliās Hanna Shabbā (*Filastīn*, Dec. 30, 1951).

[19] *Filastīn*, Feb. 21, 1952. Full details of the trial are given in *Al Muqāwama*, Feb. and Mar., 1952. The party tried to enlist support for Fuād Nāsir throughout the Middle East, with some success.

[20] At the same time the publication of two new Communist magazines was reported according to *Al Balad*, Feb. 25, 1952.

[21] *Al Hawādith*, May 18, 1953.

[22] *Jerusalem Post*, Dec., 1953.

[23] *Hamizrakh Hekhadash*, vol. 18, 1954. Qadri Tukkān, deputy for Nablus, said in the discussion that "no other country in the world had such a law." Several months later, a member of the leading Nablus family was to become one of the heads of *Al Jabha*.

[24] A seasoned observer of the Jordan scene remarked that the list of Jordan girl students at Cairo University who had signed an "Al Jabha" appeal reads like the Arab Palestine social register, all the leading families being represented: Bettina Husaini, Istiqlāl Husaini, Hiyam Dajāni, Raja Dajāni, Ikrām Dajāni, 'Aida 'Abdul Hādi, Jānib 'Abdul Latīf, *et al.* (G. Stern in *Al Hamishmar*, Tel-Aviv, July 26, 1954). It may be useful to recall the social origins of Sofia Perovska and other members of the Russian "narodnik" movement of the late nineteenth century.

[25] One of his uncles, 'Abdul Latīf Salāh, had been a leader of the Palestine Arabs under the Mandate. 'Abdul Qādir Sālih had represented his party at various conferences of the "Partisans of Peace" in Europe in previous years. Maswada quarrelled with the Communist leaders of Al Jabha and toed the party line less closely than his colleague.

CHAPTER TEN, PAGES 137–146

[1] "Meleager" (A. H. Hourani) in *Islam Today* (1943). Mr. Hourani elaborates on that theme in his book *Syria and Lebanon* (1946): "To be a Levantine is . . . to be able to go through the external forms which indicate the possession of a certain nationality, religion or culture without actually possessing it. It is no longer to have a standard of values of one's own, not to be able to create, but only able to imitate, and so not even imitate correctly, since that also needs a certain originality."

[2] *Bolshaya Sovietskaya Encyclopedia* (Soviet Encyclopædia), vol. 22, which is apparently based on a speech, delivered by Khālid Bakdāsh at a party congress in Damascus (July 26, 1946), surveying the history of the party, in which he said that the "first party cell was founded seventeen years ago." But there had been Armenian Communist cells in Beirut for at least five years prior to that date, following a split in the Social Democrat Party "Hunchag." *Bolshaya Sovietskaya Encyclopedia*, vol. 25, mentions the existence of a Communist-dominated Lebanese People's Party in 1924–25.

[3] Among them were 'Ārif Gharā'ib, Shaikh ad-Dīn Kuba, and Yūsuf Yisbek.

[4] "Die neue Krise in Syrien," *Inprecorr*, vol. 22 (1929).

[5] *Inprecorr*, May 28, 1930. For a Soviet view on the political situation in Syria and Lebanon at that period, see S. Breiter, "Blishne-Vostochnie Mandati," *Novi Vostok*, vols. 20–21.

[6] *Alīf Bā* (Beirut), May 12, 1931, quoted in *Oriente Moderno*.

[7] *Ibid.*, Nov. 12, 1931, quoted *ibid.*

[8] Another Armenian, Talakian, was named as the party leader at that time.

[9] *L'Orient* and other journals. Most of the Communist leaders were, however, arrested after this demonstration. Cf. *Rapport à la société des nations sur la situation de la Syrie et du Liban* (1933), published by the French Foreign Ministry.

[10] Bakdāsh, a Kurd by origin, and Shāwi, a Greek Orthodox, hail from rich families and had studied law. Mustafa al 'Arīs, a printer and head of the Beirut printers' union, is of working-class origin.

[11] *Rapport à la S.D.N. sur la situation de la Syrie et du Liban* (1936).

[12] Khālid Bakdāsh accused the local French administrations of Fascist and Nazi sympathies in *What Is Happening in Al Jazīra* (in Arabic), published in July, 1937. The Communists opposed the separatist movement in Al Jazīra.

[13] Such pamphlets as *"The Arab Communists and the National Movement"* (in Arabic), first published in 1937 and later re-issued.

[14] This resolution is dated May 27, 1943. A leader of the Israeli pro-Soviet MAPAM Party accused Bakdāsh of not having acted according to the spirit of proletarian internationalism: "The ideological platform of the Syrian Communist Party, published in 1939, does not even contain a demand for agrarian reform, or anything that could possibly offend the feudal landowners. But there is a paragraph which says that no land must

be sold to Zionist agencies." Cf. Aharon Cohen, *The Arab Workers' Movement* (in Hebrew), 1947. A Soviet Middle Eastern expert, V. B. Lutski, noted in 1954 that "ten years ago the demand for the abolition of feudal property had still been lacking in the Syrian party programme." But he added that the situation had changed since them. (*Voprosi Istorii*, vol. 9, 1954.)

[15] Maronite sources charged the Communists with having spent £240,000 (Lebanese) more than any other party in these elections.

[16] Several leaders, such as Fuād Qazān, visited the Soviet Union early in 1938.

[17] Barel and Gresa were among the thirty-three Communist deputies who had constituted the *groupe ouvrier et paysan* in the French parliament after the party had been declared illegal in 1939.

[18] There exist two unpublished longer works on trade unionism in the Levant: Edward W. Samuell, Jr., *A Contribution to the Study of Lebanese Labor Syndicates* (1952); and Dr. A. Levin, *Beginnings of the Workers' Movement and Labor Relations in the Middle East* (in Hebrew), 1937.

[19] This tradition has been preserved to this very day. The owner of the largest Lebanese bus company, Emile Bustāni, is a "Socialist" member of the Beirut parliament.

[20] Even earlier, in October, 1938, there had been a meeting of a "Youth Congress against Imperialism" in Beirut, which was addressed by Khālid Bakdāsh, Sa'īd ad-Dīn Ma'mūr, and Mrs. Elisa Kandalaki, among others.

[21] *Sawt ash-Sha'ab* printed, according to its own reports, 10,000 copies per issue in 1937–39. This is greatly exaggerated, but there can be no doubt that it did have one of the largest circulations in the Levant.

[22] Twenty-two Communist leaders were brought to trial (by the Vichy authorities) in Beirut in August, 1940, among them ten Arab Christians, six Moslems, and six Armenians. Nikola Shāwi (who had edited *Sawt ash-Sha'ab* from the beginning), and Bakdāsh were given five-year sentences.

CHAPTER ELEVEN, PAGES 147–153

[1] Other leaders of this group were 'Omar Fakhūri, Ra'if al Khūri, and A. Tutunji.

[2] Other newspapers and periodicals launched during 1943–44 include *At-Ta'āwun ath-Thaqāfi* (Cultural Collaboration), the mouthpiece of the friendship league with the Soviet Union; *Al 'Ummāl wa'l naqabāt* (The Workers and the Unions); and *Khayāt al 'Ummāl* (Workers' Life), the last two being Communist trade-union papers in Syria and Lebanon respectively.

[3] *Sawt ash-Sha'ab* (The People's Voice; July, 1942) had accused Fā'iz al Khūri, the Prime Minister, of not restricting the privileges of the feudal landowners.

[4] Published in Beirut, 1943. The resolution is dated May 23, 1943.

[5] *At-Tarīq* (May 8, 1944) opposed "quick and nasty arguments" as to who was to blame for the instigation of the most recent incidents.

[6] *Report of Khālid Bakdāsh to the National Congress of the Communist Party* (in Arabic), Beirut, 1944.

[7] Nikola Shāwi, *The Independence of the Syrian and Lebanese Communist Parties* (in Arabic), Beirut, July, 1944.

[8] *At-Tarīq* is edited by Antūn Thābit. 'Omar Fakhūri, who died in 1946, was one of its main contributors; so were, or are, Radwān Shagal, Kāmil 'Ayyād, and Georges Hanna.

[9] One of the few exceptions is *Wāqi' al 'ālam al 'Arabi* (The Reality of the Arab World) by Georges Hanna (Beirut, 1952). This is a somewhat unorthodox attempt by a prominent Lebanese Communist, a physician by profession, to analyse Middle Eastern problems in a Marxist-Leninist test-tube. It results, in this particular case, in mere platitudes, but what is notable is the fact that Dr. Hanna is the only Arab Communist who has so far even tried his luck in this direction.

[10] *The Strategy and Tactics of World Communism*, Supplement on Communism in the Near East, p. 16. (Washington, D.C.; U.S. Government Printing Office). At the party Congress of December, 1943, for instance, Habīb Abu Shahla, Deputy Prime Minister, represented the government.

[11] On the strike of the oil company workers, see *Sawt ash-Sha'ab*, Apr. 19, 1946; on the textile workers' strike in Damascus, see *ibid.*, Sept., 1946; on the railway workers' strike, see *ibid.*, July, 1946.

[12] *Sawt ash-Sha'ab*, Mar. 26, 1945.

[13] *Ibid.*, Nov. 23, 1945.

[14] The president of the Lebanese-Soviet friendship organization stated in December, 1947, that the association had been dissolved in reaction to the Soviet stand on Palestine. But the secretary of the association stated that the dissolution had not occurred in accordance with the association's statutes.

[15] *Sawt ash-Sha'ab*, May 22 and 29, 1946.

[16] But even their anti-fascist record was far from being stainless. During September, 1939, and July, 1941, the Lebanese and Syrian parties vacillated between taking a neutral attitude towards Fascism and supporting it. They backed, for instance, Rashīd 'Ali's *coup* in Baghdad in April, 1941. This was then called "the heroic liberation movement of the Iraqi people" in Ra'īf al Khūri's *The Ways of National Conscience* (in Arabic), p. 91, *et seq.* This book was published in Beirut in May, 1941, by a leader of the Lebanese Communist Party, who had been one of the heads of the Beirut Anti-Fascist League prior to August, 1939, and again after June 22, 1941.

[17] These figures are contained in Khālid Bakdāsh's report to the London conference of Communist Parties in March, 1947. The Arab Communist weekly *Al Ittihād* gave an even higher number of party members for Syria: 10,000 [*Al Ittihād* (Haifa), Jan. 27, 1946].

[18] Khālid Bakdāsh in Damascus polled 9886 votes and lacked only a few to be elected. The Communist candidate in Homs received 4412 and in Aleppo 7500 votes. In the Lebanese elections of 1947, Nikola Shāwi and Mustafa al 'Arīs and the other party candidates failed to secure election.

[19] *Sawt ash-Sha'ab*, Apr. 17, 1946.

[20] Khālid Bakdāsh, *Communism and Nationalism* (in Arabic), Beirut, Aug., 1944.

[21] Cf. the chapter "The Dissolution of the International" in K. Bakdāsh, *Report to the Party Congress* (Beirut), 1944.

[22] *Report to the Political Bureau* (in Arabic), Beirut, 1944.

[23] Khālid Bakdāsh, *May Day Speech* (in Arabic), Beirut, 1944. The curious emphasis on the epithet "national" is a typical feature of the nationalist line of the party at the time.

[24] *Resolutions of the 1943–44 Party Congress* (in Arabic), Beirut, 1944.

[25] Nikola Shāwi, *ibid*.

CHAPTER TWELVE, PAGES 154–170

[1] *Nidā ash-Sha'ab*, May 1, 1949.

[2] *Sawt ash-Sha'ab* (The Voice of the People), Aug., 1949. In this issue the distribution of the land belonging to the feudal landlords was demanded, as well as the nationalization of those branches of Syria's economy which were in the hands of the imperialists, but not of the "national *bourgeoisie*."

[3] Both failed to be elected. Kazab was purged soon thereafter as "Titoist."

[4] The People's Party is one of the largest Syrian parties. Its leaders represent commercial and industrial interests in the cities of North Syria and they have traditionally preserved good relations with the Communists. Most of them signed the Stockholm peace appeal.

[5] Among the arrested was Artin Makhyan, the leader of the Armenian party cells in the north.

[6] *Al Akhbār*, Oct. 16, 1950.

[7] K. Bakdāsh, *Report to the Central Command of the Communist Party in Syria and Lebanon*, Jan., 1951 (Beirut, 1951). This document is quoted here according to the English translation of Harold W. Glidden in *Middle East Journal*, spring, 1953. The main victim of this internal struggle was Farjalla al Hilu, first secretary of the Lebanese party up to 1950.

[8] There has been some interest in Yugoslavia in Kāmil Jumbalāt's Socialist Party in the Lebanon. But the talk about a "Titoist deviation" in the Syrian party appears merely to cover up a tug-of-war in which ideological issues did not play the decisive role.

[9] *Al Inshā*, July 23, 1951.

[10] Bakdāsh, *Report* (1951).

[11] The first news about its convocation was published in the pro-Communist Beirut newspaper *Al Hadaf*, Aug., 1953.

[12] Published in *Pravda*, Dec. 23, 1953.

[13] Abu 'Azīz, *Die Weltgewerkschaftsbewegung*, Mar., 1954.

[14] Bakdāsh, *Report* (1951).

[15] 'Aflaq was originally one of the leaders of the Syrian Communist Party, but left it in 1943 and founded his own left-wing nationalist group, Al Ba'ath (Renaissance).

[16] "The Peasant Movement in Syria and Lebanon" in *Nidā' ash-Sha'ab* (in Arabic), Dec., 1953.

[17] Khālid Bakdāsh, *Report* (1951).

[18] Such as, for instance, pre-election pamphlets in September, 1954, calling all voters to oppose those elements seeking to silence the voice of free Syrians and calling for a united front against imperialism in the Arab world. In an interview with the Lebanese Communist newspaper *As-Sarkha* (May 23, 1954), Bakdāsh even proposed a "national coalition from wall to wall."

[19] Bakdāsh, *Report* (1951).

[20] Khālid Bakdāsh polled 17,000 votes, 6000 more than in 1947. Born in 1912, Bakdāsh took law courses at Damascus University in the early 1930's before joining the Communist Party. He has been the party's secretary-general from 1937 on. For his writings, cf. Bibliographical Note, p. 304.

[21] "... The main attention of our organizations is directed towards the creation of a lot of sound and fury around the Party and its slogans. ... In order to acquaint public opinion with Communist ideas, [the party] was obliged to create the greatest possible noise about them. ..." Bakdāsh, *Report* (1951).

[22] Two hundred, according to *Kul Shai'* (quoted in *Moyen Orient*, Jan., 1950). There was probably some professional solidarity in that gesture; many leaders of the Lebanese party, such as Henry Muhaibar, Jean Nimr, and Khāsib Mikha'īl, defendants in the same trial, were lawyers themselves.

[23] For instance, *Kul Shai'*, Feb. 3, 1950. Many newspapers denounced police action against the Communist demonstrators, and said that it was the result of Western pressure and the Lebanese government's desire to find favour in the eyes of the West.

[24] *Al Khayāt*, Apr. 15, 1952.

[25] *Ibid.*, Nov. 8 and 9, 1952.

[26] O. M. Marashian, *Christian Science Monitor*, Aug. 11, 1953.

[27] The number of signatures reportedly collected was 60,000 up to September, 1950 (*L'Orient*, Sept. 15, 1950), and reached 200,000 by the end of 1951.

[28] Monsignor Arīda later retracted his signature, claiming that he had been misled about the true nature of this campaign.

[29] Elias Karama ("The Red Bishop") took the initiative in convening a clerical peace conference in Mount Lebanon in September, 1950. This meeting was banned, however, by the government and did not take place at the time.

[30] Sa'ad ud-Dīn Mum'a has replaced al 'Arīs as president of the Beirut Communist printers' union, a small union but the oldest, and one of the most influential ones. Al 'Arīs gave the number of the Lebanese Communist unions' members as 20,000. (*Report of the Proceedings of the Second World Trade Union Congress*, Paris, 1949.) This was, however, greatly exaggerated, especially with regard to the situation in 1949.

[31] Quoted from the memoranda of the builders' and printers' unions in "Some Aspects of Lebanese Trade Unionism," *The World Today*, Sept., 1953.

[32] *L'Orient*, July 15, 1953.

[33] Khālid Bakdāsh, *Report* (1951).

[34] The Middle Eastern Arab press reported during the summer of 1953 an "anti-Malenkov movement" in the Lebanese party, and that there were leaflets to that effect which had been seized by the Beirut police (*Mid-East Mirror*, May 30, 1953; *Filastīn*, Mar. 21, 1953). Even if these reports are true, undue importance should not be attributed to them.

[35] This very lengthy document, composed in the summer, was published only in October, 1948, apparently because of technical difficulties.

[36] Bakdāsh, *Report* (1951).

[37] This was obvious, in particular, in the election campaign of the Syrian Communist Party in August and September, 1954.

[38] Bakdāsh, *Report* (1951).

[39] Or in other words, "The emancipation of the working class could not be only the work of the intelligentsia."

CHAPTER THIRTEEN, PAGES 173–180

[1] Ray Alan in *Commentary*, Mar., 1954.

[2] S. H. Longrigg, *Iraq, 1900–1950*.

[3] In the literature of the Iraqi national movement this is called the "national war of liberation." Iraqi Communists also mention the "immortal revolution of 1920 which was enormously stimulated by the great socialist October revolution." "Report of the Iraqi Communist Party to the Conference of Communist Parties in London," *World News*, vol. 20 (London, 1954).

[4] Doreen Warriner, *Land and Poverty in the Middle East*.

[5] Longrigg, *loc. cit.*

[6] Majīd Khaddūri, *Independent Iraq* (London, 1951).

[7] Majīd Khaddūri, *loc. cit.*

[8] For the July, 1931, strike organized by the Ikha Party, which had no Communist sympathies whatsoever, cf. "Der politische Massenstreik in Baghdad," *Inprecorr*, vol. 72 (1931), which reports that "the masses made this demonstration an anti-imperialist fight."

On the 1935 insurrection, cf. "*Bolshaya Sovietskaya Encyclopedia*," *Soviet Encyclopedia*, article "Iraq," 1953, which says that though it was a religious struggle in the beginning, it "soon took on the character of an armed struggle against British imperialism and its agency. The feudal leaders of the revolt, frightened by its extent, came to an agreement with the British imperialists. The leadership of the revolt then passed into the hands of the Central Committee of the anti-imperialist front which had been founded in the course of the struggle, in which the Communist Party played an important role. . . ."

It would be interesting to know on what authority this report is based. The most likely explanation is that some over-zealous Iraqi Communist was prepared, at any price, to send comforting news to Moscow about revolutionary activities. For details of the political prehistory of this uprising, cf. *Journal of the Royal Central Asian Society*, Jan., 1936.

⁹ *Soviet Encyclopedia* (vol. 18) gives 1932 as the year of the foundation of the Iraqi Communist Party, "which from the very beginning worked under conditions of utter illegality." *Al Qā'ida* (The Foundation; April, 1954), on the other hand, says, in an editorial, that the twentieth anniversary ("twenty glorious years of sacrifice and heroism . . .") was celebrated on March 20, 1954.

¹⁰ *World News*, vol. 20 (1954). No written record of the proceedings of the 1934 conference appears to exist. There had been "Marxist circles" in Baghdad at the same time, but their members later joined the Communist opposition, while "Fahd," a native of Nasireya (he left the city in 1934), subsequently became the first secretary of the party.

¹¹ *Al Qā'ida* (The Foundation), the party mouthpiece, replacing *Ash-Sharara*, which had been published during World War II. (Undated copy, probably 1946.)

¹² Khaddūri, *loc. cit.*, contains a survey of the ideology of "Sha'biyah" (Populism), and lists some of the original sources.

¹³ He was the only Communist of renown among the members of Ahāli at that time, and his communism, too, was of a private and unorthodox nature; he did not represent any larger group. According to *El Messagero* (Nov. 6, 1942, quoted in *Oriente Moderno*), he returned to Iraq from Syria, was arrested, and released in 1942 upon the intervention of the Soviet envoy to Iraq. (There is some reason to doubt the authenticity of the second part of this story.) 'Abdul Qādir Isma'īl became a frequent contributor to the Syrian and Lebanese Communist press in 1945/6.

¹⁴ S. 'Abbūd, "The Struggle for Democracy in Iraq," *Communist International*, Feb., 1937.

¹⁵ "In 1936 the bourgeois-nationalist National Reform Party formed a bloc with the pro-Fascist officers and carried out a *coup d'état*" (*Soviet Encyclopedia*, "Iraq"). This is a far cry indeed from the enthusiasm of 1936–37.

¹⁶ "Report of H.M. Government . . . to the Council of the League of Nations on the Administration of Iraq for the year of 1929."

¹⁷ *Secret Compilation regarding the Secret Iraqi Communist Party* (in Arabic). This series will be quoted as "Secret Compilation." Evidence given by Malik Saif, member of the party Central Committee.

¹⁸ There exist no printed first-hand sources for the history of Communism in Iraq prior to 1942, apart from a few leaflets, of doubtful authenticity, usually written by people who merely expressed their private opinions on certain events or problems. Some of the early Communists, or Communist sympathizers, such as 'Abd al Fattāh Ibrāhīm or 'Azīz Sharīf, later published books and booklets (*vide* Bibliographical Note, p. 308). But in these writings they did not deal with the early history of the "democratic movement," as it had to be called, somewhat euphemistically, because of the Iraqi censorship.

CHAPTER FOURTEEN, PAGES 181–194

[1] "The *coup d'état* was launched by the German-Italian agency in Iraq," from *Strani blishnevo i srednevo Vostoka* (The Countries of the Near and Middle East; Iraq, 1944). *Soviet Encyclopedia* says that "Rashīd 'Ali and his group were connected with Germany; the masses of the people did not support them." ("Iraq," vol. 18.)

[2] The text of the Tass statement is given in *Documents on Soviet Foreign Policy* (ed. Jane Degras).

[3] Cf. M. Beloff, *The Foreign Policy of Soviet Russia*, vol. 2.

[4] Emil Habībi, the editor of the Haifa Communist weekly *Al Ittihād* and a close associate of Fuād Nāsir, claimed in a letter to the *Jerusalem Post* (Dec., 1951) that Fuād Nāsir did not collaborate with Rashīd 'Ali, but was, on the contrary, imprisoned, and released only after a lengthy hunger strike. Mr. Habībi is correct about Nāsir being arrested, but mistaken about the dates; Fuād Nāsir was indeed arrested—but by the British, when they re-entered Baghdad in May, 1941.

[5] The text of the speech is given in an Italian translation in *Oriente Moderno*, 1941.

[6] M. Khaddūri, *Independent Iraq*.

[7] *Ash-Sharara* (The Spark). When Dr. Sāmi Shawkāt, the pro-fascist leader, announced in December, 1945, the establishment of a new political club, he was attacked by K. Jadarji (*Sawt al Ahāli*, Jan. 2, 1946) because of his record. In reply, Dr. Shawkāt charged that the anti-imperialists of the left had given an enthusiastic welcome to the "national movement of 1941." (*Az-Zaman*, Jan., 1946.)

[8] The public prosecutor in the trial against him in 1947 tried to make fun of a political party the leader of which had been a "mere labourer in an ice factory!" The main sources for the history of the Iraqi party, apart from its own publications, are the "Secret Compilation" mentioned above, and a shorter book, *Muhākamat ash-Shuyu'iyīn fi'l 'Iraq* (The Communist Trial in Iraq), published by the Iraqi government press. Both, especially the former, are an ill-assorted compilation of facts, many of them irrelevant and some of them erroneous, and reflect the working of a Communist Party as seen through the eyes of a semi-literate police sergeant. As political propaganda these publications are an unqualified failure, more likely to evoke sympathy for the accused than vice versa.

[9] Malik Saif was subsequently branded a police spy by the Iraqi Communist press (*Al Qā'ida*, spring, 1950).

[10] "Secret Compilation." There is much reason to doubt the authenticity of the report.

[11] Zakki al Khairi and most members of his faction rejoined the "Fahd" group in 1947 after having reached the conclusion that "Fahd" had changed its policy and that it had become less doctrinaire in its tactics. Z. Khairi has translated articles by Lenin and Stalin into Arabic and written a series of popular booklets on problems of Communism.

[12] The leader of this group was an ex-army staff-captain, Ghadbān Mardān as-Sa'ad, and his aides included Jalāl 'Abdur-Rahmān (a lawyer

from Al Azamie), Hāshim al 'Araji (a teacher from Kazimie), and Alfred Sama'ān (a law student). Captain as-Sa'ad continued his career as an author on topical international subjects, and was arrested in March, 1951, after the publication of his book *North Korea Triumphant* (*Ash-Sha'ab*, Mar. 13, 1951).

[13] *The Communist Trial*, etc., erroneously names Dahūd as-Sayigh ("Amīn") as the founder of the Communist League. The mouthpiece of the group was Al 'Amal (Labour). Wahdat al Nidāl (Unity of the Struggle) was another faction which broke away.

[14] The League was headed by Yūsuf Harūn Zilkha and Yakov al Misri. Its programme was outlined in Zilkha's book *Zionism—the Enemy of the Arab and the Jews* (in Arabic; Dar al Hikma, Baghdad, 1946). Most of the members of the League subsequently emigrated to Israel.

[15] The weekly (later daily) paper of this group was *Al Watan* (The Fatherland).

[16] Jawahīri's poems include "The Dream" (a pæan dedicated to the late Josef Stalin), as well as odes to the battles of Stalingrad and Sevastopol.

[17] There were many pro-Communist legal, semi-legal, and illegal newspapers in 1946, most of which lasted only for a few months—apart from those already mentioned. The most important was *Al Majalla* in Baghdad, but there were also provincial newspapers of a pro-Communist character in Nejef and Kirkuk.

[18] *Ash-Sha'ab*, Jan. 10, 1946.

[19] This figure, given by the *Soviet Encyclopedia*, is exaggerated. During the second half of 1948 most of the unions were dissolved as a result of the anti-Communist measures of the government.

[20] The largest demonstration took place on June 28, 1946, in which soldiers participated, according to eye-witnesses. The demonstrators demanded that the Palestine issue be brought before the Security Council, that British soldiers be removed from Palestine, and that the Anti-Zionist League (just banned by the 'Umari government) again be recognized. The demonstrators clashed with the police in front of the British Embassy. Five of them were killed (according to *Sawt al Ahāli*, June 30, 1946).

[21] 'Abdullah Mas'ūd had been among the founders of the Communist League, Sharīf ash-Shaikh was one of the leaders of the party back in the 1930's. Mūsa ash-Shaikh Rādi subsequently became one of the leaders of the Partisans of Peace.

[22] Another question raised concerned the formation of a military committee. "Fahd" stated that for obvious reasons the party could not mention the existence of such a body. But it had clearly been said that the party would have to work in the army, which meant that a military committee did exist in accordance with the "revolutionary character of the party."

[23] Documents published in "Secret Compilation."

[24] *Ibid.*

[25] Its leaders were 'Azīz Sharīf, Tawfīq Munīr, 'Abdul Amīr, Abu Tarab and Sharīf Yūsuf—all lawyers.

[26] See Bibliographical Note.

[27] This account is given here on the authority of the "Secret Compilation," but there are weighty reasons to doubt its authenticity. A *legal* National Liberation Party never existed in Iraq; the government refused it a permit in 1945–46. The *illegal* National Liberation Party, which existed only for a short period, was headed by Zakki Muhammad Basīm, "Fahd's" principal aide, who was executed in 1949.

[28] See Chapter 17.

[29] Twenty-five, according to the "Secret Compilation."

[30] Among them Yūsuf Zilkha, Masrūr Katān, Ibrahīm Nāji, and Ya'akov Efraim.

[31] "I therefore ask to give me the punishment I deserve. . . . If you are in need—and I think you are not—of any further help or information, I am prepared to give it even in the shadow of the gallows. I demand to be punished according to the law. I do not belong to the kind of people who ask for mercy while being real criminals. I do not wish to escape or save my life—thousands of people face disaster and others are brought to trial for being simple party members. I was the man responsible for the activities of the party during a period full of criminal acts and troubles. I do not wish to go on writing, I merely want to put an end to the pangs of conscience attacking me every second," etc. ("Secret Compilation.")

[32] In the case of the Iraqi Communists, among whom were to be found the leaders of the Anti-Zionist League, this charge could easily be disproved. The change in the Soviet attitude on Palestine came several months *after* the arrest of the Iraqi party's Central Committee.

[33] Report of the Central Committee of the Iraqi party to the Second Congress of the Communist Parties in London, 1954, in *Allies for Freedom* (London, 1954).

[34] "Le soulevement de janvier 1948," *Moyen Orient*, Feb., 1950.

[35] "Secret Compilation."

CHAPTER FIFTEEN, PAGES 195–202

[1] There were almost 3000 political prisoners in Iraq in 1949–50, of whom about a third were Communists, the rest being members of other left-wing or right-wing parties in opposition to the government. The Communists, who were never inclined to understatement, mentioned 17,000 in their press. The Communists, however, won over many new friends and members among the other political prisoners.

[2] Baha ud-Dīn Nūri, Sādiq al Flakhi, Bakr Ja'far, and Kāmil Samara'i were brought to trial in July, 1953, and given lengthy prison sentences. They were defended by twenty-two lawyers, among them 'Abdul Wahāb Mahmūd, head of the lawyers' association and one of the leaders of the Partisans of Peace (*Ash-Sha'ab*, July 13, 1953).

[3] In September–October, 1954, the Iraqi government threatened all Communists with loss of their Iraqi citizenship if they would not renounce Communism. It appears that at least some of the party members were permitted to avail themselves of this offer to get out of prison; this may well be connected with the new "moderate" Communist line in

world affairs—similar temporary retreats took place in Malaya, the Philippines, and other countries.

⁴ Another Communist cell included officers, who were arrested—several of them being executed in the autumn of 1952 ("Sursis à Baghdad," Edouard Sablier in *Le Monde*, Dec. 5, 1952). The army high command had doubts about the loyalty of the second of its three divisions stationed at Ba'kouba (near Baghdad), where there was a large Communist prison camp. *Al Qā'ida*, May, 1954, reported intensified Communist activity in the Iraqi army.

⁵ Statement of the Central Committee of the Iraqi Communist Party to the *Second Conference of Communist Parties within the Sphere of British Imperialism* (London, 1954). This comparison is somewhat far-fetched because it compares the circulation of a monthly magazine with that of a daily newspaper. What cannot be doubted is that several thousand copies of *Al Qā'ida* were distributed each month.

⁶ The demonstrations on the occasion of the fourth anniversary of the rejection of the Treaty of Portsmouth (January, 1948) had started similarly. The students of the science faculty put on a demonstration, and then resisted the police for several hours. Later they proceeded to a meeting of the left-wing opposition parties, who had come out in favour of a general strike, but against demonstrations, and persuaded the opposition leaders to join the demonstrations. *Al Qā'ida* (Dec., 1952) wrote of the November riots, that "our party alone commanded and directed the struggle"—an exaggeration, to say the least. The uprising failed, according to the illegal party organ, because it was not supported by the army, and was suppressed in the capital before it could spread to the district centres.

⁷ This document was published as a booklet by the party (n.d.).

⁸ The background of the internal discussion was given in a lengthy statement headed: "The Differences of Opinion between Us and the Opportunists of the Faction of the Banner of Toilers—Agents of the Palace." (Published in *Al Qā'ida* in 1953.)

⁹ "The Heroic Fight in Iraq" in *Allies for Freedom* (London, 1954).

¹⁰ *Ibid.* This quotation is taken from the manifesto in *Al Qā'ida*.

¹¹ In the internal party discussions, the situation in Persia was frequently referred to, and this issue was one of the central ones in the debate with, or rather *against*, the Banner of the Toilers faction.

¹² *Al Qā'ida*, "The Differences of Opinion . . . .''

¹³ This appears to contradict the historical truth; "Fahd" seems to have advised Kāmil al Jadarji (who hesitated) to join the government of Nūri Sa'īd in November, 1946, "for the benefit of the whole left-wing movement." When Jadarji told "Fahd" at one of the meetings that Nūri Sa'īd planned to dissolve the Communist Party and have "Fahd" arrested, the latter replied: "I have a strong party on which I can rely without fear." Cf. documents in the "Secret Compilation." It is true, however, that the Communists were against the Palestine war, whereas Jadarji supported the government's policy.

¹⁴ *Ibid.* The Banner of the Toilers faction could refer to "Fahd's" decision to abstain from attacks against the royal family during the war years, and the party majority had some difficulty in explaining this away.

[15] *Ibid.*

[16] *Ibid.*

[17] For the simple reason that in a revolutionary situation the more extreme party generally tends to prevail over the more moderate.

[18] On al Jawahīri, see Chapter 14, note 16. His weekly was banned in April, 1951; this provoked a protest by Kāmil Jadarji, who meanwhile had been elected president of the Baghdad journalists' association. Following the arrest of a Communist cell in Baghdad in January, 1953, Al 'Ulum was given a three-year prison sentence. (On a previous occasion fifty-four lawyers had volunteered to plead his case for him, *Ash-Sha'ab*, Dec. 10, 1951.) In October, 1953, a petition sponsored by the "peace movement" and signed by 7280 citizens of Baghdad was forwarded to the government. It asked, among other things, for the release of political prisoners, the dissolution of the parliament, the revocation of the 1930 treaty with Britain, etc. (*Ash-Sha'ab*, Nov. 6, 1953.)

[19] It publishes an (illegal) magazine, *Al Talawa* (The Student).

[20] A court-martial in Basra in December, 1953, decided, for instance, to release eight Communist students on bail; a measure quite out of line with the practice of military courts in Iraq. (*Ash-Sha'ab*, Dec. 31, 1953.)

[21] *Al Qā'ida* (Nov., 1953) said that the Arabs should make peace with Israel on condition that the Jews carry out the U.N. decisions of November, 1947 (giving up about half of the territory of the country). *Al Qā'ida* (May, 1954) returned to the same subject. The same proposals had, however, been made by the Arab League and by most Arab governments, so that this was hardly sufficient reason to accuse the Iraqi Communists of high treason.

[22] This group was headed by Muhammad Reza ash-Shabībi, one of the leaders of the "Peace" Movement (from Nejef), in co-operation with several old-time Iraqi politicians who had been left out of the government coalition by Nūri as-Sa'īd. It published the newspaper *Al Hayād* (Neutrality).

[23] *Al Qā'ida* (Aug., 1954). The alliance with the "Fascists" was justified in the Communist organ by reference to the "patriotic record" of the Istiqlāl after 1945.

CHAPTER SIXTEEN, PAGES 205–217

[1] The standard work on Soviet-Turkish relations in the early period is Louis Fischer's *The Soviets in World Affairs*; for the early 1920's the third volume of E. H. Carr's *History of Soviet Russia* should be consulted. The standard work for the 1930's is M. Beloff's *Foreign Policy of Soviet Russia*. Soviet authors dealing with the same subject include Pavlovitch (1922), Gurko-Kryashin (1925), Melnik (1927), Rostovski (1941), and Danzig (1949).

[2] Such interesting episodes as the Soviet flirtation with Enver cannot be dealt with here because it had little bearing on the history of the Turkish Communist Party.

[3] *Pervyi siesd Narodov Vostoka* (1920).

[4] On the early history of the Turkish Socialist and Communist Parties, *vide* Navshirvanoff in *Novi Vostok*, Feb., 1922; Gurko-Kryashin in

Rote Gewerkschafts Internationale, Mar. 2, 1925; and M. Pavlovitch, *Revoliutsionaya Turtsiya* (1921). Subhi went as a student to France in 1905 and joined the Socialist Party in Paris. He returned to Turkey in 1908 and became one of the leaders of the Turkish Socialist Party. Arrested in 1913 in Sinope, he succeeded in escaping to Russia early in 1914.

[5] Some sources mention a conference convened by Subhi in Moscow in 1918 as the first relevant date in the history of the Turkish party.

[6] *Pervyi siesd Naradov Vostoka* (1920).

[7] *Die Kommunistische Internationale*, 2 Jahrgang, vol. 17.

[8] This group published several periodicals: *Kurtulush* (Liberation), *Kaplan* (Tiger), and later *Aidinlik* (Dawn).

[9] *Neos Antropos* (The New Man).

[10] *Die Kommunistische Internationale, loc. cit.*

[11] *Ibid.*, quoting *Yani Gun*; and Pavlovitch, *Revoliutsionaya Turtsiya*.

[12] Mahmoud Assad in *Yani Gun*, Oct. 20, 1920, quoted by Pavlovitch in *Die Kommunistische Internationale*, vol. 17 (1921).

[13] *Ibid.*

[14] The history of the "Green Movement" is given in Kemal's "Nutuk" (speech) of 1927 (Leipzig, 1929); and in Halidé Edib's *Turkish Ordeal* (1928).

[15] Among them the *Communist Manifesto*; a Lenin biography; the Constitution of the R.S.F.S.R.; the *ABC of Communism*; the programmes of the Russian and Turkish Communist Parties, etc.

[16] A letter from Tevada to Pavlovitch in *Kommunistische Internationale*, vol. 17 (1921).

[17] The letter was published in May in *Zhisn Natsionalnosti*, Oct., 1921. The publication in *Kommunistische Internationale* came only in June, 1921.

[18] The Soviet consular representative in Trebizond was accused of "lack of energy."

[19] I. Maiski, *Vneshnaya Politika R.S.F.S.R.* (1922).

[20] In 1951 it was argued that the murder of Subhi and his comrades was connected with the visit of the "American General Harboard" in Ankara at the same time. (*Novi Mir*, Oct., 1951; also *Moyen Orient*, Feb. 8, 1950.)

[21] Gurko-Kryashin, *loc. cit.*

[22] Heller in *Rote Gewerkschafts Internationale*, Aug., 1923.

[23] On the events of 1925, *vide* B. Ferdi, "Revoliutsionnoye dvishenie v Turtsii," *Kommunisticheski International*, vol. 6, 1926.

[24] B. Ferdi, "Arbeiter Bewegung in der Turkei," *Inprecorr*, Sept. 28, 1926.

[25] *Rote Gewerkschafts Internationale*, Sept.–Oct., 1926.

[26] The Turkish delegate Fakhri at the Sixth Congress of the Comintern. Text in *Inprecorr*, Oct. 4, 1928. Details on the "liquidation of *agents provocateurs*" will be found in *Novi Mir*, vol. 9 (1951).

[27] Fakhri, *ibid.*

[28] Until the late 1930's Soviet cultural relations with Turkey were closer than those with any other country. An impressive list of cultural exchange projects is given in *Strani blishnevo i srednovo Vostoka*, 1944, pp. 96 *et seq.*

[29] The attitude towards Communists in the courts was always far more severe in Turkey than in such Arab countries as Syria and Lebanon, where police chiefs and judges were more interested in political insurance than in demonstrating anti-Communism. Communist activity in Turkey was always considered tantamount to high treason; whereas the authorities in the Arab countries—with the exception of Iraq, the one nearest to the Soviet Union—took a more lenient view.

[30] Necmeddin Saddak, "Turkey Faces the Soviets," *Foreign Affairs*, Apr., 1949.

[31] *Kommunisticheski International*, Dec., 1939.

[32] The riddle of the attempt on von Papen's life has not been satisfactorily solved to this day.

[33] According to reports from Communist sources, one of the leaders of this group, Hassan Bazri, was killed by the police while in prison.

[34] Degmer, who had been secretary-general of the Communist Party as early as 1921, was given a five-year sentence in a trial which took place in July, 1948. His main aide, Zeki Bachtimar, succeeded in escaping. Among the Communist journals banned were *Sendika* (the trade-union organ), *Yiquin* (Masses), and *Soz*, and five others. Degmer, together with the other Communists, was again released under an amnesty in 1950.

[35] The text of this leaflet is contained in S. Ustyungel, "V Tiurme i na volye" (In Prison and Freedom), *Novi Mir*, Sept., 1951. This is the only Communist description available (though it is extremely fragmentary in itself) of party activities in Turkey in recent years. It shows clearly the sources of the weakness of the Turkish Communists; the author writes, for instance: "In the course of many days I had long discussions with the comrades in prison on the national and agrarian problems of Turkey. Under the influence of these talks I would like to listen today very much to my favourite opera, *Ivan Susanin* (*ibid.*). *Ivan Susanin* is Glinka's opera about a Russian peasant who sacrifices his life for the Czar. Ustyungel's predilection for Stalinism made him apparently prefer *Ivan Susanin* to *Carmen*, despite the "counter-revolutionary" content of Glinka's opera.

[36] *Kudret*, Oct. 10, 1950.

[37] *Cumhuryet*, Nov. 16, 1951, quoting the Moscow weekly *Ogonyok*.

[38] *Pravda*, June 22, 1951.

[39] *Vatan*, Oct. 15, 1953, *et seq.*

[40] The Communist "Young Turkish Progressive" organization in Paris published the above-mentioned *Baris Yolu* and another "front" periodical, *Tek Jebhe* (Unity Front). Both papers were sent from France to Turkey by mail.

[41] *Pravda*, Oct. 25, 1953.

[42] *New York Times*, Oct. 13, 1953. Also Thorossian in *Le Monde*, Nov. 11, 1953; and B. K. in *Neue Zuericher Zeitung*, Nov. 17, 1953.

[43] Also among the accused was Fuad Badaner, the husband of one of the best-known novelists of Turkey. Bashtimer had toured Russia and Eastern Europe prior to his return to Turkey with false papers.

[44] S. Ustyungel, *loc. cit.*

[1] The first newspaper, *Kurdistan*, had already been published in Egypt in 1902.

[2] Elphinston, "The Kurdish Question," *International Affairs*, Jan., 1946.

[3] *Bulletin du Centre des Études Kurdes* (Paris), Dec., 1949.

[4] Westerman, "Kurdish Independence and Russian Expansion," *Foreign Affairs*, July, 1946.

[5] David Ariel: "The Kurds in the Middle East" (in Hebrew), *Hamizrakh Hehadash* (Summer, 1951). The Kurdish point of view is given in Muhammad Shirsad: *The War of the Kurds* (in Arabic), Cairo, 1946.

[6] Majīd Mustafa, a Kurdish deputy in the Iraqi parliament, in an interview with the Damascus *Al Balad*, Mar. 21, 1946.

[7] Dr. Ja'afar Muhammad 'Abdul Karīm in *As siāsa* (Baghdad), July 12, 1946. He was one of the leaders of the left wing of Heiwa, and Foreign Minister of the Mahabad Kurdish republic.

[8] Iraqi Kurdish leaders, such as Mulla Mustafa Barazāni, have been frequently charged by Iraqi political leaders with shirking a decision in all important events, such as, for instance, the Rashīd 'Ali revolt in 1941. Mulla Mustafa is reported to have said: "I am a Kurd and, if I oppose the Rashīd 'Ali forces, it will be taken as opposition to the Arab leaders who are behind that movement." Report on Iraqi parliamentary debates, *Az Zamān*, Jan. 23–29, 1946.

[9] *Sawt al Ahāli*, Apr. 22, 1945, quoted in *Yalkut Hamizrakh Hatikhon* (Jerusalem), May–June, 1945.

[10] *Sawt al Ahāli*, quoted in *Yalkut*, Sept.–Oct., 1945.

[11] Lenczovski, *Russia and the West in Iran*, p. 249.

[12] Ruskari Kurd changed its name to Barti Demokrati Kurd in 1946, after the Communists had left it. The Popular Front in Persia had adopted this name already in September, 1945.

[13] *Bolshaya Sovietskaya Encyclopedia*, vol. 18, "Iraq."

[14] *Al Qā'ida*, Jan., 1946. This dispute, which was of great symptomatic interest, has never been reported in the West. The only periodicals to take notice at the time were *Yalkut* (1946), and G. Baer in *Beayot*, Sept., 1946 (both in Hebrew).

[15] The same argument was frequently used by right-wing politicians, too.

[16] Their reply appeared in *Shursh* (Revolution), the mouthpiece of the Kurdish Communist Party, Feb., 1946.

[17] Here we face an extremely frank admission as to how popular and national fronts are managed: "The first session of the council of the [Kurdish] Communist Party decided to establish a national front. Accordingly, representatives of democratic organizations from all over Kurdistan convened and decided to establish the national front."

[18] Details on the internal splits in the Iraqi party will be found in the chapters on Iraq.

[19] This refers apparently to the Communist "League to Combat Zionism," which was formed as a legal organization in Baghdad in 1945–46.

[20] The Kurdish Democratic Party was hardly affected by the anti-Communist measures of the Iraqi government in 1948.

[21] Archibald Roosevelt, Jr., "The Kurdish Republic of Mahabad," *Middle East Journal*, July, 1947.

[22] See also "Le mouvement national kurde," by Pierre Rondot in *En Terre d'Islam*, vol. 1, 1947. The age of Qādi Muhammad was something of a secret; *Bolshaya Sovietskaya Encyclopedia* says he was born in 1901, which would mean that he was far younger at the time of his presidency than most observers believed.

[23] Roosevelt, *loc. cit.* Baghirov, the head of the Azerbaidjan G.P.U. from 1922 to 1930, later "Prime Minister" of Azerbaidjan and first secretary of the party, was ousted from all his positions after Stalin's death and Beria's fall. He was considered the party expert for Caucasian affairs during the 1940's. His appraisal of the Kommala was contrary to the truth but quite in line with the thought-pattern of a former official of the G.P.U.

[24] M. Sergeyev in *Bolshevik*, June, 1946.

[25] *Bolshaya Sovietskaya Encyclopedia*, article on Persia.

[26] Roosevelt, *loc. cit.*

[27] *Atesh*, Nov. 28, 1946.

[28] *Az Zamān* (Baghdad), June 26, 1953.

[29] *Novoye Vremya*, June 8, 1949. Non-Communist visitors, too, have reported pro-Soviet sympathies among the Kurds. Cf. William O. Douglas, *Strange Lands and Friendly Peoples*, 1951.

[30] Though Tass reported in November, 1946, that 800,000 Armenians had asked for visas.

[31] For details about relations between Moscow and the Antiochia patriarchate, cf. *Vestnik Moskovskovo Patriarkhata*, vol. 1, 1950, and vol. 5, 1954. For relations between Alexandria and Moscow, cf. *Vestnik*, vol. 3, 1954. For relations between Jerusalem and Moscow, *ibid.*, vol. 4, 1954.

[32] *Kul Shai* (Beirut), Aug. 3, 1952.

CHAPTER EIGHTEEN, PAGES 236–259

[1] Jamāl Husaini, *Al Ikhwān ul-Muslimūn*, Beirut, 1953; Heyworth-Dunne, *Religious and Political Trends in Modern Egypt*, Washington, 1950; Y. Boehm, *The Organization of the Moslem Brotherhood in Egypt* (in Hebrew), Tel-Aviv, 1952.

[2] Y. Boehm, *ibid.*

[3] Heyworth-Dunne, in a talk over the British Broadcasting Corporation network in January, 1954, mentioned a figure of five million members. These figures appear to refer, however, not to members but, sympathizers; other observers doubt whether the membership ever exceeded 200,000.

[4] Husaini, *loc. cit.*, for the part played by the Brotherhood units in the Palestinian campaign.

[5] During the "jeep trial" in December, 1950.

[6] Several of the Communists became friendly with some of the Ikhwān leaders, and after their release the latter have stressed time and again that they came to the conclusion for the first time that "the Communists are honest patriots too." Cf. Sayyid Qutub, the foremost ideologist of the movement (*Al Akhbār*, Aug. 15, 1952): "I have demanded liberty for the Communists under the same conditions as for all others who fight against tyranny. I have claimed this liberty for them, considering them honest men who are to be met with arguments, not with bullets."

[7] Al Hudaibi stated in an interview with *Le Monde* (Aug. 11, 1952) that the army had acted without the aid of the Brotherhood.

[8] *Al-Misri*, Oct. 10, 1952; *Al Ahrām*, Nov. 7, 1952.

[9] Al Hudaibi said in an interview in *Al Misri* (Aug. 18, 1953) that the Brotherhood had a single criterion for its attitude towards the new regime: it was supporting those activities that were in accordance with their teachings and were opposing what were in contradiction.

[10] *Ruz al Yūsuf*, Oct. 12, 1953.

[11] Details are given in article by Fuād Sayyid in *Al-Musawwar* (Cairo), Dec. 3, 1954.

[12] Details in *Al Ahrām*, Dec. 11, 1954. The Communists were to be given time to broadcast from the station headed by a Brotherhood member. In exchange the Communists promised both to print and to distribute Brotherhood leaflets. This agreement was not, apparently, of great political importance. The Communists thought poorly of the organizing abilities of the Brotherhood, one of them reporting that "they spoilt everything they took into their hands." *Ibid.*

[13] *Al-Musawwar*, July 26, 1952. It should be added, however, that Hasan al Hudaibi, too, has been attacked by extremists of his own movement for alleged moral laxity, notably the fact that he was seen with women in bathing costumes on the Alexandria beach. *Shabāb Muhammad*, Aug. 2, 1952, remarked that such things could never have happened to Hasan al Banna'.

[14] Sayyid Qutub in *Ad-Da'wa*, Dec. 8, 1952.

[15] Shaikh Hasan al Baqūri stated, for instance, that there should be no religious persecution and that everybody should observe his own religious laws (*Ākhar Sā'a*, May 14, 1952); the Supreme Guide said that Moslems and Copts should always collaborate (*Al Ahrām*, May 10, 1952).

[16] The views of Hasan al Banna' are expounded in Heyworth-Dunne, *loc. cit.*; and Boehm, *loc. cit.* The Brotherhood has published a number of books and booklets on these issues, such as *Our Appeal* (in Arabic), Cairo, 1947.

[17] *Ad-Da'wa*, Dec. 8, 1952.

[18] Sālih Ashmāwi in *Ad-Da'wa*, Dec. 28, 1952.

[19] Quoted in Boehm, *loc. cit.*

[20] Interview published in *Al Musawwar*, July 26, 1952.

[21] *Ad-Da'wa*, Sept. 20, 1952.

[22] *Al Ahrām*, Oct. 26, 1952.

[23] *Ibid.*, Nov. 25, 1953.

[24] In 1946 the Communists attacked the Brotherhood in its entirety as a "Fascist" organization, *vide Al Ikhwān al muslimūn 'ala'l mizan*. After 1950 only the leadership of the Brotherhood has been attacked by the Communists, in view of their "inconsistency and lack of activity in the struggle against Imperialism." See also above, Chapter 4 (Egypt), for changing Communist attitudes towards the Brotherhood.

[25] These accusations were first voiced against Hasan al Banna' in 1946–47, when two of his chief aides resigned from their posts. They were reiterated in winter, 1951–52, by the editor of the popular weekly *Ruz al Yūsuf*. Regardless of whether such rumours have any basis in fact, they are invariably believed by at least some people in a country where more than anywhere else in the world *semper aliquid haeret*.

[26] The early history of the party (and of Ahmad Husain) is contained in his book, *Imāni* (Cairo, 1936).

[27] The programme of Misr al Fatah has been published in *Oriente Moderno*, Sept., 1938.

[28] *Il Lavoro Fascista*, July 29, 1938.

[29] *Misr al Fatah*, Aug. 18, 1938, quoted in *Oriente Moderno*, Sept., 1939.

[30] *Ibid.*, Aug. 31, 1938, quoted in *Oriente Moderno*, Sept., 1939.

[31] *Al Ahrām*, Aug. 15, 1949. It was called, however, the "Socialist Party" (Al Hizb al Ishtirāki).

[32] *Ibid.*, May 7, 1950.

[33] *Ibid.*, Aug. 27, 1951.

[34] *Ibid.*, Nov. 16, 1951.

[35] *Ibid.*, Nov. 19, 1951.

[36] A *Figaro* correspondent (June 20, 1952) gave a graphic description of Ahmad Husain before his judges: ". . . bondissant derriere sa grille, les invectiva d'abondance. Il fait penser à Charlot dans les moments les plus pathetiques de sa mimique. Petit et moustachu. Le visage dur et bute, il lance en Arabe phrase après phrase à ses juges. . . ."

[37] *Al Ishtirākiyya*, Sept. 10, 1952.

[38] *Ibid.*, Sept. 2, 1952.

[39] *Al Ahrām*, Nov. 1, 1952.

[40] Bernard Lewis, "Islamic Revival in Turkey," *International Affairs*, Jan., 1952; Lewis V. Thomas, "Recent Developments in Turkish Islam," *Middle East Journal*, winter, 1952.

[41] Nazim Hikmet is the leading Turkish Communist poet; he went to Russia in 1951 after being released from prison. He became subsequently a Stalin Prize winner. Hikmet had been called a "lower middle-class agent" by *Inprecorr*, the Comintern mouthpiece, in July, 1933.

[42] Quoted in E. Marmorstein, "Religious Opposition to Nationalism in the Middle East," *International Affairs*, July, 1952.

[43] Such as *Yesil Nur* (the Green Light) in Eskeshir; *Buyuk Cihat* (the Great Holy War) in Samsun; and *Sebiluressat* in Istanbul.

[44] *Istanbul*, vol. 17 (July 22, 1953).

[45] *Al Manār* (Damascus), Nov. 11, 1949.

[46] *Al Inshā'*, May 13, 1950.

[47] *Ibid.*, May 23, 1950.

[48] *Al Ahrām*, May 22, 1950.

[49] Dāwa'lībi was in prison at the time of the Economic Conference and could not proceed to Moscow as he had intended.

[50] Majīd Khaddūri, *Independent Iraq.*

[51] Fā'ik Samara'i and Isma'īl Ghānim, spokesmen of the party, demanded in a parliamentary debate in 1950 that all the Jews should be deported from Iraq, including those who wished to stay, and their property be seized by the state. *Liwā' ul Istiqlāl* (Baghdad), vol. 2 (Mar. 4, 1950).

[52] *Ash-Sha'ab*, Nov. 23, 1953.

[53] Fā'ik Samara'i defended the Communists in the party newspaper *Liwā' ul Istiqlāl* in May, 1954, against attacks by the government parties, saying "that their rights, like those of all other citizens, must be preserved by the constitution." There would be nothing unusual in such a statement by a liberal politician—but it is somewhat incongruous in the mouth of a fascist leader.

[54] In Israel, too, there appeared at one time a parallel trend: the anti-Western and pro-Soviet orientation of the Stern Gang in 1947–48. But this group ceased to exist in 1950, and the opinions voiced by individual Sternists thereafter belong to the realm of the history of literature.

[55] The list of public figures among signatories of the Stockholm peace appeal in 1950–51 in such countries as Syria and Lebanon should be consulted by those feeling inclined to dispute this statement.

CHAPTER NINETEEN, PAGES 260–270

[1] *Imperialisticheskaya Borba sa Afriku i Osvoboditelnoye dvishenie narodov* (Moscow, 1954), pp. 97 *et seq.*

[2] *Narodi Afriki* (Moscow, 1954), p. 213.

[3] *Mezhdunarodnaya Shisn*, vol. 7, 1955, p. 84.

[4] *Ibid.*, vol. 9, 1955, p. 111.

[5] The following quotation from Cairo radio, one among many, may serve as an illustration: "U.S. democracy leaves the capitalist free to rule the country while the masses chase dollars and watch baseball. The U.S.S.R. is a true democracy with rulers taken from the people through the Communist Party."—Cairo Radio on October 11, 1955; *Summary of World Broadcasts*, No. 615, pt. 4, p. 20.

[6] A correspondent in *L'Observateur*—a neutralist French weekly friendly to Colonel Nāsir—reported from Cairo on December 3, 1955, that the extent of Communist economic help had been greatly exaggerated, "mainly in order to bluff the Americans."

[7] According to a *New York Times* correspondent (Oct. 26, 1955), the State Department had known as early as June 3 that Moscow was getting ready to send armaments to Cairo. Gamal Abdul Nāsir revealed on September 27, 1955, that the arms deal with Czechoslovakia had been signed "about a week ago" (*Al Ahrām*, Cairo, Sept. 9, 1955). According to a speech by Mr. M. Sharett in the Israeli parliament, the prehistory of the arms deal was rather more complicated: "Egypt had not turned to Czechoslovakia to ask for arms, nor had Czechoslovakia offered

these. The initiative for such an arrangement has come from the Soviet Union. . . ." (*Jerusalem Post*, Oct. 20, 1955.)

[8] L. N. Vatolina: "Rost natsionalnovo Samosoznanya narodov arabskikh stran" ("The Growth of National Consciousness of the Peoples of the Arab Countries") in *Sovietskoye Vostokovedenie*, vol. 5 (Nov., 1955), p. 65.

CHAPTER TWENTY, PAGES 271–285

[1] The number of party members nevertheless remained comparatively small, as many sympathizers could not take the strict party discipline.

[2] Eduard Heimann, "Marxism and Underdeveloped Countries," *Social Research*, Sept., 1952.

[3] The lawyers of Cairo and Beirut, Damascus, Baghdad, and Arab Jerusalem, as well as other Middle Eastern cities, appear to feel a particularly strong predilection for Communism. Their professional associations are now, or have for long periods in the past been, headed by party members or sympathizers. To give a few examples: thirty-nine Baghdad lawyers volunteered to defend four Communist leaders (three of them lawyers themselves) in Baghdad early in 1947; twenty-five Baghdad lawyers wanted to defend their prominent colleague 'Azīz Sharīf (the head of the People's Party, a Communist "front") several months later. According to the newspaper *Ālif Ba*, 200 Damascus and Beirut lawyers volunteered to defend the Lebanese Communist leader Mustafa al 'Arīs at his trial in Beirut in December, 1949. Fifty-seven Lebanese lawyers announced that they would come to defend the first secretary of the Jordan Communist Party, Fuād Nāsir, at his trial in Amman in January, 1952. The social conscience of these lawyers, most of whom hail from rich families, appears to be very much developed, perhaps because they are better aware of their parasitic function in Middle Eastern society than others are, and feel themselves, generally speaking, as *lishnye lyudi* (superfluous people), *pace* Turgeniev and Chekhov.

[4] Theses on the "Revolutionary Movement in the Colonies and Semi-colonies," adopted at the Sixth Congress of the Communist International, 1928.

[5] Morris Watnick, "The Appeal of Communism to the Underdeveloped Peoples," *The Progress of Underdeveloped Areas*, 1952.

[6] "The Cold War," *The Twentieth Century*, April, 1953.

[7] Quoted in George Mc T. Kahin, "Indonesian Politics and Nationalism," *Nationalism and the West* (1953).

[8] M. R. Masani in *Pacific Affairs*, Mar., 1951, and the *Communist Party of India* (1954), by the same author. Eugene Staley (*The Future of Underdeveloped Countries*, 1954) says that "in their attempts to influence the peoples of underdeveloped countries, the Communists put great emphasis, I would even say chief emphasis, on appeals not to the material wants of man but rather to the human desire for status, equality, freedom from domination or oppression, especially domination by foreigners."

[9] Exact figures are not available in conditions of illegality. But if we take as our standard the social constitution of the Palestine Arab League of National Liberation during 1943–48 (which was in all respects a

NOTES TO CHAPTER TWENTY, PAGES 271-285

typical Communist group), it would appear that about 60–80 per cent. of the party members (not merely leaders or militants) belonged to the intelligentsia. A statistical breakdown of the social origins of Communists arrested and brought to trial in recent years in Egypt and Iraq tends to point to the same result, the percentage of the intelligentsia reaching, as a rule, 60–75 per cent. Morris Watnick's observations for East Asia are thus entirely borne out for the Middle East; viz. that the intellectuals are the sole group in the area which can infuse the raw social materials of agrarian discontent, etc., with the organization and leadership necessary. "And it is largely this group which has acted as the marriage broker between the international Communist movement and the manifestations of indigenous revolt" ("The Appeal of Communism to the Underdeveloped Peoples," *The Progress of Underdeveloped Areas*, ed. Bert Hoselitz, 1952).

[10] This situation may, of course, change once the Soviet Union becomes actively involved in Middle Eastern affairs.

[11] *Asian Nationalism and the West*, ed. William L. Holland, published by Institute of Pacific Relations, 1953.

[12] It was demonstrated after World War II that a Communist regime could be established even in countries without Communists; there were fewer than 1000 party members in such countries as Rumania and Hungary, Eastern Germany and Albania in 1944–45. But this took place in the wake of a world war.

[13] The Chinese Communists do not yet appear to be interested in the Middle East, but this is likely to change in the future.

[14] "The truth is that neutralism in Asia, in contrast to Europe, is the typical expression of the present stage of political development there, and can only be overcome as the nations of Asia learn from their own experience." This remark, made by Richard Loewenthal in connection with the situation in South-east Asia, is not less true for the Arab countries of the Middle East. ("Between Dulles and Nehru," *The Twentieth Century*, June, 1954.)

[15] Loewenthal, *loc. cit.*

[16] Quoted in E. Staley, *The Future of Underdeveloped Countries* (1954).

[17] *Marx-Engels Gesamtausgabe*, Abt. 1, Bd. 6, p. 487.

[18] "Communism and Islam," *International Affairs* (London), Jan., 1954.

[19] Professor Lewis also draws attention to the "uncomfortable resemblances" between the totalitarian doctrine professed by the *ulamā* (with complete and final answers to all questions on heaven and earth) and Communist propagandists. The exhilarating feeling of mission, of purpose, of being engaged in a collective adventure to accelerate the historically inevitable victory of the true faith over the evil infidels are common to classical Islam and to Communism. And it is quite true that this collectivism is not limited to the "popular sub-stratum of Islam, . . . it is discernible in many aspects of orthodox Islamic life and thought, in the attitude to society and government and even in literature" (*ibid.*). It is interesting to note that in at least one country the (Islamic) religious revival has benefited the Communists, who in Indonesia have actually formed a party known as "Parti Communist Islami." (Mohtar Lubis, quoted in *Thought* (New Delhi), Mar. 5, 1955.)

APPENDIX I, PAGES 289–299

[1] These articles are contained in vols. 9 and 10 of the Soviet (Russian) edition of the collected works of Marx and Engels. A selection was published in the United States in 1952: *The Russian Menace to Europe* (ed. Blackstock and Hoselitz). Many interesting articles of that period, such as for instance, "The Disorders in Syria . . ." or "The Revolution in Turkey," were not included in that edition and are not available in English, while the Russian edition, hard to come by in the West, is accessible only to a small circle of experts behind the Curtain.

[2] *New York Tribune*, April 15, 1854.

[3] What Marx has to say about the ignorance of Middle Eastern affairs prevailing in the West is very topical, too: ". . . the common notions floating about among the public were based more upon the *Arabian Nights Entertainment* than upon any historical facts. Official diplomatic functionaries, having been on the spot, boasted a more accurate knowledge, but this, too, amounted to nothing, as none of these officials ever troubled to learn the languages. . . . The business of these gentlemen was not with the people, the institutions, the social state of the country: it was exclusively with the court." (*New York Tribune*, April 19, 1853.)

[4] *New York Tribune*, April 7, 1853.

[5] MEGA (*Marx Engels Gesamtausgabe*), Abt. 3, Bd. 1, June 6, 1853.

[6] MEGA, Abt. 3, Bd. 1, June 14, 1853.

[7] This problem is discussed at some length by O. Jenssen: "Marxistische Beitraege zum Problem der wirtschaftlichen Entwicklung und Wirtschaftsforschung im Orient" in *Archiv fuer Wirtschaftsforschung im Orient* (Weimar, July, 1917).

[8] K. Kautsky: *Der Ursprung des Christentums* (Stuttgart, 1908).

[9] *The Foreign Policy of Russian Czarism* (1890).

[10] Letter to Bracke, June 25, 1877, in *Archiv. Marksa i Engelsa*, vol. 1 (6) (Moscow, 1933).

[11] Letter to W. Blos quoted in G. Mayer: *Friedrich Engels* (Haag, 1934).

[12] Engels, *The Foreign Policy of Russian Czarism* (1890).

[13] Otto Bauer, *Die Nationalitaetenfrage und die Sozialdemokratie* (Wien, 1907); Karl Renner, "Die Probleme des Ostens," *Kampf*, vol. 5 (1911–12).

[14] Otto Bauer, "Orientalische Revolutionen," *Kampf*, vol. 5 (1911–12).

[15] *Aus dem literarischen Nachlass von Karl Marx*, ed. Mehring, vol. 3, 1902.

[16] In Lenin, *Sotchinenya*, vol. 33 (4th ed.).

[17] In Stalin, *Sotchinenya*, vol. 4.

[18] *Der Zweite Kongress der Kommunistischen Internationale* (Hamburg, 1920).

[19] Theses (of the Sixth Congress of the Communist International) on the revolutionary movement in the colonies and semi-colonies (1928).

[20] *Resolutsii Sedmovo Vsemirnovo Kongressa Kommunisticheskovo Internatsionala* (Moscow, 1935).

[21] But the absence of experts was certainly not entirely fortuitous. Russia could undoubtedly have experts if it only attributed political importance to the Middle East.

[22] Programme of the "Democratic Movement of National Liberation" (1951).

[23] Programme for a Popular Democracy in Israel (1952).

[24] G. Dimitroff, *The United Front* (1938).

[25] To give a recent illustration: Khālid Bakdāsh sharply criticized the Syrian Republican Socialist Party in August, 1954, for insisting on the principle of state education (instead of control by the clergy). He said that such a demand was disrupting the anti-imperialist front by antagonizing the Islamic Socialist front (the Syrian branch of the Moslem Brotherhood), which was one of the staunchest pillars of anti-Westernism in the country. There have been other, similar cases.

[26] It is of course possible to publish compilations of quotations from Marx, Lenin, and Stalin purporting to show that they always attributed decisive importance to the struggle of the peoples in the "colonial and dependent countries." Akopyan in *Voprossi Ekonomiki*, vol. 1, 1951, is the most comprehensive one known to this writer. But such compilations can be made to demonstrate anything in the world.

APPENDIX II, PAGES 300–302

[1] Among them was Hanoh Bsosa, who had been Mikunis's predecessor as the deputy of Mūsa.

[2] Details about the "Eight-party Conference" in *Emet*, Oct., 1940.

[3] *Kol Ha'am*, Oct., 1940.

[4] *Emet*, Nov., 1940.

[5] On the split, cf. *Kol Ha'am*, special edition (Mikunis), June 10, 1943; and *Kol Ha'am* (Mūsa), June, 1943.

Index

References to the Notes are given thus: 313(2)¹⁵, 313 being the number of the page on which Note 15 to Chapter 2 appears.